DOCUMENTS IN THE POLITICAL HISTORY OF THE EUROPEAN CONTINENT 1815–1939

DOCUMENTS IN THE POLITICAL HISTORY OF THE EUROPEAN CONTINENT 1815-1939

Selected and Edited by
G. A. KERTESZ
MONASH UNIVERSITY

CLARENDON PRESS · OXFORD
1968

Oxford University Press, Ely House, London W. 1

GLASGOW NEW YORK TORONTO MELBOURNE WELLINGTON
CAPE TOWN SALISBURY IBADAN NAIROBI LUSAKA ADDIS ABABA
BOMBAY CALCUTTA MADRAS KARACHI LAHORE DACCA
KUALA LUMPUR HONG KONG TOKYO

PRINTED IN GREAT BRITAIN
BY BUTLER AND TANNER LTD., FROME AND LONDON

PREFACE

My aim in compiling this volume has been to provide, for the undergraduate, a collection of the most important documentary material in the field of European history between the Congress of Vienna and the outbreak of the Second World War. The lack of such a collection has long been felt by myself and my colleagues teaching in this field.

The collection has been limited to documentary material in the strict sense (laws, treaties, proclamations, party programmes, speeches, etc.) to the exclusion of what might be described as 'readings', that is, extracts from descriptions, contemporary accounts, or treatises. Collections of 'readings' are comparatively easily available, and their inclusion would have swollen this volume to impossible proportions. Descriptions and summaries, preferably contemporary, were used only in very few cases, where the original document proved either unprocurable or unsuitable for inclusion.

Except in the field of international relations, Great Britain has been excluded from the scope of the collection. The reason for this was partly lack of space, partly the availability of collections relating to the field of British history.

Selection of material proved a task more difficult than I expected. There were many documents, of course, which could not have been omitted. Beyond this category my choice has been governed by several factors. Not easily available documents are included in preference to well-known ones, short ones in preference to long ones, and, among long ones, those suitable for excerpting in preference to those not so suitable. My original hope of including complete documents only proved to be unrealistic and misguided: many detailed and machinery clauses in most of the documents would have been of interest only to the specialist to whom they would be available in any case, but of little interest and only confusing to the undergraduate. I have tried to ensure that all clauses which are either intrinsically important, or necessary for the understanding of other documents, are included. In spite of my care there will, no doubt, be criticisms of my selection. No two people could compile identical collections.

I have used two symbols only. Omissions from the original text, of whatever extent, are shown by dots . . . while square brackets [ ] enclose comment, paraphrase, explanatory words or phrases, or summaries of intervening material. Square brackets are also used around page numbers in references to the *Annual Register*, following the practice of the *Annual Register* itself which bracketed page numbers in the first part of some volumes to distinguish them from the separately numbered pages in the second part of those volumes.

The material is arranged in sections, according to country and period, with separate sections covering international affairs and Church–State relations. Within sections, documents are in most cases arranged in chronological order. This kind of arrangement might, perhaps, obscure connexions, but the copious cross-references will, I hope, minimize any inconvenience.

Editorial matter, introductions, and annotations, have been confined to the minimum needed to reveal the scope of each section, to place each document into its context, and to explain difficult or ambiguous terms in the text.

I have tried to use the best existing English translation of each document, but in some cases could find no satisfactory translation, in others no translation was available. Therefore in many cases (identified by 'trans. Ed.' following the details of source) the translation was made by myself. Several of the documents have, to the best of my knowledge, been translated into English for the first time for this collection. My wife has assisted me in some of these translations; my thanks are due to her for this, and for her patience and forbearance with me while the work of compilation was going on.

I would also like to thank my colleagues at Monash University and the University of Melbourne, particularly Professor A. M. McBriar, Mrs Alison Patrick, and Mr L. R. Fleming, for their encouragement and criticism. I gratefully acknowledge financial assistance from Monash University. Assistance from librarians at the Monash University Library, the University of

Melbourne Library, and the State Library of Victoria in making scarce material available was of great value and I am grateful for it. Mrs Joan Juliff, Mrs Audrey Allen, and Mrs Jean Thompson, their efforts concerted by Mrs Val Cook, typed a manuscript, which had been delayed by a variety of factors, with great speed, care, and enthusiasm, and my special thanks are due to them.

Monash University   G. A. K.
July 1967.

ACKNOWLEDGEMENTS

THE editor and publishers wish to thank the following publishers, authors, and editors for permission to use copyright material (the bracketed numbers below refer to the documents in this book, each of which is preceded by a note giving fuller details of its source):

George Allen & Unwin Ltd for extracts from F. C. Conybeare, *The Dreyfus Case* (No. 147)

Appleton-Century-Croft for extracts from F. A. Golder, *Documents of Russian History, 1914–1917* (Nos 137, 138, 161, 162, 163, 171(b))

G. Bell & Sons Ltd for an extract from A. de Lamartine, *History of the French Revolution of 1848* (No. 38)

Ernest Benn Ltd for an extract from P. Sabatier, *Disestablishment in France* (No. 120)

The Carnegie Endowment for International Peace for extracts from *The Hague Conventions and Declarations*, ed. by J. B. Scott (No. 105); T. J. Polner, *Russian Local Government During the War and the Union of Zemstvos* (No. 130); *Outbreak of the War: German Documents* (No. 154); *Diplomatic Documents relating to the Outbreak of the European War* (No. 156); *International Conciliation* (Nos 159, 183(b), 187)

The Clarendon Press for extracts from *The French Revolution of 1848 in its Economic Aspects*, ed. by J. A. R. Marriott (Nos 33, 35, 36, 41); R. B. Mowat, *Select Treaties and Documents* (No. 106(a)); A. J. Whyte, *The Political Life and Letters of Cavour* (No. 90(b))

Columbia University Press for extracts from *The Anti-Stalin Campaign and International Communism*, © Copyright 1956 by Columbia University Press, New York (No. 204)

Constable & Co. Ltd for extracts from J. G. Legge, *Rhyme and Revolution in Germany* (Nos 24, 26(b)); C. G. Robertson, *Bismarck* (No. 96(a))

The *Daily Telegraph and Morning Post* for an extract from the *Daily Telegraph* (No. 110)

Librairie Gallimard for an extract from A. Zévaès, *Au temps du boulangisme* (No. 146)

Editions Garnier Frères for an extract from E. Ollivier, *L'empire libéral* (No. 141)

Harper & Row, Publishers, for the abridgement of Bismarck's draft of resignation from *The Kaiser vs Bismarck: New Chapters of Bismarck's Autobiography*, as translated by Bernard Miall. Copyright 1920, 1948 by Harper & Brothers. Reprinted by permission of Harper & Row, Publishers (No. 126)

Harvard University Press for extracts from A. F. Pribram, *The Secret Treaties of Austria–Hungary*, Copyright 1920, 1921 by Harvard University Press (Nos 101, 102, 103, 104); G. Fischer, *Russian Liberalism: from Gentry to Intelligentsia*, © Copyright 1956 by the President and Fellows of Harvard College (No. 134); V. R. Lorwin, *The French Labor Movement*, © Copyright 1954 by the President and Fellows of Harvard College (No. 153)

The Controller of Her Majesty's Stationery Office for the numerous extracts from *British and Foreign State Papers*, *Parliamentary Debates, Parliamentary Papers, British Documents on the Origin of the War 1898–1914*, and Hertslet's *Map of Europe by Treaty*, for which general permission has been given by the Controller; also for the extracts from the despatch by Lord Palmerston, 11 January 1841 (F.O. 181/168) (No. 12(b)), published in W. H. Temperley and L. Penson, *Foundations of British Foreign Policy* (London, Cambridge University Press, 1938), which is Crown Copyright.

Hodder & Stoughton Ltd for an extract from *New Chapters of Bismarck's Autobiography*, translated by B. Miall (No. 126)

Holt, Rinehart and Winston, Inc., for extracts from M. J. Olgin, *The Soul of the Russian Revolution*. Copyright 1917 by Henry Holt & Co. (Nos 139(a) and (b))

Hutchinson Publishing Group Ltd for extracts from A. Werth, *France in ferment* (Nos 150(b), 151)

W. Kohlhammer Verlag for extracts from E. R. Huber, *Dokumente zur deutschen Verfassungsgeschichte* (Nos. 46, 47(b), 49(a) and (b), 61, 65(a) and (b), 70, 183(a), 186, 188, 189, 190)

Lawrence & Wishart Ltd and International Publishers, Inc., for extracts from K. Marx and F. Engels, *Selected Works* (No. 98); G. Plekhanov, *Selected Philosophical Works*, vol. i (No. 132); V. I. Lenin, *Collected Works*, vol. vi (No. 133); V. I. Lenin, *Selected Works in Three Volumes* (Nos 164, 169(a) and (b), 170); J. V. Stalin, *Works* (Nos 201, 202)

Longmans, Green & Co. Ltd for an extract from G. M. Trevelyan, *Grey of Fallodon* (No. 106(b))

Macmillan & Co. Ltd for an extract from F. H. Brabant, *The Beginning of the Third Republic in France* (No. 144)

The Macmillan Company for extracts reprinted with permission from *The Russian Revolution 1917–1921* by W. H. Chamberlin, Copyright 1935 by The Macmillan Company, renewed 1963 by W. H. Chamberlin (Nos 166, 167, 173(a), 198, 199, 200)

Oxford University Press for extracts from *The Communist International* by J. Degras (No. 197); *Documents on International Affairs* (Nos 212, 213, 214(a), (c) and (d), 218)

Paul R. Reynolds, Inc., for extracts from Benito Mussolini, *My Autobiography* [by R. W. Child] (No. 175)

Lindsay Rogers for an extract from Howard L. McBain and Lindsay Rogers, *The New Constitutions of Europe* (No. 196)

Count S. Sforza and Frederick Muller Ltd for an extract from Count Carlo Sforza, *Contemporary Italy* (No. 174)

Société Universitaire d'Éditions et de Librairie for extracts from J. Palméro, *Histoire des institutions et des doctrines pédagogiques* (Nos 111, 112, 117)

Stanford University Press for extracts reprinted from *The First Russian Revolution, 1825* by Anatole G. Mazour, Copyright 1937, renewed 1964, by Anatole G. Mazour (No. 128); *The Bolshevik Revolution 1917–1918* by James Bunyan and H. H. Fisher, Copyright 1934 by the Board of Trustees of the Leland Stanford Junior University; renewed 1961 by James Bunyan and H. H. Fisher (Nos 171(a) and (c), 172, 173(b), 195)

The Times Publishing Company Ltd for extracts from *The Times* (No. 150(a) (1)–(4))

University of Chicago Press for an extract from W. F. Dodd, *Modern Constitutions* (No. 72)

University of Nebraska Press for an extract from E. N. Anderson,

The Social and Political Conflict in Prussia 1858–1864 (No. 65(c))

D. Van Nostrand Company, Inc., for extracts from Rappard's *Source Book on European Government*, Copyright 1937, D. Van Nostrand Company, Inc., Princeton, New Jersey (Nos 176, 177, 182, 185, 193(e), 203, 205)

While every effort has been made to trace the owners of all copyright material, in a few cases this has proved impossible. In the event of this book reaching them, the publishers would be glad if they would communicate with them, so that they may acknowledge their obligation in any future edition.

CONTENTS

I · INTERNATIONAL AFFAIRS, 1815–49

AFTER the collapse of the Napoleonic Empire the initial task of the Powers in the field of international affairs was the re-establishment of a stable peace. The installation of a Bourbon king, Louis XVIII, in France, and the conclusion of a comparatively mild treaty of peace (No. 1) served this purpose, and a General Congress, which we now know as the Congress of Vienna, was called 'to regulate the arrangements necessary for completing the dispositions' of this treaty. But while the Congress was still sitting, Napoleon returned, and had to be defeated again. The treaty of 25 March 1815 (No. 2) regulated the activities of the Powers in pursuance of this aim.

The second Peace of Paris (No. 4) was less favourable to France than the first one, and the cause of a stable peace was bolstered by further agreements. Tsar Alexander I proposed the Holy Alliance (No. 3) to maintain the principles of Christian morality. This rather vague instrument, which later became a means of conservative repression, was signed by the Emperor of Austria, the King of Prussia, and the Tsar of Russia; Great Britain did not accede to it. Yet another, the Quadruple, Alliance (No. 5) was signed on the same date as the Second Peace of Paris. Austria, Great Britain, Prussia, and Russia signed this Alliance to ensure the enforcement of the terms of the peace treaty and to keep in check any further revolutionary movements. The Alliance provided for regular meetings, congresses, between the powers, and thus laid the foundations of the Congress System.

At the first Congress, held at Aix-la-Chapelle in 1818, France, having fulfilled the stipulations of the Second Peace of Paris (No. 4) was readmitted to the Concert of Europe. The Congress also formulated the principles of policy to be followed by the Concert (No. 6). In spite of this agreement on principles the Congress system did not last for long; Great Britain would not go so far as her continental allies in the repression of liberal movements, and withdrew; therefore further Congresses were largely restricted to Austria, Prussia, and Russia (Nos 7, 8, 9). From the middle twenties on, however, few international crises of great magnitude disturbed Europe. Foremost among these crises was the friction over Greece. France, Great Britain, and Russia reconciled their views in the Treaty for the Pacification of Greece in 1827 (No. 10). By 1832 an independent Greece was detached from the Ottoman Empire and guaranteed by all the Powers.

In the late thirties a Near Eastern crisis blew up again, mainly over French ambitions in the area. This was settled by the Powers through the Treaty of London in 1840 (No. 12(a)) which isolated France. A Russian proposal for a general anti-French alliance followed on France's alienation from Great Britain, but was rejected by Lord Palmerston. Palmerston's reply (No. 12(b)) is included as a typical statement of British foreign policy.

In this period we also find an unofficial diplomacy in addition to that conducted by Courts and Governments. The liberal and national movements, mainly under the influence of Mazzini, got together in 1834 and signed the Pact of Young Europe (No. 11). The pact expresses high-flown humanitarian and liberal sentiments, but had little practical significance. It is included as a forerunner of later, similar, agreements. For the same reason, we find included passages from Victor Hugo's presidential opening address at an unofficial Peace Congress held in Paris in 1849 (No. 13), interesting as an early example of a desire for a United States of Europe.

1. First Peace of Paris, 30 May 1814

The treaty of peace with France, substantial parts of which follow, was intended to establish stability in Europe after the disturbances of the Revolutionary and Napoleonic periods. Its terms are generous; the financial part, which could not be included, does not go beyond measures necessary to settle the affairs of formerly French-dominated areas, whilst the territorial settlement accepted the 1792 boundaries of France, with some corrections to France's advantage.

The text printed refers to the treaty between Great Britain and

France; an identical treaty was concluded on the same day between France and Austria, Prussia, and Russia, with additional articles in each case.

Source: E. Hertslet, *The Map of Europe by Treaty* (London, Butterworth, 1875), vol. i, pp. 2–17.

His Majesty, the King of the United Kingdom of Great Britain and Ireland, and his Allies on the one part, and His Majesty the King of France and Navarre on the other part, animated by an equal desire to terminate the long agitations of Europe, and the sufferings of mankind, by a permanent peace, founded upon a just repartition of force between its States, and containing in its stipulations the pledge of its durability; and His Britannic Majesty, together with his Allies, being unwilling to require of France, now that, replaced under the paternal Government of Her Kings, she offers the assurance of security and stability to Europe, the conditions and guarantees which they had with regret demanded from her former Government, Their said Majesties have named Plenipotentiaries to discuss, settle, and sign a Treaty of Peace and Amity, namely, [names and titles of plenipotentiaries follow]
Who having exchanged their Full Powers, found in good and due form, have agreed upon the following articles:

1. There shall be from this day forward perpetual peace and friendship between His Britannic Majesty and his Allies on the one part, and His Majesty the King of France and Navarre on the other, their heirs and successors, their dominions and subjects, respectively.

The High Contracting Parties shall devote their best attention to maintain, not only between themselves, but, inasmuch as depends upon them, between all the States of Europe, that harmony and good understanding which are so necessary for their tranquillity.

2. The Kingdom of France retains its limits entire, as they existed on the 1st of January, 1792. It shall further receive the increase of territory comprised within the line established by the following Articles . . .

5. The navigation of the Rhine . . . shall be free, so that it can be interdicted to no one:—and at the future Congress[1] attention

[1] Of Vienna.

shall be paid to the establishment of the principles according to which the duties to be raised by the States bordering on the Rhine may be regulated, in the mode the most impartial and the most favourable to the commerce of all nations.

The future Congress, with a view to facilitate the communication between nations, and continually to render them less strangers to each other, shall likewise examine and determine in what manner the above provisions can be extended to other rivers which, in their navigable course, separate or traverse different States.

6. Holland, placed under the sovereignty of the House of Orange, shall receive an increase of Territory. The title and exercise of that Sovereignty shall not in any case belong to a Prince wearing, or destined to wear, a Foreign Crown.

The States of Germany shall be independent and united by a federative bond.

Switzerland, independent, shall continue to govern herself.

Italy, beyond the limits of the countries which are to revert to Austria, shall be composed of sovereign States.

7. The island of Malta and its dependencies shall belong in full right and sovereignty to His Britannic Majesty.

8–11. [French colonial possessions which were occupied by the Allies during the war, are to be restored to France with some minor exceptions.]

12. His Britannic Majesty guarantees to the subjects of His Most Christian Majesty[1] the same facilities, privileges, and protection, with respect to commerce, and the security of their Persons and Property within the limits of the British sovereignty on the continent of India, as are now, or shall be granted to the most favoured nations.

His Most Christian Majesty, on his part, having nothing more at heart than the perpetual duration of peace between the two Crowns of England and France, and wishing to do his utmost to avoid anything which might affect their mutual good understanding, engages not to erect any fortifications in the establishments which are to be restored to him within the limits of the British sovereignty upon the continent of India, and only to place in those establishments the number of troops necessary for the maintenance of the police . . .

----

[1] Title of the King of France.

16. The High Contracting Parties, desirous to bury in entire oblivion the dissensions which have agitated Europe, declare and promise that no individual, of whatever rank or condition he may be, in the countries restored and ceded by the present treaty, shall be prosecuted, disturbed, or molested, in his person or property, under any pretext whatsoever, either on account of his conduct or political opinions, his attachment either to any of the Contracting Parties, or to any Government which has ceased to exist, or for any other reason, except for debts contracted towards individuals, or acts posterior to the date of the present treaty . . .

2. *Treaty between Austria, Great Britain, Prussia, and Russia, 25 March 1815*

Upon Napoleon's return from Elba hostilities reopened and the following treaty was concluded to regulate the proceedings of the Allied Powers. Note the explanatory declaration following the treaty which clarified the position of Great Britain.

The treaty had bilateral form and was concluded between each two of the four Powers. The text given leaves the name of the second party open.

Source: *Annual Register*, 1815, pp. 367–9.

His Majesty the King of the United Kingdom of Great Britain and Ireland, and His Majesty the   , having taken into consideration the consequences which the invasion of France by Napoleon Bonaparte, and the actual situation of that kingdom, may produce with respect to the safety of Europe, have resolved . . . to renew, by a solemn treaty, signed separately by each of the four Powers with each of the three others, the engagement to preserve against every attack the order of things so happily established in Europe, and to determine upon the most effectual means of fulfilling that engagement, as well as of giving it all the extension which the present circumstances so imperiously call for . . .

1. The High Contracting Parties above-mentioned solemnly engage to unite the resources of their respective States for the purpose of maintaining entire the conditions of the treaty of peace concluded at Paris the 30th of May, 1814 (No. 1); as also

DEC—C

the stipulation determined upon and signed at the Congress of Vienna, with the view to complete the dispositions of that treaty, to preserve them against all infringement, and particularly against the designs of Napoleon Bonaparte. For this purpose they engage . . . to direct in common, and with one accord, should the case require it, all their efforts against him, and against all those who should already have joined his faction, or shall hereafter join it, in order to force him to desist from his projects, and to render him unable to disturb in future the tranquillity of Europe and the general peace under the protection of which the rights, the liberty, and independence of nations had been recently placed and secured.

2. Although the means destined for the attainment of so great and salutary an object ought not to be subjected to limitation, and although the High Contracting Parties are resolved to devote therein all those means which, in their respective situations, they are enabled to dispose of, they have nevertheless agreed to keep constantly in the field, each, a force of 150,000 men complete, including cavalry, in the proportion of at least one-tenth, and a just proportion of artillery, not reckoning garrisons; and to employ the same actively and conjointly against the common enemy.

3. The High Contracting Parties reciprocally engage not to lay down their arms but by common consent, nor before the object of the war, designated in the first article of the present Treaty, shall have been attained; nor until Bonaparte shall have been rendered absolutely unable to create disturbance, and to renew his attempts for possessing himself of the supreme power in France . . .

7. The engagements entered into by the present treaty having for their object the maintenance of the general peace, the High Contracting Parties agree to invite all the Powers of Europe to accede to the same.

8. The present Treaty having no other end in view but to support France, or any other country which may be invaded, against the enterprises of Bonaparte and his adherents, His Most Christian Majesty[1] shall be specially invited to accede hereunto; and, in the event of His Majesty's requiring the forces stipulated in the second article, to make known what

---

[1] The King of France.

assistance circumstances will allow him to bring forward in furtherance of the object of the present Treaty.

Separate Article. As circumstances might prevent His Majesty the King of the United Kingdom of Great Britain and Ireland from keeping constantly in the field the number of troops specified in the second article, it is agreed that His Britannic Majesty shall have the option, either of furnishing his contingent of men, or of paying at the rate of thirty pounds sterling per annum for each cavalry soldier, and twenty pounds per annum for each infantry soldier, that may be wanting to complete the number stipulated in the second article.

Declaration by Viscount Castlereagh.

The undersigned, on the exchange of the ratification of the Treaty of the 25th of March last, on the part of his Court, is hereby commanded to declare, that the 8th article of the said treaty, wherein His Most Christian Majesty is invited to accede, under certain stipulations, is to be understood as binding the Contracting Parties, upon the principles of mutual security, to a common effort against the power of Napoleon Bonaparte, in pursuance of the third article of the said treaty; but it is not to be understood as binding His Britannic Majesty to prosecute the war with a view of imposing upon France any particular government.

However solicitous the Prince Regent must be to see His Most Christian Majesty restored to the throne, and however anxious he is to contribute, in conjunction with the allies, to so auspicious an event, he nevertheless deems himself called upon to make this declaration, on the exchange of the ratifications, as well in consideration of what is due to His Most Christian Majesty's interests in France, as in conformity to the principles upon which the British Government has invariably regulated its conduct.

3. *The Holy Alliance, 26 September 1815*

Tsar Alexander I, whose complex personality included traits of pietism, proposed the signing by the rulers of the Powers of the following treaty, which was to express their devotion to the principles of Christian ethics in the field of politics. The Emperor of Austria and the King of Prussia acceded to the Tsar's request; the Prince Regent abstained, giving as his reason his constitutional inability to sign a treaty without ministerial countersignature, while such countersignature would have contradicted the spirit of the document.

Source: *Annual Register*, 1816, pp. 381-2 (with emendations).

Their Majesties the Emperor of Austria, the King of Prussia, and the Emperor of Russia, having, in consequence of the great events which have marked the course of the last three years in Europe, and especially of the blessings which it has pleased Divine Providence to shower down upon those States whose Governments have placed their confidence and their hope on it alone, acquired the intimate conviction of the necessity of founding the conduct to be observed by the Powers in their reciprocal relations upon the sublime truths which the Holy Religion of our Saviour teaches——

They solemnly declare that the present act has no other object than to publish, in the face of the whole world, their fixed resolution, both in the administration of their respective states, and in their political relations with every other Government, to take for their sole guide the precepts of that Holy Religion; namely, the precepts of justice, Christian charity and peace, which, far from being applicable only to private concerns, must have an immediate influence on the Councils of Princes, and guide all their steps, as being the only means of consolidating human institutions, and remedying their imperfections. In consequence their Majesties have agreed on the following articles:—

1. Conformably to the word of the Holy Scriptures, which command all men to consider each other as brethren, the three contracting Monarchs will remain united by the bonds of a true and indissoluble fraternity, and considering each other as fellow countrymen, they will on all occasions, and in all places, lend each other aid and assistance; and regarding themselves towards their subjects and armies as fathers of families, they will lead them, in the same spirit of fraternity with which they are animated to protect religion, peace and justice.

2. In consequence, the sole principle in force, whether between the said Governments or between their subjects, shall be that of

doing each other reciprocal service, and of testifying, by un-
alterable good will, the mutual affection with which they ought
to be animated, to consider themselves all as members of one
and the same Christian nation, the three Allied Princes looking
on themselves as merely delegated by Providence to govern
three branches of the one family, namely Austria, Prussia and
Russia; thus confessing that the Christian world, of which they
and their people form a part, has, in reality, no other Sovereign
than Him to whom alone power really belongs, because in Him
alone are found all the treasures of love, knowledge and infinite
wisdom, that is to say, God, our Divine Saviour, the Word of the
Most High, the Word of Life. Their Majesties consequently
recommend to their people, with the most tender solicitude, as
the sole means of enjoying that peace which arises from a good
conscience, and which alone is durable, to strengthen themselves every day more and more in the principles and exercise
of the duties which the Divine Saviour has taught to mankind.
3. All the Powers who shall choose solemnly to avow the sacred
principles which have dictated the present act, and shall acknowledge how important it is for the happiness of nations, too
long agitated, that these truths should henceforth exercise over
the destinies of mankind all the influence which belongs to
them, will be received with equal ardour and affection into this
holy alliance.

4. Second Peace of Paris, 20 November 1815

Concluded after the defeat of Napoleon, this second Peace of Paris
is the definitive treaty of peace between France and the allies.
Note that it differs from the first Peace of Paris (No. 1) in limiting
France to the frontiers of 1790, in imposing the payment of an
indemnity, and in providing for an allied army of occupation in
France.

The text which follows is the treaty between Great Britain and
France; identical treaties with the other Powers were concluded on
the same date.

Source: E. Hertslet, *The Map of Europe by Treaty* (London, Butterworth, 1875), vol. i, pp. 342–50.

In the Name of the Most Holy and Undivided Trinity.

The Allied Powers having by their united efforts, and by the success of their arms, preserved France and Europe from the convulsions with which they were menaced by the late enterprise of Napoleon Bonaparte, and by the revolutionary system reproduced in France, to promote its success; participating at present with His Most Christian Majesty[1] in the desire to consolidate, by maintaining inviolate the Royal authority, and by restoring the operation of the Constitutional Charter (No. 14), the order of things which had been happily re-established in France, as also in the object of restoring between France and her neighbours those relations of reciprocal confidence and goodwill which the fatal effects of the Revolution and of the system of conquest had for so long a time disturbed: persuaded, at the same time, that this last object can only be obtained by an arrangement framed to secure to the Allies proper indemnities for the past and solid guarantees for the future, they have, in concert with His Majesty the King of France, taken into consideration the means of giving effect to this arrangement; and being satisfied that the Indemnity due to the Allied Powers cannot be either entirely territorial or entirely pecuniary, without prejudice to France in the one or other of her essential interests, and that it would be more fit to combine both the modes, in order to avoid the inconvenience which would result were either resorted to separately, their Imperial and Royal Majesties have adopted this basis for their present transactions; and agreeing alike as to the necessity of retaining for a fixed time in the frontier provinces of France a certain number of allied troops, they have determined to combine their different arrangements, founded upon these bases, in a definitive treaty ...

1. The frontiers of France shall be the same as they were in the year 1790, save and except the modifications on one side and on the other, which are detailed in the present article ...

2. The fortresses, places, and districts, which, according to the preceding article are no longer to form a part of the French territory, shall be placed at the disposal of the Allied Powers ...

4. The pecuniary part of the indemnity to be furnished by France to the Allied Powers is fixed at the sum of 700,000,000 of Francs. The modes, the periods, and the guarantees for the

[1] The King of France.

payment of this sum shall be regulated by a special convention which shall have the same force and effect as if it were inserted, word for word, in the present treaty.

5. The state of uneasiness and of fermentation, which after so many violent convulsions, and particularly after the last catastrophe, France must still experience, notwithstanding the paternal intentions of her King, and the advantages secured to every class of his subjects by the Constitutional Charter (No. 14), requiring, for the security of the neighbouring States, certain measures of precaution of a temporary guarantee, it has been judged indispensable to occupy, during a fixed time, by a corps of allied troops certain military positions along the frontiers of France, under the express reserve, that such occupation shall in no way prejudice the sovereignty of His Most Christian Majesty, nor the state of possession, such as it is recognized and confirmed by the present treaty. The number of these troops shall not exceed 150,000 men ... The utmost extent of the duration of this military occupation is fixed at 5 years. It may terminate before that period if, at the end of 3 years, the Allied Sovereigns, after having, in concert with His Majesty the King of France, maturely examined their reciprocal situation and interests, and the progress which shall have been made in France in the re-establishment of order and tranquillity, shall agree to acknowledge that the motives which led them to that measure have ceased to exist. But whatever may be the result of this deliberation, all the fortresses and positions occupied by the allied troops shall, at the expiration of 5 years, be evacuated without further delay, and given up to His Most Christian Majesty ...

8. All the dispositions of the Treaty of Paris of the 30th May, 1814 (No. 1) relative to the countries ceded by the treaty, shall equally apply to the several territories and districts ceded by the present treaty ...

11. The Treaty of Paris of the 30th of May, 1814 (No. 1) and the Final Act of the Congress of Vienna of the 9th of June 1815 are confirmed, and shall be maintained in all such of their enactments which shall not have been modified by the articles of the present treaty ...

5. *The Quadruple Alliance, 20 November 1815*

The aim of this treaty was to provide machinery for the enforcement of the provisions of the two peace treaties of Paris (Nos 1 and 4) and for the maintenance of a stable peace in Europe through the 'Congress System', the foundations of which are laid in article 6.

Our text gives the treaty between Great Britain and Austria; the same treaty was signed on the same day by each two of the four parties.

Source: E. Hertslet, *The Map of Europe by Treaty* (London, Butterworth, 1875), vol. i, pp. 372–5.

The purpose of the alliance concluded at Vienna the 25th day of March, 1815 (No. 2) having been happily attained by the re-establishment in France of the order of things which the last criminal attempt of Napoleon Bonaparte had momentarily subverted; Their Majesties the King of the United Kingdom of Great Britain and Ireland, the Emperor of Austria, King of Hungary and Bohemia, the Emperor of all the Russias, and the King of Prussia, considering that the repose of Europe is essentially interwoven with the confirmation of the order of things founded on the maintenance of the Royal authority and of the Constitutional Charter (No. 14), and wishing to employ all their means to prevent the general tranquillity (the object of the wishes of mankind and the constant end of their efforts) from being again disturbed; desirous moreover to draw closer the ties which unite them for the common interests of their people, have resolved to give to the principles solemnly laid down in the Treaties of Chaumont[1] of the 1st March, 1814, and of Vienna of the 25th March, 1815 (No. 2), the application the most analogous to the present state of affairs, and to fix beforehand by a solemn treaty the principles which they propose to follow, in order to guarantee Europe from dangers by which she may still be menaced . . .

1. The High Contracting Parties reciprocally promise to maintain in its force and vigour the treaty signed this day with His Most Christian Majesty[2] (No. 4) and to see that the stipulations of the said treaty . . . shall be strictly and faithfully executed in their fullest extent.

[1] Treaty between the four principal Allies which laid the foundations of the peace settlement.
[2] The King of France.

2. The High Contracting Parties, having engaged in the war which has just terminated, for the purpose of maintaining inviolably the arrangements settled at Paris last year, for the safety and interest of Europe, have judged it advisable to renew the said engagements by the present act, and to confirm them as mutually obligatory, subject to the modifications contained in the treaty signed this day with the Plenipotentiaries of His Most Christian Majesty (No. 4), and particularly those by which Napoleon Bonaparte and his family . . . have been for ever excluded from Supreme Power in France, which exclusion the Contracting Powers bind themselves by the present act to maintain in full vigour, and, should it be necessary, with the whole of their forces. And as the same revolutionary principles which upheld the last criminal usurpation, might again, under other forms, convulse France, and thereby endanger the repose of other States; under these circumstances, the High Contracting Parties solemnly admitting it to be their duty to redouble their watchfulness for the tranquillity and interests of their people, engage, in case so unfortunate an event should again occur, to concert amongst themselves, and with His Most Christian Majesty, the measures which they may judge necessary to be pursued for the safety of their respective States, and for the general tranquillity of Europe.

3. [The allied troops left in France as army of occupation are intended to ensure that the first two articles of this treaty are carried out. Should they be attacked by France, each of the Powers will furnish an additional contingent of 60,000 men.]

4. If, unfortunately, the forces stipulated in the preceding article should be found insufficient, the High Contracting Parties will concert together, without loss of time, as to the additional number of troops to be furnished by each for the support of the common cause; and they engage to employ, in case of need, the whole of their forces, in order to bring the war to a speedy and successful termination, reserving to themselves the right to prescribe, by common consent, such conditions of peace as shall hold out to Europe a sufficient guarantee against the recurrence of a similar calamity.

5. [Even after the period of occupation in France ceases, the terms of this treaty will remain in force] for the maintenance of the stipulations contained in articles 1 and 2 of the present Act.

6. To facilitate and to secure the execution of the present treaty, and to consolidate the connections which at the present moment so closely unite the four sovereigns for the happiness of the world, the High Contracting Parties have agreed to renew their meetings at fixed periods, either under the immediate auspices of the Sovereigns themselves, or by their respective ministers, for the purpose of consulting upon their common interests, and for the consideration of the measures which at each of those periods shall be considered the most salutary for the repose and prosperity of nations, and for the maintenance of the peace of Europe . . .

6. Congress of Aix-la-Chapelle, 1818

The Congress envisaged in Article 5 of the second Peace of Paris (No. 4) was held at Aix-la-Chapelle in 1818. The Powers agreed to the withdrawal of the occupation army from France and re-admitted France to the meetings of the Powers. They also considered a proposal from Tsar Alexander I for the formation of a close Union of Five Powers. While the Tsar's proposals were too far-reaching and therefore unacceptable, a form of Union or Concert was agreed to.

The proceedings of the Congress are summarized in its Protocol (a), while the principles of the new Union are discussed in the Declaration of the Five Cabinets (b).

Source: E. Hertslet, *The Map of Europe by Treaty* (London, Butterworth, 1875), vol. i, pp. 571–4.

(a) Protocol of Conference between the Plenipotentiaries of Austria, France, Great Britain, Prussia and Russia. Signed at Aix-la-Chapelle, 15 November 1818.

The Ministers of Austria, France, Great Britain, Prussia and Russia . . . have assembled in conference, to take into consideration the relations which ought to be established, in the actual state of affairs, between France and the co-subscribing Powers of the Treaty of Peace of the 20th November, 1815 (No. 4)— relations which, by assuring to France the place that belongs to her in the European system, will bind her more closely to the pacific and benevolent views in which all the Sovereigns participate, and will thus consolidate the general tranquillity.

After having maturely investigated the conservative principles of the great interests which constitute the order of things established in Europe, under the auspices of Divine Providence, by the Treaty of Paris of the 30th of May, 1814 (No. 1), the *Récès*[1] of Vienna (9th June, 1815), and the Treaty of peace of the year 1815 (No. 4), the Courts subscribing the present act do, accordingly, unanimously acknowledge and declare:—

1. That they are firmly resolved never to depart, neither in their mutual relations, nor in those which bind them to other States, from the principle of intimate union which has hitherto presided over all their common relations and interests—a union rendered more strong and indissoluble by the bonds of Christian fraternity which the Sovereigns have formed among themselves.
2. That this Union, which is the more real and durable, inasmuch as it depends on no separate interest or temporary combination, can only have for its object the maintenance of general peace, founded on a religious respect for the engagements contained in the treaties, and for the whole of the rights resulting therefrom.
3. That France, associated with other Powers by the restoration of the legitimate monarchical and constitutional power, engages henceforth to concur in the maintenance and consolidation of a system which has given peace to Europe, and which can alone insure its duration.
4. That if, for the better attaining the above declared object, the Powers which have concurred in the present act, should judge it necessary to establish particular meetings, either of the Sovereigns themselves, or of their respective ministers and plenipotentiaries, there to treat in common of their own interests, in so far as they have reference to the object of their present deliberations, the time and place of these meetings shall, on each occasion, be previously fixed by means of diplomatic communications; and that in the case of these meetings having for their object affairs specially connected with the interests of the other States of Europe, they shall only take place in pursuance of a formal invitation on the part of such of those States as the said affairs may concern, and under the express reservation of their right of direct participation therein, either directly or by their plenipotentiaries.

---

[1] Final Act.

5. That the resolutions contained in the present act shall be made known to all the Courts of Europe, by the annexed Declaration (No. 6(b)) . . .

(b) Declaration of the Five Cabinets (Great Britain, Austria, France, Prussia and Russia). Signed at Aix-la-Chapelle, 15 November 1818.

At the period of completing the pacification of Europe by the resolution of withdrawing the foreign troops from the French territory; and when there is an end of those measures of precaution which unfortunate circumstances had rendered necessary, the Ministers and Plenipotentiaries of their Majesties the Emperor of Austria, the King of France, the King of Great Britain, the King of Prussia, and the Emperor of all the Russias, have received orders from their sovereigns, to make known to all the Courts of Europe the results of their meeting at Aix-la-Chapelle, and with that view to publish the following Declaration:—

The Convention of the 9th October, 1818, which definitively regulated the execution of the engagements agreed to in the Treaty of Peace of 20th November, 1815 (No. 4), is considered by the Sovereigns who concurred therein, as the accomplishment of the work of peace, and as the completion of the political system destined to ensure its solidity.

The intimate union established among the Monarchs, who are joint parties to this system, by their own principles, no less than by the interests of their people, offers to Europe the most sacred pledge of its future tranquillity.

The object of this union is as simple as it is great and salutary. It does not tend to any new political combination—to any change in the relations sanctioned by existing treaties. Calm and consistent in its proceedings, it has no other object than the maintenance of peace, and the guarantee of those transactions on which the peace was founded and consolidated.

The Sovereigns, in forming this august union, have regarded as its fundamental basis their invariable resolution never to depart, either among themselves, or in their relations with other States, from the strictest observation of the principles of the right of nations; principles, which in their application to a state of permanent peace, can alone effectually guarantee the independence of each Government, and the stability of the general association.

Faithful to these principles, the Sovereigns will maintain them equally in those meetings at which they may be personally present, or in those which shall take place among their ministers; whether they be for purpose of discussing in common their own interests, or whether they shall relate to questions in which other Governments shall formally claim their interference. The same spirit which will direct their councils, and reign in their diplomatic communications, will preside also at these meetings; and the repose of the world will be constantly their motive and their end.

It is with these sentiments that the Sovereigns have consummated the work to which they were called. They will not cease to labour for its confirmation and perfection. They solemnly acknowledge that their duties towards God and the people whom they govern make it peremptory on them to give to the work, as far as it is in their power, an example of justice, of concord, and of moderation; happy in the power of consecrating, from henceforth, all their efforts to protect the arts of peace, to increase the internal prosperity of their States, and to awaken those sentiments of religion and morality, whose influence has been but too much enfeebled by the misfortune of the times.

7. *The Congress of Troppau, 1820*

In 1820, liberal revolutions broke out in Spain, in Naples, and in Portugal, and the Powers met at Troppau to concert their measures for the preservation of the *status quo*. At Troppau, the Powers of the Holy Alliance played the important part; and the document which follows under (a) describes the attitudes of Austria, Prussia, and Russia. Under (b) part of a note by the British Government is included to explain the reasons motivating it to differentiate itself from the Holy Alliance.

The Congress of Troppau adjourned and met again at Laibach in 1821. For that part of its activities see No. 8.

Source: *Annual Register*, 1820, pp. 735–9.

(a) Circular Note of the Courts of Austria, Russia and Prussia, 8 December 1820.

Informed of the false and extravagant reports respecting the object and the results of the conference at Troppau, which malevolent persons have put in circulation, and the credulous have further disseminated, the allied courts consider it to be necessary to give authentic explanations to their ministers at foreign courts, to enable them to correct the mistakes and false opinions occasioned by these reports. The annexed short view furnishes you with the means . . .:

The events of the 8th March, in Spain; of 2nd July, in Naples; and the catastrophe of Portugal[1] could not but excite a deep feeling of uneasiness and sorrow in all those who are bound to provide for the security of States, and at the same time to inspire them with a desire to unite and jointly to take into consideration how to eradicate all the evils which threatened to break out over Europe. It was natural that these feelings should especially influence those Powers who had lately conquered the revolution, and now see it raise its head anew; and it was equally natural that those Powers, in order to oppose it for the third time, should have recourse to the same means of which they had made so successful a use in the memorable contest which freed Europe from a yoke it had borne for twenty years. Every thing encouraged the hope, that this union, founded in the most dangerous circumstances—crowned by the most splendid success—confirmed by the negotiations of 1814, 1815, and 1818—as it had prepared, founded, and completed the peace of the world—as it had delivered the European continent from the tyranny of the revolution, would also be able to check a no less tyrannical, no less detestable power, the power of rebellion and crime.

These were the motives, this the object of the conferences at Troppau . . .

The Powers exercised an undisputed right, when they considered of joint measures of precautions against states, in which an overthrow of the Government, effected by rebellion, even considered only as an example, must give occasion to a hostile attitude. Towards all legitimate constitutions and governments the exercise of this right became the more urgent when those who had come into this situation endeavoured to communicate the misfortune which they had drawn on themselves to the neighbouring countries, and to spread around them rebellion

---

[1] Liberal revolutions.

and confusion. In such an attitude, in such conduct, there is an evident breach of the compact which insures to all European governments, besides the inviolability of their territory, the enjoyment of those peaceful relations which exclude every reciprocal encroachment.

This incontrovertible fact was the point from which the allied courts departed. The ministers who could be furnished at Troppau itself with precise instructions from their Sovereigns agreed together therefore on the principles of conduct with respect to States, whose form of government had undergone a change by force, and the amicable or compulsory measures which, in cases where a substantial and wholesome influence was to be expected, might bring back such States within the pale of the union. They communicated their deliberations to the courts of London and Paris, that these courts might take them into their own consideration.

As the revolution at Naples daily takes more root, as no other so nearly and so evidently endangers the tranquillity of the neighbouring States, and as no other can be so immediately and speedily opposed, a conviction arose of the necessity of proceeding towards the Kingdom of the Two Sicilies according to the principles above stated.

In order to lead to conciliating measures for this purpose, the Monarchs assembled at Troppau resolved to invite the King of the Two Sicilies to an interview at Laibach; a step, the sole object of which was to free the will of the King from all external constraint, and to place His Majesty in the situation of a mediator between his misled people and the States whose tranquillity was threatened. As the Monarchs were resolved not to recognize Governments which had been produced by open rebellion, they could not enter into negotiations except with the King alone. Their ministers and agents at Naples have received the necessary instructions to this effect.

France and England have been invited to participate in this step, and it is to be expected that they will not refuse their concurrence, as the principles on which the invitation is founded are perfectly conformable to the treaties they have formerly signed, and, besides, offer a pledge of the most just and peaceable sentiments.

The system adopted between Austria, Russia and Prussia is

not a new one; it reposes on the same maxims which were the basis of the treaties by which the Union of European States was founded (No. 6). The intimate harmony between the courts which are in the center of this union can only gain by it in strength and duration. The Union will consolidate itself in the same manner as it was formed by the Monarchs who founded it, and has been gradually adopted by all those who were convinced of its evident, now less than ever to be doubted, advantages. No further proof is necessary, that neither thoughts of conquest, nor the pretensions to violate the independence of other Governments in their internal administration, nor the endeavour to impede voluntary and wise ameliorations, consonant with the true interest of nations, has had any share in the resolutions of the Allied Powers. They desire nothing but to maintain peace, to free Europe from the scourge of revolution, and to prevent, or to lessen, as far as in their power, the evil which arises from the violation of all principles of order and morality. On these conditions they think themselves entitled, as the reward of their cares and exertions, to the unanimous approbation of the world.

(b) Circular Dispatch to His Majesty's Missions at Foreign Courts, 19 January 1821.

Sir,

I should not have felt it necessary to have made any communication to you, in the present state of the discussions begun at Troppau and transferred to Laibach, had it not been for a circular communication (No. 7(a)) which has been addressed by the Courts of Austria, Prussia and Russia to their several missions, and which His Majesty's Government conceive, if not adverted to, might (however unintentionally) convey, upon the subject therein alluded to, very erroneous impressions of the past, as well as of the present, sentiments of the British Government.

It has become therefore necessary to inform you, that the King has felt himself obliged to decline becoming a party to the measure in question.

These measures embrace two distinct objects—1st, the establishment of certain general principles for the regulation of the future political conduct of the Allies in the cases therein described; 2ndly, the proposed mode of dealing, under these principles, with the existing affairs of Naples.

The system of measures proposed under the former head, if to be reciprocally acted upon, would be in direct repugnance to the fundamental laws of this country. But even if this decisive objection did not exist, the British Government would nevertheless regard the principles on which those measures rest, to be such as could not be safely admitted as a system of international law. They are of opinion that their adoption would inevitably sanction, and, in the hands of less beneficent Monarchs, might hereafter lead to a much more frequent and extensive interference in the internal transactions of States, than they are persuaded is intended by the august parties from whom they proceed, or can be reconciled either with the general interest, or with the efficient authority and dignity of independent Sovereigns. They do not regard the Alliance as entitled, under existing treaties, to assume, in their character as Allies, any such general powers, nor do they conceive that such extraordinary powers could be assumed in virtue of any fresh diplomatic transaction among the Allied Courts, without their either attributing to themselves a supremacy incompatible with the rights of other States, or, if to be acquired through the special accession of such States, without introducing a federative system in Europe, not only unwieldy and ineffectual to its object, but leading to many most serious inconveniences.

With respect to the particular case of Naples, the British Government, at the very earliest moment, did not hesitate to express their strong disapprobation of the mode and circumstances under which that revolution was understood to have been effected; but they, at the same time, expressly declared to the several Allied Courts that they should not consider themselves as either called upon, or justified to advise an interference on the part of this country: they fully admitted, however, that other European States, and especially Austria and the Italian Powers, might feel themselves differently circumstanced; and they professed that it was not their purpose to prejudge the question as it might affect them, or to interfere with the course which such states might think fit to adopt, with a view to their own security, provided only that they were ready to give every reasonable assurance that their views were not directed to purposes of aggrandisement, subversive of the territorial system of Europe, as established by the late treaties . . .

Castlereagh.

8. *The Congress of Laibach, 1821*

The Congress of Troppau was adjourned late in 1820, and the Allied Sovereigns met again at Laibach early in 1821. There they were joined by the King of the Two Sicilies and concerted their measures for the restoration of order in Italy. Austrian troops were charged with the task, and they soon defeated the revolutions both in Naples and Piedmont.

The following is part of an identical circular dispatch by the Sovereigns of Austria, Prussia, and Russia, to their ministers at foreign Courts, in which they communicate their reasons for adopting a principle of intervention whenever and wherever the rights of a Monarch are threatened.

Source: *Annual Register*, 1821, pp. 599–601.

Laibach, May 12, [1821]

The assembling of the Allied Monarchs, and of their ministers, at Troppau, determined upon after the events which had overturned the legitimate Government at Naples, was destined to fix the particular point of view which it became necessary to assume with respect to those fatal events, in order to concert a common course of proceeding, and to combine, in the spirit of justice, of preservation, and of moderation, the measures necessary for protecting Italy from a general insurrection, and the neighbouring States from the most imminent dangers. Thanks to the fortunate unanimity of sentiments and intentions which prevailed between the three august Sovereigns, this first labour was soon accomplished. Principles clearly laid down, and mutually adopted with the most perfect sincerity, led to analogous resolutions; and the bases which were established at the very first conferences have been invariably followed during the whole course of a meeting rendered memorable by the most remarkable results.

This meeting, transferred to Laibach, assumed a more decisive character by the presence and the co-operation of the King of the Two Sicilies, and by the unanimous concurrence with which the princes of Italy acceded to the system adopted by the Allied Cabinets. The Monarchs were convinced that the Governments most closely interested in the destinies of the Peninsula rendered justice to the purity of their intentions; and that a Sovereign, placed in a most painful situation by acts with which perfidy and violence had contrived to associate his name, yielded with entire confidence to measures which would at once terminate this state of moral captivity, and restore to his faithful subjects that repose and that well-being of which they had been deprived by criminal factions.

The effect of these measures soon manifested itself. The edifice which had been reared by revolt—fragile in its superstructure, and weak in its foundation; resting only on the cunning of some, and upon the momentary blindness of others; condemned by an immense majority of the nation, and odious even to the army which was enrolled to defend it—crumbled to dust at the first contact with the regular troops selected to destroy it, and who at once demonstrated its nothingness. The legitimate authority is restored; the factious have been dispersed; the Neapolitan people are delivered from the tyranny of those impudent impostors, who, deluding them with the dreams of false liberty, in reality inflicted upon them the most bitter vexations; who imposed upon them enormous sacrifices solely to gratify their own ambition and rapine; and who were rapidly accelerating the ruin of the country, of which they incessantly proclaimed themselves the regenerators.

This important restoration has been completed, as far as it could, and as it ought to be, by the counsels and acts of the Allied Sovereigns. Now, when the King of the Two Sicilies is again invested with the plenitude of his rights, the Monarchs will confine themselves to the most ardent good wishes for the plans which this Sovereign is about to adopt to re-construct his Government upon a solid basis, and to secure, by laws and by wise institutions, the true interests of his subjects, and the constant prosperity of his Kingdom.

During the progress of these great transactions we saw burst forth, on more than one side, the effects of that vast conspiracy which has so long existed against all established power, and against all those rights consecrated by the social order under which Europe has enjoyed so many centuries of glory and happiness. The existence of this conspiracy was not unknown to the Monarchs; but in the midst of those agitations which Italy experienced after the catastrophe of 1820, and of those wild impulses which were hence communicated to every mind, it developed itself with increasing rapidity, and its true character stood revealed in open day. It is not, as might have been supposed at an earlier period—it is not against this or that form of government, more particularly exposed to their declamations, that the dark enterprises of the authors of these plots, and the frantic wishes of their blind partisans are directed. Those States which have admitted changes into their political system are no more secure from their attacks than those whose venerable institutions have survived the storms of time. Pure monarchies, limited monarchies, federative constitutions, republics, all are engulfed in the proscriptions of a sect who brand as an oligarchy every thing, of whatever kind, that rises above the level of chimerical equality. The leaders of the impious league, indifferent as to what may result from the general destruction they meditate, careless about all stable and permanent organization, aim merely at the fundamental bases of society. To overthrow what exists, for the chance of substituting whatever accident may suggest to their wild imaginations, or to their turbulent passions—this is the essence of their doctrines, the secret of all their machinations.

The Allied Sovereigns could not fail to perceive that there was only one barrier to oppose to this devastating torrent. To preserve what is legally established—such was, as it ought to be, the invariable principle of their policy, the point of departure, and the final object of all their resolutions. They were not to be deterred in their purpose by the vain clamours of ignorance or malice, accusing them of condemning humanity to a state of stagnation and torpor, incompatible with its natural and progressive march, and with the perfecting of social institutions. Never have these Monarchs manifested the least disposition to thwart real ameliorations, or the reform of abuses which creep into the best governments. Very different views have constantly animated them; and if this repose which Governments and nations were justified in supposing secured by the pacification of Europe, has not operated all the good which might have been expected to result from it, it is because Governments have been compelled to concentrate all their energies in the means of opposing bounds to the progress of a faction, which, disseminating everywhere error, discontent, and a fanaticism for innovation, would soon have rendered the existence of any public order whatever problematical. Useful or necessary changes in legislation, and in the administration of States, ought only to emanate from the free will and the intelligent and well-weighed conviction of those whom God has rendered responsible for power. All that deviates from this line necessarily leads to disorder, commotions, and evils far more insufferable than those which they pretend to remedy. Penetrated with this eternal truth, the Sovereigns have not hesitated to proclaim it with frankness and vigour; they have declared that, in respecting the rights and independence of all legitimate power, they regarded as legally null, and as disavowed by the principles which constitute the public right of Europe, all pretended reform operated by revolt and open hostility. They have acted conformably to this declaration, in the events which have taken place at Naples, in those of Piedmont, and those even which, under very different circumstances, though produced by combinations equally criminal, have recently made the eastern part of Europe a prey to incalculable convulsions . . .

9. The Congress of Verona, 1822

The Congress of Verona, consisting of representatives of Austria, France, Great Britain, Prussia, and Russia, met to discuss the affairs of Greece, where risings occurred against Turkish rule. Greece, however, was overshadowed by events in Spain, where the revolutionary situation was becoming more acute. Both the Tsar and the Government of France wished to intervene to restore the King to full power. Great Britain soon dissociated herself from the proceedings, and the Duke of Wellington left Verona before the Congress ended.

Austria, Prussia, and Russia finally agreed to let France restore order in Spain, and they each addressed a separate note to the Spanish Government expressing their views. Our document (a) consists of part of the Austrian note, while under (b) we have the French note threatening warlike action. France indeed invaded Spain early in 1823, and was successful in restoring the King.

Source: *Annual Register*, 1822, pp. 569–76.

(a) Dispatch of Prince Metternich to the Chargé d'Affaires of Austria at Madrid, 14 December 1822.

. . . The character of the revolution of Spain was clear to us from its origin. Conformably to eternal decrees, good can never arise to States, any more than to individuals, from a disregard of the first duties imposed upon man in the social order; the amelioration of the condition of subjects should not be commenced by criminal illusions, by perverting opinion, and by misleading the conscience: and military revolt can never form the basis of a happy and durable government.

The revolution of Spain, considered solely in regard to the destructive influence it has exercised over the kingdom which has experienced it, would be an event worthy the undivided attention and interest of foreign Sovereigns; for the prosperity or the ruin of one of the most interesting States of Europe cannot be in their eyes an indifferent alternative; only the enemies of Spain, if perchance she have any, could be capable of regarding, unmoved, the convulsions which prey upon her. A just repugnance, however, to meddle with the internal affairs of an independent nation would perhaps influence these Sovereigns not to pronounce on the situation of Spain, if the evil operated by her revolution was concentrated, or could be concentrated, within her territorial limits. But this is not the case; this revolution, even before it arrived at maturity, had been the cause of great disasters in other States; it was this revolution which, by the contagion of its principles and of its example, and by the intrigues of its principal partisans, created the revolutions of Naples and Piedmont; it was this revolution which would have excited insurrections throughout Italy, menaced France, and compromised Germany, but for the intervention of the Powers which preserved Europe from this new conflagration. Every where the destructive means employed in Spain, to prepare and consummate the revolution, have served as a model to those who flattered themselves that they were paving the way to new conquests. Every where the Spanish constitution has become the rallying point and the war whoop of faction, combined alike against the security of thrones and the repose of subjects . . .

On meeting his august allies at Verona, His Majesty, the Emperor, has had the happiness again to find in their counsels the same tutelary and disinterested dispositions which have constantly guided his own. The tone of the dispatches, which will be addressed to Madrid, will vouch for this fact, and will leave no doubt of the sincere anxiety of the Powers to serve the cause of Spain, by demonstrating to her the necessity of pursuing a different course. It is certain that the grievances which oppress her have lately augmented in fearful progression ... Civil war rages in several of her provinces; her relations with the greatest portion of Europe are deranged or suspended; and her relations with France have assumed so problematical a character as to justify serious disquietude respecting the consequences which may thence result.

Would not such a state of things justify the most fatal forebodings?

Every Spaniard, who knows the real state of his country, ought to feel that, in order to burst the fetters which now bind the Monarch and his subjects, Spain must terminate that state of separation which has been the result of late events. The relations of confidence and sincerity must be re-established between her and the other Governments; relations which, by guaranteeing on the one hand her firm intention to associate herself in the common cause of the European Monarchs, may, on the other hand, furnish the means of estimating her real will, and of rejecting every thing calculated to pervert and restrain it. But to attain this end, it is especially indispensable that her King should be free, not only as regards that personal liberty which every individual may claim under the reign of the laws, but that liberty which a Sovereign ought to enjoy in order to discharge his high vocation. The King of Spain will be free from the moment that he shall have the power of putting an end to the evils which afflict his subjects, of restoring order and peace in his Kingdom, of surrounding himself with men equally worthy of his confidence by their principles and talents; and finally of substituting for a regime acknowledged to be impracticable even by those whose egotism or pride still attaches them to it, an order of things in which the rights of the Monarch shall be happily blended with the real interests and legitimate views of all classes of the nation ...

(b) The President of the [French] Council of Ministers to the Minister at Madrid, 25 December 1822.

As your political situation may be changed in consequence of the resolutions adopted at Verona, French candour requires that you should be directed to make known the views of the Government of His Most Christian Majesty to the Government of His Catholic Majesty.[1]

Since the revolution which took place in Spain in April 1820 France, notwithstanding the dangers which that revolution presented for her, carefully endeavoured to draw close the bonds which unite the two Kings, and to maintain the relations which exist between the two nations.

But the influence, under which the changes in the Spanish monarchy were brought about, has become more powerful in consequence of the very results of these changes, as it was easy to foresee.

A constitution, which King Ferdinand on resuming the crown neither recognized nor accepted, was imposed on him by a military insurrection. The natural consequence of this transaction has been, that each dissatisfied Spaniard considers himself authorized to seek, by the same means, the establishment of an order of things more in harmony with his opinions and principles. The employment of force has created the right of force.

Hence the movements of the guards at Madrid, and the appearance of armed corps in different parts of Spain. The provinces bordering on France have been chiefly the theatre of the civil war. Thus it has become necessary for France to protect herself from this state of disorder in the Peninsula. The events which have occurred since the establishment of an army of observation have sufficiently justified the foresight of His Majesty's Government.

Meanwhile the Congress, which since last year had been looked to for deciding the affairs of Italy assembled at Verona.

As an integral part of this Congress, France was bound to explain herself with respect to the armaments to which she had been compelled to have recourse, and to the manner in which she might eventually employ them. The precautions of France appeared just to her Allies, and the continental Powers adopted the resolution of uniting with her to aid her (if there ever should be occasion) in maintaining her dignity and tranquillity.

France would be satisfied with a resolution at once so bene-

---

[1] His Most Christian Majesty: the King of France; His Catholic Majesty: the King of Spain.

volent and so honourable with respect to her; but Austria,
Prussia and Russia judged it necessary to add to the particular
act of alliance a manifestation of their sentiments. Diplomatic
notes are for that purpose addressed by these three Powers to
their respective ministers at Madrid (No. 9(a)), who will communicate them to the Spanish Government, and in their
ulterior conduct follow the orders which they shall have received from their courts.

For your part, in giving these explanations to the Cabinet of
Madrid, you will declare to it, that His Majesty's Government
is intimately united with its allies in the firm resolution to repel
by every means revolutionary principles and movements;—
that it equally concurs with its allies in the wishes which they
form, that a remedy may be found by the noble Spanish nation
itself, for these evils—evils which are of a nature to disturb the
Governments of Europe, and to impose on them precautions
which always must be painful.

You will, in particular, take care to make known that the
people of the Peninsula, restored to tranquillity, will find in
their neighbours faithful and sincere friends. You will, therefore, give to the Cabinet of Madrid the assurance that the
succours of every kind, which France can dispose of in favour
of Spain, will always be offered to her for the purpose of assuring her happiness, and increasing prosperity; but you will at
the same time declare that France will in no respect relax the
preservatory measures which she has adopted, while Spain
continues to be torn by factions. His Majesty's Government
will not even hesitate to recall you from Madrid, and to seek
guarantees in more efficacious measures, if its essential interests
continue to be compromised, and if it lose the hope of an amelioration, which it takes a pleasure in expecting from the sentiments
which have so long united Spaniards and Frenchmen in love of
their Kings, and for a wise liberty . . .

10. *Treaty for the Pacification of Greece, 6 July 1827*

The rising in Greece against Turkish rule has already been mentioned in the introduction to the previous document. In this connexion
many complications arose, too many to mention more than two:
the Austrian wish to support a legitimate government, even if

non-Christian, and the Russian wish to give support to their fellow-Orthodox, the Greeks. After prolonged negotiations, Great Britain, France, and Russia agreed on the terms of the following treaty; the Porte rejected the terms, and war ensued, in which the Powers were victorious. An independent Greece was established, with Turkish agreement, in 1830.

Source: *Annual Register*, 1827, pp. 403–5 (with emendations).

In the Name of the most Holy and undivided Trinity.

His Majesty the King of the United Kingdom of Great Britain and Ireland, His Majesty the King of France and Navarre, and His Majesty the Emperor of all the Russias, penetrated with the necessity of putting an end to the sanguinary contest which, by delivering up the Greek provinces and the isles of the Archipelago to all the disorders of anarchy, produces daily fresh impediments to the commerce of the European States, and gives occasion to piracies, which not only expose the subjects of the High Contracting Parties to considerable losses, but besides render necessary burthensome measures of protection and repression; [the Kings of the United Kingdom and France] having besides received, on the part of the Greeks, a pressing request to interpose their mediation with the Ottoman Porte, and being, as well as His Majesty the Emperor of all the Russias, animated by the desire of stopping the effusion of blood, and of arresting the evils of all kinds which might arise from the continuance of such a state of things, have resolved to unite their efforts and to regulate the operation thereof by a formal treaty, with the view of re-establishing peace between the contending parties by means of an arrangement which is called for as much by humanity as by the interest of the repose of Europe . . .

1. The Contracting Powers will offer to the Ottoman Porte their mediation, with a view of bringing about a reconciliation between it and the Greeks.

This offer of mediation shall be made to this Power immediately after the ratification of the Treaty, by means of a collective declaration signed by the Plenipotentiaries of the allied Courts at Constantinople; and there shall be made, at the same time, to the two contending parties, a demand of an immediate armistice between them, as a preliminary condition indispensable to the opening of any negotiation.

2. The arrangement to be proposed to the Ottoman Porte shall rest on the following bases: the Greeks shall hold of the Sultan as their suzerain; and in consequence of his suzerainty they shall pay to the Ottoman Empire an annual tribute, the amount of which shall be fixed, once for all, by a common agreement. They shall be governed by the authorities whom they shall themselves choose and nominate, but in the nomination of whom the Porte shall have a determinate voice.

To bring about a complete separation between the individuals of the two nations, and to prevent the collisions which are the inevitable consequence of so long a struggle, the Greeks shall enter upon possession of the Turkish property situated either on the continent or in the isles of Greece, on the condition of indemnifying the former proprietors, either by the payment of an annual sum, to be added to the tribute which is to be paid to the Porte, or by some other transaction of the same nature . . .
5. The Contracting Powers will not seek in these arrangements any augmentation of territory, any exclusive influence, any commercial advantage for their subjects which the subjects of any other nation may not equally obtain . . .

Additional and Secret Article.

In the case that the Ottoman Porte does not accept, within the space of one month, the mediation which shall be proposed, the High Contracting Parties agree upon the following measures:—

1. It shall be declared, by their representatives at Constantinople to the Porte, that the inconveniences and evils pointed out in the public treaty as inseparable from the state of things subsisting in the East for the last six years, and the termination of which, through the means at the disposal of the Sublime Porte, appears still remote, impose upon the High Contracting Parties the necessity of taking immediate measures for an approximation with the Greeks.

It is to be understood that this approximation shall be brought about by establishing commercial relations with the Greeks . . .
2. If, within the said term of one month, the Porte do not accept the armistice proposed . . . or the Greeks refuse to execute it, [the Powers will use all appropriate means to put into effect the conditions of the public treaty].

3. Finally, if contrary to all expectation these measures do not yet suffice to induce the adoption by the Ottoman Porte of the propositions made by the High Contracting Parties, or if, on the other hand, the Greeks renounce the conditions stipulated in their favour in the Treaty of this day, the High Contracting Powers will, nevertheless, continue to prosecute the work of pacification on the bases agreed upon between them; and, in consequence, they authorize from this time forward their representatives in London to discuss and determine the ulterior measures to which it may become necessary to resort . . .

11. *Pact of Young Europe, 15 April 1834*

Having organized his Young Italy movement (No. 84), Mazzini, in exile in Switzerland, formed with sixteen other young revolutionaries of several nationalities the Young Europe movement, of which the following is the charter. Although the movement itself never gained any great importance, the document is included not only to provide a contrast to the documents of the official diplomacy of the period, but also to illustrate the international character of the radical liberal movement at this time. (Cf. No. 8, p. 23.)

Source: *Life and writings of Giuseppe Mazzini*, new ed. (London, Smith-Elder, 1891), vol. iii, pp. 26–34.

We, the undersigned, men of progress and liberty:

Believing—in the equality and fraternity of all men:

Believing—that humanity is destined to achieve, through a continuous progress under the dominion of the universal moral law, the free and harmonious development of its faculties, and the fulfilment of its mission in the universe:

That this can only be achieved through the active co-operation of all its members, freely associated together:

That true, free association can only exist amongst equals; since every inequality implies a violation of independence, and every violation of independence is the destruction of free agreement and consent:

That liberty, equality and humanity are all equally sacred—that they constitute the three inviolable elements of every positive solution of the social problem—and that whensoever any one of these elements is sacrificed to the other two, the organization of human effort towards the solution of that problem is radically defective:

Convinced—That although the ultimate *aim* to be reached by humanity is essentially one, and the general principles destined to guide the various human families in their advance towards that aim, are identical for all; there are yet many paths disclosed to progress:

Convinced—That every man and every people has a special mission; the fulfilment of which determines the *individuality* of that man or of that people, and at the same time bears a part in the accomplishment of the general mission of humanity:

Convinced lastly—That the association both of individuals and peoples is necessary to secure the free performance of the individual mission, and the certainty of its direction towards the fulfilment of the general mission:

Strong in our rights as men and citizens; strong in our own conscience and in the mandate given by God and humanity to all those truly desirous of consecrating their energies, their intellect, and their whole existence to the holy cause of the progress of the Peoples:

Having already constituted ourselves in free and independent national associations as the primitive nuclei of *Young Poland, Young Germany* and *Young Italy* (No. 84):

Assembled together by common consent for the general good, this 15th April, 1834, we, constituting ourselves, as far as our own efforts are concerned, securities and pledges for the future, have determined as follows:—

1. *Young Germany, Young Poland* and *Young Italy*, being Republican associations, having the same humanitarian aim in view, and led by the same faith in liberty, equality, and progress, do hereby fraternally associate and unite, now and for ever, in all matters concerning the general aim.

2. A declaration of those principles which constitute the universal moral law in its bearings upon human society shall be drawn up and signed by the three national committees. It shall set forth and define the belief, the purpose, and the general tendency of the three associations. Any of the members who shall separate their own work from that of the association, will be regarded as guilty of culpable violation of this *Act of Fraternity*, and will take the consequences of such violation.

3. In all matters not comprehended in the Declaration of Principles, and not appertaining to the general interest, each of the three associations will be free and independent.

4. An alliance—defensive and offensive—expressive of the solidarity of the Peoples, is established between the three associations. They will work together in harmony in the cause of the emancipation of their several countries. In matters peculiarly or specially concerning their own countries, they will each have a right to the assistance of the others.

5. An assembly of the National Committees or their delegates will constitute the Committee of *Young Europe*.

6. The fraternity of the three associations is decreed, and each of them is bound to fulfil every duty arising out of that fraternity.

7. The Committee of *Young Europe* will determine upon a symbol, to be common to all the members of the three associations. A common motto will be inscribed upon all the publications of the three associations.

8. Any people desirous of sharing the rights and duties established by this alliance, may do so by formally adhering to this *Act of Fraternity*, through the medium of their representatives.

GENERAL INSTRUCTIONS
For the Initiators

1. *Young Europe* is an association of men believing in a future of liberty, equality, and fraternity, for all mankind; and desirous of consecrating their thoughts and actions to the realization of that future.

GENERAL PRINCIPLES

2. One sole God;
　　One sole ruler,—His Law;
　　One sole interpreter of that law,—Humanity.

3. To constitute humanity in such wise as to enable it throughout a continuous progress to discover and apply the law of God by which it should be governed as speedily as possible: such is the mission of *Young Europe*.

4. As our true well-being consists in living in accordance with

the law of our being, the knowledge and fulfilment of the law of humanity is the sole source of good. The fulfilment of the mission of Young Europe will result in the general good.

5. Every mission constitutes a pledge of duty. Every man is bound to consecrate his every faculty to its fulfilment. He will derive his rule of action from the profound conviction of that duty.

6. Humanity can only arrive at the knowledge of its Law of Life through the free and harmonious development of all its faculties. Humanity can only reduce that knowledge to action through the free and harmonious development of all its faculties. Association is the sole means of realizing this development.

7. No true association is possible save among free men and equals.

8. By the law of God, given by Him to humanity, all men are free, are brothers and are equals.

9. Liberty is the right of every man to exercise his faculties without impediment or restraint, in the accomplishment of his special mission, and in the choice of the means most conducive to its accomplishment.

10. The free exercise of the faculties of the individual may in no case violate the rights of others. The special mission of each man must be accomplished in harmony with the general mission of Humanity. There is no other limit to human liberty.

11. Equality implies the recognition of uniform rights and duties for all men—for none may escape the action of the law by which they are defined—and every man should participate, in proportion to his labour, in the enjoyment of the produce resulting from the activity of all the social forces.

12. Fraternity is the reciprocal affection, the sentiment which inclines man to do unto others as he would that others should do unto him.

13. All privilege is a violation of equality. All arbitrary rule is a violation of liberty. Every act of egotism is a violation of fraternity.

14. Wheresoever privilege, arbitrary rule, or egotism are introduced into the social constitution, it is the duty of every man who comprehends his own mission to combat them by every means in his power.

15. That which is true of each individual with regard to the

other individuals forming part of the society to which he belongs, is equally true of every people with regard to humanity.

16. By the law of God, given by God to humanity, all the peoples are free—are brothers and are equals.

17. Every people has its special mission, which will co-operate towards the fulfilment of the general mission of humanity. That mission constitutes its *nationality*. Nationality is sacred.

18. All unjust rule, all violence, every act of egotism exercised to the injury of a people, is a violation of the liberty, equality and fraternity of the peoples. All the peoples should aid and assist each other in putting an end to it.

19. Humanity will only be truly constituted when all the peoples of which it is composed have acquired the free exercise of their sovereignty, and shall be associated in a Republican Confederation, governed and directed by a common Declaration of Principles and a common Pact, towards the common aim —the discovery and fulfilment of the Universal Moral Law.

12. The Eastern Question, 1840–41

The weakness of the Turkish Empire, visible already in the matter of Greece (No. 10), continued and was exploited by Mehemet Ali, Pasha of Egypt, in the eighteen-thirties. The French Government sought to utilize the difficulties of the Porte for the extension of France's influence in the Near East. The other Powers wished to prevent this and therefore concluded the following treaty (a) with the Porte. Assisted by them, the Sultan defeated Mehemet Ali.

Tsar Nicholas I tried to make the alienation of Great Britain from France over Egypt permanent by proposing an alliance against France. Lord Palmerston rejected the proposal and in the dispatch that follows under (b) set out some of the fundamental principles of British foreign policy. It is included as an example of Palmerston's writing, very important in the period.

Source: (a) *Annual Register*, 1840, pp. 446–8.
　　　　 (b) H. W. Temperley and L. Penson, *Foundations of British Foreign Policy* (London, Cambridge University Press, 1938), pp. 135–8.

(a) Treaty of London for the Pacification of the Levant, 15 July 1840.

His Highness the Sultan having addressed himself to Their Majesties the Queen of the United Kingdom of Great Britain and Ireland, the Emperor of Austria . . ., the King of Prussia, and the Emperor of all the Russias, to ask their support and assistance in the difficulties in which he finds himself placed by reason of the hostile proceedings of Mehemet Ali, Pasha of Egypt—difficulties which threaten with danger the integrity of the Ottoman Empire and the independence of the Sultan's throne—Their said Majesties, moved by the sincere friendship which subsists between them and the Sultan, animated by the desire of maintaining the integrity and independence of the Ottoman empire as a security for the peace of Europe . . . and desirous, moreover, to prevent the effusion of blood, which would be occasioned by a continuance of the hostilities which have recently broken out in Syria . . . Their said Majesties and His Highness the Sultan . . . have agreed upon . . . the following articles:—

1. His Highness the Sultan having come to an agreement with their [said] Majesties . . . as to the conditions of the arrangement which it is the intention of His Highness to grant to Mehemet Ali, . . . Their Majesties engage to act in perfect accord, and to unite their efforts in order to determine Mehemet Ali to conform to that arrangement; each of the High Contracting Parties reserving itself to co-operate for that purpose according to the means of action which each may have at its disposal.

2. If the pasha of Egypt should refuse to accept the above mentioned arrangement, which will be communicated to him by the Sultan, with the concurrence of Their aforesaid Majesties, Their Majesties engage to take, at the request of the Sultan, measures concerted and settled between them, to carry that arrangement into effect. In the meanwhile, the Sultan having requested his said Allies to unite with him in order to assist him to cut off the communication by sea between Egypt and Syria, and to prevent the transport of troops, horses, arms and warlike stores of all kinds, from the one province to the other, Their Majesties . . . engage to give immediately to that effect the necessary orders to their naval commanders in the Mediterranean . . .

3. [The Powers will defend Constantinople and the Straits against attack by Mehemet Ali.]

4. It is, however, expressly understood, that the co-operation

D E C—E

mentioned in the preceding article, and destined to place the Straits of the Dardanelles and of the Bosphorus, and the Ottoman capital, under the temporary safeguard of the High Contracting Parties, against all aggression of Mehemet Ali, shall be considered only as a measure of exception, adopted at the express demand of the Sultan, and solely for his defence in the single case above mentioned: but it is agreed that such measure shall not derogate in any degree from the[1] ancient rule of the Ottoman empire, in virtue of which it has in all times been prohibited for ships of war of foreign powers to enter the Straits ... And the Sultan on the one hand, hereby declares that, excepting the contingencies above mentioned, it is his firm resolution to maintain in future this principle invariably established as the ancient rule of his empire; and as long as the Porte is at peace, to admit no foreign ships of war into the Straits ...; on the other hand, Their Majesties ... engage to respect this determination of the Sultan, and to conform to the abovementioned principle.

(b) Lord Palmerston to the Marquis of Clanricarde, ambassador at St. Petersburg, 11 January 1841.

I have received Your Excellency's despatch ... reporting the wish expressed to You by the Emperor of Russia that some engagement should be entered into between England and the other three Great Powers who are parties to the Treaty of July (No. 12(a)), with the view of providing for the contingency of an attack by France upon the liberties of Europe: and I have to instruct Your Excellency thereupon to state to His Imperial Majesty that Her Majesty's Government are much gratified by the confidence which he reposes in the Government of England, and by the frank and open manner in which he has been pleased to communicate his views and opinions to Your Excellency. Her Majesty's Government will be equally open with the Emperor, and will state to His Imperial Majesty exactly their sentiments on the subject on which he has touched in his conversation with Your Excellency.

[1] The provisions, from here to the end of the article, were incorporated in a Straits Convention of 13 July 1841, signed by all Powers, including France. Note that neither the treaty nor the convention guaranteed the independence or integrity of the Ottoman Empire.

One of the general principles which Her Majesty's Government wish to observe as a guide for their conduct in dealing with the relations between England and other States, is, that changes which foreign nations may chuse [sic] to make in their internal constitution and form of government, are to be looked upon as matters with which England has no business to interfere by force of arms, for the purpose of imposing upon such nations a form of government which they do not wish to have, or for the purpose of preventing such nations from having institutions which they desire. These things are considered in England to be matters of domestic concern, which every nation ought to be allowed to settle as it likes.

But an attempt of one nation to seize and to appropriate to itself territory which belongs to another nation, is a different matter; because such an attempt leads to a derangement of the existing Balance of Power, and by altering the relative strength of States, may tend to create danger to other Powers; and such attempts therefore, the British Government holds itself at full liberty to resist, upon the universally acknowledged principle of self-defence.

Now, it is quite true, as stated by the Emperor, that any country, such as France, for instance, may, under the plea and pretext of altering its own institutions, seek to overthrow the existing Governments of other countries, for the purpose of adding those countries to its own territories, or of associating them with its own aggressive system; and such proceedings would cease to be domestic changes of arrangement, and would assume the unquestionable character of external aggression.— Such attempts England has in former times on many occasions resisted; and it is highly probable that if a similar case were again to arise, England would again pursue a similar course.

But it is not usual for England to enter into engagements with reference to cases which have not actually arisen, or which are not immediately in prospect: and this for a plain reason. All formal engagements of the Crown, which involve the question of peace and war, must be submitted to Parliament; and Parliament might probably not approve of an engagement which should bind England prospectively to take up arms in a contingency which might happen at an uncertain time, and under circumstances which could not as yet be foreseen.

It is true that His Imperial Majesty has spoken of an understanding which need not be recorded in any formal instrument; but upon which He might rely if the turn of affairs should render it applicable to events. But this course would not be free from objections. For, in the first place, it would scarcely be consistent with the spirit of the British Constitution for the Crown to enter into a binding engagement of such a nature, without placing it formally upon record, so that Parliament might have an opportunity of expressing its opinion thereupon, and this could only be done by some written instrument; and to such a course the objection which I have alluded to above, would apply. But if the engagement were merely verbal, though it would bind the ministers who made it, it might be disavowed by their successors; and thus the Russian Government might be led to count upon a system of policy on the part of Great Britain, which might not eventually be pursued.

Under these circumstances, it seems to Her Majesty's Government that the Cabinet of St. Petersburg should be satisfied to trust to the general tendency of the policy of Great Britain, which leads her to watch attentively, and to guard with care the maintenance of the Balance of Power: and Her Majesty's Government hope that His Imperial Majesty will not think that this policy is the less deeply rooted in the minds of Her Majesty's Government, if they should not think it expedient to enter at the present moment into engagements such as those mentioned by the Emperor.

13. *Peace Congress, Paris, August 1849*

In August 1849 an entirely unofficial assembly gathered at Paris to talk about the peaceful co-operation of peoples and to press for the formation of a united Europe. In itself, the Congress is of no great importance, but some passages of Victor Hugo's presidential opening address are nevertheless included, because they illustrate well the pacific trend of certain liberal internationalists, and because they contain one of the early mentions of a United States of Europe.

Source: Victor Hugo, *Œuvres complètes: Actes et paroles* (Paris, Hetzel, Quantin, 1882), vol. i, pp. 476, 479–80, 485–6 (trans. Ed.).

. . . Gentlemen, is this religious conception—universal peace, all the nations bound together with a common bond, the Gospel as the highest law, mediation in place of warfare—is this religious conception a practical conception? Is this sacred idea a realistic idea? Many practical minds, as the expression goes, many politicians grown old, as we say, in the management of public affairs, will reply: No! I reply with you, I reply unhesitatingly, I reply: Yes! (*Applause*) . . . I would go further; I say not only: this is a realizable aim, I say: it is an inevitable end. The event may be delayed or hastened, that is all . . .

. . . The day will come, when weapons will fall from all hands. The day will come when warfare between Paris and London, St. Petersburg and Berlin, or Vienna and Turin will seem as absurd, and be as impossible, as today it would be impossible and seem absurd between Rouen and Amiens, between Boston and Philadelphia. The day will come when, without losing your distinctive qualities and your glorious individuality, all you nations of the continent, France, Russia, Italy, England, Germany, you will merge completely into a greater unity and form a European brotherhood, exactly as Normandy, Brittany, Burgundy, Lorraine, Alsace, all our provinces are joined together in the state of France. The day will come when the only battlefields will be the markets thrown open to commerce, and the minds thrown open to ideas. The day will come when bullets and bombs will be replaced by votes, by the universal suffrage of the peoples, by the revered arbitration of a great supreme council which will be to Europe what Parliament is to England, the Diet to Germany, the Legislative Assembly to France. (*Applause*) The day will come when we will see the two immense groups, the United States of America and the United States of Europe (*Applause*) facing each other, holding out their hands to each other across the seas, exchanging their products, their trade, their industry, their arts, their native genius, making the earth productive, peopling the deserts, improving creation in the eyes of the creator, and combining together those two infinite forces, the brotherhood of men and the power of God, to draw from them the well-being of all (*Sustained applause*) . . .

. . . Gentlemen, I say in closing, and may this thought encourage us, that mankind has already set forth on this providential course. In our old European world England has taken the first step, and by her centuries old example she has said to the peoples: you are free. France has taken the second step, and she has said to the peoples: you are sovereign. Let us now take the third step, and France, England, Belgium, Germany, Italy, Europe, America, let us all together say to the peoples: you are brothers! (*Tremendous cheering*)

II · THE RESTORATION
AND JULY MONARCHY IN FRANCE
1814–48

In 1814, after prolonged negotiations, the Allied Powers agreed to the restoration of the Bourbons to the French throne on the condition that Louis XVIII grant a constitutional charter. This charter was duly granted (No. 14) and it regulated the political life of France until 1830.

The great problem in France after 1814 was how to reconcile the popularly accepted 'revolutionary'—that is, liberal—principles with the claims of the royalists, in particular of the *émigré* nobles returned to France. Louis XVIII saw well that the Bourbons could retain power only if they restricted their own claims, and, in fact, Louis often allied himself with the liberals in the Chamber of Deputies, against the 'ultras', or ultra-royalists. After his death, however, his brother, the leader of the ultras, followed him on the throne as Charles X. Among the early measures of his government was a law to pay an indemnity to the *émigrés* for the estates they lost during the revolutionary period (No. 15) and a law on sacrilege, an expression of the growing clerical ties of the court (No. 16).

Measures such as these, including the dissolution of the National Guard in 1827, resulted in growing opposition to the King and his government. Having a recalcitrant chamber of deputies, the King ordered a dissolution and exerted his personal influence, in addition to using the usual measures of electoral management, in order to have a favourable majority in the Chamber. His proclamation (No. 17) was unsuccessful, and the Chamber returned had a liberal majority again. Charles therefore dissolved the Chamber again, ordered new elections conducted on the basis of an electoral law prescribed by decree, and curtailed the freedom of the press. These July decrees (No. 18) brought about what we now call the July

Revolution. The liberal middle class and the republican students and workers rose against the King. Through the astute political management of Thiers and others, the liberals gained power, and elected the Duke of Orléans Lieutenant-General of the kingdom, and then King of the French. After a proclamation (No. 19) and a speech (No. 20) of the Duke, the Chamber amended the Constitutional Charter of 1814 and incorporated a number of liberal provisions in it (No. 21). This revised charter served as the foundation of the bourgeois monarchy until 1848.

The July monarchy had to maintain itself against some internal disturbances in the early 1830s, and was involved in a number of international crises (cf. No. 12). No suitably informative documents on these matters were found, however. The educational reforms of the government are documented in Section X (No. 111).

14. *The Constitutional Charter, 4 June 1814*

The Bourbons were restored to the throne of France by the Allied Powers only on the condition that Louis XVIII grant a Constitutional Charter to the French people. The following are the most important provisions of this document, which remained in force until the July Revolution of 1830.

Source: *Annual Register*, 1814, pp. 420–2 (with emendations).

[The preamble to the Charter, too long to be included, emphasizes that the King grants and imposes the Charter voluntarily, by a free exercise of his royal authority. The Charter is granted in response to the wishes of his subjects, and to meet a real need, but as in France all power resides in the King, the provisions of the Charter are merely a rearrangement and modification—but not a diminution—of the royal power. (Cf. preamble to No. 21.)]

Public Rights of the French

1. Frenchmen are to be equal before the law, whatever may be their titles or rank.
2. They are to contribute in the proportion of their fortunes to the charges of the state.

3. They are to be equally admissible to civil and military employments.

4. Their individual liberty is hereby equally guaranteed. No person can be either prosecuted or arrested except in cases prescribed by law.

5. Each one may profess his religion with equal liberty, and shall obtain for his religious worship the same protection.

6. However, the Catholic, Apostolic and Roman religion is the religion of the State.

7. The ministers of the Catholic, Apostolic and Roman religion, and those of other Christian denominations, receive their stipends from the Royal Treasury.

8. The French are entitled to publish and print their opinions while conforming to the laws which will repress abuses of this liberty.

9. All property is to be inviolable, even that called national;[1] the law makes no distinction.

10. The State may exact the sacrifice of private property in legally proved public interest after indemnity has been paid.

11. All investigation into opinions and votes given before the Restoration is prohibited. This prohibition applies both to tribunals and to citizens.

12. Conscription is abolished. The method of recruiting the army and the navy will be prescribed by law.

Forms of the King's Government

13. The person of the King is inviolable and sacred. His ministers are responsible. Executive power belongs to the King alone.

14. The King is supreme head of the State, he commands the land and sea forces, declares war, makes treaties of peace, alliance and commerce, appoints all employees of the public administration, and makes the regulations necessary for the execution of the laws and the security of the State.

15. The legislative power is exercised collectively by the King, the Chamber of Peers and the Chamber of the Deputies of the Departments.

---

[1] Refers to noble and ecclesiastical property confiscated during the Revolution and resold.

16. The King proposes the laws.

17. Proposals for laws are taken, at the choice of the King, either to the Chamber of Peers or to the Chamber of Deputies; but tax bills must be proposed to the Chamber of Deputies first.

18. Each law must have been freely discussed and voted by the majority of each of the two Chambers.

19. The Chambers are entitled to request the King to propose a law on any subject whatever, and to suggest what it should contain . . .

22. The King alone sanctions and promulgates the laws.

23. The civil list is to be fixed for the duration of the reign by the first legislature assembled after the accession of the King.

Of the Chamber of Peers

[This section, consisting of Articles 24–34, declares the Chamber of Peers to be an essential part of the legislature, and regulates its membership and procedure. The following articles are of interest:]

27. The nomination of the peers of France is the prerogative of the King. Their number is unlimited. He can vary their dignities, and make them life or hereditary peers, at his pleasure.

32. All deliberations of the Chamber of Peers are secret.

Of the Chamber of Deputies of the Departments

[Articles 35–53 regulate the election and operation of this Chamber. The following articles are of interest:]

35. The Chamber of Deputies shall be composed of deputies elected by electoral colleges . . .

38. No deputy can be admitted into the Chamber unless he be forty years of age and pay direct taxes to the amount of one thousand francs.

40. The electors of deputies must pay direct taxes to the amount of three hundred francs and be at least thirty years of age.

44. The sittings of the Chamber are public; but the demand of five members is sufficient for forming it into a secret committee.

51. No personal restraint shall be laid upon any member of the House during the session, or within six weeks before and after it.

52. No member of the House can, during the session, be prosecuted or arrested until the Chamber has permitted his prosecution.

Of the Ministers

54. The ministers may be members of the Chamber of Peers or of the Chamber of Deputies. They have, moreover, a right to admission into either Chamber, and must be heard whenever they desire it.

55. The Chamber of Deputies has the right of impeaching the ministers before the Chamber of Peers which alone has the right to try them.

56. They cannot be accused, except for high treason or peculation.

Of the Judicial Order

[Articles 57–68 constitute this section. The most important provisions are that the King alone nominates the justices, who cannot be removed, and that the institution of juries is retained.]

Particular Rights guaranteed by the State

69. The military on active service, the officers and soldiers who have retired, the widows, officers and soldiers pensioned, shall retain their ranks, honours and pensions.

70. The public debt is guaranteed: all kinds of engagements contracted by the State with its creditors are inviolable.

71. The ancient nobility resume their titles; the new retain theirs. The King creates nobles at pleasure, but he confers on them only ranks and honours, without any exemption from the charges and duties of society.

72. The Legion of Honour is maintained: the King will fix its internal regulations and decorations.

73. The colonies shall be governed by particular laws and regulations.

74. The King and his successors shall swear at the ceremony of their anointment to the faithful observance of the present constitutional charter . . .

15. *Law of Compensation of Émigrés, 3 January 1825*

One of the early measures of the government of Charles X was the introduction of a measure to compensate *émigrés*, mainly nobles, for the losses sustained by them during the revolutionary period through the confiscation of estates. This was a very contentious measure, opposed on many different grounds, but the main opposition came from the liberal middle class who, as the main taxpayers and the main owners of *rentes*[1] stood to lose most.

Instead of including the text of the law, what follows here is a contemporary report of the contents of the bill and of the proceedings on it.

Source: *Annual Register*, 1825, pp. [136–7].

On the 3rd of January [1825] the minister brought forward three measures of the greatest importance. The first related to the settlement of the civil list; the second proposed a plan for indemnifying the emigrants or the royalist proprietors who suffered by the excesses of the Revolution; the third was a scheme for the conversion of the five per cents into a lower denomination of stock[2] . . .

The second *projet*[3] was presented by M. la Martignac, and was entitled 'Draught of law on the indemnity to be granted to the former proprietors of real property confiscated and sold for the profit of the State, in execution of the laws concerning emigrants'.

For property sold, the indemnity was to be an amount of three per cent stock, equal to twenty times the rental ascertained by the *procès-verbaux*[4] of adjudication: and where the rental was not estimated, equal to the amount of sale, making allowance for the depreciation of assignats.[5]

Where the relatives in the ascending line bought the property, or the former proprietors or their representatives had repurchased, the indemnity was to be fixed at the real amount of the prices so paid.

The *rentes* given as an indemnity were to be delivered to the

---

[1] Government bonds.
[2] The saving of interest was intended to contribute to the amounts to be paid in compensation.
[3] Bill.
[4] Protocols.
[5] Treasury notes issued during the Revolution on the security of confiscated property.

former proprietors or their representatives by fifths, in five years, to bear interest from the time of the delivery: and for this purpose a credit of 30 million of *rentes* was to be placed at the disposal of the minister of finance [between 1825 and 1829] ... Claims were to be preferred within a year by persons resident in France; within eighteen months by persons in other parts of Europe; and within two years by persons not in Europe ...

The law of indemnification gave rise to great variety of opinion. Some dissented from the principle of the measure as too anti-revolutionary; others conceived that it did not go far enough; the ultra royalists thought that the emigrants were only half compensated if what they received was not taken from those who had been gainers by their spoils; and all who disliked the financial alteration with which it was coupled, wished for its failure. The debates, though protracted, were of little interest; and M. de Villèle carried his scheme triumphantly through both chambers ...

After the law was passed, the King appointed a commission, who were to investigate the demands of those who claimed compensation, and to determine what sum ought to be allotted to each. The commission was sub-divided into five sections; each consisting of five members, and charged with the liquidation of claims in a certain number of departments.

16. *Law for the Punishment of Sacrilege, 1825*

One of the policies of Charles X was co-operation with the Roman Catholic Church, and assistance to it so that it could regain the position of dominance it had before the Revolution. Clerical influence over education was considerably extended during this reign. The measure of which a contemporary report follows is an example of laws enacted for the protection of the State Church.

Source: *Annual Register*, 1825, p. [139] (with emendations).

Another ministerial measure which excited considerable interest, especially in England, was a law introduced for the punishment of sacrilege. This law first defined the crime which it sought to coerce, in the following manner:—

'The profanation of the sacred utensils, and of the consecrated hosts, is the crime of sacrilege. Every overt act committed voluntarily and through hatred or contempt of religion, on the sacred utensils or the consecrated hosts, is declared a profanation . . .

The profanation of the sacred utensils shall be punished with death.

The profanation of the consecrated wafers shall be punished in the manner as parricide.'

This . . . law passed the Chamber of Deputies by a majority of 210 to 95; and, though the severity of the enactment was somewhat mollified, there was in its provisions, such as they were when it received the final sanction of the legislature, no deviation [from the principles stated above].

17. *Proclamation of Charles X before the Elections, 14 June 1830*

Charles X, the ultra-royalist king, could never accommodate himself to the existence of a substantial opposition to his government in the Chamber of Deputies. His Ministers and prefects had already employed various means of electoral management to bring about the election of candidates favourable to the King's ideas; they were instructed to employ such measures again, with increased intensity, in 1830. In addition, the King decided to interfere in the elections himself with the proclamation that follows.

Source: *Annual Register*, 1830, pp. [177–8].

The elections are going to commence at all points in my kingdom,—listen to the voice of your King, and maintain the Constitutional Charter, and the institutions on which it is founded, which I will preserve with my utmost efforts; but to attain this object, I must freely exercise, and cause to be respected, the sacred rights which belong to my Crown, which are the guarantee of public peace and of your liberties, as the nature of government will be altered if the culpable attempt to invade my prerogative succeed, and I shall break my oath if I submit to it. Under this Government France has become flourishing, and she owes to it her credit and her industry. France does not envy other states, and only aspires to the preservation of the advantages which she enjoys. Remain assured of your rights, which I unite with mine, and which I will protect with equal solicitude. Do not let yourselves be deceived by seditious persons, enemies to your repose; and do not yield to unfounded fears, which may excite serious disorders. Electors, hasten to join your colleagues; let the same sentiment animate you, and rally under the same standard. It is your King that demands it —it is the call of your father—fulfil your duties, and I shall fulfil mine.

18. *The July Decrees of Charles X, 25 July 1830*

When the elections returned an oppositional majority in spite of the King's intervention (No. 17) the following three ordinances were issued by the King. Had they been put into effect, the result would have been an overthrow of the Charter and the re-establishment of autocratic rule. They were, however, considered unconstitutional, and protest and revolution followed.

Source: *Annual Register*, 1830, pp. 366–70.

(a) Ordinance relating to the Press.

On the report of our Council of Ministers we have ordained and ordain as follows:—
1. The liberty of the periodical press is suspended.
2. The regulations of the . . . law of the 21st of October, 1814, are again put in force, in consequence of which no journal, or periodical, or semi-periodical writing, established, or about to be established, without distinction of the matters therein treated, shall appear either in Paris or in the departments, except by virtue of an authority first obtained from us respectively by the authors and the printer. This authority shall be renewed every three months. It may also be revoked.
3. The authority shall be provisionally granted and provisionally withdrawn by the prefects from journals . . . in the departments.
4. Journals and writings published in contravention of Article 2 shall be immediately seized. The presses and types used in the printing of them shall be placed in a public depot under seals, or rendered unfit for use.
5. No writing below twenty printed pages shall appear, except with the authority of our Minister Secretary of State for the Interior at Paris, and of the prefects in the departments. Every writing of more than twenty printed pages which shall not constitute one single work, must also equally be published under authority only . . .

(b) Ordinance dissolving the Chamber of Deputies.

Having considered Article 50 of the Constitutional Charter
(No. 14); being informed of the manœuvres which have been
practised in various parts of our kingdom to deceive and mis-
lead the electors during the late operations of the electoral
colleges; having heard our council, we have ordained and
ordain as follows:—

1. The Chamber of Deputies of Departments is dissolved.
2. Our Minister Secretary of State of the Interior is charged
with the execution of the present ordinance.

(c) Ordinance reforming the Electoral Law.

Having resolved to prevent the return of the manœuvres
which have exercised a pernicious influence on the late operations of the electoral colleges, wishing, in consequence, to
reform according to the principle of the Constitutional Charter
the rules of election, of which experience has shown the inconvenience, we have recognized the necessity of using the
right which belongs to us, to provide by acts emanating from
ourselves for the safety of the state, and for the suppression of
every enterprise injurious to the dignity of our Crown. For
these reasons, having heard our council, we have ordained and
ordain:—
[The main effect of this very complicated ordinance of thirty
articles is to reduce the already very restricted number of
electors to about a quarter of their previous number, and to
amend procedures in a way that would give added opportunity
for the exertion of official influence on the electoral colleges
by the prefects.]

19. *Proclamation by the Duke of Orléans, 30 July 1830*

The students and the workers of Paris rose in protest against the
July decrees and demanded a republic. The liberal politicians also
protested, but they had no wish for a revolution: they wanted
reform, a limited, constitutional monarchy. How the revolution
developed, how a compromise was achieved, is beyond the scope of
this note. It was agreed that the Duke of Orléans, the later Louis
Philippe, should become 'lieutenant-general', temporary head of

the state. He accepted the position in the proclamation that follows.
Source: *Annual Register*, 1830, pp. [205–6].

Inhabitants of Paris:

The deputies of France at this moment assembled at Paris
have expressed to me the desire that I should repair to this
capital to exercise the functions of lieutenant-general of the
kingdom. I have not hesitated to come and share your dangers,
to place myself in the midst of your heroic population, and to
exert all my efforts to preserve you from the calamities of civil
war and of anarchy. On returning to the city of Paris I wore
with pride those glorious colours which you have resumed, and
which I myself long wore.

The Chambers are going to assemble, they will consider the
means of securing the reign of laws, and the maintenance of the
rights of the nation. The Charter will henceforward be a reality.

20. *Speech of the Duke of Orléans, 3 August 1830*

The Chambers met on 3 August to revise the Constitutional Charter
and so to establish the new régime on a firm basis. The Duke of
Orléans, as Lieutenant-General, opened the session with the following speech.
Source: *Annual Register*, 1830, pp. 375–6.

Peers and Deputies:

Paris, troubled in its repose by a deplorable violation of the
charter and of the laws, defended them with heroic courage. In
the midst of this sanguinary struggle, all the guarantees of
social order no longer subsisted. Persons, property, rights—
every thing that is most valuable and dear to men and to
citizens, was exposed to the most serious danger.

In this absence of all public power, the wishes of my public
citizens turned towards me; they have judged me worthy to
concur with them in the salvation of the country; they have
invited me to exercise the functions of Lieutenant-General . . .

Their cause appeared to me to be just, the dangers immense
—the necessity imperative—my duty sacred—I hastened to
the midst of this valiant people, followed by my family, and
wearing those colours which, for the second time, have marked
among us the triumph of liberty.

D E C—F

I have come, firmly resolved to devote myself to all that circumstances should require of me in the situation in which they have placed me, to establish the empire of the laws, to save liberty, which was threatened, and render impossible the return of such great evils by securing for ever the power of that charter whose name, invoked during the combat, was also appealed to after the victory.

In the accomplishment of this noble task it is for the Chambers to guide me. All rights must be solemnly guaranteed, all the institutions necessary to their full and free exercise must receive the developments of which they have need. Attached by inclination and conviction to the principles of a free government, I accept beforehand all the consequences of it. I think it my duty immediately to call your attention to the organization of the national guards, to the application of the jury to the crimes of the press, to the formation of the departmental and municipal administrations, and, above all, to that fourteenth article of the charter (No. 14) which has been so hatefully interpreted.

It is with these sentiments, Gentlemen, that I come to open this session . . .

Peers and Deputies, as soon as the Chambers shall be constituted, I shall have laid before you the act of abdication of His Majesty King Charles X . . .

21. *The revised Constitutional Charter, 7 August 1830*

The Chambers duly proceeded to the revision of the Charter. The alterations were in a liberal direction, though they were not very far-reaching. In the text only the altered articles will be printed in full, for the rest reference will be made to the corresponding articles of the 1814 Charter (No. 14). Compare the 1830 preamble with the summarized contents of that of 1814.

Source: *Annual Register*, 1830, pp. 370–4.

The Chamber of Deputies, taking into consideration the imperious necessity which is the result of the 26th, 27th, 28th and 29th of July, and the following days,[1] and the situation in which France is at this moment placed in consequence of this violation of the Constitutional Charter; considering, how-

[1] The days of the July Revolution.

ever, that by this violation, and the heroic resistance of the citizens of Paris, His Majesty King Charles X, his Royal Highness Louis Antoine, his son, and the senior members of the Royal House, are leaving the kingdom of France, declares that the throne is vacant *de facto et de jure*,[1] and that there is an absolute necessity of providing for it.

The Chamber of Deputies declare, secondly, that according to the wish, and for the interest of the people of France, the preamble of the Constitutional Charter is omitted, as wounding the national dignity, in appearing to grant to them rights which essentially belong to them; and that the following articles of the same Charter ought to be suppressed or modified in the following manner:

Public Rights of the French

1–5. [As 1–5 of 1814.]
6. The ministers of the Catholic, Apostolic and Roman religion, professed by the majority of the French, and those of other Christian worship, receive stipends from the public treasury. [Cf. 6–7 of 1814.]
7. Frenchmen have the right of publishing and printing their opinions, provided they conform themselves to the laws. The Censorship can never be re-established. [Cf. 8 of 1814.]
8–11. [As 9–12 of 1814.]

Forms of the King's Government

12. [As 13 of 1814.]
13. The King is supreme head of the State, he commands the land and sea forces, declares wars, makes treaties of peace, alliance and commerce, appoints all employees of the public administration, and makes the regulations necessary for the execution of the laws, without having power either to suspend the laws themselves, or dispense with their execution. Nevertheless, no foreign troops can ever be admitted into the service of the state without an express law. [Cf. 14 of 1814.]
14. [As 15 of 1814.]
15. The proposition of the laws is to belong to the King, to the

---

[1] In fact and in law.

Chamber of Peers, and to the Chamber of Deputies. Nevertheless, all the laws of taxes are to be first voted by the Chamber of Deputies. [Cf. 16–17 of 1814.]
16. [As 18 of 1814.]
17. If a proposed law be rejected by one of the three powers, it cannot be brought forward again in the same session. [19–21 of 1814 are omitted.]
18–19. [As 22–23 of 1814.]

Of the Chamber of Peers

[Articles 20–29 of this section are substantially the same as the articles constituting this section in the Charter of 1814. The one exception is the following:]
27. The sittings of the Chamber of Peers are to be public, as those of the Chamber of Deputies. [Cf. 32 of 1814.]

Of the Chamber of Deputies of the Departments

[No changes in principle were made in this section. The main differences are in the reduction of the age limit to 30 years for Deputies, to 25 years for electors, and the effectual reduction (although this does not appear explicitly) of the property qualification. The system of indirect elections, through electoral colleges, is retained, but the presidents of the colleges are to be named by the electors, and no longer nominated by the king.]

Of the Ministers

46–47. [As 54–55 of 1814. 56 of 1814 is suppressed.]

Judicial Regulations

48–59. [Substantially as 57–68 of 1814.]

Particular Rights Guaranteed by the State

60–64. [As 69–73 of 1814.]
65. The King and his successors are to swear, on their accession,

in presence of the assembled Chambers, to observe faithfully the Constitutional Charter. [Cf. 74 of 1814.]

66. The present Charter, and the rights it consecrates, shall be entrusted to the patriotism and courage of the National Guard and all French Citizens.

67. France resumes her colours. In future there will be no other cockade than the tri-coloured.

Special Provisions

68. All the creations of peers during the reign of Charles X are declared null and void. Article 27 of the Charter [as 23 of 1814] will undergo a fresh examination during the session of 1831.

69. It is necessary to provide successively for separate laws, and that with the shortest possible delay, on the following subjects: 1) For the extension of the trial by jury to misdemeanors, and particularly those of the press; 2) For the responsibility of ministers and other agents of government; 3) For the re-election of deputies appointed to salaried public offices; 4) For the annual voting of the army estimates; 5) For the organization of the National Guard, with the election of officers by its members; 6) For a military code ... 7) For elected departmental and municipal institutions; 8) For public instruction and freedom of education; 9) For the abolition of the double vote, and for the fixing of the qualifications for electors and deputies.

70. All laws and ordinances which are contrary to the measures adopted for the reform of the Charter are from henceforward annulled and abrogated.

Upon condition of accepting these provisions and propositions, the Chamber of Deputies declares that the universal and pressing interest of the French people calls to the throne His Royal Highness Louis Phillipe d'Orléans, Duke of Orléans, Lieutenant-General of the kingdom, and his descendants for ever, from male to male, in the order of primogeniture, and to the perpetual exclusion of the female branches and their descendants.

In consequence, His Royal Highness Louis Philippe d'Orléans, Lieutenant-General of the kingdom, shall be invited to accept and make oath to the above clauses and engagements—the observance of the Constitutional Charter and the modifications indicated—and after having made oath before the assembled Chambers to assume the title of the King of the French.

III · THE RESTORATION PERIOD
IN GERMANY, 1815–48

THE Holy Roman Empire, after many centuries of existence, was dissolved by Napoleon in 1806. He then proceeded to the re-organization of Germany. The number of sovereignties was drastically reduced, a Confederation of the Rhine was formed, and French influence was established. After Napoleon's defeat, his system had to be broken up, but there was no return to the old Empire. It was decided to form a loose confederation, under the presidency of Austria, of which all German states, thirty-eight in number, would be members. The basic features of this new confederation are set out in the Act of Confederation of 1815 (No. 22), which was drawn up by the German Committee of the Congress of Vienna and incorporated in the general settlement. The conservative features of this Act were re-affirmed in the Supplementary Act of Confederation, drafted by the Vienna Conference of 1820, which served, from then on, as the basic constitutional document of the Confederation (No. 23).

But these documents expressed too conservative a view for a great portion of the German people who became imbued with liberalism through the influence of the French Revolution and Empire, and with nationalism through the wars of liberation. University students, in particular, wanted a united and free Germany, and formed the *Burschenschaften*, all-German, rather than particularistic, student unions. In 1817, the *Burschenschaften* met at the Wartburg, to celebrate the liberation of the German spirit by Luther three hundred years before, and the liberation of German lands by Blücher in the Battle of Leipzig of 1813. A contemporary description of this festival is included (No. 24).

The main direct result of these activities was the tighten-ing of controls, mainly through the Carlsbad decrees of 1819

(No. 25) which were successful in repressing overt political agitation for a time. It only began again after the French Revolution
of July 1830. Probably the most important demonstration of this
period is the Hambach Festival of 1832, at which German
radicals demanded republican institutions and liberal international fraternity. Excerpts of some of the speeches at this
festival follow (No. 26).

In spite of the strict separatist and anti-liberal views of the
Diet, some first steps towards uniformity and unification were
taken at this time. The German customs union (*Zollverein*),
which ultimately included most German states under the
leadership of Prussia, was signed in 1833 (No. 27). It can also
be regarded as one of the first steps which contributed to the
establishment of Prussian hegemony in Germany.

Comparative quiet followed until the second half of the
eighteen-forties, although the national and liberal movements
gained a great deal of support in this period. Metternich still
enforced his system. The economic crisis of the late eighteen-
forties, and the first beginnings of the industrial revolution,
brought some advances. In Prussia, in 1847, a United Diet was
called for the first time, made constitutional demands, and was
soon dissolved (No. 28). As the crisis worsened towards the end
of the year, popular demands for reform became ever stronger,
and gained public expression in the programme of the German
radicals published at Offenburg (No. 29) and the Heppenheim
resolutions of the moderate liberals (No. 30). Revolution (see
Section V) was not far behind.

22. German Act of Confederation, 8 June 1815

The Holy Roman Empire could not be re-erected as such in 1815,
because the Emperor of Austria would not assume an empty
dignity, and the King of Prussia would not accept a strong imperial
power. Yet a strong and united Germany was necessary to ensure
protection against aggression by French forces and infiltration of
French revolutionary ideas. The result was the formation of a
German Confederation, under the presidency of Austria, in which,
while the Austro-Prussian conservative partnership of 1815 remained
in existence, the Austrian Chancellor, Metternich, had the decisive
voice.

Source: *Annual Register*, 1815, pp. 390–2 (with emendations and
additions based on E. R. Huber, *Dokumente zur deutschen*

Verfassungsgeschichte (Stuttgart, Kohlhammer, 1961), vol. i, pp. 75–81).

I. General Provisions

1. The Sovereign Princes and free cities of Germany, including Their Majesties the Emperor of Austria and the Kings of Prussia, Denmark and the Netherlands, namely the Emperor of Austria and the King of Prussia for those of their possessions which formerly belonged to the German Empire, the King of Denmark for Holstein, the King of the Netherlands for the Grand Duchy of Luxemburg, unite in a perpetual league which shall be called the German Confederation.

2. The object thereof is the maintenance of the internal and external security of Germany, and of the independence and inviolability of the different German States.

3. The members of the Confederation have, as such, equal rights; they bind themselves all equally to maintain the Act of Confederation.

4. The affairs of the Confederation shall be managed by a Federal Assembly[1] in which all the members of the Confederation shall be represented by their plenipotentiaries, who shall each have one vote either severally, or as representing more than one member, as follows:

Austria 1 vote, Prussia 1, Bavaria 1, Saxony 1, Hanover 1, Württemberg 1, Baden 1, Electoral Hesse 1, Grand Duchy of Hesse 1, Denmark for Holstein 1, the Netherlands for Luxemburg 1, the Grand Ducal and Ducal Houses of Saxony 1, Brunswick and Nassau 1, Mecklenburg-Schwerin and Mecklenburg-Strelitz 1, Holstein-Oldenburg, Anhalt and Schwarzburg 1, Hohenzollern, Liechtenstein, Reuss, Schaumburg-Lippe, and Waldeck 1, the free cities of Lübeck, Frankfurt, Bremen and Hamburg 1; total, 17 votes.

5. Austria has the presidency in the Diet of the Confederation; every member of the Confederation has the power of making proposals and to bring them under discussion; and the president is bound to submit such proposals for deliberation within a period to be fixed.

[1] Usually referred to as the 'Diet' in English.

6. When these proposals relate to the enactment and amend-ment of fundamental laws of the Confederation, or to regu-lations relating to the Act of Confederation itself, or to organic federal institutions, or to other measures relating to the common good, the Federal Assembly forms itself into a plenary session, in which the component members shall have the follow-ing votes proportioned to the extent of their territories:

Austria, Prussia, Saxony, Bavaria, Hanover and Württem-berg, four votes each; Baden, Electoral Hesse, Grand Duchy of Hesse, Holstein and Luxemburg, three votes each; Brunswick, Mecklenburg-Schwerin and Nassau, two votes each; [other minor states and free cities] one vote each; total 69 votes . . .

7. The Federal Assembly decides by simple majority what proposals should be submitted to a plenary session. The pro-posals which are to be submitted to a plenary session are to be prepared by the Federal Assembly . . .; decisions in both bodies are taken by majority vote, simple in the case of the Federal Assembly, two thirds in the plenary session. In the Federal Assembly the president has a casting vote. In matters relating to the enactment or amendment of fundamental laws, to organic federal institutions, to individual rights, or religious affairs, unanimity is required in both assemblies . . .

9. The seat of the Federal Assembly is at Frankfurt am Main. It shall be opened on September 1, 1815.

10. The first business of the Federal Assembly, after its opening, will be the drafting and enactment of the fundamental laws and organic regulations of the Confederation in regard to its external, military and internal relations.

11. All members of the Confederation engage to assist in pro-tecting not only all Germany but every separate State of the Confederation against any attack, and reciprocally to guarantee to each other the whole of their possessions included within the Confederation. After war has been once declared by the Con-federation, no member may enter into separate negotiations with the enemy, nor conclude a separate armistice or peace. Although the members possess the right of alliance of every kind, yet they bind themselves to enter into no treaties hostile to the security of the Confederation or of that of any confederate State. The members of the Confederation also bind themselves not to make war on each other under any pretext, nor to decide

their differences by force, but to bring them under consideration
and decision at the Diet . . .

II. Particular Provisions . . .

13. In all confederate States there will be a constitution providing for representation by estates . . .[1]

16. Diversity of Christian religious faith in the states of the
German Confederation can occasion no difference in respect
to the enjoyment of civil and political rights. The Diet will
consider in what way the improvement of the civil standing of
the professors of the Jewish religion may best be effected . . .

18. The confederate princes and free cities agree to secure to
the subjects of the Confederate States the following rights:

The possession of landed property out of the State in which
they reside, without being subjected to greater taxes and
charges than those of the native subjects of such State;

The right of free emigration from one German confederate
State to another which shall consent to receive them for subjects; and also the rights of entering into the civil or military
service of any such confederate state; both rights, however, to
be enjoyed only in so far as no previous obligation to military
service in their native country shall stand in the way; . . .

The Diet on its first meeting shall occupy itself with the
formation of uniform regulations relative to the freedom of the
press, and the securing of the rights of authors and publishers
against unauthorized reprinting.

19. The members of the Confederation also engage, on the
first meeting of the Diet, to take into consideration the state
of commerce and intercourse between the states of the Confederation, as well as that of navigation, on the principles
adopted by the Congress of Vienna . . .

23. *Final Act of the Ministerial Conference of Vienna,*
15 May 1820

The Act of Confederation (No. 22) established only a framework
of the confederate constitution, and, in Article 10, left to the Diet
the working out of the 'fundamental laws and organic regulations'.

---

[1] This article is very difficult to translate, as the original text is vague and
ambiguous: '*In allen Bundesstaaten wird eine Landständische Verfassung statt finden*'.

Following this prescription the confederate states convened a ministerial conference at Vienna and worked out at it a document of sixty-five articles. This Final Act was accepted by the Plenary Assembly of the Confederation on 8 July 1820 as a supplement to the Act of Confederation. The first five articles, which set out the legal position of the Confederation and its members, follow.

Source: E. Hertslet, *The Map of Europe by Treaty* (London, Butterworth, 1875), vol. i, pp. 640–1.

1. The Germanic Confederation is a union according to international law of the Sovereign Princes and Free Towns of Germany, for the preservation of the independence and inviolability of the States comprised in it, and for maintaining the internal and external security of Germany.

2. As to its internal relations, this Union consists of a community of States independent of each other, with reciprocal and equal rights and obligations stipulated by treaties. As to its external relations, it constitutes a collective power, bound together in political unity.

3. The compass and the limitations, which the Confederation has assigned for its operation are laid down in the Federal Act which is the [basic treaty] and the first fundamental law of this union. While it declares the object of the Confederation, that act determines at the same time its rights and obligations.

4. The right of developing and perfecting the Confederation Act, in so far as the object proposed therein renders this necessary, belongs to the whole of the members of the Confederation. But the resolution to be adopted for this purpose must not be in contradiction to the spirit of the Federal Act, nor depart from the original character of the Federation.

5. The Confederation is established as an indissoluble union, and therefore none of its members can be at liberty to secede from it . . .

24. *The Wartburg Festival, 19 October 1817*

In 1815, as a result of the national and constitutional feeling of the Wars of Liberation, *Burschenschaften*, students' unions, were formed at all German universities, with the object of substituting an all-German organization for the clubs which had hitherto split the students up according to their state of origin. In 1817, to celebrate the three hundredth anniversary of the Reformation, and the Battle of Leipzig against Napoleon in 1813, a great student festival was held at the Wartburg. This was the most spectacular manifestation of German national and constitutionalist feeling in the early decades of the century.

What follows has been taken from a contemporary report by Lorenz Oken, professor of the University of Jena, the founder of the Congresses of German Scientists, one of the first all-German bodies that were tolerated by the authorities. It was published in his periodical *Isis*.

Source: J. G. Legge, *Rhyme and Revolution in Germany* (London, Constable, 1918), pp. 22–5.

... The students who thronged to the sacred festival were quartered in the town [of Eisenach] ...; the Hall of the Knights in the Wartburg was bedecked with wreaths, and provided with tables and benches to seat seven hundred to eight hundred men. Such was the total number present at the midday meal on the day of victory, the rest of us included. Representatives had come from Berlin, Erlangen, Giessen, Göttingen, Halle, Heidelberg, Jena, Kiel, Leipzig, Marburg, Rostock, Tübingen and Würzburg.

On the 19th at 9 a.m. the students, who had assembled in the market-place, marched to the castle, banners and a band at their head. We accompanied them. Of the professors who had this festival at heart, who saw in it the germ of some great and fruitful tree, and had come designedly to judge, from the proceedings, the students' conduct, and events that passed, what might be expected of its blossoming, there were four of us ... When general silence was obtained a student delivered a speech on very much the following lines: he spoke of the aim of this assembly of educated young men from all circles and all races of the German fatherland; of the thwarted life of the past; of the rebound, and the ideal that now possessed the German people; of hopes that had failed and been deceived; of the vocation of the student and the legitimate expectations which the fatherland founded upon it; of the destitution and even persecution to which a youth devoting himself to learning had to submit; finally how they must themselves take thought to introduce among them order, rule, and custom ...

By one and another further encouraging speeches were

delivered and then the company made for the courtyard of the castle until the tables were spread. There they formed themselves into groups large and small . . .

In one of the groups a speech of the following tenor was delivered: Dear friends, you must not let this moment of emotion and exaltation pass in smoke. It will not return. Now or never must you be united . . . All students are one; they all belong to one single nation, the German; they all follow the same precepts and customs . . . If the university man is by nature no provincialist, so is it unnatural to try and force him to be one by means of an artificial institution . . . You can and will (and the German people, including the princes, will) be nothing other than educated Germans, who are like one to the other, and whose business everywhere is free . . . Also beware of the vain thought that it is on you that Germany's being and continuance and honour depend. Germany depends only on itself, on Germany as a whole . . . Yours is not to discuss what should or should not happen in the state, what alone is seemly for you to consider is, what your business shall one day be in the State . . .

Then trumpets gave the signal for dinner. It was a merry meal . . . After dinner the procession made its way downhill . . . into the city church where the sermon aroused general emotion. Then followed a display of gymnastic exercise in the marketplace, after which darkness fell. Thus every moment was passed in praiseworthy activity.

At 7 the students, some six hundred of them, each with a torch, marched up the hill to the triumphal bonfire . . . On the hill-top songs were sung, and another speech delivered by a student.

Afterwards trial by fire was held over the following articles, which were first displayed high in the air on a pitch-fork to the assembled multitude, and then with curses hurled into the flames. The articles burnt were these: a bagwig, a guardsman's cuirass, a corporal's cane[1] . . .

Thus did the students of Germany celebrate the Festival of the Wartburg. Many of those who manage the affairs of Ger-

---

[1] At the bonfire, after the majority of the students dispersed, a small radical remnant burned a number of reactionary books; this, however, was not part of the official programme of the festival.

many, and still more, those who mismanage them, might well
take the conclave on the Wartburg as an example.

25. The Carlsbad Decrees, 20 September 1819

After the Wartburg Festival the governments watched the activities
of the university students with suspicion and, when Carl Sand, a
student, murdered the author Kotzebue because of his reactionary
activity, repression was decided on. In August 1819 a conference
of ten governments, held at Carlsbad, agreed on the text of certain
decrees, which were accepted by the Diet as laws of the Confederation on 20 September 1820. The three important laws deal
with the universities (a), the press (b), and the establishment of a
central commission for the investigation of revolutionary activities
(c).
Source: *Annual Register*, 1819, pp. 159–62 (with emendations).

(a) The University Law.

1. The Sovereign shall make choice for each university of an
extraordinary commissioner, furnished with suitable instructions and powers, residing in the place where the university is
established . . .

The duty of this commissioner shall be to watch over the most
rigorous observation of the laws and disciplinary regulations; to
observe carefully the spirit with which the professors are guided
in the scientific courses, or in the method of instruction, to give
the instruction a salutary direction, suited to the future destiny
of the students, and to devote a constant attention to everything
which may tend to the maintenance of morality, good order and
decency among the youths . . .

2. The Governments of the States members of the confederation reciprocally engage to remove from their universities . . .
the professors and other public teachers against whom it may
be proved that in departing from their duty, in overstepping the
bounds of their duty, in abusing their legitimate influence over
the minds of youth, by the propagation of pernicious dogmas,
hostile to order and public tranquillity, or in sapping the foundation of existing institutions, they have shown themselves incapable of executing the important functions entrusted to them
without any obstacle whatever being allowed to impede the
measure taken against them.

A professor thus excluded may not be admitted in any other State of the Confederation to any other establishment of public instruction.

3. The laws long since made against secret or unauthorized associations at the universities shall be maintained in all their force and rigour, and shall be particularly extended with so much the more severity against the well-known society formed some years ago under the name of the general *Burschenschaft*, as it has for its basis the idea, absolutely inadmissible, of community and continued correspondence between the different universities . . .

4. No student who, by decree of the Academic Senate confirmed by the government commissioner, or adopted on his application, shall be dismissed from a university, or who, in order to escape from such a sentence, shall withdraw, shall be received in any other university; and in general no student shall be received at another university without a sufficient attestation of his good conduct at the university he has left . . .

(b) The Press Law.

1. As long as the present decree shall be in force, no daily paper or pamphlet of less than twenty sheets shall be issued from the press without the previous consent of the public authority . . .

4. Each Government of the Confederation is accountable for the writings published under its jurisdiction, and consequently for all those comprehended in the principal regulation of Article 1; and when these writings offend against the dignity or safety of another State of the confederation, or make attacks upon its constitution or its administration, the Government which tolerates them is responsible not only to the State which suffers directly therefrom, but to the whole Confederation.

5. In order that this responsibility, founded in the nature of the Germanic Union and inseparable from its preservation, may not give rise to disagreements which might compromise the amicable relations subsisting between the confederated States, all the members of the Confederation must enter into a solemn engagement to devote their most serious attention to the superintendence which the present decree prescribes, and to exercise it in such a manner as to prevent as much as possible all reciprocal complaints and discussions.

6. [If a State cannot obtain satisfaction from another State, it may apply to the Diet.] The Diet will proceed also, without a previous denunciation, and of its own authority, against every publication comprised in the principal regulation of Article 1 in whatever state of Germany it may be published, if in the opinion of a commission appointed to consider thereof, it may have compromised the dignity of the Germanic Confederation, the safety of any of its members, or the internal peace of Germany, without any recourse being afforded against the judgment given in such a case, which shall be carried into execution by the Government that is responsible for the condemned publication.

7. The editor of a journal, or other periodical publication, that may be suppressed by command of the Diet, shall not be allowed, during the space of five years, to conduct any similar publication in any State of the Confederation . . .

(c) Law establishing a Central Commission of Investigation.

1. Within fourteen days from the date of this decree, an extraordinary commission of inquiry, appointed by the Diet and composed of seven members, including the president, shall assemble in the city of Mainz . . .

2. The object of this commission is to make careful and detailed inquiries respecting the facts, the origin and the multifarious ramifications of the secret revolutionary activities and demagogic associations, directed against the political constitution and internal repose of the confederation as well as of its individual members, of which indications have been already discovered, or may result from further investigation.

3. The Diet elects by majority vote the seven members of the confederation who are to appoint the members of the central commission . . .

5. In order to attain the end proposed, the central commission shall undertake the general direction of local investigations which have already been commenced, or may hereafter be instituted . . .

7. The central commission is authorized to examine every individual whom it may judge necessary . . .

26. *The Hambach Festival, 27 May 1832*

Over thirty thousand radicals, democrats, and republicans participated in the great open air meeting held at Hambach, the greatest
demonstration for national unity and political liberty held in
Germany in this period. It had little immediate significance: most
of the leaders were arrested or had to flee, no general movement
was founded, and repression was intensified as a result. It is none
the less important because it shows the amount of political interest,
and reveals the difference between moderate liberals and the radical
wing.

Two short pieces are included: the invitation to the festival, prepared and signed by a small committee (a) and extracts from some
of the speeches (b).

Source: (a) K. Obermann, *Einheit und Freiheit* (Berlin, Dietz, 1955),
pp. 116–17 (trans. Ed.).

(b) J. G. Legge, *Rhyme and Revolution in Germany* (London,
Constable, 1918), pp. 107–9.

(a) Invitation to the Hambach Festival.

The German May

Most peoples, when great and happy events befall their
nation, hold festivals of joy and thanksgiving. The German
people has not had such an opportunity for hundreds of years,
and even now there is no occasion for such a celebration. For
the German, the seed of great events has not yet germinated.
What he desires is a festival of hope; a festival not to celebrate
what has been achieved, but what is still to be achieved, in constitutional freedom and German national dignity, not a glorious
triumph, but a manful struggle to shake off oppression from
within and without.

All German races participate in this sacred struggle: all are
therefore invited to the great civic reunion which will be held
on Sunday, 27 May [1832] at the castle of Hambach . . .

In May, according to Teutonic custom, our famed ancestors
the Franks held their national assembly; in May heroic Poland
received its constitution; in May nature, physical and spiritual
alike, begins to stir. When the earth is adorned with flowers,
when the bud is ready to burst, how could the wish for a free
life, the desire for human dignity remain frozen in cold selfish-
ness, contemptible fear, criminal indifference?

Come hither, therefore, you German men and youths, of whatever estate, all whose breasts are aglow with the sacred spark of Fatherland and liberty. Come, German women and girls, whose political rights are so disgracefully neglected in Europe, adorn and enliven the meeting with your presence. Let all gather so that by peaceful discussion they might come to know each others' inmost heart, and form a resolute brother-hood in their devotion to their great ideal.

(b) Extracts from the Speeches of Siebenpfeiffer and Wirth.

Siebenpfeiffer:
. . . We devote our lives to science and art, we measure the stars, scrutinize sun and moon, we give poetical representations of God and man, heaven and hell, we probe the world of body and mind: but we are ignorant of the pulse of patriotism, the investigation of which (just what the Fatherland needs) is high treason, even the faint wish only to attain to a Fatherland, a home for free men, is a crime. We help to free Greece from the Turkish yoke, we drink to the resurrection of Poland, we are indignant when the despotism of kings damps the ardour of the people in Spain, in Italy, and in France, we follow with our regard England's Reform Bill, we praise the strength and the wisdom of the Sultan, who busies himself over the regeneration of his peoples, we envy the North American his happy lot that he has boldly carved out for himself; but we slavishly bow our necks under the yoke of our own oppressors . . .

The day will come, the day of noblest pride of victory when Germans from the Alps to the North Sea, from the Rhine, the Danube and the Elbe will embrace like brothers, when customs houses and toll-bars, and all the princely insignia of division and restraint and oppression will disappear, with the little constitu-tions which have been granted like playthings to a few can-tankerous children in the great family; when free roads and free waterways give evidence of the free circulation of all national activity and strength; when princes will exchange the parti-coloured ermine robes of Feudalism and the Divine Right of Kings for the manly toga of Germany's national dignity, and officials and warriors will deck themselves not in the lacquey's uniform of their lord and master but with the People's sash;

when not thirty-four towns or townlets, receiving alms from thirty-four courts, as the price of a doglike subjection, but when all towns, blossoming free in sap of their own, wrestle for the prize of patriotic deed; when every branch of our stock, with internal freedom and independence, develops with civic freedom, and a strong, homespun bond of brotherhood enfolds all in political union and strength; when the German flag, instead of carrying tribute to the barbarians, convoys the products of our industrial toil to foreign quarters of the globe, and no more catches guilt-less patriots for the executioner's axe, but bears the kiss of brother-hood to all free peoples . . .

Aye, there will come the day when a universal German Fatherland arises, that greets all its sons as citizens, and encom-passes all citizens with equal love, with equal protection . . .

Long live the free, the united Germany! Long live the Poles, the German allies! Long life the French, the Germans' brothers, who honour our nationality and independence! Long live every people that breaks its chains and swears with us the Bond of Freedom! Fatherland, Sovereign People, Union of Nations, all hail!

Wirth:

. . . But the French have no wish for reform in Germany, or only at the price of the left bank of the Rhine. It is only at this price that even liberal propagandists in France will support the efforts of a League of Freedom in Germany. That we for our part will not purchase freedom itself by the cession of the left bank of the Rhine to France, that, on the contrary, any attempt of France to rob us of a single sod of German soil will and must silence all internal opposition and rouse off Germany against France, that the re-birth of freedom in our German Fatherland, then to be hoped for, will probably have a result that turns the tables in the reincorporation of Alsace and Lorraine in Germany —on all these points there can be among Germans but one voice . . . Only when guarantees have first been given for the inviolability of German territory can a union of German patriots enter into a bond of brotherhood with the patriots of all other nations . . .

Hail to the United Free States of Germany and a con-solidated, republican Europe!

27. The Customs Union (Zollverein) Treaty, 22 March 1833

Article 19 of the Act of Confederation (No. 22) envisaged that the Diet should take steps in respect of trade and commerce within Germany, but nothing was done. Thirty-eight customs barriers, as many or more systems of money, of weight and of measure, a variety of excise duties and road tolls, made trade and even the transportation of goods very difficult. Prussia, consisting of two parts separated by other States, found the position particularly onerous. It was, therefore, on Prussian initiative that the first customs union, comprising Prussia, Hesse-Cassel, and Hesse-Darmstadt came into being. When this first union was joined by the union of Bavaria and Württemberg in 1833, the foundation was laid of the German Customs Union (Zollverein) which remained in existence until 1871 and to which most German states acceded, Austria and Hanover being the most notable abstainers.

Source: *Annual Register*, 1838, pp. 323–35.

Treaty of Customs Union between Prussia, Hesse-Cassel and Hesse-Darmstadt, and Bavaria and Württemberg.

1. The customs associations at present existing between the before-mentioned States shall, for the future, form one confederation, united by a common system of trade and customs, and comprehending all the countries included therein.

2. Into this united confederation shall be especially admitted such States as have already acceded, either with their whole territory, or with part of it, to the system of trade and customs of one or other of the Contracting States; and regard shall be had to their peculiar relations, arising out of their treaties of accession, with reference to those states with which such treaties have been concluded . . .

4. Similar laws, relative to import, export and transit duties, shall prevail within the dominions of the Contracting States . . .

6. Freedom of trade and commerce between the Contracting States, and a common interest in the customs revenues, as settled in the following articles, shall commence with the operation of the present treaty.

7. And from the same period, also, all import, export and transit duties shall be discontinued on the common boundaries of the late Prussian and Hessian, and Bavarian and Württemberg associations, and all articles which are already allowed to be freely interchanged in the territory of one, shall be freely, and

without restriction, admitted into the territory of the other,
with the following reserved exceptions . . .

[The articles that follow deal with these exceptions, the
equalization of internal (i.e. excise) duties, uniformity of road
and river tolls, steps to be taken towards uniformity in the
monetary system and in weights and measures, reduction or
abolition of transit charges, freedom of movement between the
contracting states and equal opportunity for employment or
commercial etc. activity, free use of Prussian seaports, etc.]

22. The amount of duties which are to become common property shall, after deducting [expenses and some specified items]
be divided among the Contracting States, according to the
population of each State comprehended in the union . . .

The census of the population in each separate State of the
union shall be taken every three years . . .

33. A congress, at which each of the Governments of the union
shall appoint a plenipotentiary, shall be held annually about the
beginning of June, for the purpose of general discussion . . .

41. The present treaty, which is to be brought into operation on
the 1st of January, 1834, shall continue in force until the 1st of
January, 1842; and if, during that term, and, at the latest, two
years before the expiration of it, the contrary should not be
declared, the period of its continuance shall be prolonged to
twelve years, and afterwards from twelve years to twelve
years . . .

28. The Prussian United Diet, 1847

Many of the smaller States of Germany had been granted constitutions by their rulers, and their estates had some say in legislation.
The two great German powers, Austria and Prussia, however, continued to be governed autocratically. Prussia took the first step
towards popular participation in government: the assemblies of the
estates in the provinces, which had not been called together for
several decades, were assembled in 1841 and met regularly thereafter. In spite of this concession, the new King, Frederick William IV,
had no thoughts of calling an assembly of estates for the whole of
the Kingdom, nor of granting a constitution. Only in 1847, when
the state wished to contract a loan, were the provincial estates called
together in a united Diet, which was given little more than consultative power.

Many of its members were of opinion that an assembly of provincial estates, with no guarantee of regular meeting, did not fulfil

the provisions of the laws and ordinances of Frederick William III to which the decree calling the United Diet referred. The address in reply, therefore, protested against the limitations on the competence of the Diet, and the United Diet asserted its powers by voting against many of the measures proposed by the government. A draft address, proposed by Beckerath, listed in some detail the laws infringed and the demands of the estates. This was considered to be too strong and a briefer and more general version of the second half of the address was then adopted. Even this was considered to be insulting by the King.

The decree calling the Diet is the first selection, under (a); (b) is the address as finally adopted, an asterisk marking the beginning of the amended version.

Source: *Annual Register*, 1847, pp. [374-5, 388-91].

(a) Decree calling United Diet, 3 February 1847.

We, Frederick William, by the Grace of God King of Prussia . . . give notice and herewith ordain to be known:—

Since the commencement of our Government we have constantly applied particular care to the development of the relations of the Estates of our country.

We recognize in this matter one of the weightiest problems of the kingly calling bestowed on us by God, in the solution of which a twofold aim is marked out for us—namely, to transmit the rights, the dignity, and the power of the Crown inherited from our ancestors of glorious memory intact to our successors on the throne; but at the same time to grant to the faithful Estates of our monarchy that co-operation which, in unison with those rights and the peculiar relations of our monarchy, is fitted to secure a prosperous future to our country.

In respect whereof—continuing to build on the laws given by His Late Majesty, Our Royal Father, now resting with God, particularly on the Ordinance respecting the National Debt of the 17th of January, 1820,[1] and on the Law respecting the Regulation of the Provincial Diets of the 5th of June, 1823—we decree as follows:—

1. As often as the wants of the State may require either fresh loans or the introduction of new taxes, or the increase of those

---

[1] The ordinance of 17 January 1820 requires the 'future assembly of the estates of the kingdom' to consent to new loans, and provides for annual reports on the state of the public debt to be made to this assembly.

already existing, we will call together around us the provincial Diets of the monarchy in a united Diet, in order, firstly, to call into play the co-operation of the Diets provided by the ordinance respecting the national debt; and secondly, to assure us of their consent.

2. We will for the future call together at periodical times the Committee of the United Diet.

3. To the United Diet, and, as its representative, to the Committee of the United Diet, we entrust

(a) In reference to counsel of the Diet in legislation, the same co-operation which was assigned to the provincial Diets by the law of June 5, 1823 . . .

(b) The co-operation of the Diets in paying the interest on, and liquidation of, the State debts, provided by the law of January 17, 1820, in so far as such business is not confined to the deputation of the Diet for the national debt;

(c) The right of petition upon internal though not merely provincial matters. All the above, as is more closely defined in our ordinances . . .

(b) Address in Reply voted by the United Diet, May 1847.

Most gracious Lord and King,

Since your accession to the Throne, Your Majesty has laboured incessantly at the noble development of the existence of the nation, and the country enjoys with feelings of gratitude the blessings resulting from the lively interest taken by the people in public affairs. A new and more elevated sphere has been opened for this interest. Recognizing the necessity of a representative organ common to the whole nation, and its utility for the unity of the State, Your Majesty has deigned to convoke in a united Diet the estates of all the provinces. By a free and truly kingly decision, Your Majesty has made a great step, and we fulfil a first and sacred duty when, in a spirit of immutable attachment to Your Majesty's person and family, we lay at the foot of the throne the thanks of a faithful people.

Our country is elevated by the exalted spirit of its Prince, and by the power of public opinion; its future prosperity depends upon the unison of that spirit and that public opinion. This truth is manifested anew by the fact that Your Majesty, in your

letter patent of the 3rd of February of this year (No. 28(a))
announced Your intention of continuing to build on the basis of
the laws given by His Majesty the late King, to which the people
cling as well-worn inheritance, acquired by its fidelity in the
field of battle.

Your Majesty having realized the reservation expressed in the
law of the 5th of June, 1823, and given the name of the United
Diet to the assembly which in the said law is called the General
Assembly of Estates of the Kingdom, it is plain that the rights
founded upon the laws now quoted, and upon other earlier laws,
are acquired by the said United Diet.* We entertain such a
confidence in your Majesty, that we are sure your Majesty will
not consider it a want of thankfulness on our part, if in the course
of our proceedings we enter more at length into the Ordinances
of the 3rd of February of the present year, in which many of our
number miss a full accordance with earlier laws. For, in order
that Your Majesty's faithful Estates may be a real support to the
throne—in order that we may efficiently co-operate with Your
Majesty for the profit and welfare of our beloved country—
those whom we represent must be alive to the conviction that,
while we reverence the majesty and power of the Crown, so also
the representative rights granted to us by our Kings are dear to
us, and that we preserve and cherish *both* as jewels beyond all
price.

If the Diet by its deliberations, if Your Majesty by the grounds
which it may respectfully adduce, should be convinced of the
existence of such discrepancies between the earlier laws and
these later ordinances, we do not doubt that Your Majesty's
wisdom and justice will choose a way which may lead to their
reconciliation in a manner consistent with the welfare of Prussia
—a welfare founded on the strength of the monarchic principle,
and on a secure and well-regulated representative basis.

29. *The Offenburg Resolutions of the South West German Radicals, 10 September 1847*

As the economic and social situation became worse in the crisis of
1847, and the governments remained inactive, or unable to intervene, several oppositional groups from the south-west German States
met to arrive at a common programme of reforms which, if put into
effect, could improve the situation. The first of these meetings was

that of the radicals or democrats at Offenburg, at which the following resolution was passed.

Source: *Allgemeine Zeitung* (Augsburg) No. 262, 19 September 1847, p. 2095 (trans. Ed.).

1. We demand that our State Governments repudiate the Carlsbad resolutions of 1819 (No. 25) [and other, specified, confederate repressive measures]. These resolutions violate our inalienable human rights and, at the same time, infringe the German Act of Confederation and our state constitution.

2. We demand freedom of the press: we must no longer be deprived of the inalienable right of the human spirit to publish its thought without mutilation.

3. We demand freedom of conscience and of learning . . .

4. We demand that the army swear an oath to the constitution . . .

5. We demand personal freedom. The police must stop its tutelage and torture of the citizen. The right of association, healthy community life, . . . the individual's right to move freely in the territory of the German Fatherland, . . . must remain undisturbed in future.

6. We demand representation of the people in the German Confederation . . .

7. We demand popular organization of the armed forces. Only the citizen provided with arms and trained in their use can defend the State. Let the people be given arms and let them be free of the intolerable burden of the standing armies.

8. We demand a just distribution of taxes. Let everybody contribute to the upkeep of the State according to his capacity. The present taxes should be replaced by a progressive income tax.

9. We demand that education be equally accessible to all. The means should be provided by the community . . .

10. We demand adjustment of the relationship of labour and capital. It is the duty of society to improve the position of labour and to protect it.

11. We demand laws worthy of free citizens, and application of these laws through juries . . .

12. We demand popular administration of the State. Free organs are necessary for a free life of the people . . . Over-

government by officials should be replaced by self-government.
13. We demand the abolition of all privilege . . .

30. *The Heppenheim Programme of the South West German Liberals, 10 October 1847*

A month after the Offenburg meeting of the radicals (No. 29) the moderate liberals of South West Germany met at Heppenheim to discuss a common programme. The following is a summary of their deliberations and decisions, as reported in the main liberal newspaper of the time.

Source: *Deutsche Zeitung* (Heidelberg), 15 October 1847, No. 107, pp. 852–3 (trans. Ed.).

With reference to the betterment of the state of the nation by common leadership and representation it was agreed that nothing positive could be expected of the Federal Diet as it was constituted. The Diet has so far not fulfilled the tasks set it by the Act of Confederation (No. 22) in the fields of representation by estates, free trade and communications, navigation, freedom of the press, etc.; the federal defence regulation provides neither for the arming of the population nor for a uniformly organized federal force. On the contrary, the press is harassed by censorship; the discussions of the Diet are enveloped in a secrecy lifted only to reveal decisions which hinder any free development. The only expression of common German interests in existence, the Customs Union, was not created by the Confederation, but negotiated outside its framework, through treaties between individual states; negotiations about a German law on bills of exchange, and about a postal union, are conducted not by the Confederation but by the several Governments.

From these and similar considerations followed the question: would a representation of the people in the Diet effect an improvement, and should it therefore become the aim of all patriots?

An affirmative answer was supported on several counts: the mood of the people was favourable, it would be possible to effect representation of all confederate States only through the existing organ of the confederate Governments, it could be expected that public opinion, gathering strength, would achieve a realization of the plan and thus open the way to German policies, to a vigorous development of the spiritual and material forces of the nation.

Against the proposal it was asserted that, notwithstanding the uplifting nature of this conception, there was no prospect of its realization. Some members of the Confederation, Denmark or the Netherlands, are also foreign powers and would never favour a German policy, an increase in German power; other members, again, are not wholly German powers and possess territories which, like East Prussia, may be German, but are not part of the Confederation. Further, national representation would also make the establishment of a national Government necessary; a national Government would require sovereign powers, powers which the Confederation does not possess.

A Germany unified for carrying out German policies, under a common leadership, with proper care for national interests, would probably be achieved more readily if the support of public opinion could be gained for a transformation of the Customs Union into a German Union. The Customs Union already has an administrative apparatus, however faulty, which could be given urgently needed improvements and a representative assembly elected by the Chambers of the participating States. The Customs Union already deals with a great many common interests and is in a treaty relationship with foreign powers. Not being disturbed by the presence of foreign members, this Union already contains the seed of a common policy, and to its activity in customs and trade matters other, related common interests could be added, e.g. the system of roads and waterways, uniform taxation (particularly excise taxation), regulation of crafts and trades, merchant marine, consulates, commercial code, and so on. When, through such a transformation, the German Union becomes powerful, it will exert an irresistible attraction on the remaining German states, even, in the end, on the Austrian lands of the Confederation, and thus establish a great German State.

This trend of thought . . . was finally accepted by all, with the addition, that although the immediate aim should be the development of the Customs Union and a representation of its peoples through a Customs Parliament, no opportunity should be missed for emphasizing the aim of German unity. It was undisputed and undoubted that participation of the people through their elected representatives was essential, and that in the circumstances of Germany in the present century unification could be effected only by and through liberty, never by force . . .

The liberation of the press . . ., open and oral judicial proceedings with juries, separation of the executive and judicial powers, transfer to the courts of the administration of the laws (including administrative law and police offences acts), drafting of a police criminal code, freeing the soil and its tillers from medieval burdens, independence of the communes in the administration of their affairs, reduction of the cost of the standing army and establishment of a national guard, etc. were discussed at length, as were the constitutional means that could be used to give force to the just demands of the people. Particular attention was given to possible ways of reducing impoverishment and want and, a closely related topic, of reforming the system of taxation . . .

IV · THE REVOLUTIONS OF 1848:
FRANCE

THE Paris revolution of 1848 arose from two developments, one political, the other economic and social. The middle classes wanted a reform of the franchise, still restricted to the wealthier citizens (cf. No. 21), while the workers wanted an amelioration of their living conditions which were seriously affected by the bad harvests and economic crisis of the years before 1848. The prohibition of a political reform banquet and the resulting demonstrations by the population brought concessions and then abdication by King Louis Philippe (No. 31). The people, by acclamation, appointed a Provisional Government. The first proclamation of the Government (No. 32) set out the provisional programme, and was soon followed by a decree guaranteeing the right of work of all citizens (No. 33). It was easy to reform political life by proclaiming the republic (No. 34) but rather more difficult to solve the problems of the working class, who demanded work and the establishment of National Workshops, both demands based on Louis Blanc's ideas set out in his *Organization of Labour,* a socialist treatise of great importance. The Government consisted largely of middle-class politicians who would not accept socialist principles, yet had to agree to the creation of National Workshops (No. 35(a) and (b)) without having any practical idea on how to organize them. They were relieved when a young engineer, Thomas, offered to organize the Workshops and, at the same time, influence the workers against socialism (No. 35(c)). A different line of dealing with the problem which also served the purpose of eliminating the two popularly elected socialist members of the government, Blanc and Albert, was the establishment of the so-called Luxembourg Commission, which was to discuss long-term measures for solving the workers' problems (No. 36).

The Provisional Government, having called elections for a

National Assembly (No. 37) which would, they hoped, settle
the constitution of the country in a moderate spirit, further
showed its moderation in the issue of a Manifesto to Europe
(No. 38), drafted by Lamartine, Minister of Foreign Affairs. In
this document they renounced any intention of spreading
revolution by French assistance to revolutionary movements in
other countries.

Although popular discontent continued to be manifested, as
is shown by the manifesto of one of the revolutionary societies
which is included (No. 39), the National Assembly indeed had
a moderate composition. Even the Provisional Government was
too extreme for them, and they replaced it with an executive
commission (No. 40). They also decided to liquidate the major
extremist achievement of the revolution, the National Workshops (No. 41). As a result the workers of Paris rose in arms and
were put down after a bitter and bloody fight by troops commanded by General Cavaignac during the so-called 'June
days'. Full executive power was then conferred on Cavaignac
(No. 42) whose fairly conservative government kept a tight rein
on the country while the constitution was drafted. It is regretted
that considerations of space preclude the inclusion of selections
from this constitution.

At the presidential elections in the end of 1848 Prince Louis
Napoleon Bonaparte gained a decisive victory in spite of the
treaties excluding members of Napoleon's family from the
headship of the French state (cf. article 2 of No. 5). He had
taken his seat in the National Assembly after a by-election in
September (No. 43(a)), but, even after he issued a programme
appealing to a large proportion of the population (No. 43(b)),
his chances were considered negligible and his election was a
surprise to most politicians. Section VII contains documents on
his further career.

31. Proclamations by Odilon Barrot, 24 February 1848

The revolutionaries demanded, first of all, the dismissal of the
Guizot ministry, as they held Guizot responsible for the mismanage-
ment of affairs. Louis Philippe acceded to their demands, dismissed
Guizot, and entrusted Thiers and Odilon Barrot, leaders of the two
main oppositional groups, with the formation of a Government.
With their first proclamation (a) these two politicians attempted to

stay the revolution; but the concessions were not far reaching enough, and even the abdication of the king (b) could not save the monarchy.

Source: *Annual Register*, 1848, pp. [230–1].

(a) Proclamation of Thiers and Odilon Barrot, morning of 24 February.

Citizens:

Orders are given to stop the firing. We have been charged by the King with the formation of a Ministry. The Chamber is about to be dissolved. General Lamoricière is named Commander in Chief of the National Guard of Paris. Messrs. Odilon Barrot, Thiers, Lamoricière and Duvergier de Hauranne are Ministers. Liberty! Order! Union! Reform!

(signed) Odilon Barrot   Thiers

(b) Abdication of Louis Philippe, afternoon of 24 February.

Citizens of Paris,

The King has abdicated. The crown, bestowed by the revolution of July, is now placed on the head of a child, protected by his mother. They are both under the safeguard of the honour and courage of the Parisian population. All cause of division amongst us has ceased to exist. Orders have been given to the troops of the line to return to their respective quarters. Our brave army can be better employed than in shedding its blood in so deplorable a collision.

(signed) Odilon Barrot.

32. *First Proclamation of the Provisional Government, 25 February 1848*

The population of Paris invaded the Chamber of Deputies and there, by acclamation, elected a Provisional Government from lists compiled in the editorial offices of the two main republican newspapers, the moderate *National* and the radical *Réforme*. After election the members of the Provisional Government moved, according to revolutionary tradition, to the *Hôtel de Ville*[1] where they drafted and issued the proclamation that follows.

Source: *Annual Register*, 1848, pp. [239–40].

[1] The Town Hall.

A retrograde government has been overturned by the heroism of the people of Paris. This government has fled, leaving behind it traces of blood, which will for ever forbid its return.

The blood of the people has flowed, as in July; but, happily, it has not been shed in vain. It has secured a national and popular government, in accordance with the rights, the progress, and the will of this great and generous people.

A Provisional Government, at the call of the people and some deputies in the sitting of the 24th of February, is for the moment organizing and securing the national victory. It is composed of MM. Dupont (de l'Eure), Lamartine, Crémieux, Arago, Ledru-Rollin, and Garnier Pagès. The Secretaries to the Government are MM Armand Marrast, Louis Blanc, and Ferdinand Flocon.[1] These citizens have not hesitated for an instant to accept the patriotic mission which has been imposed upon them by the urgency of the occasion.

Frenchmen, give to the world the example Paris has given to France. Prepare yourselves, by order and confidence in yourselves, for the institutions which are about to be given to you.

The Provisional Government desires a Republic, pending the ratification of the French people, who are to be immediately consulted. Neither the people of Paris nor the Provisional Government desire to substitute their opinion for the opinions of the citizens at large, upon the definite form of Government which the national sovereignty shall proclaim.

The unity of the nation, formed henceforth of all classes of the people which compose it;

The government of the nation by itself;

Liberty, equality and fraternity for its principles;

The people to devise and to maintain order.

Such is the Democratic Government which France owes to herself, and which our efforts will assure to her.

Such are the first acts of the Provisional Government.

---

[1] Albert, a worker, was later added. Most of the members were lawyers and politicians; Dupont had been a deputy in 1795 and prominent in 1830; Lamartine, historian and poet; Arago, famous astronomer; Ledru-Rollin, the leading radical republican; Blanc, journalist and socialist thinker; Marrast, editor of the moderate *National*; Flocon, editor of the radical *Réforme*.

DEC—H

33. Decree on the Right to Work, 25 February 1848

On pressure from the armed population who demanded the 'organization of labour' Louis Blanc drafted and the Provisional Government agreed to the following decree without really knowing how it could be effectively carried out.

Source: É. Thomas, *Histoire des Ateliers Nationaux*, in *The French Revolution of 1848 in its economic aspects*, ed. J. A. R. Marriott (Oxford, Clarendon Press, 1913), vol. ii, p. 19 (trans. Ed.).

The Provisional Government of the French Republic undertakes to guarantee the livelihood by work of the workers;

It undertakes to guarantee work for all citizens;

It recognizes that workers must combine in order to enjoy the legitimate benefits of their labour;

The Provisional Government returns to the workers, to whom it belongs, the million [francs] due to [be paid into] the civil list.

34. Proclamation of the Republic, 26 February 1848

Although the first proclamation of the Provisional Government (No. 32) already envisaged the establishment of a republic, it did not actually proclaim it. One day was enough, however, to impress on the members of the Provisional Government that the population of Paris would brook no further delay. Note the strong emphasis on order in the last paragraph of the excerpt.

Source: F.-A. Hélie, *Les Constitutions de la France* (Paris, Duchemin, 1880), p. 1080 (trans. Ed.).

Citizens:

Royalty in any form whatever is abolished.

No more legitimism, no more Bonapartism, no regency.

The Provisional Government has taken all the measures necessary to prevent the return of the old dynasty and the accession of a new one.

The republic is proclaimed.

The people are united.

All the forts surrounding the capital are ours.

The brave garrison of Vincennes is a garrison of brothers.[1]

---

[1] It had been feared that the garrison of the fort of Vincennes, near Paris, might invade the capital in order to put down the revolution. This fear was dispelled when the garrison declared its allegiance to the Provisional Government.

Let us maintain with respect the old republican flag whose three colours travelled around the world with our fathers. Let us show that this symbol of equality, liberty and fraternity is at the same time the symbol of order, of the most real and most lasting order, since its foundation is justice and its instrument the whole people . . .

35. *The National Workshops, February–March 1848*

The Provisional Government had undertaken to guarantee work for all citizens (No. 33) but took no practical measures to carry out its undertakings until a few days later when, again on popular pressure, the establishment of National Workshops, ostensibly (though not really) incorporating the ideas of Louis Blanc, was decreed. No thought was given to the organization of the workshops, and the Minister of Public Works was unable to cope with the influx of unemployed from all parts of Paris until a young engineer, Émile Thomas, offered to organize the Workshops on sound, that is non-socialist, lines.

Our selections include the two decrees on the formation of the Workshops (a) and (b) and part of the proposals made by Thomas (c).

Source: É. Thomas, *Histoire des Ateliers Nationaux*, in *The French Revolution of 1848 in its economic aspects*, ed. by J. A. R. Marriott (Oxford, Clarendon Press, 1913), vol. ii, pp. 27, 28, 50–52 (trans. Ed.).

(a) Establishment of Workshops, 27 February 1848.

The Provisional Government decrees the immediate establishment of National Workshops. The Minister of Public Works is responsible for the execution of this decree.

(b) Details of the National Workshops, 28 February 1848.

Workers:

By a decision of this day, 28 February 1848, the Minister of Public Works has ordered that works already begun be resumed immediately.

As from Wednesday, 1 March, important public works will be organized in different locations.

All workers who wish to take part should report to one of the mayors of Paris who will receive their application and direct them without delay to the work sites.

(c) Thomas's Proposals, 5 March 1848.

[After describing the chaotic conditions and abuses by which the paper establishment of the National Workshops was accompanied, Thomas continued, talking to the Minister of Public Works and other high officials:]

Such a state of affairs cannot continue for long without endangering public safety. Here, then, is what I propose in order to alleviate as much as possible, or even abolish, this evil.

There are no means of repression available . . . but you have at your disposal one of the most effective means which could lead to the same end, namely moral influence.

You know very well, gentlemen, how fond the people are of youths, particularly of school students, and how easily they will be guided by them. This is natural, there is nothing so like a child as the people . . .

This, then, is the useful task which I dare hope to fulfil, and which I wish to share with all my young friends from the *École Centrale*.[1] Their education destines them to direct workers in factories and workshops . . . Many of them had even been brought up among such circumstances . . .

I therefore propose, gentlemen, the establishment in a . . . distant district . . . of an administration whose task would be the centralization of the activity of the twelve municipal districts regarding the workers. On days fixed in advance each municipal district would send us its workers, bearing their cards,[2] the only—but indispensable—condition of admission. When we have noted their names, occupation and address, we shall give them a booklet intended for the various controls we shall exercise, which they shall thus be unable to evade. We shall then organize them in detachments of a fixed number of men; the detachments will form companies, each directed by one of our young friends;[3] division on this basis, recognizing

[1] *École Centrale d'Arts et Manufactures*, founded in 1838, is the equivalent of a modern technical college. It issued diplomas in industrial engineering and had a practical bias in its curriculum.

[2] A certificate of the suburban mayor certifying the eligibility of the bearer for admission to the National Workshops.

[3] Of the *École Centrale*.

the detachment as the basic unit, will allow regular payment of relief or wage, at a fixed time and under salutary inspection, with the individual assessment of each worker's paysheet.

On the other hand the Minister of Public Works as well as the municipal department of public works [of Paris] will advise us every day of the number of workers of every occupation which may be employed on new works commenced under orders from the government; similarly, we shall send every day the workers demanded from us to works either in Paris or in the provinces; our young men will still accompany them. For works under the jurisdiction of the General Council of Roads and Bridges, the direction will be in the hands of the engineers of that body, and [our young men] will only have the modest but useful position in charge of order and attention to duty.

Finally, manufacturers, mill-owners and contractors who need workers can also apply to us and engage, by mutual agreement, workers from us instead of searching for them where they congregate hoping to be hired.[1]

In one word, the institution I propose is a free and universal employment agency which, in this exceptional period, will also have the task of centralizing the distribution of relief by the municipalities . . .

36. *Decree establishing the Luxembourg Commission, 28 February 1848*

Louis Blanc, being a socialist, was distrusted by his colleagues in the Provisional Government. He was not put in charge of the National Workshops, and had to be removed somehow from active participation in the government. A means of this was found in the establishment of a Commission for the Workers, usually referred to as the Luxembourg Commission after the palace where it met. Some important reforms resulted from its deliberations, in which employers' and workers' representatives participated, but they were rescinded —and the Commission dissolved—after the meeting of the National Assembly.

Source: É. Thomas, *Histoire des Ateliers Nationaux*, in *The French*

---

[1] '*sur leur rendez-vous de grève*'. The square of the City Hall, until 1806 called Place de la Grève, was the place where unemployed or dissatisfied workers, mainly labourers, congregated, in the former case hoping to be hired, in the latter concerting strike action. Hence the word *grève* is used in two senses: strike, or, as in the above text, hiring place (or even labour exchange).

Revolution of 1848 in its economic aspects, ed. by J. A. R.
Marriott (Oxford, Clarendon Press, 1913), vol. ii, pp. 20–1
(trans. Ed.).

Since the revolution was made by the people, it ought to be
in its interests;

Whereas it is time to put an end to the long and unjust
suffering of the workers;

Whereas the question of labour is of supreme importance;

Whereas there is no higher or more suitable pre-occupation
for a republican Government;

Whereas France is particularly called upon to study and to
resolve this problem which arises in all the industrial states of
Europe;

Whereas it is necessary to consider, without the slightest delay,
how to guarantee to the people the legitimate fruits of their
labour, the Provisional Government orders as follows:

A permanent commission, which will be named Commission
of the Government for the Workers, will be appointed with the
special task of dealing with their condition.

In order to show the importance that the Provisional Government of the Republic attributes to the solution of this great
problem, it appoints one of its members, M. Louis Blanc, as
president . . . and another of its members, M. Albert, a worker,
as vice-president.

Workers will be called upon to participate in the Commission.

The seat of the Commission will be the Luxembourg Palace.

37. *Decree calling National Assembly, 5 March 1848*

In its first proclamation (No. 32) the Provisional Government
promised to consult the people at the earliest possible date. Having
taken the necessary preliminary decisions, such as basis of suffrage,
number of representatives, distribution by departments, the government called for elections on 9 April 1848 (later postponed to
23 April). The substance of the decree follows.

Source: *Annual Register*, 1848, pp. [245–6].

On the 5th of March [the Provisional Government] published
a decree by which it fixed that the elections should take place
on the 9th of April, and the constituent National Assembly meet

on the 20th of April. At the same time it announced the following as the general principles of the decree which it was about
to issue:

1. That the National Assembly shall decree the constitution.
2. That the election shall have the population for its basis.
3. That the representatives of the people shall amount to 900
in number.
4. That the suffrage shall be direct and universal, without any
limitation as to property.
5. That all Frenchmen of the age of 21 years shall be electors,
and that all Frenchmen of 25 years of age shall be eligible.
6. That the ballot shall be secret.

The decree which followed this declaration contained some
additional articles, the chief of which were the following:

1. All Frenchmen, 25 years of age, and not judicially deprived
of or suspended in the exercise of their civic rights, are eligible.
2. All the electors shall vote in the chief town of their district,
by ballot. Each bulletin shall contain as many names as there
shall be representatives to elect in the department.
No man can be named a representative of the people unless
he obtain 2000 suffrages.
3. Every representative of the people shall receive an indemnity
of 25f. per day during the Session.

38. *Lamartine's Manifesto to Europe, 7 March 1848*

The restrictions imposed on France by the settlement of 1815 (cf.
Nos 1, 4, 5) had long been resented by Frenchmen. It was expected,
in Paris as well as abroad, that the revolutionary Government would
take steps to repudiate these restrictions, and that it would also take
active steps to assist the revolutionary movements elsewhere, particularly in Poland. The following Manifesto, drafted by Lamartine
as Minister of Foreign Affairs, approved by his colleagues in the
Provisional Government, and communicated to all foreign Governments, set out in detail the official attitude on these questions.

Source: A. de Lamartine, *History of the French Revolution of 1848*
(London, Bell, 1905), pp. 278–85.

You know the events of Paris—the victory of the people;
their heroism, moderation, and tranquillity; the re-establishment of order, by the co-operation of the citizens at large, as if,

during this interregnum of the visible powers, public reason was, of itself alone, the government of France.

The French Revolution has thus entered upon its definitive period. France is a republic. The French republic does not require to be acknowledged in order to exist. It is based alike on natural and national law. It is the will of a great people, who demand the privilege only for themselves. But the French republic, being desirous of entering into the family of established Governments, as a regular power, and not as a phenomenon destructive of European order, it is expedient that you should promptly make known to the Government to which you are accredited, the principles and tendencies which will henceforth guide the foreign policy of the French Government.

The proclamation of the French republic is not an act of aggression against any form of government in the world. Forms of government have diversities as legitimate as the diversities of character,—of geographical situation,—of intellectual, moral and material development among nations. Nations, like individuals, have different ages; and the principles which rule them have successive phases. The monarchical, the aristocratic, the constitutional and the republican forms of government are the expression of the different degrees of maturity in the genius of nations. They require more liberty in proportion as they feel themselves capable of bearing more. They require greater equality and democracy in proportion as they are inspired with a greater share of justice and love for the people over whom they rule. It is merely a question of time. A nation ruins itself by anticipating the hour of that maturity; as it dishonours itself by allowing it to pass away without seizing it. Monarchy and republicanism are not, in the eyes of wise statesmen, absolute principles, arrayed in deadly conflict against each other; they are facts which contrast one with another, and which may exist face to face by mutually understanding and respecting each other.

War, therefore, is not now the principle of the French republic, as it was the fatal and glorious necessity of the republic of 1792. Half a century separates 1792 from 1848. To return, after the lapse of half a century, to the principle of 1792, or to the principle of conquest pursued during the Empire, would not be to advance, but to retrogress. The revolution of yesterday is a

step forward, not backward. The world and ourselves are
desirous of advancing to fraternity and peace . . .

The French republic, therefore, will not commence war
against any State; it is unnecessary to add, that it will accept
war should conditions incompatible with peace be offered to
the French people. The conviction of the men who govern
France at the present moment is this:—it will be fortunate for
France should war be declared against her, and should she be
thus constrained to augment her power and her glory, in spite
of her moderation; but terrible will be the responsibility to
France should the republic itself declare war without being provoked thereto! In the first case, the martial genius of France,
her impatience for action, her strength accumulated during
many years of peace, would render her invincible on her own
territory, and perhaps redoubtable beyond her frontiers: in the
second case she would turn to her own disadvantage the recol-
lections of her former conquests, which give umbrage to the
national feelings of other countries; and she would compromise
her first and most universal alliance, the good-will of nations
and the genius of civilization.

According to these principles, Sir, which are the principles
coolly and deliberately adopted by France, and which she
avows without fear and without defiance, to her friends and to
her enemies, you will impress upon your mind the following
declarations.

The treaties of 1815 have no longer any lawful existence in
the eyes of the French republic; nevertheless, the territorial
limits circumscribed by those treaties are facts which the
republic admits as a basis, and as a starting point, in her relations with foreign nations.

But if the treaties of 1815 have no existence save as facts to
be modified by common consent, and if the republic openly
declares that her right and mission are to arrive regularly and
pacifically at those modifications,—the good sense, the moderation, the conscience, the prudence of the republic exist, and they
afford to Europe a surer and more honourable guarantee than
the words of those treaties, which have so frequently been
violated or modified by Europe itself.

Endeavour, Sir, to make this emancipation of the republic
from the treaties of 1815 understood and honestly admitted,

and to show that such an admission is in no way irreconcilable
with the repose of Europe.

Thus we declare without reserve, that if the hour for the
reconstruction of any of the oppressed nations of Europe, or
other parts of the world, should seem to have arrived, according
to the decrees of Providence; if Switzerland, our faithful ally
from the time of Francis I, should be restrained or menaced in
the progressive movement she is carrying out, and which will
impart new strength to the fasces of democratical governments;
if the independent states of Italy should be invaded; if limits or
obstacles should be opposed to their internal changes; if there
should be any armed interference with their right of allying
themselves together for the purpose of consolidating an Italian
nation,—the French republic would think itself entitled to take
up arms in defence of those lawful movements for the improvement and the nationality of states.

The republic, as you perceive, has passed over at one step the
era of proscriptions and dictatorship. It is determined never to
veil liberty at home; and it is equally determined never to veil
its democratical principle abroad. It will not suffer anything to
intervene between the peaceful dawn of its own liberty and the
eyes of nations. It proclaims itself the intellectual and cordial
ally of popular rights and progress, and of every legitimate
development of institutions among nations who may be desirous
of maintaining the same principles as her own. It will not pursue
secret or incendiary propagandism among neighbouring states.
It is aware that there is no real liberty for nations except that
which springs from themselves, and takes its birth on their own
soil. But by the light of its intelligence, and the spectacle of
order and peace which it hopes to present to the world, the
republic will exercise the only honourable proselytism, the
proselytism of esteem and sympathy. This is not war, it is
nature; it is not the agitation of Europe, it is the life of nations;
it is not kindling a conflagration in the world, it is shining in our
own place on the horizon of nations, and at once to anticipate
and to direct them.

We wish, for the sake of humanity, that peace may be preserved; we also expect that it will . . .

39. *Manifesto of the Society of the Rights of Man and Citizen, 1 May 1848*

The Revolution gave rise to innumerable political clubs and societies, many of them quite radical. The manifesto which follows is
an example of their demands; the name of the society, led by
Barbès, is a clear reference to the Great French Revolution and the
Declaration of the Rights of Man and Citizen.

Source: *Annual Register*, 1848, pp. [262–3].

This Society has for its object—first to defend the rights of the
people, the exercise of which has been restored to them by the
Revolution of February; secondly, to draw from this Revolution
all its social consequences. As its point of departure, the Society
takes the declaration of the rights of man as laid down in 1793
by Robespierre. It ensues that, in a political point of view, the
Republic, one and indivisible, comprehends the inalienable
laws of the people. In a social point of view, the old constitution
is abolished; and that which is called to replace it must rest on
equality and fraternity, the fundamental principles of the new
social compact. Consequently, the social revolution, now at its
commencement, places itself between the Parias and the
Privileged of the ancient state of society. To the first it says—Be
united, but calm; for in this lies your strength. Your number is
such that it must suffice to manifest your will, and make you
obtain all you desire. It is also such that you cannot desire
anything but what is just. Your voice and your will are the voice
and the will of God. To the others it says—The old social form
has disappeared. The reign of privilege and exploitation is past.
In the point of view of the ancient social form, if the privileges
with which you were invested were acquired in a legal manner,
do not avail yourselves of them: these laws were your own work;
the immense majority of your brethren were strangers to them,
and therefore, are not bound to respect them. Rally, then, together, for you have need of the pardon of those whom you have
so long sacrificed. If, in spite of this promise of pardon, you
persist in remaining isolated in order to defend the old social
form, you will find in the vanguard, on the day of conflict, our
sections organized; and your brethren will no longer hold towards you the language of pardon, but that of justice.

40. *Law establishing Executive Commission, 9 May 1848*

When the National Assembly met, it decided to keep matters firmly in its hands. It therefore discharged the Provisional Government and decided to replace it with a five-member Executive Commission.

Source: F.-A. Hélie, *Les constitutions de la France* (Paris, Duchemin, 1880), p. 1087 (trans. Ed.).

The National Constituent Assembly entrusts the executive power to an executive commission which shall appoint ministers from outside its ranks.

The executive commission will consist of five members.

41. *Order dissolving the National Workshops, 24 May/20 June 1848*

The National Workshops had never been acceptable to the middle classes and were always considered a temporary concession for the pacification of the workers, particularly as its members had little opportunity, in Paris at any rate, to perform any useful work. One of the early decisions of the Assembly was, therefore, the dissolution of the National Workshops. The order was communicated to Thomas, the director, on 24 May, but was not made public until 20 June, after the Assembly had strengthened its position. The decree of dissolution directly led to the rising of the June days.

Source: É. Thomas, *Histoire des Ateliers Nationaux*, in *The French Revolution of 1848 in its economic aspects*, ed. by J. A. R. Marriott (Oxford, Clarendon Press, 1913), vol. ii, pp. 271–4 (trans. Ed.).

To Émile Thomas, Director of the National Workshops.

Sir, I have the honour to inform you that the Executive Commission has adopted the following measures concerning the National Workshops:

1. Unmarried workers aged between 18 and 25 years will be invited to enlist under the flag of the republic in order to complete the various regiments of the army.

Those who refuse voluntary enlistment will be deleted from the nominal rolls of the National Workshops.

2. A census of the workers of Paris will be taken without delay. It will be carried out simultaneously by municipal authorities and by employees of the central office of the National Workshops deputed for this task.

Workers who can not furnish official proof of six months' residence [in Paris] before 24 May shall be dismissed and will cease to receive wages or relief.

3. The lists of workers [compiled at the census and] arranged by municipal district and by occupation will be deposited in special offices located as near as possible to the centre of Paris; there they will be brought to the knowledge of the employers by officers of the administration. Employers will be able to requisition such numbers of workers as they declare to be necessary for the resumption or continuation of their works. Those who refuse to follow them will be instantly deleted from the nominal rolls of the National Workshops.

4. The workers who will not have been excluded by any of the above articles and who will remain for the time being on the strength of the National Workshops, shall be paid at piecework rates, not on a daily basis.[1]

5. Detachments of workers will be organized with the least possible delay and will be sent to the provinces in order to be engaged on major public works under the direction of the engineers of Roads and Bridges.

I request you, Sir, to apply yourself with the greatest possible speed to the execution of these orders . . .

42. Decree conferring power on Cavaignac, 28 June 1848

After the defeat of the June rising by General Cavaignac the National Assembly expressed its gratitude to him and, by conferring the executive power on him, made him virtual dictator.

Source: F.-A. Hélie, Les constitutions de la France (Paris, Duchemin, 1880), p. 1091 (trans. Ed.).

The National Assembly entrusts the executive power to General Cavaignac who will bear the title of President of the Council of Ministers and will appoint the ministry.

[1] As virtually no work was available, this provision amounted to a refusal to make any payment of wage or relief to members of the Workshops.

43. *Prince Louis Napoleon Bonaparte in 1848*

Although Prince Louis Napoleon Bonaparte, a nephew of Napoleon I, tried to return to France repeatedly after the February Revolution, and in fact was elected several times to the Assembly, the Government and the National Assembly prevented his return until September. He was then allowed to take his seat in the National Assembly (a), and became a candidate in the presidential elections in December, winning them with an overwhelming majority. Part of his programme is included under (b). The two selections provide an interesting contrast to the documents in section VII.

Source: *The Political and Historical Works of Louis Napoleon Bonaparte* (London, Illustrated London Library, 1852), vol. i, pp. 96–7, 101–5.

(a) Louis Napoleon's Speech on taking his Seat in the Assembly, 27 September 1848.

Citizen representatives:

I cannot longer remain silent after the calumnies directed against me. I feel it incumbent on me to declare openly, on the first day I am allowed to sit in this hall, the real sentiments which animate and have always animated me. After being proscribed during thirty-three years, I have at last recovered a country and my rights of citizenship. The Republic has conferred on me that happiness. I offer it now my oath of gratitude and devotion, and the generous fellow-countrymen who sent me to this hall may rest certain that they will find me devoted to the double task which is common to us all, namely, to assure order and tranquillity, the first want of the country, and to develop the democratical institutions which the people has a right to claim. During a long period I could only devote to my country the meditations of exile and captivity. Today a new career is open to me. Admit me in your ranks, dear colleagues, with the sentiment of affectionate sympathy which animates me. My conduct, you may be certain, shall ever be guided by a respectful devotion to the law. It will prove, to the confusion of those who have attempted to slander me, that no man is more devoted than I am, I repeat, to the defence of order and the consolidation of the Republic.

(b) Louis Napoleon's Programme, November 1848.

Fellow Citizens:

In order to recall me from exile, you elected me a representative of the people. On the eve of your proceeding to the election of chief magistrate of the republic, my name presents itself to you as a symbol of order and security.

These testimonies of a confidence so honourable are due, I am aware, much more to the name which I bear than to myself, who have as yet done nothing for my country;—but the more the memory of the Emperor protects me, and inspires your suffrages, the more I feel myself called upon to make known to you my sentiments and principles. There must not be anything equivocal in the relations between us.

I am not an ambitious man, who dreams at one time of the Empire and of war; at another of the adoption of subversive theories. Educated in free countries, and in the school of misfortune, I shall always remain faithful to the duties which your suffrages, and the will of the Assembly, may impose upon me.

If I am elected President, I should not shrink from any danger, from any sacrifice, to defend society, which has been so audaciously attacked. I should devote myself wholly, without reserve, to the confirming of a republic, which has shown itself wise by its laws, honest in its intentions, great and powerful by its acts.

I pledge my honour to leave to my successor, at the end of four years, the executive powers strengthened, liberty intact, and a real progress accomplished.

Whatever may be the result of the election, I shall bow to this will of the people; and I pledge beforehand my co-operation with any strong and honest government which shall re-establish order in principles as well as in things; which shall efficiently protect our religion, our families, and our properties—the eternal basis of every social community; which shall attempt all practicable reform, assuage animosities, reconcile parties, and thus permit a country rendered anxious by circumstances, to count upon the morrow.

To re-establish order is to restore confidence—to repair, by means of credit, the temporary depreciation of resources—to restore financial positions and revive commerce.

To protect the religion and the rights of families, is to ensure the freedom of public worship and education.

To protect property is to maintain the inviolability of the fruits of every man's labour; it is to guarantee the independence and the security of possession, an indispensable foundation for all civil liberties.

As to the reforms which are possible, the following are those which appear to me to be the most urgent:—

To adopt all those measures of economy, which, without occasioning disorder in the public service, will permit of a reduction of those taxes which press most heavily on the people —to encourage enterprises which, whilst they develop agricultural wealth, may, both in France and Algeria, give work to hands at present unoccupied—to provide for the relief of labourers in their old age, by means of provident institutions— to introduce into industrial laws modifications which may tend not to ruin the rich for the gain of the poor, but to establish the well-being of each upon the prosperity of all.

To restrict within just limits the number of employments which shall depend upon the government, and which often convert a free people into a nation of beggars.

To avoid that deplorable tendency which leads the state to do that which individuals do as well, and better, for themselves. The centralizations of interests and enterprises is in the nature of despotism: the nature of a republic is to reject monopolies.

Finally, to protect the liberty of the press from the two excesses which endanger it at present—that of arbitrary authority, on the one hand, and of its own licentiousness on the other . . .

With war we can have no relief to our ills. Peace, therefore, would be the dearest object of my desire.

V · THE REVOLUTIONS OF 1848: GERMANY AND AUSTRIA–HUNGARY

THE documents in this section are arranged in three sub-sections. Those relating to Germany as a whole are found under (i); some Prussian documents under (ii); whilst under (iii) there is a selection illustrative of the problems faced by Austria–Hungary.

The demands of the people of Nassau and of Tübingen (No. 44) are characteristic of demands made elsewhere in Germany. Such popular demands were followed up by the Heidelberg meeting of South West German liberals which, with its resolution (No. 45(a)), took the initiative for their fulfilment. The Committee of Seven appointed by this meeting called the Pre-Parliament (No. 45(b)) which set down, in a series of resolutions (No. 46) the basis of the proposed constituent assembly. At the same time the Federal Diet took steps to liquidate formally the old regime (No. 47).

One of the first steps of the National Assembly was the establishment of a Provisional Central Power (No. 48). Thereafter the activity of the Assembly largely centred on the drafting of a constitution, which was completed in March 1849. Many articles of this constitution are here included (No. 50). To illustrate the practical problems which the National Assembly had to face a selection was made of documents relating to Schleswig-Holstein (No. 49). The sub-section concludes with the speech of Frederick William IV in which he in effect rejects the offer of the imperial crown made by a delegation of the National Assembly (No. 51).

In Prussia, during the March days of 1848, not only the population supported the idea of a united liberal Germany, but also the King, as would appear from his proclamations (Nos 52, 53). He also called a constituent assembly to draft a constitution for Prussia; unfortunately considerations of space preclude the inclusion of material dealing with the calling of this assembly, its debates, its transfer to the provinces and, finally, the imposition of a constitution. But, although the King came to reject most of the ideas represented by the Frankfurt Constitution, the majority of the Chambers of this Assembly continued to hold to the ideas expressed in it (No. 54).

Frederick William IV found it ultimately impossible to reconcile Prussia's position as a Power with her absorption in a liberal united Germany. The situation in Austria–Hungary was even more difficult, as the strong non-German elements of the population also had to be considered. The imperial proclamation of 15 March 1848 (No. 55) went a long way to fulfil the demands of the people of Vienna and the Empire, and the constitution of April 1848 (No. 57), by excluding Hungary from its scope, recognized the demands of the Hungarian Parliament and people (No. 56) as justified. In addition to the Hungarians, the Slavonic elements of the empire also formulated their demands at the Slavic Congress at Prague (No. 58) which consisted mainly of Slavs from the Empire.

The defeat of the Czech nationalists by armed force inaugurated the process of reaction which led to a prolonged 'war of freedom' by the Hungarians. When all parts of the Empire, except Hungary, had been pacified a completely unitary constitution (No. 59) was imposed, which precluded the participation of Austria in a united Germany and led to a Hungarian declaration of independence (No. 60). After the defeat of Hungary with Russian help in August 1849, autocracy could reign supreme again over a unitary empire.

(i) GERMANY AS A WHOLE

44. Demands of the German People, March 1848

On 2 March 1848 a public meeting was organized at Wiesbaden, in Nassau. It was attended by some three thousand people, inhabitants of the town and of the surrounding countryside. Their demands, formulated after three hours' discussion, (a), may be compared with the petition written by the poet Uhland in Tübingen, Württemberg, on 3 March (b), and sent to the King after many signatures had been affixed to it.

Source: *Deutsche Zeitung*, No. 65, 5 March 1848, p. 516; No. 66, 6 March 1848, p. 522 (trans. Ed.).

(a) Demands of the People of Nassau, 2 March 1848.

The latest French revolution ... has shaken Europe. It is knocking on the doors of Germany. The time has come to call for the speediest development of all the national power, all the love of liberty of the German nation. There are many things that the Germans, that the people of Nassau have the right to demand. But the pressure of time does not allow everything that has been neglected during the last thirty years to be done at once. The following demands, however, must be fulfilled immediately:

1. General arming of the populace[1] with free election of the leaders ... 2. Unconditional freedom of the press. 3. Immediate calling of a German parliament. 4. The military to swear an oath to the constitution. 5. Freedom of association. 6. Public and oral [judicial] proceedings. 7. The [grand-ducal] domain to become state property, its administration to be controlled by the Estates. 8. The Second Chamber to be called immediately to devise a new electoral law based on the principle that the franchise should not be tied to a property qualification. 9. Restrictions on our freedom of religion, a constitutional right, to be lifted immediately.

(b) Petition of the People of Tübingen, 3 March 1848.

1. A constitution for the whole of Germany; [Germany] to be a federal state with popular representation through a German parliament at the Diet [sic]. 2. General arming of the populace. 3. Complete freedom of the press ... 4. Lifting of restrictions on associations and meetings for the discussion of public affairs. 5. The principle of public and oral judicial proceedings, with all its consequences, to be put into full effect. 6. The real independence of communal and district corporations to be restored completely. 7. Revision of the constitution [of Württemberg].

45. The Heidelberg Meeting of Liberals, 5 March 1848

The most prominent liberal politicians of South and South West Germany met at Heidelberg on 5 March to discuss the best way of

---

[1] That is, formation of a national guard.

achieving their twin aims of liberty and unity while maintaining order. Their resolution follows under (a), while under (b) we find the invitation to a Pre-Parliament issued by a committee of seven under the authority of the Heidelberg meeting.

Source: *Deutsche Zeitung*, No. 67, 7 March 1848, p. 529; No. 74, 14 March 1848, p. 585 (trans. Ed.).

(a) Resolution of 5 March 1848.

Fifty-one men, from Prussia, Bavaria, Württemberg, Baden, Hesse, Nassau and Frankfurt, almost all of them members of Assemblies of Estates, met here today in order to discuss the most urgent measures needed at this decisive moment.

United in their devotion to the freedom, unity, independence and honour of the German nation, they all expressed the conviction that the establishment and defence of these high principles must be attempted through the co-operation of the German races with their governments in so far as it is still possible . . .

Those at the meeting declared unanimously that, in their view, the urgent needs of the fatherland were as follows:

'Germany must not be involved in a war through interference in the affairs of a neighbouring country, or through the non-recognition of constitutional changes made there.

The Germans must not be induced to diminish or suppress, in the case of other nations, the liberty and independence that they [the Germans] demand as their right.

The Germans and their princes must rely on the loyalty and proven courage of the nation, and not on a Russian alliance, for their defence.

The calling of a national representative assembly, elected in all German States according to population, must not be postponed; [it is needed] in order to avert internal and external danger, and to develop the power and prosperity of German national life.'

In order to assist in bringing about an early and complete representation of the nation, those present have resolved:

'to approach urgently their respective governments to provide the whole German fatherland and the thrones as early and as completely as possible with this powerful bulwark.[1]

[1] i.e. a representative assembly.

At the same time they decided to work towards a more complete[1] assembly of trusted men from all the German races, which would discuss this most important matter further and would offer its co-operation to the fatherland and to the governments.'

Seven members were therefore requested to prepare proposals for the election and organization of a suitable National Representative Assembly and to issue invitations to a meeting of German men as soon as possible.

One of the main tasks of the National Representative Assembly will be [the creation] of common defence and representation abroad; through this large amounts of money will be saved for other urgent needs, while at the same time the separateness and appropriate autonomy of the individual States will be preserved.

If all Germans co-operate prudently, loyally and manfully, the fatherland may hope that liberty, unity and order can be achieved and maintained even in the most difficult situation, and it may joyfully look forward to a period of unprecedented prosperity and power.

(b) Invitation to the Pre-Parliament, 12 March 1848.

The Committee entrusted by the German men who met at Heidelberg on 5 March with the discussion of the basis of a national German parliamentary constitution has so far agreed on this basis that it can submit it for further debate to a larger assembly of men trusted by the people. We therefore invite all past and present members of the Assemblies of Estates and participants in legislative assemblies in all German states (naturally including East and West Prussia and Schleswig-Holstein[2]) to come to Frankfurt am Main on Thursday, 30 March, for this discussion. A number of men honoured by the trust of the German people who have not so far been members of Estates will receive individual invitations . . .

46. *Resolutions of the Pre-Parliament, 31 March–4 April 1848*

The members of the Pre-Parliament, called together by the previous document (No. 45(b)), passed a series of resolutions, substantial

---

[1] Than the meeting at Heidelberg.

[2] Of these only Holstein was a member of the German Confederation.

portions of which follow, in which they set down the principles which should govern the calling and activity of the National Assembly. Most of their recommendations were accepted and formalized by the Diet of the Confederation and thus formed the legal basis on which the National Assembly was called.

Source: E. R. Huber, *Dokumente zur deutschen Verfassungsgeschichte* (Stuttgart, Kohlhammer, 1961), vol. i, pp. 271–3 (trans. Ed.).

Task of the Assembly

This assembly considers its task to be the determination of the manner in which the Constituent National Assembly is to be set up. It declares expressly that any decisions about the future constitution of Germany must be left to this Constituent Assembly, which is to be elected by the people . . .

The Federal Territory

Schleswig . . . is to be incorporated in the German Federation and is to be represented in the Constituent Assembly by elected representatives like any other federal state.

East and West Prussia are to be incorporated in the German Federation in the same way.

The Assembly declares the partition of Poland to be a shameful injustice. It recognizes that it is the duty of the German people to assist in the restoration of Poland . . .

Number of Representatives . . .

There will be one representative in the German Constituent Assembly for every 50,000 of the population. States with a population of less than 50,000 shall elect one representative . . .

Mode of Election . . .

In respect to the mode of election the following applies to all German States.

The right to vote and the right to be elected must not be restricted by property qualifications, by giving an advantage to one religion, or by elections according to estates. Every adult independent citizen may vote and has the right to stand for election. Candidates need not belong to the State which they are to represent in the Assembly . . In all other respects it is left to the several German states how they wish to order the elections; the Assembly considers direct election to be the most suitable in principle . . .

Permanent Committee of the Assembly

The present Assembly will elect a permanent committee of fifty members which will remain at Frankfurt am Main until the meeting of the Constituent Assembly.

The Committee of Fifty is entrusted with the task of

inviting the Federal Diet to consult with it until the meeting of the Constituent Assembly;

advising the Federal Diet in matters relating to the interests of the nation and to the administration of federal affairs until the meeting of the Constituent Assembly . . .

calling the present Assembly together again should the fatherland be in danger . . .

All negotiations of the Committee with the Diet shall be published in the Press.

The Assembly demands that the Diet when taking in hand the foundation of a Constituent Parliament, renounce the exceptional measures which contradict the constitution[1] and remove from its body all men associated with their introduction and execution.

Fundamental Rights and Demands of the German People

The Assembly accepts in principle and recommends to the Constituent Parliament for consideration the following proposals from the people which demand certain fundamental rights as the minimum measure of liberty for the German people . . .

Equality of political rights without religious discrimination and independence of the church from the state. Complete freedom of the press. Freedom of association. Right to petition. A free representative constitution, with the popularly elected representatives having the decisive voice in legislation and taxation; responsibility of ministers. Just distribution of taxation

[1] Carlsbad decrees (No. 25) and the legislation of 1834. Cf. No. 47(b).

according to capacity. Equality of military obligation. Equal entitlement of all citizens to appointment to all communal and state offices. Unconditional right to emigrate . . . A general German citizenship law. Freedom of learning and teaching. Protection of personal freedom. Protection against denial of justice. Independence of the judiciary. Public and oral judicial proceedings; juries in criminal matters.

Further: A complete system of credit for the agricultural and working classes. Protection of labour through institutions and measures which would protect from need those unable to work, would obtain employment for those unemployed, and would modernize the system of handicrafts and factories. Education at public expense for all classes, crafts and professions. Recognition of emigration as a national matter, and its regulation in the interests of the emigrants . . .

47. Laws passed by the Diet, March–April 1848

The Federal Diet remained in existence in spite of the Revolution though as liberal ministries were appointed in the various member states, its most reactionary members were replaced. The most important resolution of the Diet is probably that appointing a Committee of Seventeen to prepare a draft constitution; this draft in fact served as the basis for the discussions of the National Assembly. Here we include two other laws as characteristic of the legislation of the period.

Source: (a) *Deutsche Zeitung*, No. 65, 5 March 1848, p. 517 (trans. Ed.).

      (b) E. R. Huber, *Dokumente zur deutschen Verfassungsgeschichte* (Stuttgart, Kohlhammer, 1961), vol. i, p. 268 (trans. Ed.).

(a) Freedom of the Press, 3 March 1848.

1. All German Confederate States may lift the censorship and introduce freedom of the press.
2. This must, however, only be done with safeguards which secure other Confederate States and the Confederation against abuse of the freedom of the press . . .

(b) Lifting of Exceptional Laws, 2 April 1848.

Whereas the [representative of] the free cities moved on 23 March on behalf of Frankfurt that the so-called exceptional laws

of the German Confederation, published since 1819, having already lost their binding force in many places because of the changed circumstances, be formally rescinded and lifted by the Confederation,
the Federal Diet resolves,
that the same exceptional laws and resolutions, which are objected to, be rescinded in all Confederate States, that they be considered null and void, and that, where it is still necessary, public notification of this decision be given.

48. Establishment of Provisional Central Power, 28 June 1848

Upon meeting in May, the Constituent National Assembly immediately assumed legislative and executive powers as well as constituent ones; to exercise the executive power it decided, after long debate, to establish a Provisional Central Power under a Regent until the constitution could regulate the form and powers of a federal ministry. Archduke Johann of Austria, a Habsburg with a liberal reputation, was elected to the regency.

Source: *Annual Register*, 1848, p. 365 (with emendations).

1. Until a Government be definitively created for Germany, a Provisional Central Power shall be formed for the administration of all affairs which affect the whole of the German nation.
2. The Central Power, shall, first, act as executive in all affairs that relate to the safety and welfare of the nation in general; 2nd, it shall take the supreme direction of the whole of the armed forces and nominate the Commander-in-Chief; 3rd, it shall provide for the political and commercial representation of Germany, and to this end appoint ambassadors and consuls.
3. The creation of the constitution remains excluded from the sphere of action of the Central Power.
4. The Central Power decides on questions of war and peace and concludes treaties with foreign Powers in agreement with the National Assembly.
5. The Provisional Central Power is confided to a Regent whom the National Assembly elects.
6. The Regent exercises his power through Ministers whom he nominates but who are responsible to the National Assembly. All his decrees, to be valid, must be countersigned by at least one responsible minister.

7. The Regent is irresponsible.

8. The National Assembly will, by a special law, fix the limits of ministerial responsibility.

9. The Ministers are entitled to be present during the sittings of the National Assembly and to be heard by the same.

10. The Ministers are bound, on the demand of the National Assembly, to appear before the same and to give information.

11. They have the right of voting in the National Assembly only when they are elected as members of the same.

12. The Position of the Regent is incompatible with the office of member of the National Assembly.

13. The German Diet ceases from the moment that the Central Power begins to exercise its functions.

14. The Provisional Central Power shall in its executive capacity act as far as compatible with its duty in understanding with the Plenipotentiaries of the German Governments.

15. The activity of the Provisional Central Power ceases as soon as the constitution for Germany is completed and put into effect.

49. *The Schleswig-Holstein Problem, 1848*

The complexities of the Schleswig-Holstein question are beyond the scope of this note. The following documents are included to illustrate the stages of the problem from the German point of view, at the same time showing the lack of power of the National Assembly. Documents (a) and (b) are resolutions of the Federal Diet in April, initiating German federal action in the matter; (c), the armistice of Malmö, was concluded in August by Prussia on English and Russian pressure without reference to the National Assembly or the Central Power (which had by then succeeded to the powers of the Diet under whose direction the war was conducted); (d) summarizes the view on the armistice of the federal government; while under (e) we find two resolutions of the National Assembly, the first rejecting the unilateral Prussian action, the second, a few days later, recognizing that the Central Power had not the means of constraining Prussia.

Further documents on Schleswig-Holstein may be found in Section VI, Nos 64, 66 and 67.

Source: (a) and (b) E. R. Huber, *Dokumente zur deutschen Verfassungs-geschichte* (Stuttgart, Kohlhammer, 1961), vol. i, pp. 458–9 (trans. Ed.).

     (c) *Annual Register*, 1848, pp. [351–2].

(d) and (e) *Stenographischer Bericht über die Verhandlungen der deutschen . . . Nationalversammlung* (Frankfurt, 1848), vol. i, pp. 1881, 1917, 2149, 2154 (trans. Ed.).

(a) Resolution of the Diet, 4 April 1848.

1. The Federal Diet declares . . . that the German Confederate State of Holstein is in danger of being attacked and it expresses its appreciation of the preparations made . . . for the defence of the confederate frontier in Holstein by Prussia and the States of the 10. Confederate Army Corps.

2. In order to ensure the unified direction of any measures still necessary for this purpose, the Diet requests Prussia to come to an agreement on this matter with the States of the 10. Army Corps.

3. The Federal Diet is prepared to mediate in order to prevent bloodshed and to bring about an agreed settlement: it requests Prussia to act as a mediator in the name of the German Confederation on the basis of the undiminished rights of Holstein, including its right to constitutional union with Schleswig . . .

(b) Resolution of the Diet, 12 April 1848.

Following on its resolution of 4 April 1848 the Federal Diet resolves

1. to declare that, if Denmark does not cease hostilities and evacuate the intruding Danish troops from Schleswig, this should be effected by force in order to preserve the Confederation-protected right of Holstein to union with Schleswig.

2. since it considers that the most secure guarantee of this union would be Schleswig's entry into the German Confederation, to request Prussia to attempt the bringing about of such entry by mediation.

3. to declare that it recognizes the Provisional Government [of Schleswig-Holstein], formed . . . to protect the rights of these states, as such, and to that extent, and it expects from the mediating Royal Prussian Government that it protect the members of the Provisional Government and its supporters.

(c) Armistice of Malmö, 26 August 1848.

. . . 6. The two Duchies, as well as the islands belonging to them, shall at once be altogether evacuated by the Danish and by the German Federal troops . . .

7. The two Contracting Parties, being desirous as speedily as possible to restore order and tranquillity in the Duchies, agree to instal a joint Government for the two Duchies for the duration of the armistice. The joint administration of the two Duchies shall be composed of five members, to be taken from the gentry of the Duchies, and who enjoy general respect and consideration. They shall administer the affairs of the Duchies according to the existing laws and ordinances, in the name of the King of Denmark, in his quality as Duke of Schleswig and Holstein, and with his authority, always excepting the legislative power . . . It is understood that neither the members of the administration before the 17th of March, nor those of whom the Provisional Government was since composed, can form part of this new administration . . .

11. The Contracting Parties request the guarantee of Great Britain for the strict execution of the articles of this present convention . . .

12. It is expressly understood that the articles of this convention shall nowise prejudice the conditions of a definitive peace, and that neither Denmark nor the Confederation give up any of the pretensions or rights which they have respectively asserted.

(d) Resolution of the German Government, 3 September 1848.

It is clear that Prussia has exceeded her powers in concluding the present treaty [of Malmö] and that the Central Power as principal cannot incur any obligation towards other states or towards Prussia under it until the Reich Government expresses its approval. The Central Power can not do so without a resolution by the National Assembly to which the treaty has to be submitted since it exceeds the limits of an armistice in the strict sense and has a political character which anticipates the peace negotiations.

(e) Motions in the National Assembly, September 1848.

Motion by Dahlmann, 5 September 1848:
That the Assembly resolve the suspension of all military and

other measures taken to put the armistice into execution. [Passed by 238 votes against 221.]

Motion by Francke, 16 September 1848:
The National Assembly resolves

1. not to hinder further the execution of the armistice of Malmö . . . so far as it can in the circumstances still be put into effect.

2. to request the Provisional Central Power to take all suitable steps towards an early agreement on the modifications of the treaty which Denmark has officially declared herself willing to introduce.

3. to request the Provisional Central Power to take the necessary steps towards an early commencement of peace negotiations. [Passed by 257 votes against 236.]

50. Sections of the Constitution, 28 March 1849

The National Assembly spent most of its time and much very conscientious work on the drafting of a constitution. One section, on the fundamental rights of the German people, was published late in 1848, but the whole document was not completed until March 1849, after some last minute concessions to ensure the support of the Left for the election of the King of Prussia as emperor. Some of the more important provisions of the constitution follow.

Source: W. Blos, *Die deutsche Revolution* (Stuttgart, Dietz, 1893), pp. 633–59 (trans. Ed.).

The Constitution of the German Reich[1]

Section I. The Reich

Article 1.

1. The German Reich comprises the territory of the German Confederation. The position of the Duchy of Schleswig will be determined at a later date.

2. If a German State has the same head of State as a non-German State, the German State must have a separate constitution, government and administration. Only German citizens

[1] Reich is the traditional word used to describe the whole of Germany and therefore it is used in the original form. There is no strictly correct translation. The same rule was applied to the word Reichstag, traditionally used to describe an all-German parliament.

may be appointed to the government and administration of a German State ...

5. The several German States retain their independence insofar as it is not limited by the Reich constitution; they retain their sovereignty and rights insofar as they are not expressly transferred to the Reich.

Section II. The Powers of the Reich

Article 1.

6. The Reich has the exclusive power of representing Germany and the several States abroad ...

Article 2.

10. The Reich has the exclusive power of declaring war and concluding peace.

Article 3.

11. All the armed forces of Germany stand at the disposal of the Reich.

12. The army of the Reich consists of the whole of the land forces of the several States. The strength and composition of these forces will be determined by laws ...

19. Naval forces are an exclusive concern of the Reich. No State is permitted to maintain naval vessels ...

Article 7.

33. The German Reich shall form one united customs and commercial territory, surrounded by a common customs boundary, with no internal customs ...

34. The Reich has the exclusive power to make laws about customs and production and excise taxes ...

Article 10.

48. Expenditure on measures and establishments of the Reich has to be paid out of the treasury of the Reich.

49. To cover its expenditure the Reich is to rely in the first place on its revenue from customs duties and from the common production and excise taxes.

50. The Reich has the right to collect matricular contributions[1] if its revenue proves to be insufficient.

51. The Reich has the power, in extraordinary circumstances, to impose Reich taxes . . .

Section III. The Head of the Reich

Article 1.

68. The position of Head of the Reich will be conferred on one of the ruling German princes.

69. The position will be hereditary in the family of the prince on whom it is conferred.

70. The title of the Head of the Reich is: Emperor of the Germans . . .

80. The Emperor exercises the legislative power in conjunction with the Reichstag . . .

Section IV. The Reichstag

Article 1.

85. The Reichstag consists of two houses, the State House and the People's House.

Article 2.

86. The State House consists of representatives of the German States . . .

88. Half the members of the State House will be nominated by the Government, half by the representative assembly of each State . . .

Article 3.

93. The People's House consists of representatives of the German people . . .

100. A resolution of the Reichstag requires the agreement of both houses.

101. A resolution of the Reichstag, to which the Reich Government does not give its assent, must not be re-introduced in the same session.

---

[1] Matricular contributions are payments to the Reich treasury by the States, in proportion to their population, to cover a deficit in the Reich budget.

If the Reichstag repeats the same resolution in unchanged form in three consecutive ordinary sessions, the resolution becomes law even without the assent of the Reich government . . .

Section VI. Fundamental Rights of the German People

130. The following fundamental rights shall be guaranteed to the German people. They shall serve as a standard for the constitutions of the several German States, and no State constitution or legislation may suspend or limit them.

Article 1.

131. The German people consists of the citizens of the States which form the German Reich.

132. All Germans have the right to German citizenship. They can exercise the rights arising [from this citizenship] in every German State . . .

Article 2.

137. There is no difference between ranks before the law. Nobility as a rank is abolished. All privileges of rank are abolished. All Germans are equal before the law . . .

Article 3.

138. The freedom of the person is inviolable . . .

140. The home is inviolable. Domiciliary search may take place [only under certain strictly defined conditions] . . .

142. The secrecy of letters is guaranteed . . .

Article 4.

143. Every German has the right to express his opinion freely in speech, writing, print, or pictorial representation . . .

Article 5.

145. Every German has full freedom of belief and conscience. No one is obliged to divulge his religious convictions . . .

Article 6.

152. The pursuit and teaching of knowledge is free . . .

Article 8.

161. The Germans have the right of assembling peacefully and without arms ...

162. The Germans have the right of forming associations ...

Article 9.

164. Property is inviolable ...

Article 12.

186. Every German State shall have a constitution with popular representation. The ministers shall be responsible to the popular representation ...

Article 13.

188. The non-German speaking races of Germany are guaranteed their racial development, namely, in the regions that they occupy, the equal right [with German] of their language in religious life, instruction, local government and judicial proceedings ...

51. *Frederick William IV rejects the Imperial Crown,* *3 April 1849*

After enacting the Constitution (No. 50), the National Assembly proceeded to elect the King of Prussia as emperor, and sent a delegation to offer this dignity to Frederick William IV. Although Frederick William was attracted by the offer (and had, a year earlier, proposed to 'undertake the leadership', cf. No. 53) he considered the constitution to be too revolutionary, too liberal. He did not reject the crown outright; he made his acceptance conditional by the reply that follows; nevertheless his temporizing put an effective end to the German unity movement for the time being.

Source: *Annual Register*, 1849, pp. [347–8] (with emendations).

Gentlemen, the message you bring me has deeply moved me. It has directed my gaze to the King of Kings, and to the sacred and august duties I have, as the King of my people, and a Prince among the mightiest in Germany. A look in that direction, gentlemen, gives clearness to the vision and certainty to the heart. In the resolution of the German National Assembly you have communicated to me I recognize the voice of the representatives of the German people. Your call gives me a right, the value of which I know how to prize. If accepted, it demands from me incalculable sacrifices, and burdens me with heavy duties. The German National Assembly has counted on me in all things which were calculated to establish the unity of Germany and the power of Prussia. I honour its confidence; please express my thanks for it. I am ready by deeds to prove that their reliance on my loyalty, love and devotion to the cause of the German fatherland has not been misplaced. But I should not justify that confidence—I should not answer to the expectations of the German people—I should not strengthen the unity of Germany—if I, violating sacred rights and breaking my former explicit and solemn promises, were, without the voluntary assent of the crowned Princes and free States of our Fatherland, to take a resolution which must be of decisive importance to them and to the States which they rule. It will now lie with the several Governments of the German States to examine together the constitution which the National Assembly has drawn up, and declare whether it will be of advantage to each and to all—whether the rights it confers on me will place me in the position to guide with a strong hand, as my position requires, the destinies of Germany and the great German fatherland, and realize the expectations of the people. But of this Germany may be certain, and you may declare it in every state— that if it needs the protection of the Prussian sword or shield from external or internal enemies, I will not fail, even without a summons. I shall follow that course from which my royal House and my people have never departed—the course of German loyalty.

(ii) PRUSSIA

52. *Proclamation of 18 March 1848*

As a result of revolutionary developments elsewhere, the King of Prussia decided to call the United Diet (cf. No. 28) for 27 April 1848. When the population of Berlin rose in revolution on 18 March, the following proclamation by the King brought forward the date of the meeting and, at the same time, outlined Frederick William's proposals for reform in Germany.

Source: *Annual Register*, 1848, p. [377].

. . . Above all, we demand that Germany be transformed from a confederation of states into one federal state. We acknowledge that this plan presupposes a reorganization of the federal constitution, which cannot be carried into execution except by a union of princes with the people, and that consequently a temporary federal representation must be formed out of the Chambers of all German States, and convoked immediately. We admit that such a federal representation imperatively demands constitutional institutions in all German states, in order that the members of that representation may sit beside each other on terms of equality.

We demand a general military system of defence for Germany, and we will endeavour to form it after that model under which our Prussian armies reaped such unfading laurels in the War of Liberation. We demand that the German federal army be assembled under one single federal banner, and we hope to see a federal commander-in-chief at its head. We demand a German federal flag; and we expect that at a period not far remote a German fleet will cause the German name to be respected, both on neighbouring and far distant seas.

We demand a German federal tribunal for the settlement of all constitutional differences between princes and their states, as well as those arising between the different German Governments.

We demand a common law of settlement for all Germany, and an entire right for all Germans to change their abode in every part of our German Fatherland.

We demand that in future no barriers of customs houses shall impede traffic upon German soil, and cripple the industry of its inhabitants. We demand, therefore, a general German union of customs, in which the same weights and measures, the same coinage, and the same German laws of commerce, will soon draw closer and closer the bond of material union.

We propose the liberty of the press throughout Germany, with the same general guarantees against its abuse . . .

In order that the accomplishment of our intentions may experience the least possible delay, and in order that we may develop the propositions which we consider to be necessary for the interior constitution of our States, we have resolved to hasten the convocation of the United Diet, and we charge the Minister of State to fix that convocation for the 2nd of April.

53. *Proclamation of 21 March 1848*

This proclamation goes even further than that of 18 March (No. 52). Frederick William not only undertakes the leadership in Germany, and offers to call a meeting of an all-German diet, but also speaks of Prussia merging into Germany.

Source: W. Blos, *Die deutsche Revolution* (Stuttgart, Dietz, 1893), pp. 485-6 (trans. Ed.).

To my people and the German nation.

Thirty-five years ago, in days of extreme danger, the King[1] spoke with confidence to his people and his confidence was not put to shame; the King, united with his people, saved Prussia and Germany from disgrace and humiliation.

With confidence I speak to-day, at a moment when the Fatherland lies in the greatest danger, to the German nation among whose most noble branches my people may count itself with pride. Internally, Germany is in a ferment, and she may be threatened by danger from without from more than one side. Salvation from the doubly pressing danger can only be got by the most intimate union of the German princes and peoples under one leadership.

I undertake to-day this leadership during the days of peril. My people, which does not shun danger, will not forsake me, and Germany will attach herself to me with confidence. I have to-day accepted the old German colours and ranged myself and my people under the venerable banner of the German empire. From this day onward Prussia is merged in Germany.

The [Prussian] Diet, which has already been convoked for the 2nd of April, in conjunction with my people, presents the ready medium and legal organ for the deliverance and pacification of Germany. It is my resolve to afford an opportunity to the Princes and Estates of Germany for a general meeting with the organs of the Diet on a plan which will be proposed without delay.

The Diet of the Germanic States, which will be thus pro-visionally constituted, must enter boldly and without delay

[1] Frederick William III, in 1813, during the Wars of Liberation.

upon the requisite preliminary measures for averting dangers both at home and abroad.

The measures at this moment urgently called for are

1. The institution of a general popular German federal army.
2. A declaration of armed neutrality . . .

At the same time as it consults on means of averting the present danger, the Diet of the Germanic States will also discuss the re-birth and foundation of a new Germany, united but not uniform, of a unity in diversity, unity with freedom.

Such higher and inner unity can only be achieved and firmly established if a true constitutional order is introduced generally, with responsible ministers in all states, public and oral judicial proceedings, based on juries in criminal cases, equal political and civil rights for all religious denominations, and a truly popular and liberal administration.

54. *Proceedings in the Prussian Landtag, 4 April 1849*

Frederick William's temporizing answer to the National Assembly (No. 51) was not acceptable to the Prussian Landtag, who urged him to fall in with the wishes of the National Assembly. A contemporary report of the proceedings follows.

Source: *Annual Register*, 1849, pp. [348–9].

When this reply (No. 51) was made known, M. Vincke, in the Second Chamber, proposed the following 'motion of urgency':

'In consideration that the answer which the Ministry has advised His Majesty to return to the deputation of the Frankfurt Assembly, and which has been received by them, is not in accordance with the address voted by the hon. Chamber in its sitting yesterday, and is calculated to produce the greatest dangers to Germany, the Chamber resolves to name a committee to draw up an address to His Majesty in reference to that answer, in which the opinion of the Chamber on the present position of the country will be expressed.'

The urgency of the motion was voted unanimously, and an address was drawn up by M. Vincke which stated—

'It is the confidence of the representatives of the German people that calls your Majesty to the glorious mission of taking into firm hands the guidance of that destiny as the head of regenerated Germany.

We recognize the earnestness of the hour; we do not forget the weight of considerations that cannot be avoided; but in face of the incalculable dangers which may arise from Germany being left without a guiding hand in the conflicting agitations of the time, in the present shattered condition of the Continent in all its relations, we trust Your Majesty's wisdom and devotion to the cause of Germany will enable you to choose the right path and to overcome all difficulties.

We, therefore, respectfully present this prayer to Your Majesty—

"That you will not refuse the summons of the National Assembly, but fulfil the hopes and expectations of the German people." '

Count Brandenburg, the head of the Ministry, took this opportunity of announcing the principle on which the Prussian Government intended to stand with reference to the German question in its present stage. It recognized the Frankfurt vote as an essential progress; it would do all in its power to ensure the attainment of the end, now so much nearer than before; but it would adhere firmly to this resolution to recognize that decision as binding only on those German Powers and Princes who should, of their own free election, confirm it by their future vote.

Various amendments were moved, but they were all rejected, and M. Vincke's address was carried by 156 to 151.

(iii) AUSTRIA–HUNGARY

55. *Proclamation of the Austrian Emperor, 15 March 1848*

The Vienna revolution broke out on 13 March and had the resignation and flight of Metternich as its immediate effect. Concession followed concession in quick succession; the following proclamation, issued when it became clear that the Vienna rising had its parallels elsewhere, particularly in Hungary, summarizes the most important concessions granted, and temporarily satisfied the population.

Source: *Annual Register*, 1848, p. [404].

By virtue of our declaration abolishing the censorship, liberty of the press is allowed in the form under which it exists in those countries which have hitherto enjoyed it. The National Guard, established on the basis of property and intelligence, already performs the most beneficial service.

The necessary steps have been taken for convoking, with the least possible loss of time, the Deputies from all our provincial States, and from the Central Congregations of the Lombardo-Venetian kingdom (the representation of the class of burghers being strengthened, and due regard being paid to the existing provincial constitutions) in order that they may deliberate on the constitution which we have resolved to grant our people.

We therefore confidently expect that excited tempers will become composed, that study will resume its wonted course, and that industry and peaceful intercourse will spring into new life.

56. *The Demands of the Hungarians, 14–15 March 1848*

The Hungarian Parliament, sitting at Pozsony (Pressburg), began on 3 March the consideration of an address to the King[1] moved by the extreme liberal, Lajos Kossuth, in which the re-estabishment of Hungarian independence and of the historic Hungarian constitution was demanded. Upon receipt of the news of the Vienna revolution of 13 March, Kossuth amended his address to bring it into line with the changed circumstances (in particular, to demand constitutional government for the Austrian parts of the empire) and it was then carried by acclamation on 14 March. Our text (a) consists of excerpts from this amended version.

On 15 March, when the news of the events of Vienna and Pozsony reached Budapest, a large meeting of the population accepted by acclamation the twelve-point demands of the Hungarian people (b) drafted by a group of university students.

Source: (a) E. Szabad, *Hungary past and present* (Edinburgh, A. & C. Black, 1854), pp. 277–9.
  (b) *Deutsche Zeitung*, No. 84, 24 March 1848, Beilage, p. 4 (trans. Ed.).

(a) Address by the Hungarian Parliament, 14 March 1848.

Your Majesty,—events which have recently transpired impose upon us the imperative duty of directing your attention to those exigencies which our fidelity towards the reigning house, the legal relations of the monarchy at large, and our love for our country prescribe. Reverting to the history of the past, we are

[1] Who was also Emperor of Austria.

reminded that for three centuries not only have we been hindered from giving free development to the constitutional spirit of our country, in accordance with the demands of the time, but our most zealous efforts have with difficulty succeeded in preserving it. The cause of this has been that the government of Your Majesty has not followed a constitutional direction, and consequently has been at variance with the independent character of our Government. This alone has hitherto prevented the development of the constitutional system in Hungary; and it is clear that unless the direction be changed, and Your Majesty's Government is made to harmonize with constitutional principles, the throne of Your Majesty, no less than the monarchy itself, endeared to us by virtue of the Pragmatic Sanction,[1] will be placed in a state of perplexity and danger, the end of which we cannot foresee, and which must entail unspeakable misery upon our country. Having been called together by Your Majesty for the purpose of carrying out measures of reform, we have resolved that upon the basis of an equal taxation we will take our share in those public burdens by which the expenses of the municipal administration have hitherto been defrayed, and provide for what farther shall be required. We have also resolved to free the country from feudal burdens, indemnifying at the same time the proprietors of the soil; and thus, by reconciling the interests of the people and the nobility, to strengthen the throne of Your Majesty, and establish it upon the well being of the country at large. One of the most important of our tasks is to alleviate the burdens of the peasantry, as regards the quarterings and the necessary provisions for the soldiery. Believing in the necessity of reform, as regards the municipalities of the towns and districts, we are likewise of opinion that the time has arrived for granting political rights to the people. The country has a right to expect measures to be carried out for raising our industrial resources, our commerce, and our agriculture. At the same time the spirit of our constitution demands free development under a true representative system, and the intellectual interests of the nation likewise demand support, based upon freedom. Our military institutions require a thorough reform,—a reform the urgency of which is pressed

[1] A law of 1722 which regulated the succession and the relationship of Hungary with the Austrian provinces.

upon us by a regard to Your Majesty's throne and the safety
of our country. We cannot longer consent to a postponement
of the constitutional application of the state revenues of
Hungary, and the rendering an exact account of the revenue
and expenditure. In entertaining several of these questions it
becomes requisite, from our relations with the hereditary
provinces, to reconcile as far as possible our mutual interests,
and reserving in all cases our national rights and independence,
we readily offer to those countries the hand of brotherhood.
We are moreover convinced, that all measures proposed as aids
to our constitutional progress, and to the elevation of the moral
and material condition of our country, can only attain real value
and vitality when a national government shall exist independent of foreign influence, which may give its sanction to
such measures; and which, based on true constitutional principles, shall be responsible to the nation, the voice of which it
will duly represent. For these reasons it is that we consider the
conversion of the present system of a government by boards and
commissions into a responsible Hungarian ministry, the chief
condition, the most essential guarantee of all measures of reform.

(b) Demands of the Hungarian People, 15 March 1848.

1. Freedom of the press; abolition of censorship.
2. A responsible ministry with its seat in the capital.[1]
3. An annual parliament in Budapest.[2]
4. Political and religious equality before the law.
5. A national guard.
6. Taxes to be paid by all.[3]
7. Abolition of serfdom.
8. Jury system. Equality of representation.
9. A national bank.
10. The military to take an oath to the constitution; Hungarian soldiers not to be stationed abroad, foreign soldiers to
be removed.

[1] The government was conducted from offices in Vienna.
[2] Parliament met at Pozsony, near Vienna, and not at the capital,
Budapest.
[3] Up to this time the nobility and the gentry were exempt from taxation.

11. Political prisoner to be freed.

12. Union with Transylvania.[1]

57. *Outline of the Austrian Constitution, April 1848*

The liberal ministry appointed after the flight of Metternich soon worked out a constitution for the empire which took into account the popularly made demands. This constitution, promulgated on 25 April 1848, is a lengthy document; instead of selections from it we include the main principles underlying it, which were announced earlier in the month.

Source: *Annual Register*, 1848, p. [406].

1. All the provinces are constituted into one body, with the exception of Hungary, Croatia, Sclavonia, Siebenbürgen,[2] and, for the present, the Italian provinces.

2. The division of the empire shall remain as it exists at present.

3. The person of the Emperor is sacred and inviolable.

4. The Emperor has full power over the land and sea forces, and the right of making war or peace.

5. Treaties of every description with foreign powers can only be made with the sanction of the two Houses of Parliament.

6. The attribute of mercy and the right of bestowing rewards belong to the Emperor; but mercy cannot be extended to the Ministers without the sanction of the Parliament.

7. The laws are to be administered publicly in open courts by verbal pleadings, and trial to be by jury. The judges will be appointed for life.

8. All projects of laws are to be proposed as well as sanctioned by the Emperor.

9. The Emperor will assemble the Parliament annually, and he must call them together at stated intervals. He has the right to prorogue and dissolve them.

10. Freedom of religion, speech, the press, petition, and public meeting is granted to every citizen, subject to future laws.

11. Entire liberty of conscience and religion.

12. The free exercise of religious worship is accorded to all Christians and Jews.

[1] Transylvania, part of the Hungarian kingdom since the tenth century, had been governed as a separate entity for several centuries.

[2] Siebenbürgen is the German name of Transylvania, which, like Croatia and Sclavonia, was part of the historic kingdom of Hungary.

13. All citizens are equal in the eye of the law, and every citizen shall be tried by his peers.

14. The responsibility of the Ministers shall be regulated by the Parliament.

15. The legislative power is in the hands of the Emperor and the Parliament.

16. Two Houses of Parliament are to be constituted. The qualifications for Members of the Upper House are birth and large landed property; and they are to be nominated by the Emperor. Members of the Lower House are to be chosen from all classes, in order that every interest may be represented.

17. The two Houses have the power to project laws and receive petitions.

18. All laws require the sanction of both Houses, particularly those relating to the expenditure, taxation, finance, and the sales of public property.

19. A law will be framed for the organization of the National Guard. The law of election is only provisional, and will be settled by the first Parliament. Amendments of the constitution can only be proposed by the Parliament.

58. *Proclamation of the first Slavic Congress in Prague to the Peoples of Europe, 12 June 1848*

German, Hungarian, and Italian national movements found their parallel among the Slavic peoples of Europe, which had only recently gained a consciousness of nationality. Representatives of these peoples, of whom only the Russians were not under foreign rule, met at Prague in June 1848 to discuss common action. Although most representatives came from the lands of the Austro–Hungarian Empire, the Congress felt called upon to address a liberal and nationalist proclamation to the peoples of Europe in the name of all Slavs. Excerpts of this follow.

Source: H. Reschauer and M. Smets, *Das Jahr 1848: Geschichte der Wiener Revolution* (Wien, Waldheim, 1872), vol. ii, pp. 340-2 (trans. Ed.).

The meeting of a Slavic Congress . . . is an unprecedented event . . . For the first time since history gave us a name, we, scattered members of a large family of peoples, have met in large numbers in order to acknowledge our brotherhood and to discuss peacefully our common concerns; we have understood each other not only through our majestic tongue, spoken by eighty millions, but also by the harmony of our heartbeats, through the identity of spiritual interest. The truth and openness of our discussions move us to announce, before God and the world, what we want, what principles have guided our deliberations.

The Latin and Germanic nations . . . have, for thousands of years, not only secured their independence with the might of the sword, but also satisfied their thirst for domination. Their policy was based mainly on the right of the stronger . . . it ruled by privilege and assigned only duties to the people; it is only now . . . that public opinion has succeeded in shattering the fetters of feudalism, in re-gaining for the individual the eternal rights of man. Among the Slavs, however . . . one tribe after another fell into subjection, and demands with a loud and resolute voice his inheritance: liberty . . . He wants no domination, no conquest, only liberty for himself as for all . . . unconditional equality before the law, the same measure of right and duty for everyone . . . the liberty, equality and fraternity of all citizens.

[But we make demands not only for the individual.] No less sacred than the human being with his inherited rights is the people in the totality of its spiritual interests . . . Nature does not know noble or ignoble people, it has not destined one to rule over another . . . But at present not even the best educated peoples recognize and respect this law as they should . . . The free Briton denies the Irishman his national equality, the German threatens many a Slavic race with force if it refuses to contribute to the political greatness of Germany, the Hungarian is not loath to claim nationality rights for his own nation alone. We Slavs condemn all such presumption unconditionally . . . Yet true to our natural character, we offer our brotherly hand to all neighbouring peoples who are ready, as we are, to recognize and protect the complete equality of rights of all nationalities, regardless of their political power or greatness . . .

[A request for a transformation of the Austro–Hungarian Empire into a federation of national states is followed by a protest against present oppression of Slavs in specified places.] If we here solemnly protest against such unworthy actions, we do so because we trust in the beneficial effects of liberty.

Freedom must and will make more just the nations which have been oppressors . . .

We propose that a general European congress of peoples be held to settle all international questions; we are convinced that free nations will reach agreement more easily than paid diplomatists. May this proposal be accepted in time, before the reactionary policies of individual courts are again successful in setting nations at each other in envy and hate.

In the name of the liberty, equality and fraternity of all peoples, given at the Congress on 12 June 1848.

59. *The Austrian Constitution, 4 March 1849*

In October 1848 the Austrian government defeated a second revolution in Vienna; by the beginning of 1849, reactionary once more, it succeeded in establishing control over most of the empire (though not over Hungary). The time was considered to be ripe for counter-acting the nationalist, centrifugal tendencies of the revolutionary period and to strengthen the empire. A unitary centralized constitution was therefore imposed which, by applying to German and non-German peoples alike, finally precluded the participation of Austria in a united Germany, and thus effectively terminated the *grossdeutsch–kleindeutsch* controversy in the National Assembly at Frankfurt. Selected articles of the new constitution follow.

Source: *Annual Register*, 1849, pp. [319–24].

[The constitution began by a definition of the territory of the empire, which included the formerly independent areas, like Hungary.]

The Crown of the Empire, and of each single Crown land, is hereditary in the house of Habsburg-Lorraine, according to the Pragmatic Sanction and the Austrian family laws . . .

The Emperor is august, inviolable and irresponsible . . .

The Emperor proclaims the laws and publishes the decrees respecting the same. Each decree must have the counter-signature of a responsible Minister.

The Emperor appoints the Ministers and he dismisses them; he appoints to all offices in all branches of the Administration . . .

For all peoples of the Empire there is but one general Austrian citizenship . . .

Serfdom, no matter of what kind or denomination, is abolished . . .

All Austrian citizens are equal before the law and before the courts . . .

Public offices are open to all persons qualified for the same . . .

The General Austrian Imperial Diet shall consist of two houses—namely, of an Upper House and of a Lower House . . .

The Upper House is formed by deputies, to be chosen by the Crown lands from the members of their respective provincial diets . . .

The Lower House proceeds from general and direct elections. The franchise belongs to every Austrian citizen who is of age, who is in the full enjoyment of civil and political rights, and who either pays the annual amount of direct taxes fixed by the electoral law, or who, on account of his personal qualities, possesses the active franchise of a parish of an Austrian Crown Land.

The votes to the elections for either House are given by word of mouth and publicly . . .

The constitution of the kingdom of Hungary shall so far be maintained that the regulations which do not tally with this constitution lose their effect, and the equality of rights of all nationalities and of the languages of the country in all relations of public and civil life shall be guaranteed by institutions framed for that purpose . . .

In the kingdoms of Croatia and Sclavonia, . . . the peculiar institutions of these dominions shall be upheld within the union of those countries with the Empire, as determined by this charter of a constitution, but with the complete independence of the said countries from the kingdom of Hungary . . .

The constitution of the kingdom of Lombardy and Venetia, and the relations of that Crown land to the empire, shall be determined by a special statute.

All the other Crown lands are to have their own special constitutions.

60. Hungarian Declaration of Independence, 14 April 1849

Hungary was far from being defeated at the time the 1849 unitary constitution (No. 59) was promulgated. She could never accept this constitution, as it contravened the national and constitutional demands of the Hungarians. The Hungarian Parliament therefore deposed the House of Habsburg and declared the independence of Hungary in the document that follows. This independence did not last long: Russian troops entered Hungary shortly after the Declaration was voted, in order to assist Austria, and the Hungarian forces were finally defeated in August 1849.

Source: E. Szabad, *Hungary past and present* (Edinburgh, A. & C. Black, 1854), p. 357.

After a conference held with closed doors, the representatives met . . . and proclaimed in the presence of an applauding audience the following decrees:

1. That Hungary, Transylvania, and the provinces belonging to it, are hereby declared a free and independent State.
2. That the House of Habsburg-Lorraine, by its treacherous conduct and armed attack on Hungary; by its attempts to destroy Hungarian independence by force of arms; and by having called in the aid of a foreign Power to assist in this murderous attempt, has torn with its own hands all the treaties binding it to Hungary; and therefore the said dynasty has forfeited all right to the Hungarian throne, and is declared banished for ever from the country.
3. That Hungary, as an independent State, desires to maintain friendly relations with all other countries, and particularly with those which were heretofore under the rule of the same house, as well as with Turkey and Italy.
4. That the future form of government shall be decided subsequently in accordance with the interests of the rest of Europe, and that in the meantime a president or governor, assisted by a ministry, shall be nominated for the provisional government of the country.

VI · GERMANY 1849–70

THE greatest number of documents in this section refers to the struggle, mainly between Austria and Prussia, over the internal organization of Germany. The King of Prussia rejected the imperial crown offered to him by the Frankfurt Assembly (No. 51) but that did not mean that Prussia agreed to a restoration of the domination of Germany by Austria. Shortly after the collapse of the Frankfurt Assembly, while its radical rump was still in session, Prussia, Saxony, and Hanover agreed to the formation of a new union, usually referred to as the Erfurt Union (No. 61), while later in the year Austria declared the reconstitution of the old German Confederation. The conflict of the two unions was finally resolved in favour of Austria in the Punctuation of Olmütz, and Austrian predominance was re-asserted (No. 62).

In the eighteen fifties and early sixties various schemes had been proposed for a reorganization of Germany, but proved non-acceptable to all parties, mainly because Austria would not agree to an amelioration of the position of Prussia. The conflict of the two countries finally came to a formal breach over Schleswig-Holstein. The affairs of these duchies (cf. No. 49) were settled by an international conference in London by a treaty (No. 64) of 1852. In 1864, however, new difficulties arose and Austria and Prussia jointly conducted a war against Denmark, in which they were victorious. In the Peace of Vienna (No. 66) the duchies became the joint possession of Austria and Prussia, and these two Powers came to an agreement in the Gastein Convention about their relationship in Schleswig and Holstein (No. 67). However, in spite of this convention, concluded in 1865, conflict between the two Powers soon arose again, and Austria invoked the assistance of the Confederation against Prussia, upon which Prussia declared the dissolution of the Confederation (No. 68) and declared war on Austria.

The Seven Weeks War ended in an overwhelming Prussian

victory; in the preliminary peace of Nikolsburg (No. 69) and
then in the Peace of Prague Austria agreed to her permanent
exclusion from Germany and thus to a reorganization of
Germany according to Prussian desires. A North German Confederation was formed under Prussian leadership (No. 71) while
Austria regulated her own internal constitutional relations with
Hungary in the compromise of 1867 (No. 72).

Another important development on which documents are included is that of Prussian internal politics. In Prussia the constitution of 1848, imposed by the King, was soon replaced by
the somewhat less liberal constitution of 1850 of which certain
provisions are included (No. 63). A liberal ministry was appointed in 1857, thus beginning the so-called 'new era' in
Prussian politics. Conflict, however, soon arose because of the
new King's plans for military reform, the House of Representatives refusing to vote for a budget unless the reorganization
of the army was carried out in accordance with their wishes.
This conflict led to the appointment of Bismarck as Prime
Minister of Prussia. Certain documents relating to the years
1862 and 1863 are included (No. 65). The settlement of the
issue took place after the victory over Austria, when Bismarck
asked for and received an indemnity for his unconstitutional
administration (No. 70).

The last document of this section has little importance for
the history of Germany in this period, but will become important later: this is the Eisenach programme of the German Social
Democratic Party, agreed to in 1869 (No. 73), the foundation
document of the Marxist branch of the German labour movement.

61. *The Erfurt Union Treaty, 26 May 1849*

All but a radical rump of the Frankfurt Assembly dissolved after
Frederick William's refusal to accept the imperial crown on the
Assembly's terms (No. 51) and Austria, now a unitary State (No. 59),
was still preoccupied in Hungary. The late spring of 1849 was
therefore considered to be a good time to assert Prussian power in
Germany, and a treaty was proposed by the Prussian Government
which would create a new form of federation, under Prussian leadership, and with a less liberal constitution than the one proposed at
Frankfurt. The treaty that follows was the foundation document of

this so-called Erfurt Union; apart from Prussia, Hanover, and Saxony, Bavaria participated in the negotiations, but would not sign the treaty. A number of German States joined this Union in the course of the ensuing year.

Source: E. R. Huber, *Dokumente zur deutschen Verfassungsgeschichte* (Stuttgart, Kohlhammer, 1961), vol. i, pp. 426–9 (trans. Ed.).

Whereas in the present situation the internal and external security of Germany [which ought to be] safeguarded by the German Confederation is endangered and thus, in order to restore united leadership in German affairs, a closer union of such Governments as are resolved to act on the basis of identical principles is necessary, the Governments of Prussia, Saxony and Hanover have concluded the following treaty.

1. The Royal Governments of Prussia, Saxony and Hanover conclude, in compliance with Article 11 of the German Act of Confederation (No. 22) of 8 June 1815 an alliance with the purpose of safeguarding the internal and external security of Germany and the independence and inviolability of the several German States . . .

2. All members of the German Confederation may join this alliance . . .

3. *1.* The supreme direction of the measures which are to be taken to achieve the aims of the alliance is vested in the Crown of Prussia . . .

2. An administrative council, to which all members shall send one or more representatives, shall be formed to conduct the business of the Alliance.

3. The Administrative Council may take a final decision on the following matters:

(1) The admission of new members to the Alliance.

(2) Steps for the calling of a constituent Reichstag and the direction of its deliberations.

(3) The appointment and direction of civil commissioners to be attached to the military when requests for assistance against internal disturbances are made.

4. Should there be diplomatic negotiations . . . they shall be conducted by the Crown of Prussia and the Administrative Council shall be kept informed of their progress . . .

5. Any military operations shall be directed by the Crown of Prussia . . .

4. In earnest of their resolve to order the affairs of Germany in accordance with the requirements of the times and the principles of justice, the Allies undertake to grant to the German people a constitution based on the draft agreed by them . . .

They shall submit this draft to a Reich Assembly called for the purpose . . .

Changes requested by this Reich Assembly will gain validity only if the Allies agree to them.

5. They also undertake to form, by 1 July at the latest, a provisional Federal Court of Arbitration . . .

62. *The 'Punctuation' of Olmütz, 29 November 1850*

Late in 1849 Austria proclaimed the revival of the German Confederation in its old form, and, although Prussia and the other states of the Erfurt Union stood aloof, a number of German states joined Austria, there being thus two unions. Conflict between them arose when there were internal disturbances in Hesse and both unions claimed the right to intervene. The crisis was settled after an intervention by Tsar Nicholas I in favour of Austria. The document embodying the main points at issue follows; at the ministerial conference mentioned in the last article the dissolution of the Erfurt Union and the renewal of the German Confederation was agreed to by all parties.

Source: E. Hertslet, *The Map of Europe by Treaty* (London, Butterworth, 1875), vol. ii, pp. 1143–5.

1. The Governments of Austria and Prussia declare that it is their intention to bring about the Final and Definitive Settlement of the Electoral Hessian and Holstein affairs, by the common decision of all the German governments.

2. In order to render the co-operation of the Governments represented at Frankfurt and of the other German Governments possible, there shall be named, as soon as may be, on the part of the members of the Confederation represented at Frankfurt, as well as on the part of Prussia and Allies, a Commissioner for each, who will have to agree upon the measures to be taken in common.

3. As it is, however, in the general interest that both in Electoral Hesse and in Holstein there should be established a legal state

of things conformable with the Fundamental Laws of the Confederation, and rendering the fulfilment of the federal duties
possible; as, moreover, Austria has given to the full, in her own
name and in that of the States allied with her, the guarantees
for the security of the interests of Prussia required by the latter
in regard to the occupation of the Electorate, the two Governments of Austria and Prussia agree, in order to proceed with the
discussion of the questions, and without prejudice to the future
decision, as follows:

A. In Electoral Hesse, Prussia will oppose no impediment
to the action of the troops called in by the Elector, and, therefore, will issue the necessary orders to the generals in command there, to allow a thoroughfare by the military roads
occupied by Prussia. The two Governments of Austria and
Prussia will, in concert with their Allies, call upon his Royal
Highness the Elector to give his consent for one battalion of
the troops called in by the Electoral Government, and one Royal
Prussian battalion to remain at Cassel, in order to maintain
tranquillity and order.

B. After consultation with their Allies, Austria and Prussia
will send to Holstein, and that as speedily as possible, joint
Commissioners, who shall demand of the Stadtholdership,[1] in
the name of the Confederation, the cessation of hostilities, the
withdrawal of the troops behind the Eyder, and the reduction
of the army to one-third of its now existing strength, threatening
common execution in case of refusal. On the other hand, both
Governments will endeavour to prevail on the Danish Government not to station in the Duchy of Schleswig more troops than
are necessary for the preservation of tranquillity and order.

4. Ministerial Conferences will immediately take place at
Dresden. The invitation to them will be issued by Austria and
Prussia conjointly, and will be so arranged that the conferences
may be opened about the middle of December.

63. Excerpts from the Prussian Constitution, 31 January 1850

After a long debate in the Prussian Landtag, the imposed constitution of December 1848 was replaced by the constitution of

---

[1] The Stadtholder was the head of the revolutionary government of the
Duchies.

31 January 1850. A small selection of its provisions is included here, mainly such articles as are important for an understanding of the constitutional conflict (Nos 65, 70) and other later internal developments in Prussia.

Source: *British and Foreign State Papers*, 1849/50 (vol. ii), pp. 1025–1039.

WE, Frederick William, by the grace of God King of Prussia, &c., make known and declare that, as the Constitution of the Prussian State, promulgated by us on the 5th of December, 1848, and acknowledged by both Chambers of our Kingdom, subject to revision in the ordinary way of legislation, has undergone the revision therein prescribed, we, in concurrence with both Chambers, have finally determined the Constitution.

We accordingly promulgate it as the fundamental law of the State . . .

12. The freedom of religious creeds, of association in religious societies, and of the common domestic and public exercise of religion is guaranteed. The enjoyment of civil rights and of the rights of citizens of the State is independent of religious creed. The fulfilment of civil duties, or of those belonging to citizens of the State must not suffer from the exercise of religious freedom.

13. Religious societies as well as ecclesiastical societies, which have no corporate rights, can only acquire these rights by special laws.

14. The Christian religion will form the basis of those ordinances of the State which are connected with the exercise of religion, without prejudice to the freedom of religion guaranteed in Article 12.

15. The Evangelical and the Roman Catholic Churches, as well as every other religious society, regulate and administer their affairs independently, and remain in possession and enjoyment of the establishments, foundations, and funds destined for the objects of their worship, instruction, and charities.

16. The intercourse of religious societies with their superiors is unimpeded. The publication of ecclesiastical ordinances is only subject to the restrictions to which all other publications are liable . . .

43. The person of the King is inviolable.

44. The Ministers of the King are responsible . . .

45. The executive power belongs to the King alone. He names and dismisses the Ministers . . .

60. The Ministers, as well as the officers of the State appointed to represent them, have access to each Chamber, and must at all times be heard at their desire. Each Chamber can desire the presence of the Ministers. The Ministers have only a right of voting in the Chamber of which they are members . . .

62. The legislative power is exercised in common by the King and the two Chambers. The agreement of the King and both Chambers is requisite for every law. Projects of financial laws and budgets will first be submitted to the Second Chamber. The latter will either be wholly adopted or rejected by the First Chamber . . .

69. The Second Chamber consists of 350 members . . .

70. Every Prussian, who has completed his 25th year, and who possesses in the commune in which he resides the qualification for the communal elections, has a right to vote as a primary elector . . .

71. For every full number of 250 souls of the population, one elector is to be chosen. The primary electors are divided, in proportion to the direct State taxes to be paid by them, into three sections, and in such manner, that upon each section, one-third of the total amount of the contributions to the taxes of all the primary electors falls . . .

The first section consists of those primary electors upon whom the highest contributions to the taxes, to the amount of one-third of the whole tax, fall.

The second section consists of those primary electors upon whom the next lower contributions to the taxes, to the amount of the second third, fall.

The third section consists of those primary electors who are the lowest taxed, upon whom the third portion falls.

Each section elects specially and actually one-third of the electors to be chosen . . .

72. The deputies are elected by the electors . . .

99. All the revenue and expenditure of the State must be estimated beforehand and brought into the budget, which is annually settled by a law.

100. Taxes and duties must only be levied for the State Treasury

in so far as they are inserted in the budget or directed by special laws . . .

104. For any excess upon the Budget, the subsequent sanction of the Chambers is necessary . . .

109. The existing taxes and duties continue to be levied, and all the enactments of existing codes of laws and of particular laws and ordinances, which are not contrary to the present Constitution, remain in force till they are altered by a law.

64. *Treaty of London, 8 May 1852*

While the Schleswig-Holstein conflict of 1848-49 (cf. No. 49) was an expression of German national claims, strictly it was caused by a conflict of legal rules on the succession to the thrones of Denmark and the Duchies. Under the auspices of Great Britain and Russia, the disputed succession was settled by the following treaty, thus ostensibly eliminating any cause of future conflict between Denmark and Germany.

Source: E. Hertslet, *The Map of Europe by Treaty* (London, Butterworth, 1875), vol. ii, pp. 1151-4.

1. After having taken into serious consideration the interests of his Monarchy, His Majesty the King of Denmark, with the assent of His Royal Highness the Hereditary Prince, and of his nearest cognates, entitled to the succession by the Royal Law of Denmark, as well as in concert with His Majesty the Emperor of All the Russias, Head of the elder Branch of the House of Holstein-Gottorp, having declared his wish to regulate the order of succession in his dominions in such manner that, in default of issue male in a direct line from King Frederick III of Denmark, his Crown should devolve upon His Highness the Prince Christian of Schleswig-Holstein-Sonderbourg-Glücksbourg . . .; the High Contracting Parties[1] appreciating the wisdom of the views which have determined the eventual adoption of that arrangement, engage by common consent, in case the contemplated contingency should be realized, to acknowledge in His Highness the Prince Christian . . . the Right of Succeeding to the whole of the Dominions now united under the sceptre of His Majesty the King of Denmark . . .

3. It is expressly understood that the reciprocal rights and

[1] Great Britain, Austria, France, Prussia, Russia, and Sweden and Norway.

obligations of His Majesty the King of Denmark, and of the Germanic Confederation, concerning the Duchies of Holstein and Lauenburg, rights and obligations established by the Federal right, shall not be affected by the present Treaty . . .

65. *The Constitutional Conflict in Prussia, 1862-63*

King William I of Prussia (while Regent) and the Landtag agreed that a reform of the Prussian army was necessary, but they did not agree on the way the reform should be carried out, as the King's plan would have reduced the importance of the Landwehr, or reserve army, which was officered by middle-class officers. In 1861 the Landtag provisionally granted funds to the government to begin the reforms, subject to agreement on details; when such agreement was not forthcoming, it reduced military expenditure in the Estimates of 1862. From this time on, even after the appointment of Bismarck to the Prime Ministership in September 1862, the government administered the country and carried out the army reforms without legislative sanction, and without a valid budget; the conflict was only settled in September 1866, after the victory over Austria (No. 70; cf. also the relevant articles of the Constitution, No. 63).

The documents on this subject consist of a declaration of the Prussian government (a), a resolution of the House of Representatives in which it declares the proceedings of the government unconstitutional (b) and Bismarck's famous speech in which he expounds his theory of the 'gap' in the constitution (c).

Source: (a) and (b) E. R. Huber, *Dokumente zur deutschen Verfassungsgeschichtte* (Stuttgart, Kohlhammer, 1964), vol. ii, pp. 44–46 (trans. Ed.).

(c) E. N. Anderson, *The Social and Political Conflict in Prussia 1858–1864* (Lincoln, University of Nebraska, 1954), pp. 218–20.

(a) Declaration of the Prussian Ministry, 29 September 1862.

Since the House has deleted all expenses relating to the reorganization of the army from the Estimates for 1862, the Royal Government must assume that the same action will be taken in respect of the Estimates for 1863 when they come to be debated . . . During the debates it has also become clear that agreement to a budget which would really correspond to the needs of the country can only be made possible by agreement on another Bill, on Obligation to Military Service, which the Royal Government expects to introduce in the next session.

On the submission of the Royal Government His Majesty the

King has therefore ... directed that ... the Bill concerning the Determination of the Budget for 1863 ... be withdrawn.

The Royal Government does not intend to depart from the principle of introducing the budget early enough to allow its determination before the beginning of the year to which it refers. It merely considers as its duty, in the present case, not to allow the obstacles to an agreement to become any greater than they already are. It will introduce the budget for 1863, together with a Bill on Universal Military Service (which will maintain the measures of army reform already taken) at the beginning of the next session and will introduce the budget for 1864 in sufficient time for the House to debate it in accordance with the Constitution.

(b) Resolution of the Prussian House of Representatives, 7 October 1862.

Consisting

that, according to the Constitution, state expenditure may only be incurred or justified on the basis of a budget agreed to in advance for each year, or, exceptionally, on the basis of special laws or permission by the Landtag,

that, therefore, the Royal State Government is not entitled to incur expenditure in the current year on the basis of a budget determined for the previous year;

further considering

that the withdrawal of the budget for 1863, which had already been introduced and to a large extent debated, and the proposed long delay in introducing a new budget, extend the present wrongful way of conducting the administration without a previously determined budget, and endangers the right of the Representation to determine the budget in advance,

that a determination of the budget for 1863 in good time still appears to be practicable;

finally considering

that, as a consequence of the Declaration by the Royal State Government of 29 September 1862 (No. 65(a)) the fear exists that the Government will continue, on its own responsibility, the military expenditure which the Chamber of Deputies disallowed already for 1862, and whose disallowance for 1863 is likely, as is admitted by the Royal Government,

that, therefore, it seems necessary to expressly safeguard the rights of the Representation;
the House of Representatives declares:

1. It is demanded that the Royal State Government introduce the budget for 1863 in the House of Representatives for its determination according to the Constitution early enough to allow a decision before 1 January 1863.
2. It is a breach of the Constitution if the Royal Government directs expenditure to be made which has been definitely and expressly disallowed by a resolution of the House of Representatives.

(c) Bismarck's Speech in the House of Representatives, 27 January 1863.

. . . You clothe this demand in the form of a declaration that the constitution is violated in so far as the Crown and the Upper House do not bow to your will. You direct the accusation of violation of the constitution against the ministry, not against the Crown, whose loyalty to the constitution you place beyond all doubt . . . You know as well as anyone in Prussia that the ministry acts in Prussia in the name of and on behalf of His Majesty the King, and that in this sense it has executed those acts in which you see a violation of the constitution. You know that in this connexion a Prussian ministry has a different position from that of the English. An English ministry, let it call itself what it will, is a parliamentary one, a ministry of the parliamentary majority; but we are ministers of His Majesty the King. I do not reject the separation of the ministers and the Crown, as you have assumed in the address . . . in order to protect the ministry behind the shield of the Crown. We do not need this protection; we stand firmly on the ground of our good rights. I repudiate the separation because by it you conceal the fact that you find yourself not in conflict with the ministry, but in conflict with the Crown for domination over the country.

Article 99 reads, if I remember correctly: all income and expenditure of the state must be estimated each year in advance and brought together in a state budget.

If it followed that 'the latter will be fixed annually by the

Lower House' then you were entirely correct in your complaints
in the address, for the constitution would be violated. But the
text of Article 99 continues: The budget will be fixed annually
by law. Now, Article 62 states with incontrovertible clarity how
a law is passed. It says that for the passage of a law, including
a budget law, agreement of the Crown and of both Houses is
necessary. That the Upper House is justified in rejecting a
budget approved by the Lower House but not acceptable to the
Upper is, moreover, emphasized in the article.

Each of these three concurrent rights is in theory unlimited,
one as much as the other. If agreement among the three powers
is not reached, the constitution is lacking in any stipulation
about which one must give in. In earlier discussions one passed
over this difficulty with ease; it was assumed according to
analogy of other countries, whose constitution and laws,
however, are not published in Prussia and have no validity here,
that the difficulty could be settled with the two other factors
giving in to the Lower House, that if agreement over the budget
is not reached between the Crown and the Lower House, the
Crown not only submits to the Lower House and dismisses the
ministers who do not have the confidence of the Lower House,
but in case of disagreement with the Lower House the Crown
also forces the Upper House by mass appointments to place itself on the plane of the Lower House. In this way, to be sure,
the sovereign and exclusive rule of the Lower House would be
established; but such exclusive rule is not constitutional in
Prussia. The constitution upholds the balance of the three legislative powers on all questions, also with respect to the budget.
None of these powers can force the others to give way. The constitution therefore points to the way of compromise for an understanding. A statesman of constitutional experience has said
that the entire constitutional life is at every moment a series of
compromises. If the compromise is thwarted in that one of the
participating powers wishes to enforce its own views with
doctrinaire absolutism, the series of compromises will be inter-
rupted and in its place will occur conflicts. And since the life
of a state cannot remain still, conflicts become questions of
power. Whoever has the power in hand goes ahead with his
views, for the life of a state cannot remain still even a moment . . .

66. *Peace of Vienna with Denmark, 30 October 1864*

When a succession crisis arose again in connexion with Schleswig-Holstein because of a proposed Danish breach of the Treaty of London (No. 64), great German national feeling arose and the German Confederation was pressed to take action. Instead of acting through the Confederation, however, Prussia and Austria, as signatories of the Treaty of London, took individual action and together defeated the Danes easily. As a result the King of Denmark renounced his sovereignty over the Duchies; they were not, however, incorporated in the German Confederation as sovereign states, or given to the heir according to German law, the Duke of Augustenburg, but became the joint property of Austria and Prussia.

Source: E. Hertslet, *The Map of Europe by Treaty* (London, Butterworth, 1875), vol. iii, pp. 1630–3.

1. There shall be in future peace and friendship between Their Majesties the King of Prussia and the Emperor of Austria and His Majesty the King of Denmark as well as between their heirs and successors, their respective States and subjects in perpetuity.
2. All the treaties and conventions concluded before the war between the High Contracting Parties are re-established in force in so far as they are not abrogated or modified by the tenor of the present treaty.
3. His Majesty the King of Denmark renounces all his rights over the Duchies of Schleswig, Holstein and Lauenburg, in favour of Their Majesties the King of Prussia and the Emperor of Austria, pledging himself to recognize the dispositions which Their said Majesties shall make with regard to these Duchies.
4. The cession of the Duchy of Schleswig includes all the islands belonging to that Duchy as well as the territory situated on *terra firma* . . .
[The rest of Article 4, and further twenty articles, regulate the details of the transfer of the Duchies.]

67. *The Gastein Convention, 14 August 1865*

Austro-Prussian joint administration of Schleswig and Holstein soon led to friction between the two Governments. It was therefore decided to settle the differences by the following convention, which divides the historically indivisible twin duchies, Austria to receive Holstein, Prussia Schleswig.

Source: E. Hertslet, *The Map of Europe by Treaty* (London, Butterworth, 1875), vol. iii, pp. 1638–42.

Their Majesties the Emperor of Austria and the King of Prussia have become convinced that the co-sovereignty which has hitherto existed in the territories ceded by Denmark in the Treaty of Peace of 30th October 1864 (No. 66) leads to untoward results, which at the same time endanger both the good understanding between their Governments and the interests of the Duchies. Their Majesties have therefore resolved for the future not to exercise in common the rights which have accrued to them by Article 3 of the above-mentioned treaty, but to divide the exercise thereof geographically until a further agreement may be made . . .

1. The exercise of the rights acquired in common by the High Contracting Parties in virtue of Article 3 of the Vienna Treaty of Peace . . . (No. 66) shall, without prejudice to the continuance of those rights of both Powers to the whole of both Duchies, pass to His Majesty the Emperor of Austria as regards the Duchy of Holstein, and to His Majesty the King of Prussia as regards the Duchy of Schleswig.

2. The High Contracting Parties will propose to the Diet the establishment of a German fleet, and will fix upon the harbour of Kiel as a federal harbour for the said fleet . . .

6. The High Contracting Parties entertain in common the intention that the Duchies shall enter the *Zollverein* . . .

9. His Majesty the Emperor of Austria cedes to His Majesty the King of Prussia the rights acquired in the aforementioned Vienna Treaty of Peace (No. 66) with respect to the Duchy of Lauenburg; and in return the Royal Prussian Government binds itself to pay to the Austrian Government the sum of 2,500,000 Danish rix-dollars, payable at Berlin in Prussian silver . . .

10. The carrying into effect of the foregoing division of the co-sovereignty which has been agreed upon, shall begin as soon as possible after the approval of this convention by their Majesties . . . and shall be accomplished at the latest by the 15th September.

The joint Command-in-Chief, hitherto existing, shall be dissolved . . .

68. *Prussian Declaration to the Federal Diet, 14 June 1866*

In spite of the Gastein convention (No. 67) friction between Austria and Prussia over Schleswig and Holstein continued; not surprisingly, as it was merely a reflection of the two Powers' struggle for predominance in Germany. Austria accused Prussia of breaches of agreements, took the matter to the Federal Diet, and moved for armed federal action against Prussia. Prussia protested and, in the Declaration which follows, announced her withdrawal from the Confederation and its dissolution.

Source: E. Hertslet, *The Map of Europe by Treaty* (London, Butterworth, 1875), vol. iii, pp. 1652–4.

. . . For three months past the most powerful member of the Confederation,[1] violating the fundamental laws of the Federal Act, has . . . armed against Prussia; that circumstance had already seriously shaken the confidence of the Prussian Government in the protection which the Germanic Confederation has guaranteed to each of its members. The Royal Government having, therefore, appealed for the protection of Prussia against an arbitrary attack by Austria, to the action of the Confederation and of its Members; that appeal had no other result than the armament of other Confederated States, armaments the objects of which have remained without explanation. The Royal Government, after such precedents, necessarily considered their external and internal security as endangered . . .

The motion[2] . . . drawn up by Austria and the adoption of the motion by a part of the Confederated States, no doubt after a previous understanding, could only confirm and strengthen the views of the Royal Government.

By virtue of the federal law, no declaration of war can be made against any member of the Confederation. The Austrian motion, therefore, and the vote of the States adhering to it, being a declaration of war against Prussia, the Royal Government considers the dissolution of the federal pact as accomplished.

In the name and by the august order of His Majesty the King, his gracious master, the Envoy therefore declares that Prussia considers the federal pact in force up to the present

[1] i.e. Austria.   [2] To take armed action against Prussia.

time as dissolved; that so far from considering it henceforth obligatory, it will consider it as having expired, and will act accordingly.

His Majesty the King, nevertheless, does not consider the national basis on which that Confederation has been established as destroyed from the fact of the extinction of the old Confederation. Prussia, on the contrary, holds firmly to those bases and to the unity of the German nation, unity soaring above temporary forms, and considers it the bounden duty of the German States to find in that unity the most suitable expression.

The Royal Government here submits, on its part, the constitutive basis of a new Union of States more in keeping with the wants of the period, and declares itself ready to conclude, on the modified basis of the old Confederation, a new Confederation with such of the German States as would join it with that object . . .

69. *The Treaty of Nikolsburg, 26 July 1866*

When war broke out, Prussia, unaided, easily defeated the forces of Austria and of the German states which assisted Austria. Bismarck, however, did not impose very rigorous terms on Austria; he was satisfied with the withdrawal of Austria from German affairs, and a free hand in Germany north of the river Main.

The Preliminary Treaty of Peace of Nikolsburg, part of which follows, sets out the principles of settlement; the final peace treaty, of Prague, differs only by including many more detailed provisions.

Source: E. Hertslet, *The Map of Europe by Treaty* (London, Butterworth, 1875), vol. iii, pp. 1698–701.

1. With the exception of the Lombardo-Venetian Kingdom,[1] the territory of the Austrian Monarchy remains intact. His Majesty the King of Prussia engages to withdraw his troops from the Austrian territories occupied by them . . .

2. His Majesty the Emperor of Austria recognizes the dissolution of the Germanic Confederation as it has existed hitherto and consents to a new organization of Germany without the participation of the Empire of Austria. His Majesty likewise promises to recognize the closer union which will be founded by

---

[1] This was ceded by Austria to Italy by the Treaty of Prague, 23 August 1866.

His Majesty the King of Prussia, to the north of the line of the
Main, and he declares that he consents to the German States
south of that line entering into a union, the national relations
of which, with the North German Confederation, are to be the
subject of an ulterior agreement between the two Parties.

3. His Majesty the Emperor of Austria transfers to His Majesty
the King of Prussia all the rights which the Treaty of Vienna
of 30th October, 1864 (No. 66) recognized as belonging to him
over the Duchies of Schleswig and Holstein, with this reservation, that the people of the northern districts of Schleswig shall
be again united to Denmark if they express a desire to be so
by a vote freely given.

4. [Austria to pay the war expenses of Prussia.]

5. In conformity with the wish expressed by His Majesty the
Emperor of Austria His Majesty the King of Prussia declares
his willingness to let the territorial state of the Kingdom of
Saxony continue in its present extent . . . On the other hand,
His Majesty the Emperor of Austria promises to recognize the
new organization which the King of Prussia will establish in
the north of Germany . . .

70. *Settlement of the Constitutional Conflict in Prussia,*
September 1866

The majority of Prussians, in or out of the House of Representatives,
received the news of victory with great joy. The success of the
Government made the opposition pre-disposed to settle the constitutional conflict on the Government's terms, and thus, while
nominally reaffirming the rights of the House, in fact confirmed
Bismarck's position. The Prime Minister's speech in which he offers
settlement (a) and the Law of Indemnity (b) follow.

Source: E. R. Huber, *Dokumente zur deutschen Verfassungsgeschichte*
(Stuttgart, Kohlhammer, 1964), vol. ii, pp. 87–9 (trans.
Ed.).

(a) Bismarck's Speech on Indemnity, 1 September 1866.

. . . The more sincerely the Royal Government desires peace,
the more its members feel bound to renounce retrospective
criticism, be it in defence, be it in attack. During the last four
years we have frequently expressed our views on both sides
with more or less bitterness or good will, but nobody succeeded

in converting anyone. Everyone thought he was right in acting as he did . . . We desire peace not because we are unable to continue the fight, on the contrary, the tide is flowing more in our favour than it has for years; we do not desire peace in order to evade a possible future charge on the basis of a possible future law . . .; I don't believe we shall be charged, I don't believe we should be convicted if we were, and whatever opinions one may have, the ministry has been reproached with many things, but not with cowardice.

We desire peace because, in our opinion, the fatherland needs it more at present than it had before; we desire it and seek it because we believe we may find it at the present moment; we should have sought it earlier, if we could have hoped to find it; we believe we may find it now because you will have recognized that the Royal Government is not so far removed from the tasks which the majority also wish to see completed as you may have thought a few years ago . . .

This is the reason why we believe we shall find peace, and we seek it honestly; we have offered you our hand, and the report of your committee is the token of your acceptance. We shall then complete the tasks which are still unaccomplished together with you. I by no means exclude from these tasks improvements [of the constitution]. But it is only together that we shall be able to complete them, with identical good will, without doubting the sincerity of the other . . .

(b) Law of Indemnity, 14 September 1866.

1. For the purpose of the accountability and discharge from liability of the Government, the schedules of Receipts and Expenditure of the State for the years 1862, 1863, 1864 and 1865, attached to this Law, shall serve in place of the Estimates which, according to the Constitution, are to be agreed upon yearly before the beginning of the financial year.
2. The State Government is granted an indemnity for the administration conducted without lawfully determined Estimates since the beginning of the year 1862 . . . The retrospective responsibility of the Government shall be the same as if the administration . . . had been conducted . . . on the basis of Estimates lawfully approved and published in time.

3. For the purpose of current administration in 1866 the government is granted 154 million *Thaler.* . . .

4. The State Government shall submit the accounts of Receipts and Expenditure for 1866 to the Landtag in the course of the year 1867.

71. *Constitution of the North German Confederation,* *14 June 1867*

To replace the German Confederation, a new Confederation was formed in Germany north of the river Main, under Prussian leadership. Some of the more important articles of the constitution of this Confederation follow.

Source: *British and Foreign State Papers,* Vol. lvii (1866/67), pp. 296–313.

[The rulers of the German states situated to the north of the river Main[1]] enter into a perpetual Confederation for the defence of the federal territory and of the rights prevailing therein, as well as for fostering the welfare of the German people. The said Confederation will bear the name of the North German Confederation, and the following will be its Constitution.

1. The territory of the Confederation consists of the States of Prussia with Lauenburg, Saxony, Mecklenburg-Schwerin, Saxe-Weimar, Mecklenburg-Strelitz, Oldenburg, Brunswick, Saxe-Meiningen, Saxe-Altenburg, Saxe-Coburg-Gotha, Anhalt, Schwarzburg-Rudolstadt, Schwarzburg-Sonderhausen, Waldeck, Reuss of the elder line, Reuss of the younger line, Schaumburg-Lippe, Lippe, Lübeck, Bremen, Hamburg, and the parts of the Grand Duchy of Hesse situated north of the Main.

2. The Confederation exercises the right of legislation within the aforesaid territory, according to the provisions of this constitution, and to the effect that the federal laws take precedence of the laws of the respective countries . . .

4. The following matters are subject to the supervision of the Confederation and to its legislation.

   1. The regulations on freedom of expatriation, on domiciliation and settlement, right of citizenship, passports, and

---

[1] For a list of the states see Article 1.

police for foreigners, also on matters of business, including the system of insurance . . .;

2. The customs and commercial legislation, and the taxes
to be applied to Federal purposes;

3. The regulation of the systems of weights, measures and
money . . .;

4. The general regulations for banking;

5. Patents of invention;

6. The protection of intellectual property;

7. The organization of a common protection for German
commerce abroad . . .;

8. Railways . . . roads, and water-communications . . .;

9. . . . Waterways common to several States . . .;

10. The postal and telegraph service . . .;

13. The common legislation on contract law, penal law,
commercial law, the law of bills of exchange, and the
legal procedure;

14. The military affairs of the Confederation and the
navy . . .;

5. The legislation of the Confederation is performed by the
Federal Council (Bundesrat) and the Diet (Reichstag). The
concurrence of the resolutions passed by the majorities of the
two Assemblies is necessary and sufficient for a federal law . . .
6. The Federal Council consists of the representatives of the
members of the Confederation, amongst whom the votes are
divided according to the rules for the full assembly of the late
Germanic Confederation, so that Prussia, with the late votes of
Hanover, Hesse-Cassel, Holstein, Nassau and Frankfurt,[1] has
17 votes, Saxony 4, . . . Mecklenburg-Schwerin 2, . . . Brunswick 2, [all other States one each], Total 43 . . .
11. The Presidency of the Confederation appertains to the
Crown of Prussia, which, in the exercise thereof, has the right
of representing the Confederation internationally, of declaring
war and concluding peace, of entering into alliances and other
treaties with foreign States, of accrediting and receiving ambassadors in the name of the Confederation . . .
15. The Chancellor of the Confederation, who is to be

[1] The five States here listed were incorporated into Prussia after the war
of 1866.

appointed by the Presidency, presides over the Federal Council and has the direction of the business . . .

20. The Diet (Reichstag) emanates from general and direct elections with secret voting . . .

53. The Federal Navy is an undivided one under the commander-in-chief of Prussia . . .

57. Every North German is liable to military service and cannot perform that service by substitute.

58. The costs and burdens of the whole military affairs of the Confederation are to be borne by all the federal States and those who belong to them, so that neither the advantage nor the overburdening of individual States or classes is admissible in principle . . .

60. The effective strength of the federal army in time of peace is regulated up to December 31, 1871, at one per cent. of the population of 1867, and is furnished *pro rata* thereof by the separate federal States. For the later times the . . . strength . . . will be settled by way of federal legislation.

61. After the publication of this Constitution the Prussian military legislation is to be immediately introduced into the whole federal territory . . .

63. All the land forces of the Confederation form one single army, which in war and peace is under the command of His Majesty the King of Prussia, as Federal Commander-in-Chief . . .

69. All the receipts and expenses of the Confederation must be estimated for each year, and brought into the federal budget. This is to be settled by law before the beginning of the financial year, according to the following principles.

70. To provide for all common expenses any surpluses of the preceding year are first of all made use of, as well as the common revenues arising from the customs, from the common taxes on consumption, and from the postal and telegraph services. In so far as these are not sufficient to cover the expenses, they are to be made up, so long as federal taxes are not introduced, by contributions from the separate federal States in proportion to their population,[1] and those contributions will be imposed by the Presidency until they reach the amount fixed in the budget . . .

[1] The so-called matricular contributions.

78. Alterations of the Constitution take place by way of legislation, but a majority of two-thirds of the votes represented in the Federal Council is necessary thereto.

72. *The Austro-Hungarian Compromise (Ausgleich) of October 1867*

The period between 1848 and 1867 saw a number of changes in the structure of the Austrian Empire, none of them lasting or successful mainly because of opposition by the Hungarians, the second largest nationality in the monarchy. After Austria's exclusion from Germany it was considered expedient to come to a lasting settlement with the Hungarians. As a result a Compromise (*Ausgleich*) was negotiated, which transformed the unitary Empire into a Dual Monarchy, in which Hungary was given important rights. The relationship of the two parts (Austrian and Hungarian) of the monarchy was defined in two similar laws, one enacted in Austria, one in Hungary. Some of the more important articles of the Austrian law follow.

Source: W. F. Dodd, *Modern Constitutions* (Chicago, University of Chicago Press, 1909), vol. i, pp. 114–22.

1. The following affairs are declared common to Austria and Hungary:

   a. Foreign affairs, including diplomatic and commercial representation abroad, as well as measures relating to international treaties . . .
   b. Military and naval affairs; excluding the voting of contingents and legislation concerning the manner of performing military service . . .
   c. The finances, with reference to matters of common expense . . .

2. Besides these, the following affairs shall not indeed be administered in common, but shall be regulated upon uniform principles to be agreed upon from time to time:

   1. Commercial affairs, especially customs legislation.
   2. Legislation concerning indirect taxes . . .
   3. The establishment of the monetary system and monetary standards.
   4. Regulations concerning railway lines which affect the interests of both parts of the empire.

5. The establishment of a system of defence.

3. The expenses of affairs common to both Austria and Hungary shall be borne by the two parts of the Empire in a proportion to be fixed from time to time by an agreement between the two legislative bodies, approved by the Emperor . . .

5. The administration of common affairs shall be conducted by a joint responsible ministry, which is forbidden to direct at the same time the administration of joint affairs and those of either part of the Empire . . .

6. The legislative power belonging to the legislative bodies of each of the two parts of the Empire shall be exercised by them, in so far as it relates to joint affairs, by means of Delegations . . .

10. Delegates and their substitutes shall be elected annually by . . . the Reichsrat.

11. The delegations shall be convened annually by the Emperor . . .

13. The powers of the Delegations shall extend to all matters concerning common affairs . . .

15. For the passage of a law concerning matters within the power of the Delegations the agreement of both Delegations shall be necessary, or in default of such agreement, a vote of the full assembly of the two Delegations sitting together; in either case the approval of the Emperor shall be necessary.

16. The right to hold the joint ministry to its responsibility shall be exercised by the Delegations . . .

36. Agreement concerning matters which, though not managed in common, yet are to be regulated upon the same principles, shall be reached in one of the following ways: (1) The responsible ministries by an agreement between themselves shall prepare a project of law which shall be submitted to the representative bodies of the two parts of the Empire and the project agreed upon by the two representative bodies shall be submitted for the approval of the Emperor. (2) Each representative body shall elect from its members a Deputation composed of an equal number of members, which shall prepare a project upon the initiative of the respective ministries; such project shall be submitted to each of the legislative bodies by the ministries, shall be regularly considered, and the identical law of the two assemblies shall be submitted for the approval

of the Emperor. The second procedure shall be followed especially in reaching an agreement concerning the distribution of
the cost of affairs administered in common . . .

73. *The Eisenach Programme of the Social Democratic Labour Party, August 1869*

The socialist movement had been fairly strong in Germany since
the late eighteen fifties but it was dominated by Ferdinand Lassalle
and his German socialism. The influence of Marx was felt only in
the late eighteen sixties. A group of German Marxists met at
Eisenach in August 1869 to form an organization; the Social Democratic Labour Party was the result. Substantial parts of its
programme follow.

Source: A. Bebel, *My Life* (London, T. Fisher Unwin, 1912),
        pp. 167–70.

1. The Social Democratic Labour Party aims at the establishment of a free democratic State.

2. Every member of the party pledges himself to insist with all
his might on the following principles:

   (a) The present political and social conditions are in the
highest degree unjust and therefore to be opposed . . .

   (b) The struggle for the emancipation of the working classes
is not a struggle for class privileges and prerogatives, but for
equal rights and equal duties and for the abolition of all class
domination.

   (c) The economic dependence of the worker on the capitalist
is the basis of his servitude in all its forms, and the Social
Democratic party aims, by the abolition of the present method
of production (the wages system), at assuring, by means of
co-operative labour, that every worker shall receive the full
product of his work.

   (d) Political freedom is the indispensable basis of the
economic emancipation of the working classes. The social
question is therefore inseparable from the political question;
its solution depends upon the solution of the political question
and is only possible in a democratic state.

   (e) In consideration of the fact that the political and economic emancipation of the working class is only possible if this
class wages war in common and united, the Social Democratic Labour Party adopts a united organization which yet

makes it possible for every one of its members to make his influence felt for the benefit of the whole.

(f) Considering that the emancipation of labour is neither a local nor a national but a social question, which embraces all countries in which there is a modern society, the Social Democratic Labour Party regards itself, as far as the laws of association permit, as a branch of the 'International' (cf. No. 98) and adopts its aims.

3. The following are to be regarded as the most urgent questions of propaganda:

(a) Equal universal and direct suffrage by secret ballot for all men over twenty . . . The deputies are to be paid salaries.

(b) The introduction of direct legislation (initiative and referendum) by the people.

(c) Abolition of all privileges of class, property, birth and creed.

(d) Substitution of a national militia for standing armies.

(e) Separation of church and state and secularization of schools.

(f) Compulsory education in elementary schools and gratuitous instruction in all public educational establishments.

(g) Independence of the courts, introduction of the jury system, industrial courts, public and oral procedure, and gratuitous jurisdiction.

(h) Abolition of all legal restriction of the press, the right of association and combination, the introduction of a normal working day, the restriction of female labour, and the abolition of child labour.

(i) Abolition of all indirect taxation and the introduction of a single direct progressive income tax and a tax on inheritance.

(j) State help for co-operative undertakings and state credit for free productive co-operative associations, with democratic guarantees. [The rest of the programme deals with the internal organization of the party.]

VII · SECOND REPUBLIC
AND SECOND EMPIRE IN FRANCE
1851–70

THE documents in this section have been selected to illustrate political developments under the personal rule of Napoleon III. The documents of the *coup d'état* serve as an introduction: the decree dissolving the National Assembly (No. 74), the decree calling for a plebiscite (No. 75), and the resolution of certain members of the National Assembly protesting against the decrees (No. 76).

After the approval of the *coup d'état* by an overwhelming majority in a plebiscite, Louis Napoleon proceeded to a formal establishment of his rule, by the constitution of 1852, explained in the decree promulgating it (No. 77). Later in 1852, by an overwhelming popular vote, the imperial dignity was re-established and Louis Napoleon declared to be emperor as Napoleon III (No. 78).

From 1860 we find a number of measures which liberalize the autocratic system and grant more political liberty to the subjects. No attempt at explaining the reasons for these measures can be made here, but some of the more important measures are included: the *senatus consultum*[1] of 1861, which permitted the publication of debates in the Senate and the Legislative Body (No. 79), that of the same year which granted the right to debate the budget by sections rather than as a whole (No. 80), and the imperial decree of 1867 which granted the right to interpellate the government (No. 81).

These measures culminated in 1869–70 when the 'liberal empire' was formally established with a new constitution (No. 82).

---

[1] Originally, an important resolution of the Senate in ancient Rome; here a resolution of the Senate amending the Constitution.

74. Decree dissolving the National Assembly, 2 December 1851

Louis Napoleon Bonaparte, having been elected president in 1848 (cf. No. 43(b)) worked hard at making himself and his policies popular in the country and, indeed, by 1851, was assured of substantial support not only among the population, but also in the National Assembly. Many thought that only his continuance in the presidency could assure the maintenance of internal peace and order, but re-election of a president after his four-year term was prohibited by the 1848 constitution.

Petitions for the revision of this provision were received in large numbers during 1851 (many of them organized by the prefects), and the National Assembly voted by a large majority in favour of such revision, but it was short of the constitutionally required two-thirds majority. Louis Napoleon and his entourage therefore decided on a *coup d'état* which, after several postponements, took place in the early hours of 2 December 1851. The first step was the dissolution of the National Assembly.

Source: *The Political and Historical Works of Louis Napoleon Bonaparte* (London, Illustrated London Library, 1852), vol. ii, p. 354.

In the name of the French people the President of the Republic decrees:

1. The National Assembly is dissolved.
2. Universal suffrage is re-established. The law of the 31st of May[1] is abrogated.
3. The French people is convoked for their votes from the 14th December to the 21st December following.
4. The state of siege is decreed throughout the first military division.
5. The Council of State is dissolved.
6. The Minister of the Interior is charged with the execution of the present decree.

75. Proclamation and Decree on the Plebiscite, 2 December 1851

The dissolution of the National Assembly (No. 74) was justified by Louis Napoleon in the proclamation that follows (a). In it, he also indicated the main constitutional changes he wanted to introduce and announced the holding of a plebiscite to ascertain the will of the people. The terms of the plebiscite are contained in his decree (b).

Source: *Annual Register*, 1851, pp. [254–5, 201].

[1] In this law the Assembly, against the wishes of the president, re-introduced restrictions on the suffrage.

(a) Proclamation of 2 December 1851.

Frenchmen,

The present situation cannot last much longer. Each day the situation of the country becomes worse. The Assembly, which ought to be the firmest supporter of order, has become a theatre of plots. The patriotism of 300 of its members could not arrest its fatal tendencies. In place of making laws for the general interest of the people it was forging arms for civil war. It attacked the power I hold directly from the people; it encouraged every evil passion; it endangered the repose of France. I have dissolved it, and I make the whole people judge between me and it. The Constitution, as you know, had been made with the object of weakening beforehand the powers you entrusted to me. Six millions of votes were a striking protest against it, and yet I have faithfully observed it. Provocations, calumnies, outrages, found me passive. But now that the fundamental part is no longer respected by those who incessantly invoke it, and the men who have already destroyed two monarchies wish to tie up my hands in order to overthrow the Republic, and to save the country by appealing to the solemn judgment of the only sovereign I recognize in France—the people.

I, then, make a loyal appeal to the entire nation; and I say to you, if you wish to continue this state of disquietude and uneasiness that degrades you and endangers the future, choose another person in my place, for I no longer wish for a place which is powerless for good, but which makes me responsible for acts that I cannot hinder, and chains me to the helm when I see the vessel rushing into the abyss. If, on the contrary, you have still confidence in me, give me the means of accomplishing the grand mission I hold from you. That mission consists in closing the era of revolution, in satisfying the legitimate wants of the people, and in protecting them against subversive passions. It consists especially in the power to create institutions which survive men, and which are the foundation on which something durable is based. Persuaded that the instability of power, that the preponderance of a single Assembly, are the permanent causes of trouble and discord, I submit to your vote the fundamental bases of a constitution which the assemblies will develop hereafter.

1. A responsible chief named for ten years.
2. The Ministers dependent on the Executive alone.
3. A Council of State formed of the most distinguished men preparing the laws and maintaining the discussion before the Legislative Body.
4. A Legislative Body, discussing and voting the laws, named by universal suffrage, without the *scrutin de liste*[1] which falsifies the election.
5. A second Assembly formed of all the illustrious persons of the nation; a preponderating power, guardian of the fundamental pact and of public liberty.

This system, created by the First Consul[2] in the beginning of the present century, has already given to France repose and prosperity. It guarantees them still. Such is my profound conviction. If you partake it, declare so by your votes. If, on the contrary, you prefer a Government without force, monarchical or republican, borrowed from some chimerical future, reply in the negative. Thus, then, for the first time since 1804[3] you will vote with complete knowledge of the facts and knowing for whom and for what you vote.

If I do not obtain the majority of the votes I shall summon a new Assembly, and lay down before it the mission I have received from you. But if you believe that the cause of which my name is the symbol, that is, France regenerated by the revolution of '89, and organized by the Emperor, is still yours; proclaim it to be so by ratifying the powers I demand of you. Then France and Europe will be preserved from anarchy, obstacles will be removed, rivalries will have disappeared for all will respect, in the will of the people, the decree of providence.

(b) Decree on the Plebiscite, 2 December 1851.

Considering that the sovereignty resides in the universality of the citizens, and that no fraction of the people can attribute to itself the exercise thereof; considering the laws and decrees which have hitherto regulated the mode of appeal to the

[1] Voting for lists of candidates in multi-member constituencies.
[2] Napoleon I.
[3] When the establishment of a hereditary empire under Napoleon I was approved by popular vote.

people, and particularly [a number of decrees is listed]; the President of the Republic decrees as follows:

[The people are convoked in their electoral colleges on 14 December to accept or reject the following plebiscite:]

'The French people wills the maintenance of the authority of Louis Napoleon Bonaparte, and delegates to him the powers necessary to frame a Constitution on the basis proposed in his proclamation of the 2nd of December (No. 75(a)).'

76. Resolution in Protest by Members of the National Assembly, 2 December 1851

The *coup d'état* did not proceed entirely without opposition, although there was little fighting. The most significant protest came from some three hundred deputies of the National Assembly who, after the dissolution, met in the city hall of the tenth district of Paris, and there passed the resolution which follows.

Source: *The Political and Historical Works of Louis Napoleon Bonaparte* (London, Illustrated London Library, 1852), vol. ii, p. 412.

The Legislative Assembly . . . taking into consideration Art. 68 of the Constitution[1] and looking at the fact that the Assembly is prevented by violence from exercising its mandate; Decrees as follows:

Louis Napoleon Bonaparte is deprived of his functions as President of the Republic; all citizens are bound to refuse him obedience; the executive power passes *de jure* into the hands of the Legislative Assembly. The judges of the high court of Justice are bound to assemble immediately, to proceed to the trial of the President of the Republic and his accomplices.

[1] Article 68: 'The President of the Republic, the Ministers, the agents, the depositaries of public authority, are responsible, each in what concerns themselves respectively, for all the acts of the Government and the Administration—any measure by which the President of the Republic dissolves the National Assembly, prorogues it, or places obstacles in the exercise of its powers, is a crime of high treason. By this act merely, the President is deprived of all authority, the citizens are bound to withhold their obedience, the executive power passes in full right to the National Assembly. The judges of the High Court of Justice will meet immediately under pain of forfeiture; they will convoke the juries in the place which they will select to proceed to the judgment of the President and his accomplices; they will nominate the magistrates charged to fulfil the duties of public ministers.'

In consequence, all functionaries and depositories of the public force and authority are enjoined to obey all the requisitions made in the name of the Assembly, under penalty of high treason.

77. *The Constitution of 14 January 1852*

A new constitution was drawn up shortly after the plebiscite to give effect to the principles enunciated by Louis Napoleon in his proclamation of 2 December (No. 75(a)). The constitution itself is a lengthy document, which was promulgated by a lengthy proclamation explaining its most important principles. Large sections of the explanatory text of the proclamation follow.

Source: *The Political and Historical Works of Louis Napoleon Bonaparte* (London, Illustrated London Library, 1852), vol. i, pp. 146–152.

Frenchmen—

In my Proclamation of the 2nd of December (No. 75(a)), when I loyally explained to you what, according to my ideas, were the vital conditions of government in France, I had not the pretension, so common in these days, of substituting a personal theory for the experience of centuries. On the contrary, I sought in the past the examples that might best be followed, what men have given them, and what benefits had resulted.

I have thought it reasonable to prefer the precepts of genius to the specious doctrines of men of abstract ideas. I have taken as models the political institutions which already at the commencement of the century under analogous circumstances have strengthened tottering society and raised France to a lofty degree of prosperity and grandeur . . .

In one word, I said to myself, since France makes progress in the last fifty years in virtue alone of the administrative, military, judicial, religious and financial organization of the Consulate and the Empire, why should we not also adopt the political institutions of that epoch? Created by the same thought, they must bear the same character of nationality and practical utility.

In effect . . . it is essential to aver that our present state of society is nought else than France regenerate by the revolution of '89, and organized by the Emperor. Nothing remains of the old regime but great *souvenirs* and great benefits; all that was organized under it was destroyed by the revolution, and all that has been organized since the revolution, and still exists, has been the work of Napoleon . . . The First Consul, alone, re-established unity, hierarchy, and the true principles of Government. They are still in vigour.

It may, then, be affirmed that the frame of our social edifice is the work of the Emperor—which has stood firm—resisting his fall and the shocks of three revolutions.

Wherefore, since they have the same origin, should not his political institutions have the same chance of duration?

My own conviction has been formed for a long time; and therefore it was that I submitted to your judgement the principal bases of a Constitution borrowed from that of the year VIII. Approved of by you, they are to become the foundation of our political Constitution. Let us now examine its spirit.

In our country—for the last eight hundred years monarchical—the central power has always existed by increasing. Royalty destroyed the great vassals; the revolutions themselves caused to disappear the obstacles which opposed the rapid and uniform exercise of authority. In this country of centralization, public opinion has invariably referred everything, good and evil, to the chief of the Government: so that to write at the head of a charter that the chief is irresponsible, is to lie to public feeling. It is to endeavour to establish a fiction which has three times disappeared at the sound of revolution.

The present Constitution, on the contrary, proclaims that the chief whom you have elected is responsible to you. That he has the right of appeal to your sovereign judgement, in order that in grave circumstances you may always be able to continue your confidence in him, or to withdraw it.

Being responsible, his actions must be free and without hindrance. Hence arises the obligation of his having ministers who may be honoured and powerful auxiliaries of his thought, but who no longer form a responsible council, composed of jointly responsible members, a daily obstacle to the special influence of the chief of the state—a council, the expression of a policy emanating from the Chambers, and for that very reason exposed to frequent changes which render impossible a continuous policy or the application of a regular system.

Nevertheless, in proportion to the loftiness of position in which a man is placed, and in proportion to his independence and to the confidence that the people place in him, is his need of enlightened and conscientious counsel. Hence the creation of a Council of State, in future the real Council of Government, the first wheelwork of our new organization—a reunion of practical men elaborating projects of law in special committee, then discussing them behind closed doors, and without oratorical ostentations in general assembly, next presenting them to the acceptation of the Legislative Body. Thus the Government is free in its movements and enlightened in its progress . . .

A Chamber which bears the title of the Legislative Body will vote the laws and the taxes. It will be elected by universal suffrage, without the ballot . . . The Legislative Body freely discusses the laws, adopts or rejects them, but does not introduce those unforeseen amendments which often derange the whole economy of the system . . . it does not possess that parliamentary initiative which was the source of such grave abuse . . .

Another Assembly bears the name of Senate. It will be composed of those elements which in every country create a legitimate influence; such as an illustrious name, wealth, talent, and services rendered to the country . . . It intervenes either to resolve any grave difficulty which might arise during the absence of the Legislative Body, or to explain the text of the Constitution, and to secure whatever may be necessary to its progress. It has the right to annul any illegal or arbitrary act . . .

The Emperor said to the Council of State: 'A constitution is the work of time: it is impossible to leave in it too large a margin for ameliorations.' Accordingly, the present Constitution has only settled that which it was impossible to leave uncertain. It has not shut up within insurmountable barriers the destinies of a great people. It has left for change a margin sufficiently large to allow in great crises other means of safety than the disastrous expedient of revolution.

The Senate can, in concert with the Government, modify all that is not fundamental in the Constitution; but as to any modifications of the fundamental bases sanctioned by your suffrages, they can only become definite after having your ratification. Thus the people remains master of its destiny. Nothing fundamental is effected without its will.

Such are the ideas, such the principles, that you have authorized me to apply. May this Constitution give to our country calm and prosperous days; may it prevent the return of those intestine struggles in which victory, however legitimate, is always dearly bought. May the sanction which you have given to my efforts be blessed by Heaven. Then peace will be assured at home and abroad, my ardent hopes will be fulfilled, my mission will be accomplished.

78. The Re-Establishment of the Empire, November–December 1852

After Louis Napoleon took power as president for ten years in 1851, it was clear that it would not be long before he assumed the imperial dignity. In November 1852 a *senatus consultum* (a) was passed proposing this modification of the constitution, and was approved by a large majority in a plebiscite (b).
Source: *Annual Register*, 1852, pp. [263–4, 267] (with emendations).

(a) *Senatus Consultum*, 7 November 1852.

1. The imperial dignity is re-established. Louis Napoleon Bonaparte is Emperor of the French under the name of Napoleon III.
2. The imperial dignity is hereditary in the direct descendants, natural and legitimate, of Louis Napoleon Bonaparte . . .
8. The following proposition shall be submitted to the people for acceptance in the form determined by decrees: 'The people desires the re-establishment of the imperial dignity in the person of Louis Napoleon Bonaparte, with the succession in his direct descendants natural and legitimate or adopted; and gives him the right to regulate the order of succession to the throne in the Bonaparte family . . .'

(b) Decree on the Re-establishment of the Empire, 2 December 1852.

Seeing the *senatus consultum*, dated 7 November 1852, which submitted to the people the following plebiscite:
[text in paragraph 8 of No. 78(a)];
D E C—N

Seeing the declaration of the Legislative Body, which proves that the operations of the vote have been everywhere freely and regularly accomplished;

That the general summing up of the votes on the plebiscite has given seven millions eight hundred and twenty-four thousand one hundred and eighty-nine (7,824,189) bulletins bearing the word 'Yes';

Two hundred and fifty-three thousand one hundred and forty-five (253,145) bulletins bearing the word 'No';

Sixty-three thousand three hundred and twenty-six (63,326) invalid bulletins:

We have decreed and decree as follows:

1. The *senatus consultum* of the 7th of November, 1852, ratified by the plebiscite of the 21st and 22nd of November, is promulgated and becomes the law of the State.

2. Louis Napoleon Bonaparte is Emperor of the French under the name of Napoleon III.

79. *Senatus Consultum amending Article 42 of the Constitution, 2 February 1861*

The first of the liberalization measures which, though still with restrictions, enabled the public at large to be informed of the debates of the Chambers.

Source: F.-A. Hélie, *Les constitutions de la France* (Paris, Duchemin, 1880), p. 1272 (trans. Ed.).

Article 42 of the Constitution[1] is amended as follows:

The debates in the sessions of the Senate and the Legislative Body shall be taken down in shorthand and inserted, in full, in the official gazette of the following day.

In addition, reports of these sessions, compiled by editorial secretaries under the authority of the president of each Chamber, shall be put at the disposal of all newspapers each evening.

Reports on the sessions of the Senate or of the Legislative Body in newspapers or other means of publication must not

[1] The original Article 42 reads: 'The account of the proceedings of the sittings of the Legislative Body given by newspapers or other means of publication shall consist only of the reproduction of the minutes drawn up at the close of each sitting by the care of the President of the Legislative Body.'

consist of anything but the debates inserted in full in the official gazette or the reports compiled under the authority of the president in accordance with the preceding paragraphs hereof.

Nonetheless, when several bills or petitions are debated in the same session, it will be permissible to publish the debates relating to one bill or petition only. In such a case, if the debate extends over several sessions, publication of the debates or reports must be continued until the vote is taken.[1]

80. Senatus Consultum amending articles 4 and 12 of the Senatus Consultum of 25 December 1852, 31 December 1861

This is another important liberalization measure. Before it, the budget had to be debated and voted as a whole: under the new arrangement it became possible to discuss the estimates of each ministry separately. At the same time, the control of the Legislative Body over supplementary or extraordinary estimates was extended.

Source: F.-A. Hélie, *Les constitutions de la France* (Paris, Duchemin, 1880), pp. 1274–5 (trans. Ed.).

1. The estimates of expenditure shall be presented to the Legislative Body set out in sections, chapters and articles. The estimates of each ministry shall be voted by sections. The appropriations voted for each section shall be allocated to its chapters by a decree of the Emperor made in the Council of State.

2. Special decrees, made in the same form, may authorize transfers from one chapter to another within the estimates of the same ministry.

3. Supplementary or extraordinary appropriations may only be granted by law . . .

81. Imperial decree concerning the Relations of the Government with the Senate and the Legislative Body, 19 January 1867

The importance of this decree is that it enables members of the two Chambers to raise questions in public session, asking for an explanation by the minister concerned. In this way grievances could be aired, and actions of the executive criticized. While it is true that

---

[1] That is, selection of parts for publication, or editorial comment, is prohibited.

the general debate on the address in reply was abolished as part of this reform, the possibility of raising specific matters amply compensated for the loss.

Source: F.-A. Hélie, *Les constitutions de la France* (Paris, Duchemin, 1880), p. 1283 (trans. Ed.).

1. Members of the Senate and of the Legislative Body may address interpellations to the Government.

2. All requests for interpellations must be in writing and signed by at least five members. Such requests must explain the subject of the interpellation in summary form; they are to be sent to the president who communicates them to the minister of state and sends them to committees for examination.

3. If two committees of the Senate or four committees of the Legislative Body are of opinion that the interpellations may take place, the Chamber shall set a day for the debate.

4. After the close of the debate, the Chamber may resolve the return to the order of the day, or to communicate with the government.

5. Return to the order of the day always has priority.

6. Communication to the Government must always be couched in the following terms: 'The Senate or the Legislative Body brings the subject of the interpellations to the attention of the Government.'—In this case an extract of the debate is sent to the minister of state . . .

8. Articles 1 and 2 of our decree of 24 November 1860 which order that the Senate and the Legislative Body shall each year, at the beginning of the session, vote an address in reply to our speech, are abrogated.

82. *The Liberal Empire, 21 May 1870*

After further measures of liberalization in 1869, the Emperor submitted, on 23 April 1870, a *senatus consultum* to the people, who were asked to approve the new constitution contained in it. The document that follows consists of the proclamation making public the result of the plebiscite and introducing the new constitution, the most important new provisions of which are included in summary form.

Source: F.-A. Hélie, *Les constitutions de la France* (Paris, Duchemin, 1880), pp. 1323–7 (trans. Ed.).

Napoleon, by the grace of God and the national will Emperor of the French, to all present and to come, greeting.

In view of our decree of 23rd of April last which convoked the French people in its electoral assemblies to accept or reject the following proposition:

'The people approves the liberal reforms of the Constitution introduced by the Emperor, with the consent of the great bodies of the State, since 1860 and it ratifies the *senatus consultum* of the 20th of April 1870';

In view of the declaration of the Legislative Body which states that the operations of the vote have been everywhere freely and regularly accomplished; and that the general summing up of the votes on the proposition has given 7,350,142 bulletins bearing the word 'Yes'; 1,538,825 bulletins bearing the word 'No'; and 112,975 invalid bulletins;

We have sanctioned and sanction, we have promulgated and promulgate as the constitution of the State the *senatus consultum* adopted by the Senate on the 20th of April 1870, the text of which is as follows:

Senatus Consultum Establishing the Constitution of the Empire.

[The following are some of the more important changes from the Constitution of 1852, the provisions of which, if not expressly superseded, remain in force:

The Senate and the Legislative Body as well as the Emperor now have the initiative in introducing legislation;

A Council of Ministers is established; the ministers are responsible; they may be members of the Senate or the Legislative Body;

The Constitution can be altered only by the people on the proposal of the Emperor.]

VIII · REVOLUTION AND UNIFICATION IN ITALY, 1830-70

THE Vienna settlement of 1815 re-established the old régime in Italy by dissolving the Napoleonic State structure. Autocracy and separatism again became the order of the day. But important sections of the population, particularly members of the urban middle class, were not satisfied with this state of affairs. Conspiratorial secret societies, based on vaguely liberal principles, loosely connected with each other, were formed all over the Peninsula. There were several waves of insurrections in Italy, pressing for constitutional reform, national unification, and, as its pre-condition, the exclusion of Austria from Lombardy and Venetia. The most important of these waves took place in 1831, after the July Revolution in France. Some of the proclamations of the insurgents follow (No. 83).

The insurrections were defeated by the forces of order, but from their failure Giuseppe Mazzini drew important lessons, which he incorporated in the General Instructions to members of his newly founded revolutionary society, Young Italy (No. 84). From this time on Mazzini and Young Italy remained an important influence in keeping awake liberal and national sentiment in the Italian people. Yet they had little direct influence; when revolutionary events began in January 1848, at Palermo in Sicily, there was little connexion with Mazzini and his followers.

The first important events occurred in the most backward of the Italian States, Naples, which incorporated Sicily. The King was forced to promise a constitution (No. 85). In this he was soon followed by the King of Sardinia (No. 86), the most up-to-date and most powerful State of the Peninsula, and even by the States of the Church (No. 87).

At the same time Milan, in Austrian-occupied Lombardy, also rose, the Austrians, sorely pressed everywhere, had to withdraw temporarily, and Milan asked for help from the other states of Italy (No. 88). In the short war that followed, Sardinia —the only power really actively involved—was soon defeated. Later in the year, and in the beginning of 1849, republics were founded in Rome (No. 89) under the leadership of Mazzini, and in Venice, and Sardinia attempted again to expel Austria, but was again defeated. By August 1849, the old régime was re-established all over Italy except in Sardinia, where the constitution (or *statuto*) continued in force.

The movement for the unification of Italy continued, however, after the revolutionary years, largely under the leadership of Sardinia, and her Prime Minister, Cavour. An important step on the way toward unification was Cavour's appearance at the Congress of Paris in 1856 (No. 90) where the topic of Italy was discussed over the protest of the Austrian representative. In 1859, France in alliance with Sardinia defeated the Austrians in a short campaign and gained Lombardy for Sardinia in the armistice of Villafranca (No. 91), confirmed by the treaties of Zürich. The Central Italian principalities also joined Sardinia, and thus the Kingdom of Italy came into being.

In 1860 Garibaldi and his volunteer troops landed in Sicily and, with lightning speed, occupied the island and most of the Kingdom of Naples. The population of these parts, on whose behalf Garibaldi issued a proclamation (No. 92), gave Garibaldi considerable support. The manœuvring of the Sardinian Government in connexion with Garibaldi's activities is beyond the scope of this note, but it resulted in the incorporation of the parts occupied by Garibaldi and of a large part of the Papal States into the Kingdom of Italy. Venetia was gained as a result of Austrian defeat in the Austro–Prussian war in 1866, and the final remaining part, Rome, was occupied in 1870, when the French protecting troops were withdrawn to participate in the Franco–Prussian war. The position of the Papacy, no longer ruler of a sovereign state, had to be safeguarded, and for this purpose the Italian parliament passed a Law of Guarantees in 1871, which is included in Section X (No. 115).

83. *Insurrectionary Manifestoes, 1831*

In 1831, largely as a result of the July 1830 revolution in France, a wave of insurrections broke out, particularly in Central Italy.

These insurrections, led by local conspiratorial groups, were not co-ordinated, and their aims often clashed. Some local success was achieved and the tacitly accepted leadership, the revolutionaries of Bologna, tried to extend the scope of the rising to Lombardy (a) and to Naples (b). Their call to revolt was unsuccessful, and Austrian forces soon succeeded in restoring order all over Italy.

Source: *Annual Register*, 1831, p. [453].

(a) Bolognese proclamation to the people of Lombardy.

Fellow-countrymen of Lombardy,

Follow the example of France—imitate the patriots of Central Italy—burst asunder the degrading chains which the Holy Alliance has riveted upon you. We were slaves, and wretched under the despotism of priests,[1] but our oppressors were still Italians. You are the slaves of foreigners, who enrich themselves by despoiling you, and render you daily more miserable. On the day of your rising, 40,000 of our patriots will march to assist you in crushing the Austrians. Let there be no delay, for there is danger in hesitation. Display your courage, fellow-countrymen, and despotism will flee from our country. Our country, liberty, and national independence for ever!

(b) Bolognese proclamation to the people of Naples.

In 1820 you won your liberty, and obtained a constitution without bloodshed. Your king, and all the civil and military authorities, swore to observe it, but treachery and perjury have deprived you of it. The enlightened nations have represented you as having lost your constitution by your cowardice. Avenge the national honour; do not suffer yourselves to be deceived by fallacious promises and amnesties which are only snares. To arms! Neapolitan patriots: shake off the yoke; become free again, for you have it in your power.

84. *General Instructions for the Members of Young Italy, 1831*

Guiseppe Mazzini participated in the insurrectionary activities of 1831, but then left Italy for exile in Switzerland, disillusioned by their failure. He considered, however, that the insurrectionaries themselves were at fault: there was too little cohesion among their local groups, there was no overall aim that united them all. To

---

[1] Bologna was part of the States of the Church.

remedy this, he founded the association he called *Young Italy*, and in the general instructions to members, which follow, he developed his revolutionary and political ideas.

Compare this document with the *Pact of Young Europe* (No. 11) in which he extended his organization over other countries of Europe.

Source: *Life and Writings of G. Mazzini.* New ed. (London, Smith-Elder, 1891), vol. i, pp. 96–113.

Liberty—Equality—Humanity—Independence—Unity.

Section 1.

Young Italy is a brotherhood of Italians who believe in a law of *Progress* and *Duty*, and are convinced that Italy is destined to become one nation—convinced also that she possesses sufficient strength within herself to become one, and that the ill success of her former efforts is to be attributed not to the weakness, but to the misdirection of the revolutionary elements within her—that the secret of force lies in constancy and unity of effort. They join this association in the firm intent of consecrating both thought and action to the great aim of re-constituting Italy as one independent sovereign nation of free men and equals.

Section 2.

By Italy we understand—1, Continental and peninsular Italy, bounded on the north by the upper circle of the Alps, on the south by the sea, on the west by the mouths of the Varo, and on the east by Trieste; 2, The islands proved Italian by the language of the inhabitants, and destined, under a special administrative organization, to form a part of the Italian political unity.

By the Nation we understand the universality of Italians bound together by a common Pact, and governed by the same laws.

Section 3.

Basis of the Association

The security, efficacity, and rapid progress of an association, are always in proportion to the determination, clearness, and precision of its aims.

The strength of an association lies, not in the numerical cypher of the elements of which it is composed, but in the homogeneousness of those elements; in the perfect concordance of its members as to the path to be followed, and the certainty that the moment of action will find them ranged in a compact phalanx, strong in reciprocal trust, and bound together by unity of will, beneath a common banner.

Revolutionary associations, which admit heterogeneous elements into their ranks, and possess no definite programme, may remain united in apparent harmony during the work of destruction; but will inevitably prove impotent to direct the movement the day after, and be undermined by discords all the more dangerous, in proportion as the necessities of the time call for unity of action and of aim.

A principle implies a method; or, in other words, as the aim is, so must the means be.

So long as the true practical aim of a revolution remains uncertain, so long will the means adopted to promote or consolidate it remain futile and uncertain also. The revolution will proceed without faith: and hence its progress will be wavering and weak. The history of the past has proved this.

Whosoever would assume the position of initiator in the transformation of a nation—whether individual or association—must know clearly to what the proposed changes are to lead. Whosoever would presume to call the people to arms, must be prepared to tell them wherefore. Whosoever would undertake a work of regeneration, must have a faith; if he have not, he can but create *émeutes*,[1] nothing more, and become the author of an anarchy he is neither able to remedy nor overcome. For, indeed, no whole nation ever rises to battle in ignorance of the aim to be achieved by victory.

For these reasons the members of Young Italy make known to their fellow-countrymen, without reserve, the programme in the name of which they intend to combat.

The aim of the association is revolution; but its labours will be essentially educational, both before and after the day of revolution; and it therefore declares the principles upon which the national education should be conducted and from which alone Italy may hope for safety and regeneration . . .

[1] Riots.

Young Italy is *Republican* and *Unitarian*.

Republican—because theoretically every nation is destined, by the law of God and humanity, to form a free and equal community of brothers; and the republican is the only form of government that insures this future.

Because all true sovereignty resides essentially in the nation, the sole progressive and continuous interpreter of the supreme moral law . . .

Because, when the sovereignty is recognized as existing not in the whole body, but in several distinct powers, the path to usurpation is laid open, and the struggle for supremacy between these powers is inevitable; distrust and organized hostility take the place of harmony, which is society's law of life. Because the monarchical element being incapable of sustaining itself alone by the side of the popular element, it necessarily involves the existence of the intermediate element of an aristocracy—the source of inequality and corruption to the whole nation.

Because both history and the nature of things teach us that elective monarchy tends to generate anarchy; and hereditary monarchy tends to generate despotism.

Because, when monarchy is not—as in the middle ages—based upon the belief now extinct in right divine, it becomes too weak to be a bond of unity and authority in the state.

Because the inevitable tendency of the series of progressive transformations taking place in Europe, is towards the enthronement of the republican principle, and because the inauguration of the monarchical principle in Italy would carry along with it the necessity of a new revolution shortly after.

Young Italy is republican, because practically there are no monarchical elements in Italy. We have no powerful and respected aristocracy to take the intermediate place between the throne and the people; we have no dynasty of Italian princes possessing any tradition either of glory or of important services rendered to the development of the nation, and commanding the affection and sympathy of the various states.

Because our Italian tradition is essentially republican; our great memories are republican; the whole history of our national progress is republican . . .

Because, while the populations of the various Italian States would cheerfully unite in the name of a principle which could give no umbrage to local ambition, they would not willingly submit to be governed by a man—the offspring of one of these states; and their several pretensions would necessarily tend to federalism . . .

Young Italy is *Unitarian*.

Because, without unity, there is no true nation.

Because, without unity, there is no real strength; and Italy, surrounded as she is by powerful, united and jealous nations, has need of strength before all things.

Because federalism, by reducing her to the political impotence of Switzerland, would necessarily place her under the influence of one of the neighbouring nations.

Because federalism, by reviving the local rivalries now extinct, would throw Italy back upon the middle ages.

Because federalism would divide the great national arena into a number of smaller arenae; and, by thus opening a path for every paltry ambition, become a source of aristocracy.

Because federalism, by destroying the unity of the great Italian family, would strike at the root of the great mission Italy is destined to accomplish towards humanity.

Because Europe is undergoing a progressive series of transformations, which are gradually and irresistibly guiding European society to form itself into vast and united masses.

Because the entire work of internal civilization in Italy will be seen, if rightly studied, to have been tending for ages to the formation of unity.

Because all the objections raised against the unitarian system do but apply, in fact, to a system of administrative centralization and despotism which has really nothing in common with unity.

National unity, as understood by Young Italy, does not imply the despotism of any, but the association and concord of all. The life inherent in each locality is sacred. Young Italy would have the *administrative* organization designed upon a broad basis of religious respect for the liberty of each commune, but the political organization, destined to represent the nation in Europe, should be one and central.

Without unity of religious belief, and unity of social pact; without unity of civil, political, and penal legislation, there is no true nation.

These principles, which are the basis of the association, and their immediate consequences, set forth in the publications of the association, form the creed of Young Italy; and the society only admits as members those who accept and believe in this creed . . .

The general principles held by the members of Young Italy, in common with men of other nations, and those herein indicated having special regard to Italy, will be evolved and popularly explained by the initiators to the initiated, and by the initiated, as far as possible, to the generality of Italians.

Both initiators and initiated must never forget that the moral application of every principle is the first and the most essential; that without morality there is no true citizen; that the first step towards the achievement of a holy enterprise is the purification of the soul by virtue; that, where the daily life of the individual is not in harmony with the principles he preaches, the inculcation of those principles is an infamous profanation and hypocrisy; that it is only by virtue that the members of Young Italy can win over others to their belief; that if we do not show ourselves far superior to those who deny our principles, we are but miserable sectarians, and that Young Italy must be neither a sect nor a party, but a faith and an apostolate.

As the precursors of Italian regeneration, it is our duty to lay the first stone of its religion.

Section 4.

The means by which Young Italy proposes to reach its aim are—education and insurrection, to be adopted simultaneously, and made to harmonize with each other.

Education must ever be directed to teach by example, word and pen the necessity of insurrection. Insurrection, whenever it can be realized, must be so conducted as to render it a means of national education.

Education, though of necessity secret in Italy, will be public out of Italy . . .

The mission of the Italian exiles is to constitute an apostolate.

The instructions and intelligence indispensable as preparatory to action will be secret, both in Italy and abroad.

The character of the insurrection must be national; the programme of the insurrection must contain the germ of the programme of future Italian nationality. Wheresoever the initiative of insurrection shall take place, the flag raised, and the aim proposed, will be Italian.

That aim being the formation of a nation, the insurrection will act in the name of the nation, and rely upon the people, hitherto neglected, for its support. That aim being the conquest of the whole of Italy, in whatever provinces will be conducted on a principle of invasion and expansion the most energetic, and the broadest possible . . .

Convinced that Italy is strong enough to free herself without external help; that, in order to found a nationality, it is necessary that the feeling and consciousness of nationality should exist; and that it can never be created by any revolution, however triumphant, if achieved by foreign arms; convinced, moreover, that every insurrection that looks abroad for assistance, must remain dependent upon the state of things abroad, and can therefore never be certain of victory;—Young Italy is determined that while it will ever be ready to profit by the favourable course of events abroad, it will neither allow the character of the insurrection nor the choice of the moment to be governed by them.

Young Italy is aware that revolutionary Europe awaits a signal, and that this signal may be given by Italy as well as by any other nation. It knows that the ground it proposes to tread is virgin soil; and the experiment untried. Foregone insurrections have relied upon the forces supplied by one class alone, and not upon the strength of the whole nation.

The one thing wanting to twenty millions of Italians, desirous of emancipating themselves, is not power, but *faith*.

Young Italy will endeavour to inspire this faith—first by its teachings, and afterwards by an energetic initiative.

Young Italy draws a distinction between the period of insurrection and that of revolution. The revolution begins as soon as the insurrection is triumphant.

Therefore, the period which may elapse between the first initiative and the complete liberation of the Italian soil, will be governed by a provisional dictatorial power, concentrated in the hands of a small number of men.

The soil once free, every authority will bow down before the National Council, the sole source of authority in the State.

Insurrection—by means of guerrilla bands—is the true method of warfare for all nations desirous of emancipating themselves from a foreign yoke. This method of warfare supplies the want—inevitable at the commencement of the insurrection—of a regular army; it calls the greatest number of elements into the field, and yet may be sustained by the smallest number. It forms the military education of the people, and consecrates every foot of the native soil by the memory of some warlike deed.

Guerrilla warfare opens a field of activity for every local capacity; forces the enemy into an unaccustomed method of battle; avoids the evil consequences of a great defeat; secures the national war from the risk of treason, and has the advantage of not confining it within any defined and determinate basis of operations. It is invincible, indestructible.

The regular army, recruited with all possible solicitude, and organized with all possible care, will complete the work begun by the war of insurrection.

All the members of Young Italy will exert themselves to diffuse these principles of insurrection . . .

Section 5.

All the members of Young Italy will pay into the treasury of the Society a monthly contribution of 50 *centimes*. Those whose position enables them to do so will bind themselves to pay a monthly contribution of a larger amount.

Section 6.

The colours of Young Italy are *white*, *red*, and *green*. The banner of Young Italy will display these colours, and bear on the one side the words—*Liberty, Equality, Humanity*; and on the other—*Unity, Independence* . . .

85. Constitutional Promises in Naples, 28 January 1848

The first revolution in Italy in 1848 broke out in January in Palermo, Sicily, where the Sicilians demanded separation from Naples. The insurrection soon spread to Naples itself, the most autocratically governed of the Italian States (cf. No. 83(b)), where a constitution was demanded. As the first among the Italian rulers, King Ferdinand II made promises of a constitution, the terms of which follow. The full constitution was granted in February.

Source: *Annual Register*, 1848, p. [334].

The legislative power shall be exercised by Us [the King] and by two Chambers—namely a Chamber of Peers and a Chamber of Deputies. The members of the first Chamber shall be nominated by Us; the deputies shall be nominated by electors on the basis of a property qualification which shall be fixed.

The only dominating religion of the State shall be the Roman Catholic and Apostolic religion, and no other form of worship shall be tolerated.

The person of the King shall always be sacred, inviolable, and not subject to responsibility.

The Ministers shall always be responsible for all the acts of the Government.

The land and sea services shall always be dependent on the King.

The national guard shall be organized in all the kingdom on a uniform mode, similar to that of the capital.

The press shall be free, and only subject to a repressive law for all that may offend religion, morality, public order, the King, the Royal Family, foreign Sovereigns and their families, as well as the honour and interests of private individuals.

86. *Constitutional Promises in Sardinia, 8 February 1848*

A few days after the King of Naples, the King of Sardinia, Charles Albert, also considered it necessary to promise a constitution to his people. The short document which follows sets out the principles on which the fundamental statute would be based; the statute itself was granted on 4 March 1848, and, unlike other Italian constitutions of this period, continued in force even after unification.

Source: *Annual Register*, 1848, pp. [317–18].

[We,] Charles Albert, by the grace of God King of Sardinia . . . have resolved and determined to adopt the following bases of a fundamental statute for the establishment in our States of a complete system of representative Government.

1. The Catholic, Apostolic, and Roman religion is the sole religion of the state. The other forms of public worship at present existing are tolerated in conformity with the law.

2. The person of the Sovereign is sacred and inviolable. His ministers are responsible.

3. To the King alone appertains the executive power. He is the supreme head of the State. He commands all the forces, both naval and military; declares war, concludes treaties of peace, alliance and commerce; nominates to all offices and gives all the necessary orders for the execution of the laws without suspending or dispensing with the observance thereof.

4. The King alone sanctions and promulgates the laws.

5. All justice emanates from the King, and is administered in his name. He may grant mercy and commute punishment.

6. The legislative power will be collectively exercised by the King and by two Chambers.

7. The first of these Chambers will be composed of Members nominated by the King for life; the second will be elective, on the basis of the census to be determined.

8. The proposal of laws will appertain to the King and to each of the Chambers, but with the distinct understanding that all laws imposing taxes must originate in the elective Chamber.

9. The King convokes the two Chambers annually, prorogues their sessions, and may dissolve the elective one; but in this case he will convoke a new assembly at the expiration of four months.

10. No tax may be imposed or levied if not assented to by the Chambers and sanctioned by the King.

11. The press will be free, but subject to repressive laws.

12. Individual liberty will be guaranteed.

13. The judges . . . will be irremovable, after having exercised their functions for a certain space of time, to be hereafter determined.

14. We reserve to ourselves the power of establishing a district militia, composed of persons who may pay a rate, which will be fixed upon hereafter. This militia will be placed under the command of the administrative authority, and in dependence on the Minister of the Interior. The King will have the power of suspending or dissolving it in places where he may deem it opportune so to do.

87. *Fundamental Statute for the Temporal Government of the States of the Church, 14 March 1848*

Until 1846, the accession of Pius IX to the papacy, the States of the Church were among the most backward of the Peninsula. Pius soon made some alterations in the existing system, of government purely by the church hierarchy, and, in March 1848, at a time when he was still being acclaimed as the 'liberal pope', he granted a constitution to his States. The preamble to this document, and some of its general provisions, give a good indication of its content.

Source: *British and Foreign State Papers*, vol. xxxvi (1847–58), pp. 879–81.

In the institutions we [the Pope] have hitherto bestowed on our subjects it has been our intention to reproduce certain ancient institutions which were for a long time a mirror of the wisdom of our august predecessors, and which, as the age advanced, it was desired should be adapted to altered circumstances . . .

Proceeding in this course we had come to the resolution of establishing a consultive representation of all the provinces, whose duty it should be to assist our Government in legislative labours and the administration of the State; and we expected that the advantages of the results would have justified the experiment which we had been first to make in Italy. But since our neighbours have deemed their people already mature for receiving the benefits of a representation not merely consultive, but deliberative; we do not desire to hold our people in less esteem or confide less in their gratitude,—not merely towards our humble person, for which we take no heed, but towards the Church and this Apostolic See, the inviolable and supreme rights of which God has committed to our keeping, and the presence of which has been, and ever will be, a source of so much good to this people. Our communes had anciently the privilege each of governing itself by laws chosen by its own act under the sovereign sanction. An order of things by which the diversity of laws and customs often separated one commune from concert with others, would not certainly be permitted to be renewed, under the same forms, by the present state of civilization. But we intend to intrust this prerogative to two councils of upright and prudent citizens in the one nominated by ourselves, in the other deputed by every part of the State through means of a form of election to be opportunely established; which may both represent the individual interests of every place in our dominions, and wisely reconcile them with that highest interest of every commune and every province, that is the general interest of the State.

As, however, the more grave interests of the political independence of the Head of the Church, by which the independence of this portion of Italy has indeed been preserved, cannot be separated from the temporal interests of its internal prosperity; we not only reserve to ourselves and our successors the supreme sanction and promulgation of all the laws that the above-named Councils shall have deliberated on, and the full exercise of the sovereign authority in the provinces not regarded by this Act; but we likewise intend to maintain entire our authority in matters naturally connected with the Catholic religion and morals; and to this we are bound, out of regard to the security of all Christendom, that in the States of the Church, thus constituted under a new form, the liberties and rights of the same Church and of the Holy See may never suffer diminution, nor any example be given of violating the sanctity of that religion which we have received the mission and obligation to preach to all the universe as the sole symbol of the alliance of Deity with mankind, as the sole pledge of that celestial benediction by which states exist and nations prosper.

Having in the meantime implored the Divine aid, and listened to the unanimous opinion of our venerable brethren the Cardinals of the Holy Roman Church, for this object united expressly in Consistory, we have decreed and do decree as follows:

General Dispositions.

1. The Sacred College of Cardinals, the electors of the Supreme Pontiff, forms a Senate inseparable from him.
2. Two deliberative Councils are instituted for the formation of laws—the High Council and the Council of Deputies.
3. Although all justice emanates from the Sovereign and is administered in his name, the judicial order is independent in the application of the laws to individual cases, the right of pardon being always reserved to the Sovereign himself. The

judges of the collegiate tribunals are irremovable after having exercised their functions for three years, dating from the promulgation of the present Statute.

4. No extraordinary tribunals or commissions can be instituted. Everyone, whether in civil or criminal matters, shall be judged by the tribunal expressly determined by law; before which all are equal.

5. The Civic Guard is to be considered as a State institution . . .

6. No restriction can be placed upon personal liberty except in the cases and according to the forms prescribed by law. Hence no one can be arrested unless in virtue of an act emanating from the competent authority . . .

7. The public debt and all other State obligations are guaranteed.

8. All property, whether of private individuals, of corporate bodies, or any pious or public institutions, contributes equally and without distinction to the State burdens, whoever may be its possessor . . .

9. In like manner the right of property is inviolable in all, with the sole exception of expropriations demanded by public utility, and compensated at a legal valuation.

10. Literary property is also recognized.

11. The existing government or political preventive censure for the press is abolished, and repressive measures, to be determined by a special law, will be substituted for it. No innovation is made in the Ecclesiastical Censure . . .

13. The Communal and Provincial Administration will be exercised by citizens and regulated by appropriate laws . . .

Of the Ministers

53. The governmental authority provides by ordinances and regulations for the execution of the laws.

54. The laws and all acts of Government . . . are signed by the respective Ministers, who are responsible for them . . .

88. *Rising in the Austrian provinces, March 1848*

The revolutionary movement soon extended to the provinces of Austria. The population of Milan rose, temporarily expelled the

Austrian troops, formulated an immediate programme (a) and, in a proclamation, asked for assistance by all Italy (b). Venice soon followed suit and established a provisional government, which declared its will to co-operate with the Milanese (c).

Source: *Annual Register*, 1848, pp. 319–21.

(a) Demands of the Milanese, 17 March 1848.

1. The suppression of the old police, and the establishment of a new corps, under the orders of the Municipality.
2. The abolition of the laws regarding state offences, and the immediate liberation of the political prisoners.
3. A provisional regency of the kingdom.
4. Liberty of the press.
5. The convocation of the district councils for the purpose of electing a National Assembly.
6. The institution of a Civic Guard under the orders of the Municipality.

(b) Proclamation to all Italians by the Provisional Government at Milan, 23 March 1848.

Fellow Citizens,—

We have conquered. We have compelled the enemy to fly, oppressed by his own shame as much as by our valour, but scattered in our fields—wandering like wild beasts—united in bands of plunderers, he prolongs for us all the horrors of war without affording any of its sublime emotions. This makes it easily to be understood that the arms we have taken up—that we still hold—can never be laid down as long as one of his band shall be hid under the cover of the Alps. We have sworn, we swear it again, with the generous Prince[1] who flies with the common impulse to associate himself with our glory—all Italy swears it, and so it shall be!

To arms then, to arms, to secure the fruits of our glorious revolution—to fight the last battle of independence and the Italian Union.

A moveable army shall be at once organized. Theodore Lechi is named General-in-Chief of all the forces of the Provisional Government. A soldier of long standing in the old army of Italy,

---

[1] King Charles Albert of Sardinia.

he will join the glorious traditions of the Napoleon military epoch to the new honours which the Italian army now prepares in the great war of liberty.

(c) Proclamation of the Provisional Government of Venice, 26 March 1848.

We hailed with infinite joy the account of the emancipation of our generous sister of Lombardy.

On the very day when you shook off the Austrian yoke, a Provisional Government of the Venetian Republic was proclaimed here, under the glorious banner of St. Mark.[1]

We are influenced by no local prejudice—we are, above all, Italians, and the insignia of St. Mark figures on the tricoloured banner.

We are united to you, Lombards, not only by the tie of affection, but also by a community of misfortunes and hopes.

When the hallowed soil of the country shall have ceased to be sullied by the feet of the foreign oppressor, we shall join you in discussing the form of government most conducive to our common glory.

89. *Proclamation of the Roman Republic, 8 February 1849*

In the first months of 1849, only three attempts can still be seen against the re-establishment of the *status quo ante*, all the rest having been defeated. These are the unlucky renewal of the war against Austria by Sardinia, quickly defeated; the resistance of the Venetian republic, which held out until August 1849; and the popular movement at Rome, whence the Pope had to flee. Led by Mazzini, the Roman movement attempted to establish a democratic state, a focus for the establishment of a republic embracing all Italy.

Source: *Annual Register*, 1849, pp. 293–4.

1. Papacy has fallen, *de facto* and *de jure*,[2] from the temporal throne of the Roman State.
2. The Roman Pontiff shall enjoy all the guarantees necessary for the exercise of his spiritual power.
3. The Government of the Roman State is to be a pure democracy, and to assume the glorious name of the Roman Republic.

---

[1] Patron saint of Venice.
[2] In fact and in law.

4. The Roman Republic shall maintain with the rest of Italy relations required by a common nationality.

90. *Cavour at the Congress of Paris, 1856*

The Congress of Paris was called to settle the affairs of Europe upon the conclusion of the Crimean war (cf. No. 93, 94). Having participated in the war on the side of the allies, Sardinia was invited to participate, and Cavour used the occasion to bring the state of Italy, particularly the evils resulting from continued Austrian influence, to the notice of the Powers in a note, part of which follows (a). In spite of the opposition of Austria the matter was discussed and France and Great Britain expressed their sympathy, although neither undertook any obligations. In a speech to the Sardinian Chamber of Deputies, extracts of which follow (b), Cavour summed up the results of the Congress as far as Italy was concerned.

Source: (a) *Annual Register*, 1856, pp. [230–2].
      (b) A. J. Whyte, *The Political Life and Letters of Cavour* (Oxford, Clarendon Press, 1930), pp. 222–3.

(a) Sardinian Note to the Powers, 16 April 1856.

[The Sardinian government regrets that the Congress, in its deliberations, did not concern itself with the affairs of Italy, although the continued repression and reaction, originally set in after 1848 in the Austrian-occupied provinces, and in the States influenced by Austria, render the situation in Italy very unstable and dangerous. The extension of Austrian influence is to be feared, particularly as it would encourage revolutionary activity all over the Peninsula. Particular dangers and events are discussed in some detail.]

The facts that the undersigned have exposed suffice to make appreciated the dangers of the position in which the Government of the King of Sardinia finds itself placed. Disturbed within by the action of revolutionary passions, excited all round by a system of violent repression and by the foreign occupation, threatened by the extension of Austrian power, it may at any moment be forced by an inevitable necessity to adopt extreme measures of which it is impossible to calculate the consequences.

The undersigned do not doubt but that such a state of things will excite the solicitude of the Governments of France and England, not only on account of the sincere friendship and real sympathy that these Powers profess for the Sovereign who alone, among all, at the moment when their success was most uncertain, declared himself openly in their favour[1] but, above all, because it constitutes a real danger for Europe.

Sardinia is the only State in Italy that has been able to raise an impassable barrier to the revolutionary spirit, and at the same time remain independent of Austria. It is the counterpoise to her invading influence.

If Sardinia succumbed, exhausted of power, abandoned by her Allies,—if she also was obliged to submit to Austrian domination, then the conquest of Italy by this Power would be achieved; and Austria, after having obtained without it costing her the least sacrifice, the immense benefit of the free navigation of the Danube and the neutralization of the Black Sea,[2] would acquire a preponderating influence in the West.

This is what France and England would never wish: this they will never permit.

Moreover, the undersigned are convinced that the Cabinets of Paris and London, taking into serious consideration the state of Italy, will decide, in concert with Sardinia, on the means for applying an efficacious remedy.

(b) Cavour's Report to the Chamber of Deputies, 7 May 1856.

. . . The great solutions are not carried into effect with the pen. Diplomacy is powerless to change the condition of a nation. At most, it can but sanction completed facts and give them legal form. What benefit then has Italy obtained from the Congress? We have gained two things, first, that the anomalous and unhappy condition of Italy has been proclaimed to Europe, not by demagogues, or revolutionaries, excited journalists, or party men, but by representatives of the greatest nations in Europe; by distinguished men accustomed to consult the dictates of reason rather than the impulse of emotion. That is the first fact, which I consider of the greatest value. The second is that these same powers have declared that, not only in the interests of Italy herself, but in the interests of Europe, a remedy must be found for the evils from which Italy is suffering. I cannot believe

[1] This refers to Sardinian participation in the Crimean war.
[2] Austria, although neutral in the Crimean war, benefited from the settlement.

that the sentiments expressed and the advice given by such nations as France and England can remain for long sterile of results . . .

As a result of the policy pursued these last few years we have taken a great step forward and discussed before a European Congress, not as at Laibach and Verona (cf. Nos 8 and 9) with a view to aggravating the evils of Italy and riveting more tightly her chains, but with the manifest intention of bringing some remedy to her wounds and of expressing strongly the sympathy felt for her by the Great Powers. The Congress over, the cause of Italy is now carried before the bar of public opinion; before that tribunal which, in the memorable words of the French Emperor, must deliver the final verdict and proclaim the ultimate victory. The struggle may be long, the fluctuations of fortune, perchance, many; but we, trusting in the righteousness of our cause, await with confidence the final issue.

91. *The Armistice of Villafranca, 11 July 1859*

The sympathy of Napoleon III towards the Italian cause increased in the late 1850s and when, in 1859, war broke out between Austria and Sardinia he intervened with overwhelming force on the side of the latter. Austria was decisively defeated in a short war, and Italians began to hope for the unification of at least Northern Italy as a result, when Napoleon III, without consulting Sardinia, concluded an armistice at Villafranca for reasons of his own. According to the terms, elaborated but not changed by the treaties of Zürich of November 1859, Lombardy was ceded to France, to be passed on to Sardinia, and an Italian confederation was accepted in principle. This confederation never came into being, but the Central Italian States, in spite of opposition from the Powers, decided to join Sardinia; thus a Kingdom of Italy, incorporating all but the Papal States, Naples, and Venetia, came into being.

Source: *Annual Register*, 1859, p. 224.

Between His Majesty the Emperor of Austria and His Majesty the Emperor of the French it has been agreed as follows:—

The two Sovereigns favour the creation of an Italian Confederation. This Confederation shall be under the honorary presidency of the Holy Father.

The Emperor of Austria cedes to the Emperor of the French his rights over Lombardy, with the exception of the fortresses of Mantua and Peschiera.

The Emperor of the French shall present the ceded territory
to the King of Sardinia.

Venetia shall form part of the Italian Confederation, remaining, however, subject to the Crown of the Emperor of Austria.

The Grand Duke of Tuscany and the Duke of Modena return
to their states, granting a general amnesty.

The two emperors shall request the Holy Father to introduce
in his States some indispensable reforms.

Full and complete amnesty is granted on both sides to persons
compromised on the occasion of the recent events in the territories of the belligerents.

92. *Proclamation of Garibaldi to the Italians, April 1860*

Early in 1860 Garibaldi and his volunteers, with the connivance
of some members of the Sardinian government, landed in Sicily to
overthrow the Neapolitan government and thus bring about the
incorporation of the kingdom in the united Italy. With great popular
support Garibaldi achieved great success; the whole of the territory
of Naples soon came under his control and only on reaching the
border of the Papal States was he stopped by Sardinian troops who
had, by then, occupied most of the States of the Church. Naples
and Sicily were then offered by Garibaldi to King Victor Emmanuel
and became part of the Kingdom of Italy.

The proclamation that follows sets out Garibaldi's aim clearly.

Source: *Annual Register*, 1860, pp. 281–2.

Italians!

The Sicilians are fighting against the enemies of Italy, and for
Italy. It is the duty of every Italian to succour them with words,
money, and arms, and, above all, in person.

The misfortunes of Italy arise from the indifference of one
province to the fate of the others. The redemption of Italy began
from the moment that men of the same land ran to help their
distressed brothers. Left to themselves the Sicilians will have to
fight not only the mercenaries of the Bourbon, but also of
Austria and the Priest of Rome.

Let the inhabitants of the free provinces lift their voices on
behalf of their struggling brethren, and impel their brave youth
to the conflict. Let the Marches, Umbria, Sabina, Rome, the
Neapolitan, rise to divide the forces of our enemies.

Where the cities suffice not for the insurrection, let them send bands of their bravest into the country. The brave man finds an arm everywhere. Listen not to the voice of cowards, but arm, and let us fight for our brethren, who will fight for us tomorrow.

A band of those who fought with me the country's battles marches with me to the fight. Good and generous, they will fight for their country to the last drop of their blood, nor ask for other reward than a clear conscience.

'Italy and Victor Emmanuel!' they cried, on passing the Ticino. 'Italy and Victor Emmanuel!' shall re-echo in the blazing caves of Mongibello.

At this cry, thundering from the great rock of Italy to the Tarpeian, the rotten Throne of tyranny shall crumble, and, as one man, the brave descendants of Vespro shall rise.

To arms! Let us put an end, once for all, to the miseries of so many centuries. Prove to the world that it is no lie that Roman generations inhabited this land.

IX · INTERNATIONAL AFFAIRS
1849–1914

THE main feature of this period in international affairs is the breakup of the system established at the Congress of Vienna, first by the Crimean War, and then by the rise of Germany as a great Power. On the first point, the British ministerial declaration on the reasons of the war (No. 93) and the Treaty of Paris, with the Straits Convention (No. 94) are included.

The rise of Prussia has already been illustrated by some documents in Section VI (Nos. 66–69, 71). In the present section documents on the outbreak of the Franco-Prussian War (No. 96) are followed by the preliminary peace treaty (No. 97) between France and the newly constituted German Empire.

After the establishment of the Empire Bismarck and his system of alliances dominated international relations between the Powers, and the most important of the alliances follow: the Austro–German alliance of 1879 (No. 100), the League of the Three Emperors of 1881 (No. 101), the Triple Alliance of 1882 (No. 102), and the Reinsurance Treaty of 1887 (No. 103). Yet it seems to have been largely Bismarck's personality which was responsible for the success in keeping together such conflicting interests as those of Austria–Hungary and Russia; after his resignation in 1890 (cf. No. 135) Russia was quickly alienated and concluded an alliance with France (No. 104). The threat from an expansive German policy also brought together Great Britain and France in 1904 (No. 106) and Great Britain and Russia in 1907.

Bismarck in convoking and presiding over the Congress of Berlin in 1878 (No. 99) was largely responsible for bringing about an at least temporary settlement of the differences between the Powers in the Near East. After his dismissal, however, German foreign policy became much more aggressive, concerned with gaining advantages and prestige for Germany overseas, particularly in North Africa. The Emperor's speech at Tangier in 1905 (No. 107) and the international conference on the affairs of Morocco at Algeciras in 1906 (No. 108) which resulted in a setback for Germany, illustrate the process, while the interview with William II published in the *Daily Telegraph* (No. 110) show how Germany and Great Britain were being alienated.

Two more lines of development are illustrated in this section. The first shows intergovernmental co-operation in alleviating the effects of war. The Geneva Conventions of 1864 (No. 95) and 1868, negotiated on Swiss initiative, were mainly concerned with improving the condition of the wounded, while the Hague Conferences of 1899 and 1907, though unsuccessful in their main aim of negotiating a limitation to armaments, were successful in agreeing on a series of conventions (No. 105) which regulated the conduct of war and attempted to settle international disputes peacefully.

The other line of development to be illustrated is the growth of the international workers' movement. The General Rules of the International Working Men's Association (founded by Marx and known as the First International) (No. 98) are the statutes of the first international body of workers. The Second International, founded in 1889, lasted much longer than the first and passed quite a number of important resolutions at its Congresses; from these, the 1907 Stuttgart resolutions on militarism and international conflict (No. 109) have been selected for inclusion.

93. *Lord John Russell's Speech on the Outbreak of the Crimean War, 31 March 1854*

The dispute in the Near East which evolved between Turkey, Russia, and France was over comparatively trivial matters, but the underlying principles (cf. No. 12) were important ones. In his speech, excerpts of which follow, Lord John Russell, who as Minister without Portfolio represented the Foreign Secretary, the Earl of Clarendon, in the House of Commons, expounded the underlying issues and explained why the war, which signified the end of the Vienna system, was necessary.

Source: *Hansard's Parliamentary Debates*, 3rd Series, vol. 132, col. 198–217.

. . . For the period of nearly forty years this country has been in the enjoyment of the blessings of peace, and those blessings have never been more widely nor more extensively valued . . . it is impossible to think of war without reflecting at the same time of the bloodshed that it occasions, of the prosperity that it interrupts, and of the misery that it inflicts. It is therefore . . . only from a paramount sense of necessity that we should engage in this war that I appear here to advise this House . . . In performing this task . . . I shall endeavour . . . to point to the course which Russia has pursued, and to show that, unless we are content to submit to the further aggrandizement of that Power, and, possibly, to the destruction of Turkey—whose integrity and independence have been so often declared essential to the stability of the system of Europe—we have no choice left us but to interpose by arms . . .

I will now proceed to state . . . the great outline of what has occurred . . . In treating of this subject I shall keep wholly out of view the dispute which has furnished, not the cause, but a pretext for the interference of the Emperor of Russia . . . the question of the Holy Places. I will not touch upon the silver star, or the key of the great gate, or the key of the little gate, or any of those questions which were put forward as subjects of discussion. All these matters of dispute, whether they deserved the contention that took place about them or not, were settled by the agreement of all the Powers concerned. What I have to treat of are other questions and other demands. Now . . . in referring to the relations between Russia and Turkey, we must always keep in view that the Empress Catherine,[1] after a successful war, obtained from the Sultan an article which I will read to the House with respect to the Christians generally residing in the Sultan's dominions . . . The seventh article of the Treaty of Kainardji runs thus:—'The Sublime Porte promises to protect constantly the Christian religion and its churches, and it also allows the Ministers of the Imperial Court of Russia to make, upon all occasions, representations as well in favour of the new church at Constantinople, . . . as on behalf of its officiating ministers . . .'

The House will perceive at once . . . that there is an assurance that the Porte will protect the Christian religion of its subjects.

[1] 1762-96.

And if there had been any persecution of that religion . . . the Emperor of Russia might justly have complained of the infraction of the treaty. But there is another thing likewise very obvious—namely, that there is . . . no interference stipulated for with the ordinary administration of the affairs of the Sultan in his own dominions . . .

Coming to the events which took place last year, the House will have perceived that no sooner was the question of the Holy Places settled than further demands, which had already been put forward, were insisted upon by the Ambassador of Russia. In the first place, according to rumour, these demands had taken the shape of a treaty offensive and defensive. They afterwards took the shape of a convention. After this there was a formal document requiring the Sultan to give certain pledges to Russia. Again, a note was insisted upon, but a note which was to be an agreement with Russia, a stipulation with Russia that the privileges and immunities which the Christians held in the Turkish empire should be enjoyed for the future without molestation . . . Prince Menchikoff ended with a demand for certain privileges and immunities for the Christians residing in Turkey . . .

The Minister of the Sultan declared that the Porte had already come to a decision and that that decision was adverse to the demands of Russia put forward by Prince Menchikoff. Prince Menchikoff having . . . pronounced threats of the calamities that would follow the rejection of his terms . . . proceeded with great state and ceremony to leave Constantinople and returned to the Russian territory . . .

When the intelligence arrived at St. Petersburg that the last demands of Prince Menchikoff had been refused, it was decided there that a message should be sent, conveying a letter of Count Nesselrode's, demanding, in the most peremptory terms, that Prince Menchikoff's note should be signed within eight days, and announcing that, in default of such signature, the Principalities,[1] part of the Sultan's territories, would be occupied by Russian troops. It was quite impossible for the Sultan, with any regard to his honour, to assent to such terms; and the menaced invasion by Russian troops immediately took place . . .

The Sultan offered, by the advice of his Ministers, fresh

[1] Of Moldavia and Wallachia, which later formed Romania.

terms of peace. These terms arrived at a moment when a note had been agreed upon by the representatives of the four Powers at Vienna, and therefore the Sultan's terms were set aside, and the other proposals were transmitted to Constantinople. The Sultan agreed to those proposals, with some modifications ... The Vienna note, as modified by the Porte ... conceded to the Emperor every security he could have wished as to the privileges and immunities of the Christian subjects of the Porte ...

The Russian proposal, on the contrary, was, not for increasing the immunities and privileges of the Christian subjects of the Porte ... but that all those privileges and immunities should be confirmed by a special treaty with Russia, and thereby the Russian Minister would have had the power, on every question of spiritual, nay, on every question of civil privilege, of interfering between the Sultan and 12,000,000 of his subjects ... The question was, whether the sovereignty of these 12,000,000 of people should be transferred from their own sovereign, the Sultan, to a foreign sovereign who possessed an overwhelming force ...

[Upon the invasion of the principalities the Sultan declared war on Russia. Even after the declaration of war, however, the four power conference at Vienna continued to mediate, though its proposals were rejected by Russia. France and Great Britain then sent a note demanding that the Russians evacuate the principalities within a certain number of days.]

The Emperor of Russia ... has declined to give any answer to that proposal and it remained for Her Majesty and the Emperor of the French to consider if any other step, and what, remained. They considered that no other course but war did remain ... They considered that the safety of Europe depended upon the maintenance of the equilibrium of which the integrity and independence of Turkey form a part. They considered that it would be impossible to hope to maintain that integrity and independence if Russia was allowed unchecked and uninterrupted to impose her own terms upon Turkey. It was therefore decided by Her Majesty's Government ... to issue a declaration of war. That declaration of war has been issued. We can none of us be insensible to the gravity and importance of such a declaration—we should all have been glad to have avoided it;

but I hold that, consistently with our position—consistently with our duties to Europe—consistently even with the general interests of this country, we cannot permit the aggrandizement of Russia to take any shape that her arms might enable it to assume . . .

94. *The Congress of Paris, 1856*

After the defeat of Russia in the Crimean war, the Powers met in congress at Paris to settle the terms of the peace. The terms of the Treaty of Paris (a) were a humiliation for Russia, while the Ottoman Empire was assured of support. An effort was made to eliminate future conflict by making the principalities of Moldavia and Wallachia independent and by prohibiting the maintenance of warships in the Black Sea. The Straits Convention (b), signed on the same day, again agreed to the closing of the Straits to ships of war in times of peace (cf. No. 12(a), Article 4).

Source: E. Hertslet, *The Map of Europe by Treaty* (London, Butter-worth, 1875), vol. ii, pp. 1250–64 (a); 1266–8 (b).

(a) General Treaty of Peace . . . Paris, 30 March 1856.

1. From the day of the exchange of the ratifications of the present treaty there shall be peace and friendship between Her Majesty the Queen of the United Kingdom . . ., the Emperor of the French, . . . the King of Sardinia, . . . the Sultan, on the one part, and . . . the Emperor of All the Russias, on the other part . . .

7. [The Contracting Parties] declare the Sublime Porte admitted to participate in the advantages of the public law and system (*Concert*) of Europe. Their Majesties engage, each on his part, to respect the independence and the territorial integrity of the Ottoman Empire; guarantee in common the strict observance of that engagement; and will, in consequence, consider any act tending to its violation as a question of general interest . . .

8. [The Powers undertake to mediate should any dispute arise with Turkey.]

9. . . . The Sultan having . . . issued a Firman[1] which . . . records his generous intentions towards the Christian population of his Empire . . . has resolved to communicate [it] to the Contracting Parties . . .

[1] Decree.

The Contracting Powers recognize the high value of this communication. It is clearly understood that it cannot, in any case, give to the said Powers the right to interfere, either collectively or separately, in the relations of . . . the Sultan with his subjects, nor in the internal administration of his empire.

10. The Convention of 13 July 1841,[1] which maintains the ancient rule of the Ottoman Empire relative to the closing of the Straits of the Bosphorus and of Dardanelles, has been revised by common consent (No. 94(b)) . . .

11. The Black Sea is neutralized; its water and its ports, thrown open to the mercantile marine of every nation, are formally and in perpetuity interdicted to the flag of war, either of the powers possessing its coasts, or of any power . . .

22. The Principalities of Wallachia and Moldavia shall continue to enjoy under suzerainty of the Porte, and under the Guarantee of the Contracting Powers, the Privileges and Immunities of which they are in possession . . . There shall be no separate right of interference in their internal affairs.

23. The Sublime Porte engages to preserve to the said Principalities an independent and national administration as well as full liberty of worship, of legislation, of commerce, and of navigation . . .

(b) The Straits Convention, 30 March 1856.

1. His Majesty the Sultan, on the one part, declares that he is firmly resolved to maintain for the future the principle invariably established as the ancient rule of his empire, and in virtue of which it has, at all times, been prohibited for the ships of war of foreign powers to enter the Straits of the Dardanelles and of the Bosphorus; and that, so long as the Porte is at peace, His Majesty will admit no foreign ship of war into the said straits.

And Their Majesties the Queen of the United Kingdom . . ., the Emperor of Austria, the Emperor of the French, the King of Prussia, the Emperor of All the Russias, and the King of Sardinia, on the other part, engage to respect this determination of the Sultan, and to conform themselves to the principle above declared.

[1] Cf. No. 12(a), Article 4, note.

2. The Sultan reserves to himself, as in past times, to deliver firmans of passage for light vessels under flag of war, which shall be employed as is usual in the service of the missions of foreign powers.

3. The same exception applies to the light vessels under flag of war which each of the contracting powers is authorised to station at the mouths of the Danube . . .

95. *Convention for the Amelioration of the Condition of the Wounded in Times of War* [*Geneva Convention*], *22 August 1864*

The war of 1859, between France, Sardinia, and Austria, brought to the attention of the world the great suffering wounded have to undergo in modern large scale war. To help in alleviating their suffering, the International Red Cross Society was founded on private initiative, but the Swiss government also initiated an international conference to negotiate internationally accepted rules for dealing with wounded in land warfare. The most important provisions of the Convention incorporating these rules follows. A further convention, which established rules applicable to naval warfare, was signed on 20 October 1868.

Source: E. Hertslet, *The Map of Europe by Treaty* (London, Butterworth, 1875), vol. iii, pp. 1621–26.

1. Ambulances and military hospitals shall be acknowledged to be neuter [*sic*], and, as such, shall be protected and respected by belligerents so long as any sick or wounded may be therein. Such neutrality shall cease if the ambulances or hospitals should be held by a military force.

2. Persons employed in hospitals and ambulances, comprising the staff for superintendence, medical service, administration, transport of wounded, as well as chaplains, shall participate in the benefit of neutrality whilst so employed, and so long as there remain any wounded to bring in or succour.

3. The persons designated in the preceding article may, even after occupation by the enemy, continue to fulfil their duties in the hospital or ambulance which they serve, or may withdraw in order to rejoin the corps to which they belong . . .

6. Wounded or sick soldiers shall be entertained and taken care of, to whatever nation they may belong.

Commanders-in-chief shall have the power to deliver immediately to the outposts of the enemy soldiers who have been wounded in an engagement, when circumstances permit this to be done, and with the consent of both parties.

Those who are recognized, after their wounds are healed, as incapable of serving, shall be sent to their country.

The others may also be sent back, on condition of not again bearing arms during the continuance of the war . . .

7. A distinctive and uniform flag shall be adopted for hospitals, ambulances and evacuations. It must, on every occasion, be accompanied by the national flag. An arm-badge (*brassard*) shall also be allowed for individuals neutralized, but the delivery thereof shall be left to military authority.

The flag and the arm-badge shall bear a red cross on a white ground . . .

96. *The Outbreak of the Franco-Prussian War, July 1870*

One of the central documents of the outbreak of the war is the so-called 'Ems telegram', a despatch sent by Privy Councillor Abeken, from the Emperor's personal office, to Bismarck, and published by the latter in edited form. The text of the original telegram and of Bismarck's version follow in parallel columns (a). In addition, the official French announcement of the causes of the war (b) and the speech of the King of Prussia giving the Prussian view (c) are included.

Source: (a) C. G. Robertson, *Bismarck* (London, Constable, 1918), pp. 496–7.

(b) and (c) E. Hertslet, *The Map of Europe by Treaty* (London, Butterworth, 1875), vol. iii, pp. 1880–2.

(a) The 'Ems telegram', 13 July 1870.

The original text

His Majesty writes to me: 'Count Benedetti spoke to me on the promenade, in order to demand from me, finally in a very importunate manner, that I should authorize him to telegraph at

Bismarck's version

After the news of the renunciation of the hereditary Prince of Hohenzollern had been officially communicated to the Imperial Government of France by the Royal Government of Spain the French Ambassador further demanded of His Majesty, the King, at Ems, that he once that I bound myself for all future time never again to give my consent if the Hohenzollerns should renew their candidature. I refused at last somewhat sternly, as it is neither right nor possible to undertake engagements of this sort *à tout jamais*.[1] I told him that I had as yet received no news, and as he was earlier informed from Paris and Madrid than myself, he could see clearly that my government had no more interest in the matter.'

His Majesty has since received a letter from Prince Charles Anthony. His Majesty, having told Count Benedetti that he was awaiting news from the Prince, has decided, with reference to the above demand, on the suggestion of Count Eulenburg and myself, not to receive Count Benedetti again, but only to let him be informed through an aide-de-camp: 'That his Majesty has now received from the Prince confirmation of the news which Benedetti had already received from Paris, and had nothing further to say to the ambassador'. His Majesty leaves it to your Excellency to decide whether Benedetti's fresh demand and its

would authorize him to telegraph to Paris that His Majesty, the King, bound himself for all time never again to give his consent, should the Hohenzollerns renew their candidature.

His Majesty, the King, thereupon decided not to receive the French Ambassador again, and sent the aide-de-camp on duty to tell him that His Majesty had nothing further to communicate to the ambassador.

[1] For ever.

rejection should be at once
communicated to both our
ambassadors, to foreign
nations, and to the Press.

(b) French Announcement to the Prussian Government of the
     Causes of War with Prussia, 19 July 1870.

The Government of His Majesty the Emperor of the French,
being unable to consider the proposal to raise a Prussian
Prince to the Throne of Spain otherwise than as an attempt
against the territorial security of France, was compelled to ask
the King of Prussia for an assurance that such an arrangement
could not be carried out with his consent.

His Majesty the King of Prussia having refused to give this
assurance, and having, on the contrary, given the Ambassador
of His Majesty the Emperor of the French to understand that
he intended to reserve for this eventuality, and for every other,
the power of acting according to circumstances, the Imperial
Government could not but see in the King's declaration a
reservation threatening to France and to the general Balance
of Power in Europe. This declaration was further aggravated
by the notification made to the Cabinets of the refusal to receive
the Emperor's Ambassador and to enter into any new explanation with him.

The Government of His Imperial Majesty has consequently
thought itself obliged to provide immediately for the defence of
its honour and its compromised interests; and being resolved to
take for this purpose all the measures enjoined by the position
in which it has been placed, considers itself from henceforth in
a state of war with Prussia.

(c) Part of the Speech of the King of Prussia at the opening of
     the North German Reichstag, 19 July 1870.

... The candidature of a German Prince to the Spanish
Throne [with the] proposal and withdrawal of whom the Confederation Governments were equally strangers, and was only
so far of interest to the North German Confederation, that the
Government of that friendly nation seemed to build upon it the
hope of finding therein the guarantee for the orderly and peace-

ful Government of a country which had undergone many trials, has afforded a pretext to the Government of the Emperor of the French to put forward the *casus belli* in a manner long unknown in diplomatic intercourse, and in spite of the removal of this pretext, to adhere to it with that disregard of the rights of the people to the blessings of Peace, of which history furnishes analogous examples in the case of former rulers of France.

If Germany in past centuries has silently borne with such outrages upon her rights and honour, she did so because in her disunion she knew not how strong she was. To-day, when the bands of intellectual and just unity, which the Wars of Freedom began to draw together, binds the German races indeed closer, and therefore, more intimately: to-day, when the armaments of Germany no longer leave an opening to the enemy, Germany possesses in herself the will and the power to repulse renewed acts of French violence . . .

The German, as well as the French people, both of them equally enjoying and desiring the blessings of Christian civilization and increasing prosperity, should be destined to a more holy contest than the bloody one of arms. Yet the Governing Power of France have known how to work on the well-balanced but susceptible feelings of our great neighbouring people by calculated misrepresentation for personal interests and passions.

The more Confederated Governments have felt that they have done all which honour and dignity permit to maintain for Europe the blessings of Peace; and the clearer it appears to all eyes that the sword has been forced into our hand, with greater confidence we turn, supported by the unanimous will of the German Governments of the South, as well as of the North, to the love of the Fatherland and willingness for sacrifice of the German people to the summons to protect her honour and independence.

We will, after the examples of our Father, do battle for our freedom and our right against violence of a foreign conqueror; and in this struggle, in which we have no good but the attainment of lasting Peace for Europe, God will be with us as He was with our Fathers.

97. Preliminary Treaty of Peace between France and Germany, Versailles, 26 February 1871

After the defeat of France and the abdication of Napoleon III the new French Government negotiated a preliminary peace treaty with the German Empire (as it was by this time, cf. No. 130). The most important provisions of the preliminary peace treaty follow. The definitive treaty of peace, signed at Frankfurt on 10 May 1871, made some slight alterations in the territorial settlement, but otherwise differs only in containing more detail.

Source: E. Hertslet, *The Map of Europe by Treaty* (London, Butterworth, 1875), vol. iii, pp. 1912–17.

1. France renounces in favour of the German Empire all her rights and titles over the territories situated on the East of the frontier hereafter described ... The German Empire shall possess these territories in perpetuity in all sovereignty and property ... The frontier, such as it has just been described, is marked in green on two identic copies of the map of the territory forming the Government of Alsace, ... a copy of which shall be annexed to both copies of the present treaty.

Nevertheless, the alteration of the above tracing has been agreed to by the two Contracting Parties. In the former Department of the Moselle, the villages of Marie-aux-Chênes ... and Vionville ... shall be ceded to Germany. In exchange thereof, France shall retain the town and fortifications of Belfort ...

2. France shall pay to His Majesty the Emperor of Germany the sum of 5 milliards francs. The payment of at least 1,000,000,000 (one milliard) francs shall be effected within the year 1871, and the whole of the remainder of the debt in the space of 3 years, dating from the ratification of the present treaty.

3. The evacuation of the French territory occupied by German troops shall begin after the ratification of the present treaty by the National Assembly sitting at Bordeaux. Immediately after that ratification, the German troops shall quit the interior of Paris, as well as the forts on the left bank of the Seine and within the shortest possible delay ... they shall entirely evacuate the Departments as far as the left bank of the Seine ... The garrison of Paris is excepted from this disposition, the number

of which shall not exceed 40,000 men, and the garrisons indispensably necessary for the safety of the strongholds.

The evacuation of the Departments between the right bank of the Seine and the eastern frontier by German troops shall take place gradually after the ratification of the Definitive Treaty of Peace and the payment of the first 500,000,000 (half milliard) of the contribution stipulated by Article 2 . . .

98. General Rules of the International Working Men's Association, 1871

The International Working Men's Association founded at a workers' congress at London in 1864, was the first large-scale international organization of the working class. It lasted officially until 1876, though after 1871 it had lost its effectiveness because of controversies between Marx and the anarchist wing.

The rules that follow were written by Marx and are based on his provisional rules accepted at the foundation congress in 1864. The definitive form was adopted at the Congress of 1871.

Source: K. Marx and F. Engels, *Selected Works in two volumes* (Moscow, 1951), vol. i, pp. 350–3.

CONSIDERING,

That the emancipation of the working classes must be conquered by the working classes themselves; that the struggle for the emancipation of the working classes means not a struggle for class privileges and monopolies, but for equal rights and duties, and the abolition of all class rule;

That the economical subjection of the man of labour to the monopolizer of the means of labour, that is, the sources of life, lies at the bottom of servitude in all its forms, of all social misery, mental degradation and political dependence;

That the economical emancipation of the working classes is therefore the great end to which every political movement ought to be subordinate as a means;

That all efforts aiming at that great end have hitherto failed from the want of solidarity between the manifold divisions of labour in each country, and from the absence of a fraternal bond of union between the working classes of different countries;

That the emancipation of labour is neither a local nor a

national, but a social problem, embracing all countries in which modern society exists, and depending for its solution on the concurrence, practical and theoretical, of the most advanced countries;

That the present revival of the working classes in the most industrious countries of Europe, while it raises a new hope, gives solemn warning against a relapse into the old errors, and calls for the immediate combination of the still disconnected movements;

For These Reasons—

The International Working Men's Association has been founded.

It declares:

That all societies and individuals adhering to it will acknowledge truth, justice and morality as the basis of their conduct towards each other and towards all men, without regard to colour, creed, or nationality;

That it acknowledges *no rights without duties, no duties without rights*;

And in this spirit the following rules have been drawn up.

1. This Association is established to afford a central medium of communication and co-operation between Working Men's Societies existing in different countries and aiming at the same end; *viz.*, the protection, advancement, and complete emancipation of the working classes.

2. The name of the Society shall be 'The International Working Men's Association'.

3. There shall annually meet a General Working Men's Congress, consisting of delegates of the branches of the Association. The Congress will have to proclaim the common aspirations of the working class, take the measures required for the successful working of the International Association, and appoint the General Council of the Society.

4. Each Congress appoints the time and place of meeting for the next Congress ... The Congress appoints the seat and elects the members of the General Council annually ...

5. The General Council shall consist of working men from the different countries represented in the International Association ...

6. The General Council shall form an international agency between the different national and local groups of the Association, so that the working men in one country be constantly informed of the movements of their class in every other country; that an inquiry into the social state of the different countries of Europe be made simultaneously, and under a common direction; that the questions of general interest mooted in one society be ventilated by all; and that when immediate practical steps should be needed—as, for instance, in case of international quarrels—the action of the associated societies be simultaneous and uniform. Whenever it seems opportune, the General Council shall take the initiative of proposals to be laid before the different national or local societies. To facilitate the communications, the General Council shall publish periodical reports.

7. . . . The members of the International Association shall use their utmost efforts to combine the disconnected working men's societies of their respective countries into national bodies, represented by central national organs . . .

9. Everybody who acknowledges and defends the principles of the International Working Men's Association is eligible to become a member. Every branch is responsible for the integrity of the members it admits . . .

11. While united in a perpetual bond of fraternal co-operation, the working men's societies joining the International Association will preserve their existing organizations intact . . .

99. *The Treaty of Berlin, 13 July 1878*

In the mid-1870s, after risings in Bosnia and Bulgaria, the Eastern question assumed crisis proportions once more. The Powers met in conference at Constantinople to reform the Ottoman Empire. The Turks evaded the proposals of the Powers, and Russia retaliated with an armed attack, in which, although initial successes were gained, she could not attain a decisive victory, while Great Britain was ready to threaten war in support of the Turks. Russia concluded the Peace of San Stefano with Turkey in March 1878, in which the two countries agreed on the establishment of a Great Bulgaria, of predominantly Slavonic population, from territories of the Ottoman Empire. This was unacceptable to Great Britain and the crisis worsened until the Powers agreed to meet in a Congress called to Berlin by the German Government. Under Bismarck's presidency a compromise was negotiated, the most important provisions of which follow.

Source: E. Hertslet, *The Map of Europe by Treaty* (London, H.M.S.O., 1891), vol. iv, pp. 2759–99.

1. Bulgaria is constituted an autonomous and tributary principality under the suzerainty of His Imperial Majesty the Sultan; it will have a Christian Government and a national militia . . .

3. The Prince of Bulgaria shall be freely elected by the population and confirmed by the Sublime Porte, with the assent of the Powers . . .

5. The following points shall form the basis of the public law of Bulgaria:[1]

The difference of religious creeds and confessions shall not be alleged against any person as a ground for exclusion or incapacity in matters relating to the enjoyment of civil and political rights, admission to public employments, functions, and honours, or the exercise of the various professions and industries in any locality whatsoever.

The freedom and outward exercise of all forms of worship are assured to all persons belonging to Bulgaria, as well as to foreigners, and no hindrance shall be offered either to the hierarchical organization of the different communions, or to their relations with their spiritual chiefs . . .

13. A province is formed south of the Balkans which will take the name of 'Eastern Roumelia', and will remain under the direct political and military authority of His Imperial Majesty the Sultan, under conditions of administrative autonomy. It shall have a Christian Governor-General . . .

18. The Governor-General of Eastern Roumelia shall be nominated by the Sublime Porte, with the Assent of the Powers, for a term of five years . . .

25. The Provinces of Bosnia and Herzegovina shall be occupied and administered by Austria–Hungary. The Government of Austria–Hungary, not desiring to undertake the administration of the Sandjak of Novi-Bazar, which extends between Servia

---

[1] Similar provisions are included in the treaty for every autonomous country mentioned, and somewhat milder ones of the same sense for the rest of the Turkish Empire.

and Montenegro ... the Ottoman Administration will continue to exercise its functions there. Nevertheless, in order to
assure the maintenance of the new political state of affairs, as
well as freedom and security of communications, Austria–
Hungary reserves the right of keeping garrisons and having
military and commercial roads in the whole of this part of the
ancient Vilayet of Bosnia. To this end the Governments of
Austria–Hungary and Turkey reserve to themselves to come to an
understanding on the details.

26. The independence of Montenegro is recognized by the
Sublime Porte and by all those of the High Contracting Parties
who had not hitherto admitted it ...

34. The High Contracting Parties recognize the independence
of the Principality of Servia ...

43. The High Contracting Parties recognize the independence
of Romania ...

100. *The Austro-German Alliance, 7 October 1879*

The Treaty of Berlin (No. 99) settled the Eastern crisis, but it did
not settle the Eastern question. Russia and Great Britain, and even
more Russia and Austria–Hungary, continued to suspect each other's
intentions. To prevent a possible upset of the European balance of
power by war between the last two states, Bismarck concluded an
alliance with Austria–Hungary, which became the foundation of
the foreign policy of both empires until the first world war.

Source: *British and Foreign State Papers*, vol. cxxi (1925, pt. 1),
pp. 1014–15.

1. Should, contrary to the hope and the sincere desire of the
two High Contracting Parties, one of the two Empires be
attacked by Russia, the High Contracting Parties bind themselves to come to the assistance of each other with the whole
military strength of their Empire and accordingly only to conclude peace in common and by mutual agreement.

2. Should one of the High Contracting Parties be attacked by
another Power, the other party binds itself hereby not only to
refrain from assisting the aggressor against its High Ally, but
to observe at least a benevolent neutral attitude towards its
fellow contracting party.

Should, however, the attacking party in such a case be

supported by Russia, either by active co-operation or by military measures which constitute a menace to the party attacked, the obligation of reciprocal assistance with the whole fighting force which is stipulated in Article 1 of this treaty becomes equally operative, and the conduct of the war by the two High Contracting Parties shall in this case also be joint until the conclusion of a common peace ...

4. This treaty shall, in conformity with its peaceful character, and to avoid any misinterpretation, be kept secret by both High Contracting Parties and only communicated to a third Power upon a joint understanding between the two parties and according to the terms of a special agreement ...

101. The League of the Three Emperors, 18 June 1881

A further step (cf. No. 100) by Bismarck to prevent the distrust between Austria–Hungary and Russia from endangering the balance of power by a war between them was the negotiation of the League of the Three Emperors in 1881, the terms of which would deter such war, and enable disputed problems to be settled peacefully. At the same time it prevented France from gaining an ally either in Austria–Hungary or in Russia.

Source: A. F. Pribram, *The Secret Treaties of Austria–Hungary, 1879–1914* (Cambridge, Mass., Harvard University Press, 1920), vol. i, pp. 37–47.

The Courts of Austria–Hungary, of Germany, and of Russia, animated by an equal desire to consolidate the general peace by an understanding intended to assure the defensive position of their respective States, have come into agreement on certain questions which more especially concern their reciprocal interests.

1. In case one of the High Contracting Parties should find itself at war with a fourth Great Power, the two others shall maintain towards it a benevolent neutrality and shall devote their efforts to the localization of the conflict.

This stipulation shall apply likewise to a war between one of the three Powers and Turkey, but only in the case where a previous agreement shall have been reached between the three Courts as to the results of this war ...

2. Russia, in agreement with Germany, declares her firm resolution to respect the interests arising from the new position
assured to Austria–Hungary by the Treaty of Berlin (No. 99,
Art. 25).

The Three Courts, desirous of avoiding all discord between
them, engage to take account of their respective interests in the
Balkan Peninsula. They further promise one another that any
new modifications in the territorial *status quo* of Turkey in
Europe can be accomplished only in virtue of a common
agreement between them . . .

3. The three Courts recognize the European and mutually
obligatory character of the principle of the closing of the
Straits of the Bosphorus and of the Dardanelles, founded on
international law . . .

They will take care in common that Turkey shall make no
exception to this rule in favor of the interests of any Government whatsoever . . .

102. *The Triple Alliance, 1882–1912*

An important feature of the Bismarckian system, particularly in the
initial years of its existence, was the Triple Alliance of Austria–
Hungary, Germany, and Italy. First concluded in 1882, it was
renewed in 1887, 1891, 1902, and 1912, with small alterations and
additions. The full text of the important paragraphs included in all
renewals follows (a), followed by the text of a ministerial declaration
made separately by each government (b). In 1887, while the main
treaty was renewed unchanged, additional treaties were negotiated
between Germany and Italy and Austria–Hungary and Italy respectively, in both cases dealing with the Ottoman Empire. The
operative paragraph of the Austro-Italian treaty is here included
(c). These separate agreements were incorporated in the main treaty
in 1891 and subsequent renewals, and no other important additions
or alterations were made in them.

Source: A. F. Pribram, *The Secret Treaties of Austria–Hungary, 1879–*
1914 (Cambridge, Mass., Harvard University Press, 1920),
vol. i, pp. 65–71, 109.

(a) The Triple Alliance, 20 May 1882.

1. The High Contracting Parties mutually promise peace and
friendship, and will enter into no alliance or engagement
directed against any one of their States. They engage to proceed

to an exchange of ideas on political and economic questions of a general nature which may arise, and they further promise one another mutual support within the limits of their own interests.

2. In case Italy, without direct provocation on her part, should be attacked by France for any reason whatsoever, the two other Contracting Parties shall be bound to lend help and assistance with all their forces to the Party attacked. This same obligation shall devolve upon Italy in case of any aggression without direct provocation by France against Germany.

3. If one, or two, of the High Contracting Parties, without direct provocation on their part, should chance to be attacked and to be engaged in a war with two or more Great Powers nonsignatory to the present treaty, the *casus foederis* will arise simultaneously for all the High Contracting Parties.

4. In case of a Great Power nonsignatory to the present Treaty should threaten the security of the States of one of the High Contracting Parties, and the threatened Party should find itself forced on that account to make war against it, the two others bind themselves to observe towards their Ally a benevolent neutrality. Each of them reserves to itself, in this case, the right to take part in the war, if it should see fit, to make common cause with its Ally.

5. If the peace of any of the High Contracting Parties should chance to be threatened under the circumstances foreseen by the preceding articles, the High Contracting Parties shall take counsel together in ample time as to the military measures to be taken with a view to eventual co-operation. They engage henceforward, in all cases of common participation in a war, to conclude neither armistice, nor peace, nor treaty, except by common agreement among themselves.

6. The High Contracting Parties mutually promise secrecy as to the contents and existence of the present treaty . . .

(b) Text of the Ministerial Declaration issued by the Contracting Parties at different dates of May 1882.

The . . . Government declares that the provisions of the secret Treaty concluded May 20, 1882, between Italy, Austria–Hungary and Germany, cannot, as has been previously agreed, in any case be regarded as being directed against England . . .

(c) Separate Treaty between Austria–Hungary and Italy, 20 February 1887.

1. The High Contracting Parties, having in mind only the maintenance, so far as possible, of the territorial *status quo* in the Orient, engage to use their influence to forestall any territorial modification which might be injurious to one or other of the Powers signatory to the present treaty. They shall communicate to one another all information of a nature to enlighten each other mutually concerning their own dispositions, as well as those of other Powers.

However, if, in the course of events, the maintenance of the *status quo* in the regions of the Balkans or of the Ottoman coasts and islands in the Adriatic and in the Aegean Sea should become impossible, and if, whether in consequence of the action of a third Power or otherwise, Austria–Hungary or Italy should find themselves under the necessity of modifying it by a temporary or permanent occupation on their part, this occupation shall take place only after a previous agreement between the two Powers aforesaid, based upon the principle of a reciprocal compensation for every advantage, territorial or other, which each of them might obtain beyond the present *status quo*, and giving satisfaction to the interests and well founded claims of the two Parties . . .

103. *The 'Reinsurance Treaty', 18 June 1887*

Continuing Austro-Hungarian-Russian distrust resulted in the breaking down of the League of the Three Emperors (No. 101) which was not renewed in 1887. In order to still keep Russia in German alliance, and so to prevent her alliance with France, Bismarck negotiated the so-called 'Reinsurance Treaty' with Russia, which supplemented, from the German point of view, the treaties with Austria–Hungary (Nos 100, 102).

Source: A. F. Pribram, *The Secret Treaties of Austria–Hungary, 1879–1914* (Cambridge, Mass., Harvard University Press, 1920), vol. i, pp. 275–81.

1. In case one of the High Contracting Parties should find itself at war with a third great Power, the other would maintain a benevolent neutrality towards it, and would devote its efforts to

the localization of the conflict. This provision would not apply to a war against Austria or France in case this war should result from an attack directed against one of these two latter Powers by one of the High Contracting Parties.

2. Germany recognizes the rights historically acquired by Russia in the Balkan Peninsula, and particularly the legitimacy of her preponderant and decisive influence in Bulgaria and in Eastern Roumelia. The two Courts engage to admit no modification of the territorial *status quo* of the said peninsula without a previous agreement between them, and to oppose, as occasion arises, every attempt to disturb this *status quo* or to modify it without their consent . . .

104. *The Franco-Russian Military Convention, 17 August 1892*

After Bismarck's resignation in 1890 (cf. No. 135) the Emperor, William II, and the new chancellor, Caprivi, did not renew the Reinsurance Treaty with Russia (No. 103). Russia and France now both being isolated, diplomatic and financial co-operation developed between them, and conversations between their representatives resulted, in 1892, in the conclusion of a military convention, followed later (1912) by a naval convention.

Source: A. F. Pribram, *The Secret Treaties of Austria–Hungary, 1879– 1914* (Cambridge, Mass., Harvard University Press, 1920), vol. ii, pp. 215–16.

France and Russia, being animated by an equal desire to preserve peace, and having no other object than to meet the necessities of a defensive war, provoked by an attack of the forces of the Triple Alliance against the one or the other of them, have agreed upon the following provisions:

1. If France is attacked by Germany, or by Italy supported by Germany, Russia shall employ all her available forces to attack Germany.

If Russia is attacked by Germany, or by Austria supported by Germany, France shall employ all her available forces to fight Germany.

2. In case the forces of the Triple Alliance, or of one of the Powers composing it, should mobilize, France and Russia, at the first news of the event and without the necessity of any

previous concert, shall mobilize immediately and simultaneously the whole of their forces and shall move them as close as
possible to their frontiers.

3. The available forces to be employed against Germany shall
be, on the part of France, 1,300,000 men, on the part of Russia,
700,000 or 800,000 men.

These forces shall engage to the full, with all speed, in order
that Germany may have to fight at the same time on the East
and on the West . . .

5. France and Russia shall not conclude peace separately.

6. The present Convention shall have the same duration as the
Triple Alliance.

105. *The Hague Conventions, 1899–1907*

In May 1899, on the initiative of Tsar Nicholas II, an International
Peace Conference met at The Hague, primarily to discuss the
limitation of armaments and the pacific settlement of international
disputes. Agreement could not be reached on the first point; nevertheless some important conventions were agreed to, one of which
resulted in the setting up of a Permanent Court of Arbitration, a
direct forerunner of the International Court of Justice.

A second Peace Conference, also at The Hague, was called in
1907, on the initiative of Theodore Roosevelt, president of the
United States of America. Sitting for some four months, this Conference supplemented the work of the first by agreeing to a large
number of conventions, as well as filling out the details of some of the
conventions of 1899.

Our selections consist of excerpts from the Final Act of the 1899
Conference (a), which summarizes its work, followed by excerpts
of the Final Act of 1907 (b), in order to show the progress achieved.
In addition, some articles of the Convention for the Pacific Settlement of International Disputes of 1899 (c) will reveal the principles
accepted by the Contracting Parties.

Source: *The Hague Conventions and Declarations of 1899 and 1907*, ed.
by J. B. Scott (New York, 1915) (Carnegie Endowment for
International Peace), pp. 1–31, 41–81.

(a) Final Act of the International Peace Conference, 29 July
1899.

The International Peace Conference . . . in a series of meetings, between the 18th May and the 29th July 1899 . . . has

agreed ... on the text of the Conventions and Declarations enumerated below:

I. Convention for the pacific settlement of international disputes.
II. Convention regarding the laws and customs of war on land.
III. Convention for the adaptation to maritime warfare of the principles of the Geneva Convention of the 22nd August 1864 (No. 95).
IV. Three Declarations:

1. To prohibit the launching of projectiles and explosives from balloons or by other similar new methods.
2. To prohibit the use of projectiles, the only object of which is the diffusion of asphyxiating or deleterious gases.
3. To prohibit the use of bullets which expand or flatten easily in the human body, such as bullets with a hard envelope, of which the envelope does not entirely cover the core or is pierced with incisions ...

Guided by the same sentiments, the Conference has adopted unanimously the following Resolution:

The Conference is of opinion that the restriction of military charges, which are at present a heavy burden on the world, is extremely desirable for the increase of the material and moral welfare of mankind.

It has besides formulated the following [wishes]:

1. The Conference, taking into consideration the preliminary step taken by the Swiss Federal Government for the revision of the Geneva Convention, expresses the wish that steps may be shortly taken for the assembly of a special Conference having for its object the revision of that Convention.

This wish was voted unanimously.

2. The Conference expresses the wish that the questions of the rights and duties of neutrals may be inserted in the program of a Conference in the near future ...

4. The Conference expresses the wish that the Governments, taking into consideration the proposals made at the Conference, may examine the possibility of an agreement as to the limitation of armed forces by land and sea, and of war budgets.

5. The Conference expresses the wish that the proposal, which

contemplates the declaration of the inviolability of private property in naval warfare may be referred to a subsequent Conference for consideration.

6. The Conference expresses the wish that the proposal to settle the question of the bombardment of ports, towns and villages by a naval force may be referred to a subsequent Conference for consideration.

The last five wishes were voted unanimously, saving some abstentions . . .

(b) Final Act of the Second International Peace Conference, 18 October 1907.

The Second International Peace Conference . . . at a series of meetings, held from the 15th June to the 18th October 1907 . . . drew up . . . the text of the Conventions and of the Declaration enumerated below . . .:

I. Convention for the pacific settlement of international disputes.

II. Convention respecting the limitation of the employment of force for the recovery of contract debts.

III. Convention relative to the opening of hostilities.

IV. Convention respecting the laws and customs of war on land.

V. Convention respecting the rights and duties of neutral powers and persons in case of war on land.

VI. Convention relative to the status of enemy merchant ships at the outbreak of hostilities.

VII. Convention relative to the conversion of merchant ships into war-ships.

VIII. Convention relative to the laying of automatic submarine contact mines.

IX. Convention respecting bombardment by naval forces in time of war.

X. Convention for the adaptation to naval war of the principles of the Geneva Convention.

XI. Convention relative to certain restrictions with regard to the exercise of the right of capture in naval war.

XII. Convention relative to the creation of an International Prize Court.

XIII. Convention concerning the rights and duties of neutral Powers in naval war.

XIV. Declaration prohibiting the discharge of projectiles and explosives from balloons . . .

The Conference, actuated by the spirit of mutual agreement and concession characterizing its deliberations, has agreed upon the following Declaration, which, while reserving to each of the Powers represented full liberty of action as regards voting, enables them to affirm the principles which they regard as unanimously admitted:

It is unanimous—

1. In admitting the principle of compulsory arbitration.

2. In declaring that certain disputes, in particular those relating to the interpretation and application of the provisions of international agreements, may be submitted to compulsory arbitration without any restriction.

Finally, it is unanimous in proclaiming that, although it has not yet found feasible to conclude a Convention in this sense, nevertheless the divergences of opinion which have come to light have not exceeded the bounds of judicial controversy, and that, by working together here during the past four months, the collected Powers not only have learnt to understand one another and to draw closer together, but have succeeded in the course of this long collaboration in evolving a very lofty conception of the common welfare of humanity.

The Conference has further unanimously adopted the following Resolution:

The Second Peace Conference confirms the Resolution adopted by the Conference of 1899 in regard to the limitation of military expenditure; and inasmuch as military expenditure has considerably increased in almost every country since that time, the Conference declares that it is eminently desirable that the Governments should resume the serious examination of this question . . .

(c) Convention for the Pacific Settlement of International Disputes, 29 July 1899.

1. With a view to obviating, as far as possible, recourse to force in the relations between States, the signatory Powers agree to

use their best efforts to insure the pacific settlement of international differences.

2. In case of serious disagreement or conflict, before an appeal to arms, the signatory Powers agree to have recourse, as far as circumstances allow, to the good offices or mediation of one or more friendly Powers.

3. Independently of this recourse, the signatory Powers recommend that one or more Powers, strangers to the dispute, should, on their own initiative, and as far as circumstances may allow, offer their good offices or mediation to the States at variance . . .

4. The part of the mediator consists in reconciling the opposing claims and appeasing the feelings of resentment which may have arisen between the States at variance . . .

9. In differences of an international nature involving neither honor nor vital interests, and arising from a difference of opinion on points of fact, the signatory Powers recommend that the parties, who have not been able to come to an agreement by means of diplomacy, should as far as circumstances allow, institute an international commission of inquiry, to facilitate a solution of these differences by elucidating the facts by means of an impartial and conscientious investigation.

10. The international commissions of inquiry are constituted by special agreement between the parties in conflict . . .

14. The report of the international commission of inquiry is limited to a statement of facts, and has in no way the character of an arbitral award. It leaves the conflicting Powers entire freedom as to the effect to be given to this statement . . .

15. International arbitration has for its object the settlement of differences between States by judges of their own choice, and on the basis of respect for law.

16. In questions of a legal nature, and especially in the interpretation or application of international conventions, arbitration is recognized by the signatory Powers as the most effective, and at the same time the most equitable, means of settling disputes which diplomacy has failed to settle . . .

20. With the object of facilitating an immediate recourse to arbitration for international differences, which it has not been possible to settle by diplomacy, the signatory Powers undertake to organize a Permanent Court of Arbitration, accessible at all

times and operating, unless otherwise stipulated by the parties, in accordance with rules of procedure inserted in the present Convention . . .

23. . . . Each signatory Power shall select four persons at the most, of known competency in questions of international law, of the highest moral reputation, and disposed to accept the duties of arbitrators.

The persons thus selected shall be inscribed, as members of the Court, in a list which shall be notified . . . to all the signatory Powers.

24. When the signatory Powers desire to have recourse to the Permanent Court for the settlement of a difference that has arisen between them, the arbitrators called upon to form the competent tribunal to decide this difference must be chosen from the general list of members of the Court . . .

106. *The Anglo-French Entente, 1904*

In 1899 strained relations still existed between Great Britain and France because of differences in Africa. In subsequent years, however, the pressure of aggressive German policy brought them much closer, and, by 1904, they were ready to settle all their differences amicably in the treaty that follows (a). The two governments continued to co-operate closely, and while there was no formal alliance, as emphasized by (b), it was generally understood that Great Britain would support France if she were attacked by Germany.

Source: (a) R. B. Mowat, *Select Treaties and Documents* (Oxford, Clarendon Press, 1916), pp. 1–5.

(b) G. M. Trevelyan, *Grey of Fallodon* (London, Longmans, Green, 1937), p. 129.

(a) Agreement between Great Britain and France respecting Egypt and Morocco, 8 April 1904.

1. His Britannic Majesty's Government declare that they have no intention of altering the political status of Egypt.

The Government of the French Republic, for their part, declare, that they will not obstruct the action of Great Britain in that country by asking that a limit of time be fixed for the British occupation or in any other manner . . .

2. The Government of the French Republic declare that they have no intention of altering the political status of Morocco.

His Britannic Majesty's Government, for their part, recognize that it appertains to France, more particularly as a power whose dominions are conterminous for a great distance with those of Morocco, to preserve order in that country, and to provide assistance for the purpose of all administrative, economic, financial, and military reforms which it may require.

They declare that they will not obstruct the action taken by France for this purpose . . .

4. The two Governments, being equally attached to the principle of commercial liberty both in Egypt and Morocco, declare that they will not, in those countries, countenance any inequality either in the imposition of customs duties or other taxes, or of railway transport charges.

The trade of both nations with Morocco and with Egypt shall enjoy the same treatment in transit through the French and British possessions in Africa . . .

(b) Notes on an interview with the French Ambassador, P. Cambon, made by the Foreign Secretary, Sir Edward Grey, 10 January 1906.

The French Ambassador asked me to-day whether, in the event of an attack by Germany upon France arising out of the Morocco difficulty, France could rely upon the armed support of England.

I said I could not answer this question: I could not even consult the Prime Minister or the Cabinet during the elections. I was sure that there would be a strong sentiment and sympathy on the part of the English public; more than that I could not say and all I could promise was diplomatic support now. M. Cambon said he did not believe that there would be war, but that there would be no danger of war, if the German Emperor knew that we should fight to help France.

I said that I thought the German Emperor probably did expect this; but that it was one thing to let it be supposed in Germany that we should join in a war; it was a different thing to take an engagement to France to do it; it would be a very grave mistake to make a promise of that kind till one was absolutely certain it would be fulfilled.

M. Cambon mentioned the word neutrality and I said at once that neutrality—benevolent neutrality, if there was such a thing, I would promise, but that was all.

Our great desire was to see the Morocco Conference (cf. No. 108) have an issue favourable to the Anglo-French Entente, but a pacific issue; if that failed, I could not say what England would do; much might depend upon the manner in which war broke out . . .

107. *The Tangier Crisis, 1905*

In the Anglo-French Entente (No. 106(a)) Great Britain recognized the special interest of France in Morocco, but this recognition was not general. Germany, in particular, desired to participate in the exploitation of Morocco and to establish the German interest in this area. Emperor William II, when voyaging in the Mediterranean in March 1905, landed at Tangier and in several speeches demanded equal rights for Germany. A summary report of the speeches is taken from the report of the British representative at Tangier.

Source: *British documents on the Origin of the War, 1898–1914*, ed. by G. P. Gooch and H. Temperley (London, H.M.S.O., 1928), vol. iii, p. 63.

. . . When the German Emperor landed on the pier he was warmly greeted by Mulai Abdelmalek, who saluted him in the Sultan's name and stated that His Shereefian Majesty's joy at receiving the visit was not only on His Majesty's own account but also on that of his subjects.

The Emperor replied that it gave him great pleasure and satisfaction to salute a near relative of the Sultan, and he requested him to convey to the Sultan his thanks for having sent the special embassy to greet him, and also for the magnificent preparations made for his reception. His Imperial Majesty added that he was deeply interested in the welfare and prosperity of the Moorish Empire. It was to the Sultan as an independent sovereign that he was paying a visit and he trusted that, under His Shereefian Majesty's sovereignty, Morocco would remain free, and open to the peaceful competition of all nations without monopolies and exclusion.

. . . Later on at the German Legation Mulai Abdelmalek handed to the Emperor the Sultan's letter . . . The Emperor in reply thanked Mulai Abdelmalek more especially for the expressions of sincere friendship contained in the message. He entirely concurred in the Sultan's sentiments. It proved emphatically the omnipotence of the divine wisdom, which, as the Ambassador knew, directed the fate of nations. He personally most sincerely wished the development and the prosperity of the Moorish Empire as much for the good of His Shereefian Majesty's own subjects as for that of the nations of Europe trading in this country, as he hoped, on a footing of perfect equality.

His Imperial Majesty added that he had visited Tangier resolved to do all that lay in his power to efficiently safeguard German Interests in Morocco. He considered the Sultan an absolutely independent Sovereign and it was with His Majesty that he desired to come to an understanding as to a means of safeguarding those interests . . .

I am informed that the foregoing account of the speeches . . . was furnished to a journalist by the German Chargé d'Affaires . . .

108. *The Treaty of Algeciras, 7 April 1906*

The German diplomatic offensive to gain a share of Morocco which was opened by the Emperor's visit to Tangier (No. 107) remained unsuccessful because of French resistance. Germany was successful only in achieving the calling of an international conference, at Algeciras, to discuss the affairs of Morocco. Germany was supported only by Austria–Hungary and thus the only advantage she gained at the conference was the recognition that Moroccan affairs were of international interest; the lengthy General Act of the Conference, a contemporary summary of which follows, generally protected the interests of France.

Source: *Annual Register*, 1906, pp. [301–2].

The final convention, signed on April 7, was to the following effect:

1. The police to be placed under the sovereign authority of the Sultan and . . . distributed among the eight ports open to commerce.
2. To assist the Sultan in the organization of the police, Spanish and French instructors, officers and non-commissioned officers

were to be placed at his disposal by their respective Governments, which would submit their appointments to the approval of the Sultan.

3. These instructors were to insure the instruction and discipline of the police, see that the men possessed aptitude for military service, and in a general way supervise their administration.

4. The total effective of the police troops not to be more than 2,500 or less than 2,000, of the Spanish and French officers from sixteen to twenty, and of the non-commissioned officers from thirty to forty.

5. Their appointment to be for five years.

6. The inspector-general of the police was to be a superior officer of the Swiss Army . . .

7. A new State Bank was to be established, to be known as the State Bank of Morocco, it would have the exclusive privilege of issuing banknotes, would fulfil the functions of Treasurer and Paymaster of the Empire, and would make advances to the Moorish Government to the amount of 1,000,000 francs, and open a credit not exceeding two thirds of its initial capital to be employed in meeting, first, the expense of the police, and, secondly, that of works of general interest; the initial capital to be divided into as many equal parts as there were Powers represented at the Conference, each Power having the right to subscribe to the capital which was to be not less than 15,000,000 francs nor more than 20,000,000.

8. Foreigners to have the right of acquiring property in any part of Morocco and building upon it.

9. In the frontier region of Algeria the enforcement of the regulations to be the exclusive right of France, and in the frontier region of the Spanish possessions, of Spain.

[10.] None of the public services of the Empire might be alienated to the profit of private interests.

109. *The Second International: Stuttgart Resolution on Militarism and International Conflict, 1907*

The Second International was founded in 1889, the centenary of the outbreak of the French Revolution, to replace the First International (cf. No. 98) which dissolved in 1876. It held regular congresses, established an International Socialist Bureau, and, in general, became a large and fairly stable organization, in spite of clashes within it of groups with differing political views and attitudes. At the congresses many important resolutions were passed, including a series defining the socialist attitude to war. At the seventh congress, at Stuttgart in 1907, the French delegates moved for a resolution which would condemn war and call on workers everywhere to engage in general strike and insurrection in order to make a continuation of hostilities impossible. This motion was not acceptable to the large German delegation, but a sub-committee was appointed to draw up a compromise text which was accepted.

Source: J. Longuet, *Le mouvement socialiste international* (Paris, Quillet, 1913), pp. 57–8 (Encyclopédie Socialiste, vol. v) (trans. Ed.).

[The first half of the resolution considered the causes of wars, which it attributed to the working of the capitalist system. The worker, therefore, has no interest in war, and should take action to prevent it.]

The International is not able to define in advance the type of action, necessarily diverse according to the times and the circumstances of the several national parties, but its duty lies in intensifying and co-ordinating the endeavours of the working class against militarism and war as much as possible.

In fact, since the International Congress at Brussels, the proletariat, through its unceasing fight against militarism by its refusal to grant funds for military and naval expenses, and through its efforts to democratize the army, has used the most varied forms of action with growing power and efficacy to prevent wars or to end them or to make use of the upheaval of society caused by war for the purpose of freeing the working class; so, notably, in the agreement between English and French trade unions after the Fashoda incident. [Some other examples are also given.] All these efforts testify to the growing strength of the working class and its growing concern to maintain peace by its energetic intervention.

The action of the working class will be the more successful the more its spirit is prepared for a vigorous effort by unceasing propaganda, and the more the action of the several national parties is encouraged and co-ordinated by the International.

The Congress is convinced that, under the pressure of the proletariat, the serious use of international arbitration will be substituted, in the case of all disputes, for the pitiful attempts of the bourgeois Governments, and that thus the people will be assured of the benefits of general disarmament which will allow the use for cultural purposes of the immense resources of power and money now swallowed by armaments and war.

The Congress declares:

If war threatens to break out, it is the duty of the working class in the countries concerned, and of their parliamentary representatives, with the aid of the co-ordinating activity of the International Bureau, to do all they can to prevent the outbreak of war by whatever means seem to them most appropriate, which will naturally vary with the intensity of the class war and the general political situation.

Should war nevertheless break out, it is their duty to intercede for its speedy end and to make use, with all their power, of the economic and political crisis caused by the war to rouse all strata of the people and to hasten the fall of capitalist domination.

110. *The Daily Telegraph Interview, 27 October 1908*

The aggressiveness of German foreign policy and the German naval construction programme alienated not only the British Government but also the British people. To counteract this trend the Emperor decided to get an interview with himself published in one of the English papers through the mediation of an English friend. Although he sent the text to Chancellor Bülow for his perusal, it was only cursorily looked at by the officials. The intention was to bring to expression Germany's friendship with Great Britain; in fact, for reasons which will be obvious upon reading the text, British public opinion became even more distrustful of Germany's intentions.

Source: *The Daily Telegraph* (London), 28 October 1908.

We have received the following communication from a source of such unimpeachable authority that we can without hesitation commend the obvious message which it conveys to the attention of the public . . .

I have decided to make known the substance of a lengthy conversation which it was my recent privilege to have with his Majesty the German Emperor. I do so in the hope that it may help to remove that obstinate misconception of the character of the Kaiser's feelings towards England which, I fear, is deeply rooted in the ordinary Englishman's breast. It is the Emperor's sincere wish that it should be eradicated. He has given repeated proofs of his desire by work and deed. But, to speak frankly, his patience is sorely tried, now that he finds himself so continually misrepresented, and has so often experienced the mortification of finding that any momentary improvement of relations is followed by renewed outbursts of prejudice, and a prompt return to the old attitude of suspicion.

As I have said, his Majesty honoured me with a long conversation, and spoke with impulsive and unusual frankness. 'You English,' he said, 'are mad, mad as March hares. What has come over you that you are so completely given over to suspicions quite unworthy of a great nation? What more can I do than I have done? I declared with all the emphasis at my command, in my speech at Guildhall, that my heart is set upon peace, and that it is one of my dearest wishes to live on the best terms with England. Have I ever been false to my word? Falsehood and prevarication are alien to my nature. My actions ought to speak for themselves, but you listen not to them, but to those who misinterpret and distort them. That is a personal insult which I feel and resent. To be forever misjudged, to have my repeated offers of friendship weighed and scrutinized with jealous, mistrustful eyes, taxes my patience severely. I have said time after time that I am a friend of England, and your Press— or, at least, a considerable section of it—bids the people of England refuse my proffered hand, and insinuates that the other holds a dagger. How can I convince a nation against its will?' . . .

'I have referred,' he said, 'to the speeches in which I have done all that a Sovereign can to proclaim my goodwill. But, as actions speak louder than words, let me also refer to my acts. It is commonly believed in England that throughout the South African War Germany was hostile to her. German opinion undoubtedly was hostile—bitterly hostile . . . But what of official Germany? Let my critics ask themselves what brought to a sudden stop, and, indeed, to absolute collapse, the European tour of the Boer delegates who were striving to obtain European intervention? . . . When they asked me to receive them—I refused . . . Was that, I ask, the action of a secret enemy?

Again, when the struggle was at its height, the German Government was invited by the Governments of France and Russia to join with them in calling upon England to put an end to the war. The moment had come, they said, not only to save the Boer Republics, but also to humiliate England to the dust. What was my reply? I said that so far from Germany joining in any concerted European action to put pressure upon England and bring about her downfall, Germany would always keep aloof from politics that could bring her into complications with a Sea Power like England . . .

But, you will say, what of the German navy? Surely, that is a menace to England! Against whom but England are my squadrons being prepared? If England is not in the minds of those Germans who are bent on creating a powerful fleet, why is Germany asked to consent to such new and heavy burdens of taxation? My answer is clear. Germany is a young and growing Empire. She has a world-wide commerce, which is rapidly expanding, and to which the legitimate ambition of patriotic Germans refuses to assign any bounds. Germany must have a powerful fleet to protect that commerce, and her manifold interests in even the most distant seas. She expects those interests to go on growing, and she must be able to champion them manfully in any quarter of the globe. Germany looks ahead. Her horizons stretch far away . . . She must be prepared for any eventualities in the Far East.   Who can foresee what may take place in the Pacific in the days to come, days not so distant as some believe, but days, at any rate, for which all European Powers with Far Eastern interests ought steadily to prepare? Look at the accomplished awakening of Japan; think of the possible national awakening of China; and then judge of the vast problems of the Pacific. Only those Powers which have great navies will be listened to with respect, when the future of the Pacific comes to be solved; and if for that reason only Germany must have a powerful fleet. It may even be that England herself will be glad that Germany has a fleet when they speak together on the same side in the great debates of the future.'

Such was the purport of the Emperor's conversation. He spoke with all that earnestness which marks his manner when speaking on a deeply-pondered subject. I would ask my fellow-countrymen who value the cause of peace to weigh what I have written, and to revise, if necessary, their estimate of the Kaiser and his friendship for England by his Majesty's own words. If they had enjoyed the privilege, which was mine, of hearing them spoken, they would doubt no longer either his Majesty's firm desire to live on the best of terms with England or his growing impatience at the persistent mistrust with which his offer of friendship is too often received.

X · EDUCATION, THE CHURCH
AND THE STATE

I T might have been possible to incorporate some at least of the documents in this section in the sections dealing with the various states. It was considered, however, that it would be more useful to keep them all together, thus giving a picture of the relationship of the increasingly secularistic European society with the Roman Catholic Church.

The section begins with the first important educational measure of the period, the French law of 1833 (*Loi Guizot*) (No. 111) which established a state-controlled secular system of education. The controversy over the role of the Church in education can be best followed through in France, where the *Loi Falloux* of 1850 (No. 112) returned to the Church some of its former rights, but the laws introduced by Jules Ferry in 1880–2 (No. 117) completely excluded the Church from education. The controversy between Church and State did not stop with these measures; the Church was submitted to increasing control of which the Law of Associations of 1901 (No. 119) is an example, and then was completely separated from the state in 1905 (No. 120).

Education also played a part in the so-called *Kulturkampf*, the Church-State controversy in Germany (No. 116), though here the conflict was aggravated by fears resulting from the declaration of the primacy and infallibility of the Pope made by the Vatican Council in 1870 (No. 114). It was thought that these decrees would increase the influence and power of the Pope over Catholics also in temporal matters, and thus affect the allegiance of the Catholics (and particularly of the South German Catholics recently incorporated in the Empire) to their rulers and the state.

The attitude of Pope Pius IX contributed nothing to a diminution of such fears. Pius always differentiated the Church from modern civilization, many of whose ideas he condemned in the Syllabus of Errors of 1864 (No. 113). Nor did the gradual Italian occupation of the Papal States, ending in the occupation of Rome in 1870, and the unilaterally imposed settlement of the Pope's position in the Italian Law of Guarantees of 1871 (No. 115) make Pius more ready to accept modern attitudes. It was his successor, Leo XIII, who attempted a reconciliation of the Church and the modern world, and, although he was not very successful in the political field, his social encyclical *Rerum novarum* (No. 118) gained a lasting influence as one of the most important statements on social justice in this period.

111. *French Law on Primary Instruction (Loi Guizot), 28 June 1833*

In the early nineteenth century in most of Europe such public education as existed was in the hand of the churches. It was, therefore, a pioneer measure in which, during the period of the July Monarchy, Guizot, then Minister for Education, proposed not only the establishment of secular control of education, but also that of officially acceptable qualifications for teachers. The law also prescribed that each commune was to maintain a lower primary school, and each Department a teacher training institution.

Source: J. Palméro, *Histoire des institutions et des doctrines pédagogiques* (Paris, Société Universitaire d'Éditions et de Librairie, 1951), pp. 296-7 (trans. Ed.).

Title I. The Primary instruction and its purpose.

1. Primary instruction is elementary or higher. Elementary primary instruction necessarily comprises moral and religious instruction, reading, writing, elements of the French language and of arithmetic, the legal system of weights and measures . . .
3. Primary instruction is private or public . . .

Title II. Public primary schools.

8. Public primary schools are those that are maintained, wholly or partly, by the communes, the Departments, or the State.
9. Each commune is obliged, by itself or together with one or more other neighbouring communes, to maintain at least one elementary primary school . . .

10. Communes which are capitals of Departments and those which have a population of more than six thousand souls, must also maintain a higher primary school.

11. Each Department is obliged, by itself or together with one or more neighbouring Departments, to maintain a primary teachers' college . . .

112. The French Law of Education (Loi Falloux), 15 March 1850

The conservative majority (the 'Party of Order') in the National Assembly of the Second Republic wished to re-establish the Church as a stabilizing factor in society, and therefore to increase its influence in education. It therefore passed a law, introduced by Count Falloux, which gave the Church a number of privileges in the field of education. Excerpts of this law follow.

Source: J. Palméro, *Histoire des institutions et des doctrines pédagogiques* (Paris, Société Universitaire d'Éditions et de Librairie, 1951), pp. 299–300 (trans. Ed.).

. . . 18. The inspection of the institutions of public or free education is carried out by:

1. The general inspectors and chief inspectors;
2. The rectors and inspectors of the educational districts [*académies*];
3. The inspectors of primary instruction;
4. In the case of primary instruction, by cantonal delegates, the mayor, and the parish priest, minister, or delegate of the Israelite consistory . . .

24. Primary instruction is given without charge to children whose families are unable to pay.

25. Every Frenchman who has completed his twenty-first year may engage in primary teaching anywhere in France provided that he possesses a trained teacher's certificate [*brevet de capacité*].

A probationer's certificate [*certificat de stage*], matriculation certificate, a certificate stating that its owner has been admitted to one of the Higher Schools of the State, or the licence of a priest or minister issued by one of the denominations recognized by the State and neither suspended nor revoked, may be substituted for the trained teacher's certificate . . .

49. An ecclesiastical licence to teach [*lettre d'obédience*] will take the place of a trained teacher's certificate in the case of woman teachers who belong to a religious teaching congregation recognized by the State . . .

113. *The Syllabus of Errors, 8 December 1864*

Papal condemnation of views opposed to Catholic belief is by no means new; but such views were rather more wide-spread and influential in the nineteenth century than they had been before. Thus Pius IX and his predecessors in the Papal See had frequently found occasion to condemn them in encyclicals, apostolic letters, or consistorial allocutions. In the early eighteen sixties Pope Pius IX found it expedient to have a syllabus prepared of the most important errors of modern philosophy, theology, political and social thought which had been condemned by him or his predecessors; he sent it to all bishops, accompanied by the encyclical letter *Quanta Cura*, which discusses some of the most important errors in detail. It is important to note that the syllabus, the full text of which follows, is merely a summary of earlier condemnations, and that each error listed is followed, in the original, by a reference to the original documents. These references are here omitted; their nature can be seen from the text of Section IV of the document.

Source: W. E. Gladstone, *The Vatican Decrees in their Bearing on Civil Allegiance: a Political Expostulation; to which are added a History of the Vatican Council; together with the Latin and English text of the Papal Syllabus and the Vatican Decrees* by . . . P. Schaff (New York, Harper & Brothers, 1875), pp. 109–29.

The syllabus of the principal errors of our time, which are stigmatized in the Consistorial Allocutions, Encyclicals, and other Apostolical Letters of our Most Holy Father, Pope Pius IX.

I. PANTHEISM, NATURALISM, AND ABSOLUTE RATIONALISM

1. There exists no supreme, most wise, and most provident divine being distinct from the universe, and God is none other than nature, and is therefore subject to change. In effect, God is produced in man and in the world, and all things are God, and have the very substance of God. God is therefore one and the same thing with the world, and thence spirit is the same thing with matter, necessity with liberty, true with false, good with evil, justice with injustice.

2. All action of God upon man and world is to be denied.

3. Human reason, without any regard to God, is the sole arbiter of truth and falsehood, of good and evil; it is its own law to itself, and suffices by its natural force to secure the welfare of men and of nations.

4. All the truths of religion are derived from the native strength of human reason; whence reason is the master rule by which man can and ought to arrive at the knowledge of all truths of every kind.

5. Divine revelation is imperfect, and, therefore, subject to a continual and indefinite progress, which corresponds with the progress of human reason.

6. Christian faith contradicts human reason, and divine revelation not only does not benefit, but even injures the perfection of man.

7. The prophecies and miracles set forth and narrated in the Sacred Scriptures are the fictions of poets; and the mysteries of the Christian faith are the result of philosophical investigations. In the books of both Testaments there are contained mythical inventions, and Jesus Christ is himself a mythical fiction.

II. MODERATE RATIONALISM

8. As human reason is placed on a level with religion, so theological matters must be treated in the same manner as philosophical ones.

9. All the dogmas of the Christian religion are, without exception, the object of scientific knowledge of philosophy, and human reason, instructed solely by history, is able, by its own natural strength and principles, to arrive at the true knowledge of even the most abstruse dogmas: provided such dogmas be proposed as subject-matter for human reason.

10. As the philosopher is one thing, and philosophy is another, so it is the right and duty of the philosopher to submit to the authority which he shall have recognized as true; but philosophy neither can nor ought to submit to any authority.

11. The Church not only ought never to animadvert upon philosophy, but ought to tolerate the errors of philosophy, leaving to philosophy the care of their correction.

12. The decrees of the Apostolic See and of the Roman Congregations fetter the free progress of science.
13. The method and principles by which the old scholastic doctors cultivated theology are no longer suitable to the demands of the age and the progress of science.
14. Philosophy must be treated of without any account being taken of supernatural revelation.

III. INDIFFERENTISM, LATITUDINARIANISM

15. Every man is free to embrace and profess the religion he shall believe true, guided by the light of reason.
16. Men may in any religion find the way of eternal salvation, and obtain eternal salvation.
17. We may entertain at least a well-founded hope for the eternal salvation of all those who are in no manner in the true Church of Christ.
18. Protestantism is nothing more than another form of the same true Christian religion, in which it is possible to be equally pleasing to God as in the Catholic Church.

IV. SOCIALISM, COMMUNISM, SECRET SOCIETIES, BIBLICAL SOCIETIES, CLERICO-LIBERAL SOCIETIES

Pests of this description are frequently rebuked in the severest terms in the Encyc. *Qui pluribus*, Nov. 9, 1846; Alloc. *Quibus quantisque*, April 20, 1849; Encyc. *Noscitis et Nobiscum*, Dec. 8, 1849; Alloc. *Singulari quadam*, Dec. 9, 1854; Encyc. *Quanto conficiamur moerore*, Aug. 10, 1863.

V. ERRORS CONCERNING THE CHURCH AND HER RIGHTS

19. The Church is not a true, and perfect, and entirely free society, nor does she enjoy peculiar and perpetual rights conferred upon her by her Divine Founder, but it appertains to the civil power to define what are the rights and limits within which the Church may exercise authority.
20. The ecclesiastical power must not exercise its authority without the permission and assent of the civil government.

21. The Church has not the power of defining dogmatically that the religion of the Catholic Church is the only true religion.

22. The obligation which binds Catholic teachers and authors applies only to those things which are proposed for universal belief as dogmas of the faith, by the infallible judgment of the Church.

23. The Roman Pontiffs and oecumenical Councils have exceeded the limits of their power, have usurped the rights of princes, and have even committed errors in defining matters of faith and morals.

24. The Church has not the power of availing herself of force, or any direct or indirect temporal power.

25. In addition to the authority inherent in the Episcopate, a further and temporal power is granted to it by the civil authority, either expressly or tacitly, which power is on that account also revocable by the civil authority whenever it pleases.

26. The Church has not the innate and legitimate right of acquisition and possession.

27. The ministers of the Church, and the Roman Pontiff, ought to be absolutely excluded from all charge and dominion over temporal affairs.

28. Bishops have not the right of promulgating even their apostolical letters, without the permission of the Government.

29. Dispensations granted by the Roman Pontiff must be considered null, unless they have been asked for by the civil Government.

30. The immunity of the Church and of ecclesiastical persons derives its origin from civil law.

31. Ecclesiastical courts for temporal causes of the clergy, whether civil or criminal, ought by all means to be abolished, even without the concurrence and against the protests of the Apostolic See.

32. The personal immunity exonerating the clergy from military service may be abolished, without violation either of natural right or of equity. Its abolition is called for by civil progress, especially in a community constituted upon principles of liberal government.

33. It does not appertain exclusively to ecclesiastical jurisdiction, by any right, proper and inherent, to direct the teaching of theological subjects.

34. The teaching of those who compare the Roman Pontiff to a free sovereign acting in the universal Church is a doctrine which prevailed in the middle ages.

35. There would be no obstacle to the sentence of a general council, or the act of all the universal peoples transferring the pontifical sovereignty from the Bishop and City of Rome to some other bishopric and some other city.

36. The definition of a national council does not admit of any subsequent discussion, and the civil power can regard as settled an affair decided by such national council.

37. National churches can be established, after being withdrawn and plainly separated from the authority of the Roman Pontiff.

38. Roman Pontiffs have, by their too arbitrary conduct, contributed to the division of the Church into eastern and western.

VI. ERRORS ABOUT CIVIL SOCIETY, CONSIDERED BOTH IN ITSELF AND IN ITS RELATION TO THE CHURCH

39. The Commonwealth is the origin and source of all rights, and possesses rights which are not circumscribed by any limits.

40. The teaching of the Catholic Church is opposed to the well-being and interests of society.

41. The civil power, even when exercised by an unbelieving sovereign, possesses an indirect and negative power over religious affairs ...

42. In the case of conflicting laws between the two powers, the civil law ought to prevail.

43. The civil power has a right to break, and to declare and render null, the conversations (commonly called Concordats) concluded with the Apostolic See, relative to the use of rights appertaining to the ecclesiastical immunity, without the consent of the Holy See, and even contrary to its protest.

44. The civil authority may interfere in matters relating to religion, morality, and spiritual government. Hence it has control over the instructions for the guidance of consciences issued, conformably with their mission, by the pastors of the Church. Further, it possesses power to decree, in the matter of

administering the divine sacraments, as to the dispositions necessary for their reception.

45. The entire direction of public schools, in which the youth of Christian States are educated, except (to a certain extent) in the case of episcopal seminaries, may and must appertain to the civil power, and belong to it so far that no other authority whatsoever shall be recognized as having any right to interfere in the discipline of the schools, the arrangement of the studies, the taking of degrees, or the choice and approval of the teachers.

46. Much more, even in clerical seminaries, the method of study to be adopted is subject to the civil authority.

47. The best theory of civil society requires that popular schools open to the children of all classes, and, generally, all public institutes intended for instruction in letters and philosophy, and for conducting the education of the young, should be freed from all ecclesiastical authority, government and interference, and should be fully subject to the civil and political power, in conformity with the will of rulers and the prevalent opinions of the age.

48. This system of instructing youth, which consists in separating it from the Catholic faith and from the power of the Church, and in teaching exclusively, or at least primarily, the knowledge of natural things and the earthly ends of social life alone, may be approved by Catholics.

49. The civil power has the right to prevent ministers of religion, and the faithful, from communicating freely and mutually with each other, and with the Roman Pontiff.

50. The secular authority possesses, as inherent in itself, the right of presenting bishops, and may require of them that they take possession of their dioceses before having received canonical institution and the apostolic letters from the Holy See.

51. And, further, the secular Government has the right of deposing bishops from their pastoral functions, and it is not bound to obey the Roman Pontiff in those things which relate to episcopal sees and the institution of bishops.

52. The Government has of itself the right to alter the age prescribed by the Church for the religious profession, both of men and women; and it may enjoin upon all religious establishments to admit no person to take solemn vows without its permission.

53. The laws for the protection of religious establishments, and securing their rights and duties, ought to be abolished; nay more, the civil Government may lend its assistance to all who desire to quit the religious life they have undertaken, and break their vows. The Government may also suppress religious orders, collegiate churches, and simple benefices, even those belonging to private patronage, and submit their goods and revenues to the administration and disposal of the civil power.

54. Kings and princes are not only exempt from the jurisdiction of the Church, but are superior to the Church, in litigated questions of jurisdiction.

55. The Church ought to be separated from the State, and the State from the Church.

VII. ERRORS CONCERNING NATURAL AND CHRISTIAN ETHICS

56. Moral laws do not stand in need of the divine sanction, and there is no necessity that human laws should be conformable to the law of nature, and receive their sanction from God.

57. Knowledge of philosophical things and morals, and also civil laws, may and must depart from divine and ecclesiastical authority.

58. No other forces are to be recognized than those which reside in matter; and all moral teaching and moral excellence ought to be made to consist in the accumulation of riches by every possible means, and in the enjoyment of pleasure.

59. Right consists in the material fact, and all human duties are but vain words, and all human acts have the force of right.

60. Authority is nothing else but the result of numerical superiority and material force.

61. An unjust act, being successful, inflicts no injury upon the sanctity of right.

62. The principle of non-intervention, as it is called, ought to be proclaimed and adhered to.

63. It is allowable to refuse obedience to legitimate princes: nay, more, to rise in insurrection against them.

64. The violation of a solemn oath, even every wicked and flagitious action repugnant to the eternal law, is not only not

blameable, but quite lawful, and worthy of the highest praise, when done for the love of country.

VIII. THE ERRORS CONCERNING
CHRISTIAN MARRIAGE

65. It can not be by any means tolerated, to maintain that Christ has raised marriage to the dignity of a sacrament.

66. The sacrament of marriage is only an adjunct of the contract, and separable from it, and the sacrament itself consists in the nuptial benediction alone.

67. By the law of nature, the marriage tie is not indissoluble, and in many cases divorce, properly so called, may be pronounced by the civil authority.

68. The Church has not the power of laying down what are diriment impediments[1] to marriage. The civil authority does possess such a power and can do away with existing impediments to marriage.

69. The Church only commenced in later ages to bring in diriment impediments, and then availing herself of a right not her own, but borrowed from the civil power.

70. The canons of the Council of Trent, which pronounce censure of anathema against those who deny to the Church the right of laying down what are diriment impediments, either are not dogmatic, or must be understood as referring only to such borrowed power.

71. The form of solemnizing marriage prescribed by the said Council, under penalty of nullity, does not bind in cases where the civil law has appointed another form, and where it decrees that this new form shall effectuate a valid marriage.

72. Boniface VIII is the first who declared that the vow of chastity pronounced at ordination annuls nuptials.

73. A merely civil contract may, among Christians, constitute a true marriage; and it is false either that the marriage contract between Christians is always a sacrament, or that the contract is null if the sacrament be excluded.

74. Matrimonial causes and espousals belong by their very nature to civil jurisdiction.

[1] Impediments which render a marriage null and void.

IX. ERRORS REGARDING THE CIVIL POWER
OF THE SOVEREIGN PONTIFF

75. The children of the Christian and Catholic Church are not agreed upon the compatibility of the temporal with the spiritual power.

76. The abolition of the temporal power, of which the Apostolic See is possessed, would contribute in the greatest degree to the liberty and prosperity of the Church.

X. ERRORS HAVING REFERENCE TO
MODERN LIBERALISM

77. In the present day, it is no longer expedient that the Catholic religion shall be held as the only religion of the State, to the exclusion of all other modes of worship.

78. Whence it has been wisely provided by law, in some countries called Catholic, that persons coming to reside therein shall enjoy the public exercise of their own worship.

79. Moreover, it is false that the civil liberty of every mode of worship, and the full power given to all of overtly and publicly manifesting their opinions and their ideas, of all kinds whatsoever, conduce more easily to corrupt the morals and minds of the people, and to the propagation of the pest of indifferentism.

80. The Roman Pontiff can and ought to reconcile himself to, and agree with, progress, liberalism, and civilization as lately introduced.

114. *Decrees of the First Vatican Council, 18 July 1870*

In 1869, for the first time since the Council of Trent (1545–63), which dealt with matters arising from the Reformation, the Pope called an oecumenical council of the Roman Catholic Church. The Council was to formulate the Church's teaching on a great variety of matters: faith and dogma, canon law, the Church, religious orders, church–state relations, etc. A dogmatic constitution, *Dei Filius*, dealing with matters of faith, was proclaimed on 24 April 1870; from this time on, the Council concerned itself mainly with the first sections of the draft of the dogmatic constitution on the Church, which included definitions of the primacy and infallibility of the Pope. After prolonged and sometimes acrimonious debate, in which even the opportuneness of making such definitions was discussed at length, the dogmatic constitution *Pastor Aeternus* was passed by the Council with only two dissentients, but with a large number of absentees. The day after the proclamation of the constitution war broke out between France and Prussia (cf. No. 96) resulting in the withdrawal of French troops from Rome. Italian troops then occupied the city and the Council dispersed, being formally suspended on 20 October 1870. It did not meet again.

Two selections from the dogmatic constitution *Pastor Aeternus* follow, the first (a) defining the primacy, the second (b) the infallibility of the Pope.

Source: W. E. Gladstone, *The Vatican Decrees in their Bearing on Civil Allegiance: a Political Expostulation; to which are added a History of the Vatican Council; together with the Latin and English text of the Papal Syllabus and the Vatican Decrees* by ... P. Schaff (New York, Harper & Brothers, 1875), pp. 159–68.

(a) ... Chapter III. On the Power and Nature of the Primacy of the Roman Pontiff.

Wherefore resting on plain testimonies of the Sacred Writings, and adhering to the plain and express decrees both of our predecessors, the Roman Pontiffs, and of the General Councils, we renew the definition of the oecumenical Council of Florence, in virtue of which all the faithful of Christ must believe that the holy Apostolic See and the Roman Pontiff possesses the primacy over the whole world, and that the Roman Pontiff is the successor of blessed Peter, Prince of the Apostles, and is true vicar of Christ, and head of the whole Church, and father and teacher of all Christians; and that full power was given to him in blessed Peter to rule, feed, and govern the universal Church by Jesus Christ our Lord; as is also contained in the acts of the General Councils and in the sacred Canons.

Hence we teach and declare that by the appointment of our Lord the Roman Church possesses a superiority of ordinary power over all other churches, and that this power of jurisdiction of the Roman Pontiff, which is truly episcopal, is immediate; to which all, of whatever rite and dignity, both pastors and faithful, both individually and collectively, are bound, by their duty of hierarchical subordination and true obedience, to submit not only in matters which belong to faith and morals, but also in those that appertain to the discipline and government of the Church throughout the world ... This is the teaching of Catholic truth, from which no one can deviate without loss of faith and salvation . . . They err from the right course who assert that it is lawful to appeal from the judgments of the Roman Pontiffs to an oecumenical Council, as to an authority higher than that of the Roman Pontiff . . .

(b) Chapter IV. Concerning the Infallible Teaching of the Roman Pontiff.

Moreover, that the supreme power of teaching is also included in the Apostolic primacy, which the Roman Pontiff, as the successor of Peter, Prince of the Apostles, possesses over the whole Church, this Holy See has always held, the perpetual practice of the Church confirms, and oecumenical Councils also have declared, especially those in which the East with the West met in the union of faith and charity. For the Fathers of the Fourth Council of Constantinople [869], following in the footsteps of their predecessors, gave forth this solemn profession: The first condition of salvation is to keep the rule of the true faith. And because the sentence of our Lord Jesus Christ can not be passed by, who said: 'Thou art Peter, and upon this rock I will build my Church', these things which have been said are approved by events, because in the Apostolic See the Catholic religion and her holy and well known doctrine has always been kept undefiled . . .

Therefore faithfully adhering to the tradition received from the beginning of the Christian faith, for the glory of God our Saviour, the exaltation of the Catholic religion, and the salvation of Christian people, the sacred Council approving, we teach and define that it is a dogma divinely revealed: that the Roman Pontiff, when he speaks *ex cathedra*, that is, when in discharge of the office of pastor and doctor of all Christians, by virtue of his supreme Apostolic authority, he defines a doctrine regarding faith or morals to be held by the universal Church, by the divine assistance promised to him in blessed Peter, is possessed of that infallibility with which the divine Redeemer willed that his Church should be endowed for defining doctrine regarding faith and morals; and that therefore such definitions of the Roman Pontiff are irreformable of themselves and not from the consent of the Church.

But if any one—which may God avert—presume to contradict this our definition: let him be anathema.

115. *The Italian Law of Guarantees, 13 May 1871*

Rome and the remainder of the Papal States were incorporated into the Kingdom of Italy after their occupation by Italian troops in 1870 (cf. introduction to Section VIII), but the Italian government realized that it would still have to pay some respect to the position of the Pope if it did not want to encounter internal and external difficulties. As Pope Pius IX refused to negotiate, the Italian government drafted a law, duly passed by parliament, which defined the relationship of the Papacy and Italy unilaterally. The most important articles of this law follow. The Papacy never accepted the validity of this law, and an agreed settlement on its relations with the government of Italy was only reached in the Treaty of the Lateran of 1929 (No. 180).

Source: *British and Foreign State Papers*, vol. lxv (1873/4), pp. 638–42.

Section I. Prerogatives of the Pontiff and of the Holy See.

1. The person of the Supreme Pontiff is sacred and inviolable.
2. Any attempt against the person of the Supreme Pontiff, or any provocation to commit the same, shall be punished with the same penalties as are established by law for a similar attempt or provocation against the person of the King . . .
3. The Italian Government shall render to the Supreme Pontiff, in the territories of the Kingdom, the honours which are due to royal rank, and shall maintain the privileges of honour which are paid to him by Catholic Sovereigns . . .
4. The annual donation of 3,225,000 lire in favour of the Holy See is maintained . . . for the diverse ecclesiastical wants of the Holy See, for ordinary and extraordinary repairs to and for the custody of the apostolic palaces and their dependencies; for all allowances, gratuities and pensions to the guards . . . and to all persons attached to the Pontifical Court, and for eventual expenditure; as well as for the ordinary repairs and custody of the museums and library thereto annexed, and for allowances, stipends, and pensions to persons employed for that purpose . . .
5. The Supreme Pontiff shall . . . have free enjoyment of the apostolic palaces of the Vatican and the Lateran . . . as also of the villa of Castel Gandolfo . . .

6. During the vacancy of the Pontifical See, no judicial or political authority shall . . . offer any impediment or limitation to the personal liberty of the Cardinals. The Government shall take proper measures in order that the assemblies of the Conclave and the Oecumenical Councils be not disturbed by any external violence . . .

12. The Supreme Pontiff shall be at liberty to correspond with the Episcopate and with the whole Catholic world, without any interference on the part of the Italian Government. To this effect he shall be free to establish in the Vatican, or in any other of his residences, postal and telegraphic offices, and to employ therein persons of his choice.

Section II. Relations of Church and State.

14. Every special restriction of the right of assemblage of members of the Catholic clergy is hereby annulled.

15. . . . Bishops shall not be required to take oath of allegiance to the King. The higher and lesser benefices shall be conferred solely upon citizens of the Kingdom, with the exception of such benefices as are situate in the city of Rome and in the suburban sees . . .

16. The *exequatur* and the *placet*[1] of the Crown and every other form of Government warrant for the publication and execution of acts emanating from ecclesiastical authorities are hereby abolished . . .

17. No complaint or appeal from acts issued by the ecclesiastical authorities, in matters spiritual or disciplinary, shall be allowed, no compulsory execution, however, shall be acknowledged or granted to the acts aforesaid . . .

18. Provision shall be made by a further enactment for the reorganization, the conservation, and the administration of ecclesiastical property throughout the Kingdom . . .

116. *The Kulturkampf in Germany*

A Catholic party, the so-called *Zentrum* or Centre, had already existed in the Prussian Parliament before 1871, representing mainly the Rhenish provinces of Prussia. It gained considerable strength

---

[1] Two forms of royal permission necessary in some countries before papal directions to bishops etc. could be published or carried out.

in the Reichstag after unification, when the predominantly Catholic states of Bavaria and Württemberg joined the Reich. Many of the Catholic politicians had been opponents of unification under Prussian leadership, or on Bismarck's terms. This in itself was reason enough for Bismarck to distrust them, but his distrust was further increased by his suspicion, shared by many non-Catholic politicians in Germany and elsewhere, that the Vatican decrees (No. 114) would result at least in dividing, at worst in alienating the allegiance of Catholic subjects.

In alliance with the National Liberal Party he therefore began what was described as a *Kulturkampf*, battle of civilizations, against the Catholic Church, intending to subject it to a large measure of control by the state. The Law against Jesuits (a) was the only important measure he succeeded in having enacted in the Reichstag; thereafter he transferred the field of battle to Prussia and, in the May laws of 1873, excerpts of two of which follow (b), enacted strong repressive measures. The Catholic Church in Germany reacted with public protest and passive resistance; Pope Pius IX himself protested, but unsuccessfully (c). Later legislation (d) even reinforced the May laws.

The repressive measures made no impression on the Catholics' will to resist, and did not affect the number of their representatives, and so Bismarck's aims were not achieved; neither were his fears proven correct. So after the accession of Pope Leo XIII better relations gradually grew up, the execution of the laws became more lenient, and, in the mid-eighties, they were repealed.

Source: (a) *Reichsgesetzblatt*, 1872, No. 22, 4 July 1872, p. 253 (trans. Ed.).

     (b) *Gesetzsammlung für die Königlichen Preussischen Staaten*, 1873, No. 14, pp. 191–7, 205–6 (trans. Ed.).

     (c) *Annual Register*, 1873, pp. [194–5].

     (d) *Reichsgesetzblatt*, 1874, 6 May 1874, pp. 43–4 (trans. Ed.).

(a) Imperial Law concerning Jesuits, 4 July 1872.

1. The Order of the Society of Jesus, and orders and congregations related to it, are excluded from the territory of the German Reich. No further establishments [of such orders] may be founded. The establishments now in existence must be dissolved within a time limit to be set by the Bundesrat, which must not exceed six months.

2. Members of the Society of Jesus ... if they are foreigners, may be expelled from the federal territory; if they are [Germans], they may be excluded from specified districts or localities, or may be settled in such ...

(b) The Prussian 'May Laws' of 1873.

(1) Law concerning the Education and Appointment of Priests, 11 May 1873.

1. An ecclesiastical office in one of the Christian churches may only be conferred upon a German who has pursued his studies in accordance with the provisions of this law and whose appointment has not been objected to by the government . . .

4. Pre-requisites for an appointment to an ecclesiastical position are the passing of the leaving examination in a German high school [*Gymnasium*], the pursuit of theological studies for three years at a German State university, and the passing of a State examination . . .

6. [In provinces where there is no Faculty of Theology, studies at an ecclesiastical seminary may replace the prescribed university studies, provided that the Minister for Religious Affairs recognizes their suitability] . . .

9. All ecclesiastical institutions concerned with the education of [priests and ministers] . . . shall be under the supervision of the state . . .

10. Their teachers must be Germans who have proven their scholarly qualifications . . . and whose appointment is not objected to by the Government.

13. If these provisions are not adhered to, the Minister has the right to order the closing of the institution . . .

15. . . . [The State] has the right to object to the appointment and transfer of a priest or minister, or to the transformation of a temporary into a permanent appointment . . .

(2) Law on the Limitations of the Ecclesiastical Power of Discipline and Punishment, 13 May 1873.

1. No Church or religious body has the right to threaten men with other forms of punishment and correction, nor to proclaim or publish any other forms, than those which belong to the purely religious field or consist either in the deprivation of some right exercised within the Church or religious body, or else in exclusion from it. Corporal methods of punishment or correction, and such as fall on property, liberty and civic honour, are forbidden.

2. The penalties allowed in Article 1 may not be pronounced against a member . . . for the following reasons:

(1) Because that member has done something which he is obliged to do by the law of the land or the ordinances issued by legal authority acting within the limits of its competence.

(2) Because that member has exercised or declined to exercise the general right of taking part in elections or giving a vote in a certain way . . .

(c) Exchange of Letters between Pope Pius IX and Emperor William I.

(1) Letter of the Pope, 7 August 1873.

The measures which have been adopted by Your Majesty's Government for some time past all aim more and more at the destruction of Catholicism. When I seriously ponder over the causes which may have led to these very hard measures, I confess that I am unable to discover any reasons for such a course. On the other hand I am informed that Your Majesty does not countenance the proceedings of your Government, and does not approve the harshness of the measures adopted against the Catholic religion. If, then, it be true that Your Majesty does not approve thereof—and the letters which Your august Majesty has addressed to me formerly might sufficiently demonstrate that you cannot approve that which is now occurring—if, I say, Your Majesty does not approve of your Government continuing in the path it has chosen of further extending its rigorous measures against the religion of Jesus Christ, whereby the latter is more injuriously affected—will Your Majesty, then, not become convinced that these measures have no other effect than that of undermining Your Majesty's own throne? I speak with frankness, for my banner is truth; I speak in order to fulfil one of my duties, which consists in telling the truth to all, even to those who are not Catholics— for every one who has been baptized belongs in some way or other, which to define more precisely would be here out of place—belongs, I say, to the Pope. I cherish the conviction that Your Majesty will receive my observations with your usual goodness, and will adopt the measures necessary in the present case . . .

(2) Letter of the Emperor, 3 September 1873.

I am glad that Your Holiness has, as in former times, done me the honour to write to me. I rejoice the more at this since an opportunity is thereby afforded me of correcting errors which, as appear from the contents of the letter of Your Holiness of the 7th of August, must have occurred in the communications you have received relative to German affairs. If the reports which are made to Your Holiness respecting German questions only stated the truth, it would not be possible for Your Holiness to entertain the supposition that my Government enters upon a path which I do not approve. According to the Constitution of my States such a case cannot happen, since the laws and Government measures in Prussia require my consent as Sovereign. To my deep sorrow, a portion of my Catholic subjects have organized for the past two years a political party which endeavours to disturb, by intrigues hostile to the State, the religious peace which has existed in Prussia for centuries. Leading Catholic priests have unfortunately not only approved this movement, but joined in it to the extent of open revolt against existing laws. It will not have escaped the observation of Your Holiness that similar indications manifest themselves at the present time in several European and some Transatlantic States. It is not my mission to investigate the causes by which the clergy and the faithful of one of the Christian denominations can be induced actively to assist the enemies of all law; but it certainly is my mission to protect internal peace and preserve the authority of the laws in the States whose Government has been entrusted to me by God. I am conscious that I owe hereafter an account of the accomplishment of this my kingly duty. I shall maintain order and law in my States against all attacks as long as God gives me the power; I am duty bound to do it as a Christian Monarch, even when to my sorrow I have to fulfil this royal duty against servants of a Church which I suppose acknowledges no less than the Evangelical Church that the commandment of obedience to secular authority is an emanation of the revealed will of God. Many of the priests in Prussia subject to your Holiness disown, to my regret, the Christian doctrine in this respect, and place my Government under the necessity, supported by the great majority of my loyal Catholic and Evangelical subjects, of extorting obedience to the law by worldly means. I willingly entertain the hope that Your Holiness, upon being informed of the true position of affairs, will use your authority to put an end to the agitation carried on amid deplorable distortion of the truth and abuse of priestly authority. The religion of Jesus Christ has, as I attest to Your Holiness before God, nothing to do with these intrigues, any more than has truth, to whose banner invoked by Your Holiness I unreservedly subscribe. There is one more expression in the letter of Your Holiness which I cannot pass over without contradiction, although it is not based upon the previous information, but upon the belief of Your Holiness— namely, the expression that every one that has received baptism belongs to the Pope. The Evangelical creed, which, as must be known to Your Holiness, I, like my ancestors and the majority of my subjects, profess, does not permit us to accept in our relations to God any other mediator than our Lord Jesus Christ . . . The difference of belief does not prevent my living in peace with those who do not share mine . . .

(d) Law concerning the Prevention of the Unauthorized Exercise of Ecclesiastical Office, 4 May 1874.

1. If an ecclesiastic or minister of religion deprived of his functions by a judicial decision does anything which implies a claim on his part to continue in the exercise of the functions from which he has been removed, the State police may command or forbid him to reside in certain districts or places.

If the act in question takes the form of an actual exercise of his functions, or an express claim to exercise them, or, again, if the ecclesiastic contravenes the order given him by the State police, he may be declared to have forfeited his nationality by order of the central authority and he may be expelled from the territory of the Confederation . . .

117. *Educational Reforms in France, 1880–2*

After the consolidation of the Third Republic, the republican Governments tackled educational reform with two aims in mind: to improve the educational level of the French people, and to reduce the influence of the Roman Catholic Church. The latter was an

important aim, resulting partly from the generally secularistic conviction of the republican leaders but also from the fact that the
Church still supported the monarchical movement and remained
hostile to the Republic.

The following measures are all associated with the name of Jules
Ferry, who as Minister for Education and as Premier was responsible
for their introduction.

Source: J. Palméro, *Histoire des institutions et des doctrines pédagogiques*
(Paris, Société Universitaire d'Éditions et de Librairie,
1951), pp. 311–12 (trans. Ed.).

(a) Law concerning the Freedom of Higher Education, 15
March 1880.

1. Examinations and practical tests which lead to the conferring
of degrees must be taken in the faculties of the State . . .
2. Enrolments in the faculties of the State are free . . .
4. Independent establishments of higher education must not, in
any case, take the name of a university . . .
5. University degrees or titles may only be borne by persons
who have obtained them after the prescribed tests or competitive examinations taken before professors or commissions of
the State.

(b) Law establishing Absolute Freedom of Primary Education,
16 June 1881.

1. No more tuition fees shall be collected in the public primary
schools or public kindergartens . . .

(c) Law concerning the Compulsoriness and Neutrality of
Primary Education, 28 March 1882.

1. Primary education includes:
   Moral and civic instruction;[1]
   Reading and writing . . .
2. Public primary schools will keep one day a week free, in
addition to Sunday, to enable parents, if they so wish, to have
their children given religious instruction outside the public
school building.

Religious instruction is optional in private schools.

[1] No longer 'moral and religious' as in Article 23 of the *Loi Falloux*
(No. 112).

3. Articles 18 and 44 of the law of 15 March 1848 (No. 112), insofar as they give ministers of religion the right of inspection, superintendence and direction of public and private primary schools . . . are abrogated.

4. Primary instruction is compulsory for children of both sexes from the completion of their sixth year to the completion of their thirteenth year . . .

118. *The Encyclical Rerum novarum, 15 May 1891*

While Pope Pius IX saw his task in the preservation of traditional Catholic doctrine through the condemnation of modern trends (cf. No. 113), his successor, Leo XIII, wanted to reconcile the Church and modern civilization. In the so-called Leonine corpus of political and social encyclicals he defined the spheres of spiritual and temporal power, discussed the freedom of citizens, and by upholding the dignity of the state, whether monarchy or republic, emphasized the compatibility of the Church's teaching with modern democracy. Most important of these encyclicals was, however, *Rerum novarum*, 'on the condition of the working classes', regarded as revolutionary by many, in which he applied the Church's traditional teaching to the conditions created by the industrial revolution. Only brief excerpts of this long document, one of the most important pronouncements on social justice, can be included.

Source: *Encyclical letter of our Holy Father . . . Pope Leo XIII on the Condition of Labour* (Official translation) (Sydney, Finn Brothers, 1891).

. . . Every man has by nature the right to possess property as his own . . . Man not only can possess the fruits of the earth, but also the earth itself; for of the products of the earth he can make provision for the future . . . Nor must we at this stage have recourse to the State. Man is older than the State: and he holds the right of providing for the life of his body prior to the formation of any State . . .

That which is required for the preservation of life, and for life's well-being, is produced in great abundance by the earth, but not until man has brought it into cultivation and lavished upon it his care and skill. Now, when man thus spends the industry of his mind and the strength of his body in procuring the fruits of nature, by that act he makes his own that portion of nature's field which he cultivates—that portion on which he leaves, as it were, the impress of his own personality; and it cannot but be just that he should possess that portion as his own, and should have a right to keep it without molestation.

These arguments are so strong and convincing that it seems surprising that certain obsolete opinions should now be revived in opposition to what is here laid down. We are told that it is right for private persons to have the use of the soil and the fruits of their land, but that it is unjust for anyone to possess as owner either the land on which he has built or the estate which he has cultivated. But those who assert this do not perceive that they are robbing man of what his own labour has produced . . .

With reason, therefore, the common opinion of mankind, little affected by the few dissentients who have maintained the opposite view, has found in the study of nature, and in the law of nature herself, the foundations of the division of property, and has consecrated by the practice of all ages the principle of private ownership, as being pre-eminently in conformity with human nature, and as conducing in the most unmistakable manner to the peace and tranquillity of human life . . .

Thus it is clear that the main tenet of socialism, the community of goods, must be utterly rejected; for it would injure those whom it is intended to benefit, it would be contrary to the natural rights of mankind, and it would introduce confusion and disorder into the commonwealth. Our first and most fundamental principle, therefore, when we undertake to alleviate the condition of the masses, must be the inviolability of private property . . .

There naturally exist among mankind innumerable differences of the most important kind; people differ in capability, in diligence, in health, and in strength; and unequal fortune is a necessary result of inequality of condition. Such inequality is far from being disadvantageous either to individuals or to the community; social and public life can only go on by the help of various kinds of capacity and the playing of many parts; and each man, as a rule, chooses the part which peculiarly suits his case . . .

The great mistake that is made in the matter now under consideration is to possess oneself of the idea that class is naturally hostile to class; that rich and poor are intended by nature to live at war with one another . . . These two classes should exist in harmony and agreement, and should, as it were, fit into one another, so as to maintain the equilibrium of the body politic. Each requires the other; capital cannot do without labour, nor labour without capital. Mutual agreement results in pleasantness and good order; perpetual conflict necessarily produces confusion and outrage. Now in preventing such strife as this, and in making it impossible, the efficacy of Christianity is marvellous and manifold. First of all, there is nothing more powerful than Religion (of which the Church is the interpreter and guardian) in drawing rich and poor together, by reminding each class of its duties to the other, and especially of the duties of justice. Thus religion teaches the labouring man and the workman to carry out honestly and well all equitable agreements freely made; never to injure capital, or to outrage the person of an employer; never to employ violence in representing his own cause, or to engage in riot and disorder; and to have nothing to do with men of evil principles, who work upon the people with artful promises . . . Religion teaches the rich man and the employer that their work-people are not their slaves; that they must respect in every man his dignity as a man and as a Christian; that labour is nothing to be ashamed of, if we listen to right reason and to Christian philosophy, but is an honourable employment, enabling man to sustain his life in an upright and creditable way; and that it is shameful and inhuman to treat men like chattels to make money by, or to look upon them merely as so much muscle or physical power. Thus, again, Religion teaches that, as among the workman's concerns are Religion herself and things spiritual and mental, the employer is bound to see that he has time for the duties of piety; that he be not exposed to corrupting influences and dangerous occasions; and that he be not led away to neglect his home and family or to squander his wages. Then, again, the employer must never tax his work-people beyond their strength, nor employ them in work unsuited to their sex or age. His great and principal obligation is to give to every one that which is just. Doubtless before we can decide whether wages are adequate, many things have to be considered; but rich men and masters should remember this—that to exercise pressure for the sake of gain, upon the indigent and the destitute, and to make one's profit out of the need of another, is condemned by all laws, human and divine . . .

We have said that the State must not absorb the individual or the family; both should be allowed free and untrammelled action as far as is consistent with the common good and the interests of others. Nevertheless, rulers should anxiously safeguard the community and all its parts; the community, because the conservation of the community is so emphatically the business of the supreme power, that the safety of the commonwealth is not only the first law, but it is a Government's whole reason of existence; and the parts, because both philosophy and the Gospel agree in laying down that the object of the administration of the State should be, not the advantage of the ruler, but the benefit of those over whom he rules . . . Whenever the general interest or any particular class suffers or is threatened with evils which can in no other way be met, the public authority must step in to meet them . . . When there is a question of protecting the rights of individuals, the poor and helpless have a claim to special consideration . . .

It is most true that by far the larger part of the people who work prefer to improve themselves by honest labour rather than by doing wrong to others. But there are not a few who are imbued with bad principles and are anxious for revolutionary change, and whose great purpose is to stir up tumult and bring about a policy of violence. The authority of the State should intervene to put restraint upon these disturbers, to save the workmen from their seditious arts, and to protect lawful owners from spoliation.

When work-people have recourse to a strike, it is frequently because the hours of labour are too long, or the work too hard, or because they consider their wages insufficient. The grave inconvenience of this not uncommon occurrence should be obviated by public remedial measures; for such paralysis of labour not only affects the masters and their work-people, but is extremely injurious to trade, and to the general interests of the public . . . The laws should be beforehand, and prevent these troubles from arising; they should lend their influence and authority to the removal in good time of the causes which lead to conflicts between masters and those whom they employ . . .

Wages, we are told, are fixed by free consent; and, therefore, the employer, when he pays what was agreed upon, has done his part and is not called upon for anything further. The only way, it is said, in which injustice could happen would be if the master refused to pay the whole of the wages, or the workmen would not complete the work undertaken; when this happens the State should intervene, to see that each obtains his own— but not under any other circumstances.

This mode of reasoning is by no means convincing to a fair minded man, for there are important considerations which it leaves out of view altogether. To labour is to exert oneself for the sake of procuring what is necessary for the purposes of life, and, most of all, for self-preservation. In the sweat of thy brow thou shalt eat bread.[1] Therefore, a man's labour has two notes or characters. First of all, it is *personal*; for the exertion of individual power belongs to the individual who puts it forth, employing this power for that personal profit for which it was given. Secondly, man's labour is *necessary*; for without the results of labour a man cannot live; and self-conservation is a law of Nature, which it is wrong to disobey. Now if we were to consider labour merely so far as it is *personal*, doubtless it would be within the workman's right to accept any rate of wages whatever; for in the same way as he is free to work or not, so he is free to accept a small remuneration or even none at all. But this is a mere abstract supposition; the labour of the working man is not only his personal attribute, but it is *necessary*; and this makes all the difference. The preservation of life is the bounded duty of each and all, and to fail therein is a crime. It follows that each one has a right to procure what is required in order to live; and the poor can procure it in no other way than by work and wages.

Let it be granted, then, that, as a rule, workman and employer should make free agreements, and in particular should freely agree as to wages; nevertheless, there is a dictate of nature more imperious and more ancient than any bargain between man and man, that the remuneration must be enough to support the wage-earner in reasonable and frugal comfort . . .

If a workman's wages be sufficient to enable him to maintain himself, his wife, and his children in reasonable comfort, he will not find it difficult, if he is a sensible man, to study economy; and he will not fail, by cutting down expenses, to put by a little property; nature and reason would urge him to do this. We

---

[1] Genesis 3.19.

have seen that this great Labour question cannot be solved
except by assuming as a principle that private ownership, and
its policy should be to induce as many of the people as possible
to become owners . . . If working people can be encouraged to
look forward to obtaining a share in the land, the result will be
that the gulf between vast wealth and deep poverty will be
bridged over, and the two orders will be brought nearer
together. Another consequence will be the greater abundance
of the fruits of the earth. Men always work harder and more
readily when they work on that which is their own; nay, they
learn to love the very soil which yields in response to the labour
of their hands not only food to eat, but an abundance of good
things for themselves and those that are dear to them . . .

   In the last place—employers and workmen may themselves
effect much in the matter of which We treat by means of those
institutions and organizations which afford opportune assistance to those in need, and which draw the two orders more
closely together. Among these may be enumerated: societies for
mutual help; various foundations established by private persons
for providing for the workman, and for his widow or his or-
phans in sudden calamity, in sickness, and in the event of
death . . . The most important of all are workmen's associations; for these virtually include the rest . . . Such associations
should be adapted to the requirements of the age in which we
live—an age of greater instruction, of different customs, and of
more numerous requirements in daily life. It is gratifying to
know that there are actually in existence not a few societies of
this nature, consisting either of workmen alone or of workmen
and employers together; but it were greatly to be desired that
they should multiply and become more effective . . . To enter
into 'society' of this kind is the natural right of man; and the
State must protect natural rights, not destroy them; and if it
forbids its citizens to form associations it contradicts the very
principle of its own existence; for both they and it exist in virtue
of the same principle, viz., the natural propensity of man to
live in society.

   There are times, no doubt, when it is right that the law
should interfere to prevent association; as when men join together for purposes which are evidently bad, unjust, or dangerous to the State. In such cases the public authority may justly

forbid the formation of associations, and may dissolve them when they already exist. But every precaution should be taken not to violate the rights of individuals and not to make unreasonable regulations under the pretence of public benefit . . .

119. *The French Law of Associations, 1 July 1901*

We have seen (No. 117) the trend of the republican governments in France to reduce and control the Roman Catholic Church's influence in education; when, in the Dreyfus affair (cf. No. 147) many Catholics, and even religious orders, openly revealed their anti-republican tendencies, the Government of republican consolidation under Waldeck-Rousseau introduced a measure to control religious congregations[1] and to force the dissolution of the most anti-republican ones. Although the law, excerpts of which follow, purports to deal with associations in general, large sections of it are applicable to religious orders and congregations only.[1]

Source: *British and Foreign State Papers*, vol. xcv (1901/2), pp. 1029–1035 (in French) (trans. Ed.).

I

1. An association is an agreement by which two or more persons permanently join their knowledge or efforts towards an aim other than their [personal] profit . . .
2. Persons may freely form associations without any need of authorization or legal notice, but [such associations] will not be considered legally incorporated unless the provisions of article 5 are observed . . .
5. [Legal notice, giving particulars of the name and objects of the association, the address of its establishments, and of the name, profession and address of its directors or chief administrators is required, accompanied by two copies of its statutes. The notice is to be handed in at the Prefecture of the Department.] . . .

III

13. No religious congregation may be formed without authorization by a law which determines the conditions of its activity. New establishments may only be founded by a religious con-

---

[1] Orders: societies of religious under solemn vows. Congregations (not to be confused with local parish congregations): societies of religious under simple vows.

gregation if it is given permission by a decree of the Council of State. The dissolution of a congregation or closing of its establishments may be ordered by a decree of the Council of Ministers.

14. No one who belongs to an unauthorized religious congregation is allowed to direct . . . an educational institution . . . or teach in one . . .

15. Every religious congregation [must keep full records of its financial transactions, and a complete and detailed list of its members] . . .

18. The congregations which are in existence at the time of the promulgation of this law, and have not been previously authorized or recognized, must prove within three months that they have taken all steps necessary to conform to the provisions of this law. In the absence of such proof, they are to be considered dissolved. This applies also to congregations whose authorization was refused . . .

120. *The French Law of Separation, 9 December 1905*

As a consequence of a series of new disputes between the Roman Catholic Church and the Government (partly over the Law of Associations, No. 119), and of the growing anti-clericalism of French political opinion, it was decided in 1905 to effect the separation of the State from the Church to whose maintenance the State was still contributing under the terms of the Concordat of 1801. The most important provisions of the law, which contradicted the traditional Catholic doctrine on the organization of the Church, follow hereunder.

Source: P. Sabatier, *Disestablishment in France* (London, T. Fisher Unwin, 1907), pp. 139–68.

1. The Republic assures liberty of conscience, and guarantees the free practice of religions, subject only to the restrictions hereinafter enacted in the interest of public order.

2. The Republic neither recognizes nor salaries nor subsidizes any religion. Consequently, on and after the first day of January next after the promulgation of the present law all expenses connected with the practice of religions will be omitted from the budgets of the State, of the departments and of the communes . . . The public religious establishments are hereby suppressed . . .

3. ... Immediately after the promulgation of the present law, the inspectors of the Department of Public Lands shall proceed to a descriptive inventory and valuation

(1) of the real and personal property of the said establishments;
(2) of the property of the State, of the departments, and of the communes, of which the same establishments have the use ....

4. Within a year from the date of the promulgation of the present law, the real and personal property of public religious establishments ... shall be transferred ... to the associations complying with the general rules of organization of the religion of which they propose to ensure the practice, which shall be legally formed according to the provisions of Article 19 ...

5. That portion of the property denoted in the foregoing Article which issues from the State ... shall revert to the State ...

9. In default of any association to take over the property of a public religious establishment, such property shall be assigned by decree to the communal institutions for poor relief or to the public charities ...

11. Ministers of religion who, at the time of the promulgation of the present law, shall have completed their sixtieth year and shall have held ecclesiastical offices salaried by the State for at least thirty years, shall receive an annual pension for life ...

18. The associations formed to provide for the cost, maintenance and public worship of a religion must be constituted in accordance with ... the law of 1st July 1901 (No. 119). They shall, moreover, be subject to the provisions of the present law.

19. These associations must have for their exclusive object the practice of a religion, and must have a minimum membership as follows:

In communes of less than 1,000 inhabitants, seven persons;
In communes of 1,000 to 20,000 inhabitants, fifteen persons;
In communes the inhabitants of which number over 20,000, twenty-five adult persons, domiciled or resident within the ecclesiastical district.

Any of their members may retire at any time after payment of the subscriptions that are due, and of those of the current year, notwithstanding any clause to the contrary ...

20. These associations may . . . form unions having a central administration or directorate . . .

30. . . . Religious teaching may be given to children between the ages of six and thirteen on the registers of the public schools only outside school hours . . .

35. If a discourse delivered or a document placarded or publicly distributed in the places in which worship is held, contains a direct provocation to resist the execution of the laws or the legal acts of public authority, or tends to arouse or arm one section of the citizens against the others, the minister of religion who shall be guilty of it shall be punished with an imprisonment of three months to two years . . .

XI · GERMANY 1871–1914

THE documents in this section deal with internal politics in the newly formed German Empire between its formation and the first world war. Foreign policy has been covered in some detail in Section IX (cf. Nos 96, 97, 100–3, 107, 110) and some documents of the *Kulturkampf* have been included in Section X (No. 116).

The proclamation by which William I accepted the imperial dignity (No. 121) begins the section. The constitution of the German Empire is not here included because, except for some slight concessions made to Bavaria and Württemberg, it follows closely the constitution of the North German Confederation (No. 71).

Several documents deal with the rise of socialism, and its consequences. The Gotha Programme (No. 122) of the first united German social democratic party is followed by legislation introduced by Bismarck to prohibit socialist activity (No. 123). But Bismarck was concerned with an improvement of the condition of the workers as well, and introduced a pioneering social welfare programme, some basic documents of which follow (No. 124). The series is concluded with the programme of the Social Democratic Party of Germany agreed to at its Erfurt Congress in 1891, after the party was legalized again (No. 127).

Soon after the establishment of the Empire pressure arose within Germany for the establishment or acquisition of German colonies, and a German Colonial Society was founded in 1880 (No. 125(a)). Bismarck originally opposed German' colonization, but he changed his views in 1883; an explanation of his views and intentions is included (No. 125(b)) followed by the text of the charter of the Society for German Colonization (No. 125(c)). Some further documents connected with German policy from the time after Bismarck's resignation in 1890 (No. 126) can be found in Section IX (Nos 107, 108, 110).

121. *Proclamation of William I on the Imperial Dignity,*
18 January 1871

While the Franco-Prussian war was still in progress (cf. Nos 96, 97) the rulers of the South German States (Bavaria, Baden, and Württemberg), which had joined Prussia in the war, agreed to join the States of the North German Confederation in forming a German Empire, and they asked William I, King of Prussia and President of the Confederation (cf. No. 71) to assume the imperial crown. William I accepted the dignity in the following proclamation.

Source: *Annual Register*, 1871, pp. [220–1].

We, William, by God's grace King of Prussia, hereby announce that the German Princes and Free Towns having addressed to us a unanimous call to renew and undertake with the re-establishment of the German Empire the dignity of Emperor, which now for sixty years has been in abeyance, and the requisite provisions having been inserted in the constitution of the German Confederation, we regard it as a duty we owe to the entire Fatherland to comply with this call of the United German Princes and Free Towns, and to accept the dignity of Emperor.

Accordingly, we and our successors to the Crown of Prussia henceforth shall use the Imperial title in all our relations and affairs of the German Empire and we hope to God that it may be vouchsafed to the German nation to lead the Fatherland on to a blessed future under the auspices of its ancient splendour ...

122. *The Gotha Programme, May 1875*

As industrialization proceeded in Germany, socialism also gained strength, but the working class was still divided between two major movements (cf. No. 73). After the unification of Germany, however, unity in the German workers' movement became more important than ever. To bring it about, representatives of the Lassallean General German Workers' Union, and of the Marxist Social-Democratic Labour Party, met in 1875 in the unity congress of Gotha, and there formulated the following joint programme of their now united party, the Social Democratic Party of Germany, often referred to by its German initials SPD.

Source: Schönberg, *Handbuch der politischen Oekonomie* (3rd ed.), vol. i, pp. 131 ff., in J. H. Robinson and C. A. Beard, *Readings in Modern European History* (Boston, Ginn, 1909), vol. ii, pp. 493–5.

1. Labour is the source of all wealth and of all civilization; and since it is only through society that generally productive labour is possible, the whole product of labour, where there is a general obligation to work, belongs to society,—that is, to all its members, by equal right, and to each according to his reasonable needs.

In the society of to-day the means of production are a monopoly of the capitalistic class; the dependence of the working class, which results from this, is the cause of misery and servitude in all its forms.

The emancipation of labour requires the conversion of the means of production into the common property of society and the social regulation of all labour and its application for the general good, together with the just distribution of the product of labour.

The emancipation of labour must be the work of the labouring class itself, opposed to which all other classes are reactionary groups.

2. Proceeding from these principles, the socialist labour party of Germany endeavours by every lawful means to bring about a free State and a socialistic society, to effect the destruction of the iron law of wages by doing away with the system of wage labour, to abolish exploitation of every kind, and to extinguish all social and political inequality.

The socialist labour party of Germany, although for the time being confining its activity within national bounds, is fully conscious of the international character of the labour movement, and is resolved to meet all the obligations which this lays upon the labourer, in order to bring the brotherhood of all mankind to a full realization.

The socialist labour party of Germany, in order to prepare the way for the solution of the social question, demands the establishment of socialistic productive associations with the support of the State and under democratic control of the working people. These productive associations, for both industry and agriculture, are to be created to such an extent that the socialistic organization of all labour may result therefrom.

[In addition to the demand for universal suffrage for all above twenty years of age, secret ballot, freedom of the press, free and compulsory education, etc.,] the socialist labour party of Germany demands the following reforms in the present social organization: (1) the greatest possible extension of political rights and freedom in the sense of the above-mentioned demands; (2) a single progressive income tax, both State and local, instead of all the existing taxes, especially the indirect ones, which weigh heavily upon the people; (3) unlimited right of association; (4) a normal working day corresponding with the needs of society, and the prohibition of work on Sunday; (5) prohibition of child labour and all forms of labour by women which are dangerous to health or morality; (6) laws for the protection of the life and health of workmen, sanitary control of workmen's houses, inspection of mines, factories, workshops, and domestic industries by officials chosen by the workmen themselves, and an effective system of enforcement of the same; (7) regulation of prison labour.

123. *The Anti-Socialist Law, 21 October 1878*

The formation of a united socialist party (cf. No. 122) and its electoral success revealed to Bismarck the extent to which this, in his view, subversive movement was gaining influence among the German workers. Using repeated attempts at assassinating the Emperor as his excuse, Bismarck introduced legislation in the Reichstag to prohibit socialist activity. There was some initial opposition to the measure among the representatives, but Bismarck managed to carry it through after an election was fought on the issue. Some of the principal provisions of the law follow; it is worthy of note that the law did not prohibit the candidature and election of socialists to the Reichstag.

Source: *Reichsgesetzblatt*, 1878, No. 34, 21 October 1878, pp. 351-8 (trans. Ed.).

1. Associations which aim, by social-democratic, socialistic or communistic agitation, at the destruction of the existing order in State or society are forbidden. The same holds of associations in which such activity makes its appearance in a manner likely to endanger the peace, in particular, the harmony between different classes of the population . . .

9. Meetings in which social-democratic, socialistic, or communistic tendencies, directed to the destruction of the existing order in State or society, make their appearance are to be dissolved. Such meetings as appear to justify the assumption that

they are destined to further such tendencies are to be forbidden. Public festivities and processions are placed under the same restriction . . .

11. All printed matter, in which social-democratic, socialistic, or communistic tendencies appear . . . is to be forbidden. In the case of periodical literature, the prohibition can be extended to any further issue, as soon as a single number has been forbidden under this law . . .

16. The collection of contributions for the furthering of social-democratic, socialistic, or communistic endeavours . . . as also the public instigation to the furnishing of such contributions, are to be forbidden by the police . . . The money seized [by the police] from forbidden collections, or the equivalent of the same, is to fall to the poor-relief fund of the neighbourhood.

28. For districts and localities in which, because of the above-mentioned agitation, public safety is endangered, the following provisions can be put into effect, for the space of a year at most, by the central police of the State in question, subject to the permission of the Bundesrat.

(1) That public meetings may only take place with the previous permission of the police; this prohibition does not extend to meetings for an election to the Reichstag or the diet.

(2) That the distribution of printed matter may not take place in public roads, streets, squares, or other public localities.

(3) That residence in such districts or localities can be forbidden to all persons from whom danger to the public safety or order is to be feared . . .

124. *Bismarck's Social Legislation Programme*

Bismarck realized that repressive legislation alone could not prevent the success of social-democratic ideas among the workers. The workers could only be transformed into contented subjects if steps were taken to safeguard their welfare. He therefore devised a system of accident and invalidity insurance and age pensions well in accordance with the paternalistic traditions of the Prussian State and well in advance of similar legislation in other European States. He had some difficulty in carrying his various measures through the Reichstag where the strong liberal group viewed State interference in the relationship of employer and employee with disfavour, particularly as financial contributions were expected from employers as well as workers. Nevertheless, in spite of minor defeats, Bismarck was successful in carrying his most important measures.

Our selections consist of imperial speeches to the Reichstag which give an outline of the programme.

Source: H. Kohl, *Dreissig Jahre preussisch-deutscher Geschichte in amtlichen Kundgebungen* (Giessen, Ricker, 1888), pp. 246, 249–50 (trans. Ed.).

(a) Speech opening the Reichstag, 15 February 1881.

. . . At the opening of the Reichstag in February 1879 His Majesty the Emperor with reference to the [anti-socialist] law of 21 October 1878 (No. 123) expressed the hope that the Reichstag would not refuse its continuing co-operation in remedying social ills by means of legislation. Such remedy shall be sought not only in the repression of socialistic excesses, but also in the promotion of the welfare of the workers. In this respect the care of such workers as are incapable of earning their livelihood is the first step. In their interest His Majesty the Emperor had a bill on the insurance of workers against the result of accidents presented to the Bundesrat—a bill which is intended to meet a need felt equally by workers and employers. His Majesty the Emperor hopes that the bill will receive the assent of the Governments of the States, and that it will be welcomed by the Reichstag as a complement of the legislation on protection against social-democratic activity (No. 123). The now existing provisions which should have protected the worker from becoming helpless through the loss of his earning capacity by accident or old age have proved inadequate, and their inadequacy has contributed no little to turning the members of this class to participation in social-democratic activity in order to seek help . . .

(b) Imperial Message opening the Reichstag, 17 November 1881.

. . . Already in February of this year We expressed our conviction that the healing of social disorders must not proceed exclusively through the repression of social-democratic excesses, but must also be sought through the promotion of the welfare of the workers. We consider it to be Our Imperial duty to urge the Reichstag to the execution of this task, and We would look back on the achievements with which God has blessed Our government with all the more satisfaction if We succeeded in taking with Us the knowledge that We leave to the Fatherland a new and lasting assurance of internal peace, that We leave to those who need help . . . an increased certainty and amount of assistance. In Our endeavours to this end We count on the assent of the Federated Governments and the support of the Reichstag without party distinction . . .

The Bill on insurance of workers against industrial accidents will be redrafted in the light of the debate in the Reichstag in the last session, to prepare for its re-submission for debate. As a supplement to it a new bill will be introduced which will provide for the concurrent establishment of industrial sickness benefit organizations. But also those who have become incapable of earning a living through age or invalidity have a justified claim on society to a greater measure of state assistance than they have received up to now.

To find the correct means and methods for this state assistance is one of the most difficult, but also one of the highest tasks of every community which stands on the moral foundations of a Christian public life . . .

125. *Colonial Affairs*

Germany, which had been a confederation of continental States, only became a first-class power in 1871 and had no colonies. In the trend to imperial expansion which is characteristic of this period, Germans wanted to become participants in the race for colonies. The motives were partly commercial—German trading interests wanted support in colonial trade—partly nationalistic—possession of colonies added to national prestige. Many societies were formed to propagate the idea of colonization, culminating in the Colonial Society (*Kolonialverein*) whose aims follow (a).

Bismarck long opposed colonization. He appears to have changed his mind in 1883—his motives are still being debated—and in a speech in 1884 (b) he explained his views and intentions. The charter of the German company which established German East Africa (c) characterizes Bismarck's colonial policy.

After Bismarck's resignation (cf. No. 126) German colonial policy became rather more expansive, though also less successful. On this aspect see Nos 107, 108, and 110 in Section IX.

Source: (a) and (b) : H. Blum, *Das deutsche Reich zur Zeit Bismarcks*

(Leipzig und Wien, Bibliographisches Institut, 1892), pp. 607, 601–2 (trans. Ed.).

(c) H. Kohl, *Dreissig Jahre preussisch-deutscher Geschichte in amtlichen Kundgebungen* (Giessen, Ricker, 1888), pp. 277–8 (trans. Ed.).

(a) Article 2 of the Statutes of the *Kolonialverein*, 6 December 1880.

The German Colonial Society has adopted as its objects [the following]:

to spread, in ever wider circles, a realization of the necessity of devoting the national effort to the field of colonization;

to serve as a centre for the movements with such an aim which have come into being in many parts of the fatherland; and

to prepare the way for a practical solution of the problem of colonization.

As a first step towards larger undertakings the Society demands the establishment of trading stations.

(b) Bismarck's Speech in the Reichstag, 26 June 1884.

. . . The genesis of the colonial question is as follows: The enterprises of hanseatic merchants, connected with the purchase of land followed by requests for protection by the Reich first caused us to consider closely the question, whether we could promise such protection to the extent desired. I still retain today my earlier aversion to colonies as they were in the last century, what we would now call the French system—here a territory is acquired as the basis, and then emigrants are sought, officials appointed and garrisons established. It is a different question whether it is expedient, and, secondly, whether it is the duty of the German Reich, to afford protection and certain kinds of support to such subjects as devote themselves to enterprises of this kind trusting in protection by the Reich. This question I answer affirmatively, with less certainty as to expediency (I cannot foretell what will come out of it), but with absolute certainty as to the duty of the state.

I cannot avoid this answer. I first approached the matter with hesitation and asked myself: how could I justify it if I were to say to these entrepreneurs, whose courage . . ., whose audacity, whose enthusiasm for their task pleased me so much: all this is very well, but the German Empire is not strong enough, it would attract the ill-will of other States, it would . . . come to unpleasant encounters with others, it would receive raps on the nose [*sic*] without being able to retaliate. I did not have the courage as Chancellor of the Reich to make to the entrepreneurs this declaration of bankruptcy of the German nation in respect to overseas undertakings.

We do not intend to engage in a colonial policy of exclusion, used, unfortunately, by other, less powerful states, like England, which hinder the development and trade of their colonies through it.

[It has been] mentioned that our colonial enterprises would be extraordinarily costly, and would cause our distressed Reich treasury to get into an even worse condition. This would be true if we were to begin, as happened in earlier attempts, by sending out a number of higher and lower officials, followed by the dispatch of a garrison, the construction of barracks, ports and fortifications. But this is far from being our intention. Our intention . . . is to leave the responsibility for the material development and establishment of colonies to the activity and spirit of enterprise of our seafaring and trading citizens, and rather than to proceed in the form of annexing overseas territories to the German Reich, to use the device of charters . . . which would, in essence, leave the [colonizing company] to govern the colony, and would only afford it a European judicial system and such protection as can be given without standing garrisons. Our intention is not to found provinces, but to protect in their development commercial enterprises, even those in the highest stage of development, those which acquire a sovereignty, a trading sovereignty which might ultimately be transferred to the German Reich, to protect them not only from attacks from their immediate vicinity, but also from oppression and damage from other European powers . . .

(c) Imperial Letter of Protection to the Society for German Colonization, 27 February 1885.

. . . The Chairmen of the Society for German Colonization, Dr. Carl Peters and . . . Felix Count Behr-Bandelin having requested Our protection for the territorial acquisitions of the Society in East Africa . . . and having submitted to Us the contracts by which these territories have been ceded to them [by the local rulers] with rights of sovereignty with the request that We receive these territories under Our sovereignty, We herewith declare that We have accepted the sovereignty and placed the territories . . . under Our imperial protection.

We grant to the said Society, on condition that it remains a German Society, and that the members of its board of directors are German citizens, . . . the power to exercise all rights based on the contracts submitted to us, including the right of jurisdiction, under the supervision of our government, over natives and over citizens of the Reich and of other nations who will settle in these territories, go there for trading or other purposes . . .

126. *Bismarck's Resignation, 18 March 1890*

Soon after the accession of William II in 1888 it became clear that the old Chancellor and the young Emperor both laid claim to the direction of policy, internal as well as external. Clashes occurred over the policy to be followed towards Russia, the renewal of the anti-socialist legislation, and several other matters. The final breach, however, came over a comparatively minor matter, William's insistence that Prussian ministers should have direct access to him, bypassing the Prime Minister, Bismarck.

The following excerpts from Bismarck's letter of resignation reveal his attitude.

Source: *New Chapters of Bismarck's Autobiography*, tr. by Bernard Miall (London, Hodder & Stoughton, 1920), pp. 189–98. Also contained in *The Kaiser vs. Bismarck: New Chapters of Bismarck's Autobiography*, as translated by Bernard Miall (New York, Harper, 1920), pp. 113–17.

In connection with my respectful proposal of the 15th of this month Your Majesty has commanded me to present a draft order by which the Royal Order of the 8th September, 1852, which has since then regulated the position of the Prime Minister in respect of his colleagues, should be annulled . . .

In the time of absolute sovereignty, there was no need of the post of Prime Minister. The need was first demonstrated in . . . 1847 . . . of clearing the way for a constitutional state of affairs by the appointment of a Prime Minister whose duty it would be to watch over the unification of the policy of the responsible

Ministers, and to carry out the same, and to accept the responsibility for the joint results of the Cabinet's policy. With the year 1848 the constitutional habit became part of our life, and Prime Ministers were appointed . . . It was incumbent upon them to maintain, in the Cabinet, and in its relations with the monarch, that unity and stability without which ministerial responsibility, as constituting the essence of constitutional life, cannot be realized. The relations of the Ministry and its individual members to this new institution of the Premiership very soon necessitated a stricter regulation, corresponding with the Constitution, such as was effected, in agreement with the Ministry of the day, by the Order of the 8th September, 1852. This Order has since then remained of decisive importance to the position of the Prime Minister, and has alone given the Prime Minister the authority which makes it possible to accept that measure of responsibility for the joint policy of the Cabinet which is expected of him . . . If every individual Minister can extract orders from the Sovereign, without a previous understanding with his colleagues, a united Cabinet policy, for which each Minister shall be responsible, is not possible . . . In this connection, as was established in yesterday's Cabinet meeting, my colleagues are as a whole in agreement with me, and also in this respect, that any successor of mine in the Premiership would be unable to assume the responsibility for his administration if the authority bestowed by the Order of 1852 were lacking to him. To each of my successors this necessity will appeal even more forcibly than to me, because he will not immediately be assisted by the authority which many years of the Premiership and the confidence of both the late Kaisers has lent me. I have not hitherto found it necessary expressly to refer my colleagues to the Order of 1852. Its existence, and the certainty that I possessed the confidence of the late Kaisers Wilhelm and Friedrich, were sufficient securely to establish my authority in the Ministry. This certainty no longer exists to-day, either for myself or my colleagues. On this account I have been obliged to fall back upon the Order of 1852, that I might securely establish the necessary centralization of your Majesty's service.

For the foregoing reasons I am not in a position to carry out Your Majesty's command, according to which I was to accomplish and countersign the abrogation of the Order of 1852, of which I had been only lately reminded, but was nevertheless to continue in the Premiership . . .

I ventured to assume that it would be acceptable to Your Majesty if I resigned my posts in the Prussian service, but remained in the Imperial service. I have, after close examination of this question, permitted myself respectfully to draw attention to a few critical results of this division of my offices, particularly in respect of the future appearances of the Imperial Chancellor in the Reichstag, while refraining from recapitulating in this place all the results which such a separation between Prussia and the Imperial Chancellor would produce . . .

Even if it were practicable to carry out our foreign policy so independently of our domestic policy, and our Imperial policy so independently of our Prussian policy, as would be the case if the Imperial Chancellor had as little to do with Prussian as with Bavarian or Saxon politics, and had no interest in increasing the strength of the Prussian vote in the Federal Council and the Reichstag, yet I should find it impossible, in accordance with the latest decision of Your Majesty, concerning a direction of our foreign policy, . . . to undertake the execution of Your Majesty's written commands in respect of our foreign policy. I should thereby call in question all the results of importance to the German Empire which our foreign policy has, for decades, under unfavourable circumstances, achieved, in the opinion of both your Majesty's predecessors, as regards our relations with Russia . . .

It is very painful to me, in my attachment to the service of the Royal House, and to Your Majesty, and after long years of familiarity with conditions which I had regarded as permanent, to sever myself from the accustomed relations with Your Majesty and the general policy of the Empire and of Prussia; but after conscientious consideration of Your Majesty's intentions, which I should have to be prepared to carry out were I to remain in the service, I cannot do otherwise than most humbly beseech Your Majesty graciously to please to release me, with the statutory pension, from the offices of Imperial Chancellor, Prime Minister, and Prussian Minister of Foreign Affairs.

After my impressions of the last few weeks and the disclosures which I gathered yesterday from the communications of Your Majesty's Civil and Military Cabinets, I may in all respects assume that I am meeting Your Majesty's wishes by this my request for leave to resign, and I may also with safety assume that Your Majesty will graciously grant my request.

I would have submitted the request for my discharge from my office to Your Majesty a long time ago, if I had not had the impression that it was Your Majesty's wish to make use of the experience and the capacities of a faithful servant of your predecessors. Now that I am sure that Your Majesty does not require these, I am able to retire from public life, without the fear that my decision will be condemned as untimely by public opinion.

127. The Erfurt Programme of the Social-Democratic Party of Germany, October 1891

On the Emperor William's insistence the anti-socialist legislation (No. 123) was not renewed when it expired in 1890 and thus the Social-Democratic Party of Germany could be legally re-established. At its congress in 1890 it decided that the Gotha programme of 1875 (No. 122) no longer met the needs of the times. A committee was therefore set up and it drew up a new party programme, rather more militant in tone, which was duly adopted by the party congress at Erfurt in 1891.

Source: *Manifesto of the Social-Democratic Party in the German Empire as adopted at the Erfurt Congress of 1891* (Melbourne, Melbourne Fabian Society, 1895), pp. 3–6.

. . . Ever greater grows the mass of the proletariat, ever vaster the army of the unemployed, ever sharper the contrast between oppressors and oppressed, ever fiercer that war of classes between bourgeoisie and proletariat, which divides modern society into two hostile camps, and is the common characteristic of every industrial country. The gulf between the propertied classes and the destitute is widened by the crisis arising from capitalist production, which becomes daily more comprehensive and omnipotent, which makes universal uncertainty the normal condition of society, and which furnishes a proof that the forces of production have outgrown the existing social order, and that private ownership of the means of production has become incompatible with their full development and their proper application.

Private ownership of the means of production, formerly the means of securing his product to the producer, has now become the means of expropriating the peasant proprietors, the artisans, and the small tradesmen, and placing the non-producers, the capitalists, and large land-owners in possession of the products of labour. Nothing but the conversion of capitalist private ownership of the means of production—the earth and its fruits, mines and quarries, raw material, tools, machines, means of exchange—into social ownership, and the substitution of socialist production carried on by and for society in the place of the present production of commodities for exchange, can effect such a revolution that, instead of large industries and the steadily growing capacities of common production being, as hitherto, a source of misery and oppression to the classes whom they have despoiled, they may become a source of the highest well-being and of the most perfect and comprehensive harmony.

This social revolution involves the emancipation, not merely of the proletariat, but of the whole human race, which is suffering under existing conditions.

The struggle of the working classes against capitalist exploitation must of necessity be a political struggle. The working classes can neither carry on their economic struggle nor develop their economic organization without political rights. They cannot effect the transfer of the means of production to the community without being first invested with political power.

It must be the aim of social democracy to give conscious unanimity to this struggle of the working classes, and to indicate the inevitable goal.

The interests of the working classes are identical in all lands governed by capitalist methods of production . . . Therefore the emancipation of labour is a task in which the workmen of all civilized lands have a share. Recognizing this, the Social Democrats of Germany feel and declare themselves at one with the workmen of every land, who are conscious of the destinies of their class.

The German Social Democrats, are not, therefore, fighting for new class privileges and rights, but for the abolition of class government, and even of classes themselves, and for universal equality in rights and duties, without distinction of sex or rank. Holding these views, they are not merely fighting against the exploitation and oppression of the wage-earners in the existing social order, but against every kind of exploitation and oppression, whether directed against class, party, sex or race.

Starting from these principles, the German Social Democrats demand, to begin with:—

1. Universal, equal and direct suffrage by ballot, in all elections, for all subjects of the Empire over twenty years of age, without distinction of sex. Proportional representation, and, until this system has been introduced, fresh division of electoral districts by law after each census. Two years' duration of the legislature. Holding of elections on a legal day of rest. Payment of the representatives elected. Removal of all restrictions upon political rights, except in the case of persons under age.

2. Direct legislation by the people by means of the right of initiative and of veto. Self-government by the people in empire, state, province, and commune. Election of magistrates by the people, with the right of holding them responsible. Annual vote of taxes.

3. Universal military education. Substitution of militia for a standing army. Decision by the popular representatives of questions of peace and war. Decision of all international disputes by arbitration.

4. Abolition of all laws which restrict or suppress free expression of opinion and the right of meeting or association.

5. Abolition of all laws which place the woman, whether in a private or a public capacity, at a disadvantage as compared with the man.

6. Declaration that religion is a private matter . . .

7. Secularization of education. Compulsory attendance at public national schools. Free education, free supply of educational apparatus, and free maintenance to children in schools, and to such pupils, male and female, in higher educational institutions, as are judged to be fitted for further education.

8. Free administration of the law and free legal assistance. Administration of the law by judges elected by the people . . . Abolition of capital punishment.

9. Free medical assistance, and free supply of remedies. Free burial of the dead.

10. Graduated income and property tax to meet all public

expenses, which are to be met by taxation. Self-assessment. Succession duties, graduated according to the extent of the inheritance and the degree of relationship. Abolition of all indirect taxation . . .

For the protection of labour, the German Social Democrats also demand to begin with:—

1. An effective national and international system of protective legislation on the following principles:—

   a. The fixing of a nominal working day which shall not exceed eight hours.

   b. Prohibition of the employment of children under fourteen.

   c. Prohibition of night work . . .

   d. An unbroken rest of at least thirty-six hours for every workman every week.

   e. Prohibition of the truck system.

2. Supervision of all industrial establishments . . . by an Imperial labour department . . . A thorough system of industrial sanitary regulation.

3. Legal equality of agricultural labourers and domestic servants with industrial labourers . . .

4. Confirmation of the rights of association.

5. The taking over by the Imperial Government of the whole system of workmen's insurance, though giving the workmen a certain share in its administration.

XII · PRE-REVOLUTIONARY RUSSIA
1825–1917

THE selection of documents for this section presented greater difficulties than for any other, because of the wealth of important material available. Government documents and revolutionary writings could easily have filled a whole volume by themselves. It was decided, therefore, to include few documents, mainly such as are not easily available, and to aim at illustration rather than at full coverage.

Documents of the first Russian revolution, the Decembrist rising of 1825 (No. 128), open the section, followed by documents relating to the most important reform measures of Alexander II, the emancipation of the serfs (No. 129) and the establishment of zemstvos (No. 130).

Oppositional and revolutionary movements did not cease with the defeat of the Decembrist movement, nor even with the enactment of the great reforms. On the contrary, they continued to gain strength in spite of repression, and to split up into several distinct groups. It was not possible to include excerpts of writings of revolutionaries, which would have been best suited to reveal their thought, nor could be more than illustrative material selected: some *narodnik* manifestoes of 1881 (No. 131), the programme of the first Russian Marxist group (No. 132), the rules of the Russian Social-Democratic Labour Party, drafted by Lenin (No. 133), and the programme of the Union of Liberation (No. 134). It is regretted that the programme of the Socialist Revolutionary Party could not be included.

The first great crisis the Russian Government had to surmount was the Revolution of 1905. The petition of the workers of St. Petersburg (No. 135) and brief selections which throw a light on the activity of the Soviet of Workers' Deputies (No. 139) illustrate the revolutionaries' side of the Revolution, while the manifestoes which grant political (Nos 136, 137) and economic (No. 138) concessions illustrate the Government's side. The main achievement of the 1905 revolution was the calling of a representative legislative assembly, the State Duma, and the promulgation of new fundamental laws (No. 140(a)). The State Duma soon embarked on the discussion of a liberal reform programme, but this was not acceptable to the Tsar who dissolved the Duma after a few months (No. 140(b)). Considerations of space and unsuitability unfortunately preclude the inclusion of documents dealing with the Duma and the Government's activity (mainly Stolypin's reform programme) between 1906 and 1917.

Documents on Russian foreign policy may be found in Sections I (where most documents have a relevance), IX (Nos 93, 94, 99, 101, 103–5) and XIV (No. 157).

Dates in this section have been given in accordance with the Julian Calendar in use in Russia at the time. This was twelve days behind the Gregorian Calendar used in Western Europe during the nineteenth century, thirteen days behind in the twentieth century.

128. *The Decembrist Rising, December 1825*

During the Napoleonic Wars, for the first time in history, a large number of educated Russians, mainly army officers, gained a first-hand knowledge of Western Europe and, by making a comparison, came to a realization of the backwardness of Russia and the necessity of reform. As the Government of Alexander I hardly went beyond the discussion of some half-hearted proposals, a great deal of conspiratorial activity ensued, centred on the capital, St. Petersburg, and on the Ukraine. Largely influenced by the French Enlightenment, the conspirators of the several secret societies wished to take power to introduce fairly far-ranging reforms. Their plans were by no means perfected when the confusion following the death of Alexander I moved them to action. There were military risings at both centres of the conspiracy but, because of lack of co-ordination and the absence of popular support, they were easily defeated.

Our documents include a manifesto drawn up by the leader of the St. Petersburg group, Trubetskoi (a), which was to be promulgated if the rising was successful, and which sets out the programme of the revolutionaries; the appeal to the people written by S. Muravev-Apostol and M. Bestuzhev-Riumin (b) shows, by contrast, the traditional type of argument by which the conspirators hoped to gain popular support.

Source: A. G. Mazour, *The First Russian Revolution: 1825* (Stanford, Calif., Stanford University Press, 1937), pp. 283–5.

(a) Trubetskoi's Manifesto, 13 December 1825

The Manifesto of the Senate should proclaim:

1. abolition of the former Government;
2. establishment of a Provisional Government until a permanent one is decided upon by representatives;
3. freedom of the press, hence abolition of censorship;
4. religious tolerance of all faiths;
5. abolition of the right to own men;
6. equality of all classes before the law . . .
7. announcement of rights for every citizen to occupy himself with whatever he wishes [regardless of class] . . . to acquire all kinds of property . . .
8. cancellation of poll tax and arrears;
9. abolition of monopolies on salt and alcohol . . .
10. abolition of recruiting and military colonies;
11. reduction of the term of military service . . .
12. retirement . . . of all privates who have served fifteen years;
13. the creation of Community, County, Gubernia and Regional administrations, which are to be substituted for all civil service men appointed formerly by the Government;
14. public trials;
15. introduction of a jury system . . .

There shall be created an administration of two or three persons to which all the highest officers of the Government shall be subordinated . . . the entire Supreme Executive Government, but not the legislative nor judicial . . .

The Provisional Government is instructed to:

1. equalize all classes;
2. form all local, Community, County, Gubernia and Regional administrations;
3. form a National Guard;
4. form a judicial branch with a jury;
5. equalize recruiting obligations among all classes;

6. abolish a permanent army;
7. establish a form of election of representatives to the Lower Chamber which will have to ratify the future form of Government.

(b) An Appeal to the People.

The Lord took pity on Russia and sent death to our tyrant. Christ said: you shall not be slaves of men, for you were redeemed by my blood. The world did not listen to this sacred command and fell into misery. But our suffering moved the Lord, and today He is sending us freedom and salvation. Brethren! Let us repent of our long servility and swear: let there be a sole Tsar in Heaven and on Earth, Jesus Christ.

All misfortunes of the Russian people derived from autocratic government. It broke down. By the death of the tyrant the Lord signifies His will—that we throw off from ourselves the chains of slavery, which are repugnant to Christian law. From now on Russia is free. But as true sons of the Church, let us not attempt any crime, but, without civil strife, establish a government of the people, based on the law of God which proclaims: 'And whosoever will be chief among you, let him be your servant.'

The Russian army hopes to establish a government of the people, based upon sacred law. And so, let this pious people of ours remain in peace and tranquillity and pray the Lord for the most speedy accomplishment of our sacred undertaking. The servants of the altar who have been forsaken in poverty and scorned to this day by the impious tyrant now pray the Lord for us in restoring in all glory the Temples of God.

129. *The Emancipation of the Serfs*

Most reform-minded Russians considered that the fundamental measure, on which all reforms were to be based, should be the emancipation of the serfs. Some steps were taken by Alexander I and Nicholas I to improve the condition of the serfs, particularly the State serfs, but none of these reforms was far-reaching. It was only after defeat in the Crimean War (cf. Nos 93, 94), in which the Russian soldier showed up badly in comparison with his Western counterpart, that the new Tsar, Alexander II, began taking steps towards general reforms, including emancipation.

In his speech to the Assembly of Nobility of Moscow Province

(a) Alexander merely expressed his concern, but followed this up by the appointment of a series of committees to consider the reforms. The outcome was the emancipation ukaze (b) of 19 February 1861, which sets out the principles of the measure emancipating the privately owned serfs. State serfs were emancipated soon afterwards, under similar conditions.

Unfortunately the decree which prescribes the methods in which emancipation, redemption, etc. is to be carried out is far too long and detailed for excerpts to be at all meaningful, while its inclusion in full would have been impossible.

Source: (a) A. Rambaud, *History of Russia from the Earliest Times to 1882* (Boston, Estes and Lauriat, 1886), vol. iii, p. 221.
      (b) *Annual Register*, 1861, pp. [207-12].

(a) Speech of Alexander II to the Moscow Nobility, March 1856.

. . . For the removal of certain unfounded reports I consider it necessary to declare to you that I have not at present the intention of annihilating serfage; but certainly, as you yourselves know, the existing manner of possessing serfs cannot remain unchanged. It is better to abolish serfage from above than to await the time when it will begin to abolish itself from below. I request you, gentlemen, to consider how this can be put into execution, and to submit my words to the Noblesse for their consideration . . .

(b) Emancipation Ukaze, 19 February 1861

. . . In considering the various classes and conditions of which the State is composed we came to the conviction that the legislation of the Empire, having wisely provided for the organization of the upper and middle classes and having defined with precision their obligations, their rights, and their privileges, has not attained the same degree of efficiency as regards the peasants attached to the soil, thus designated because whether from ancient law or from custom they have been hereditarily subjected to the authority of the proprietors, on whom it was incumbent at the same time to provide for their welfare. The rights of the proprietors have been hitherto very extended and very imperfectly defined by the law, which has been supplied by tradition, custom, and the good pleasure of the proprietors . . .

As the paternal character of the relations between the proprietors and the peasants became weakened, and, moreover, as the seigneurial authority fell sometimes into hands exclusively occupied with their personal interests, those bonds of mutual good-will slackened, and a wide opening was made for an arbitrary sway, which weighed upon the peasants, was unfavourable to their welfare, and made them indifferent to all progress under the conditions of their existence . . .

We thus came to the conviction that the work of a serious improvement of the condition of the peasants was a sacred inheritance bequeathed to us by our ancestors, a mission which, in the course of events, Divine Providence called upon us to fulfil . . .

Having invoked the Divine assistance, we have resolved to carry this work into execution.

In virtue of the new dispositions . . . the peasants attached to the soil will be invested within a term fixed by the law with all rights of free cultivators.

The proprietors retaining their rights of property on all the land belonging to them, grant to the peasants for a fixed regulated rental the full enjoyment of their close; and, moreover, to assure their livelihood and to guarantee the fulfilment of their obligations towards the Government, the quantity of arable land is fixed by the said dispositions, as well as other rural appurtenances.

But, in the enjoyment of these territorial allotments, the peasants are obliged, in return, to acquit the rentals fixed by the same dispositions . . . In this state, which must be a transitory one, the peasants shall be designated as 'temporarily bound'.

At the same time, they are granted the right of purchasing their close, and, with the consent of the proprietors, they may acquire in full property the arable lands and other appurtenances which are allotted to them as a permanent holding. By the acquisition in full property of the quantity of land fixed, the peasants are free from their obligations towards the proprietors for land thus purchased, and they enter definitively into the condition of free peasant landholders.

By a special disposition concerning the domestics, a transitory state is fixed for them . . . On the expiration of a term of two years . . . they shall receive their full enfranchisement and some temporary immunities . . .

We leave it to the proprietors to come to amicable terms with the peasants and to conclude transactions relative to the extent of the territorial allotment and to the amount of rental to be fixed in consequence, observing, at the same time, the established rules to guarantee the inviolability of such agreements.

As the new organization, in consequence of the inevitable complexity of the changes which it necessitates, cannot be immediately put into execution, as a lapse of time is necessary, which cannot be less than two years or thereabouts; to avoid all misunderstanding and to protect public and private interests during this interval, the system actually existing on the properties of landowners will be maintained up to the moment when a new system shall have been instituted . . .

For which end we have deemed it advisable to ordain:—

1. To establish in each district a special court for the question of the peasants; it will have to investigate the affairs of the rural communes established on the land of the lords of the soil.

2. To appoint in each district justices of the peace to investigate on the spot all misunderstandings and disputes which may arise on the occasion of the introduction of the new regulation, and to form district assemblies with these justices of the peace.

3. To organize in the seigneurial properties communal administrations . . . and to open in the large villages district administrations . . .

4. To formulate, verify and confirm in each rural district or estate a charter of rules in which shall be enumerated, on the basis of the local Statute, the amount of land reserved to the peasants in permanent enjoyment, and the extent of the charges which may be exacted from them . . .

5. To put these charters into execution . . . within the term of two years . . .

6. Up to the expiration of this term, the peasants and domestics are to remain in the same obedience towards their proprietors, and to fulfil their former obligations without scruple.

7. The proprietors will continue to watch over the maintenance of order on their estates, with the right of jurisdiction and of police, until the organization of the districts and of the district tribunals has been effected . . .

To render the transactions between the proprietors and the

peasants more easy, in virtue of which the latter may acquire in full property their close (homestead) and the land they occupy, the Government will advance assistance, according to a special regulation, by means of loans or a transfer of debts encumbering an estate . . .

130. *The Establishment of the Zemstvos, January 1864*

The emancipation of the serfs having provided the foundation, Alexander II continued his reform of Russian institutions, and the following years reformed the administration of justice, municipal law, the army, etc. Most important among these measures was the decree issued in January 1864 which provided that districts and provinces should each elect a zemstvo or assembly to carry out the functions of local government. A summary of the provisions of the decree follows.

Source: T. J. Polner, *Russian Local Government during the War and the Union of Zemstvos* (New Haven, Yale University Press, 1930) (Economic and Social History of the World War, Russian Series, Carnegie Endowment for International Peace), pp. 16–22.

The zemstvos were introduced in only thirty-four of the central provinces of the Empire. None were established in Siberia, Turkestan, the Caucasus, Trans-Caucasia, Poland, the Baltic Provinces, and the Cossack territories. Nine provinces in the West and North-West, where many of the big landlords were Poles were also denied zemstvo government. But even where the zemstvos were established they were considered not as links in the machinery of government, nor as authoritative organs of public law, but as private corporate associations formed in order to satisfy such local needs as are distinct from the interests of the State . . .

The competence of the zemstvo institutions was wide from the outset, nevertheless. The Law of 1864 left to the zemstvos the charge of public education, health, welfare, agricultural development, stock-breeding, trade, industry, construction and upkeep of roads, bridges and harbours, fire insurance and measures of fire prevention, food supply, local postal service, and similar matters. In short, there was hardly a branch of local activity that was left outside the competence of the zemstvo.

In addition to the care for local needs, the zemstvos were entrusted with a number of duties and obligations of an official nature. Thus, they were required to maintain gaols, pay the expenses of travelling police authorities and judiciary officials, and assume other similar responsibilities. In case of war the zemstvos were obliged to assist the families of men called to the colours from the reserve . . . The zemstvos were empowered, moreover, to issue certain ordinances of a police character, and, upon confirmation by the Government administration, these ordinances acquired all the force of laws.

However, this very wide sphere left to the competence of the zemstvo institutions was in practice hedged in by the narrow limits of their authority in the most essential fields. Thus, in the educational domain, the zemstvo was to attend only to the economic needs of the schools (construction and maintenance of buildings, supply of books and other necessaries, payment of teachers' salaries, etc.). It was denied the right to alter the curricula in its own schools, nor was it permitted to appoint or dismiss the teachers, and whenever it wished to open a new school it had to obtain special permission . . .

In conformity with the administrative division of the Empire into provinces and districts, the zemstvos were likewise classified as provincial and district zemstvos. But the sphere of the two different institutions was not sharply separated by law; they were free to divide their work among themselves as might seem best to them . . .

The general guidance of zemstvo activities and the preparation of the annual budgets was in the hands of the zemstvo assemblies. These were collegiate bodies composed of delegates, or deputies, elected by the population. The latter chose the delegates to the district zemstvo assemblies, and these, in turn, would elect among their own members the delegates to the provincial zemstvo assemblies. They were presided over by the marshals of the local nobility elected by the members of their own corporation. An arrangement of this kind was necessary as some concession to the class principle prevailing in the social organization of the Russian Empire previous to the era of the Great Reforms. The assemblies then chose, on the collegiate principle, their executive organs, known as zemstvo boards, but the appointment of the presiding officers of these boards, after they had been elected to office, required the approval of the Government.

Delegates to the several zemstvo organs were elected on a basis of property qualification, on the 'curial' system. The first curia was composed of private individuals possessing real estate outside the cities; the second, of those owning real estate within the city limits; and the third was represented by the peasant communes. The number of delegates to be chosen by each curia in each district was prescribed in a special schedule appended to the law . . .

The budgets of the zemstvos were built largely on the principle of self-assessment. The chief source of zemstvo revenues was furnished by taxation of real estate (mainly land and forests). The rates of this taxation were not fixed by law, but were prescribed afresh by the zemstvo assemblies every year, in accordance with the expenditure contemplated . . .

Within the limits of the jurisdiction granted them by law the zemstvos were absolutely independent. All that the representatives of the Central Government—the provincial governors— were supposed to do was to watch that the decisions adopted by the zemstvo assemblies should not violate any law . . .

131. *The Narodnik movement*

The *narodnik* or populist movement originated in the eighteen sixties and gained its greatest spread in the early seventies, with the 'going to the people' movement. It is difficult, however, to find suitable documentary—as opposed to literary—sources for this period. Our documents are, therefore, taken from a later period, when the never very coherent movement had broken up into two main branches, the *Narodnaia Volia* or People's Will, the terrorist branch, and the *Chernii Peredel* or Black Partition, a more peaceful group.

In 1881, after a series of assassinations of high officials carried out successfully, *Narodnaia Volia* succeeded in killing Tsar Alexander II. The Executive Committee of the group then issued two manifestoes, one to the peoples of Europe, the second to the new Tsar, Alexander III. The former (a) follows.

Later in the same year the leaders of *Narodnaia Volia* and *Chernii Peredel* together drew up an agreed programme of demands and made it public (b). This document is the nearest approach to a coherent *narodnik* programme.

Source: *Annual Register*, 1881, pp. [271, 278–9].

(a) Manifesto to Europe, March 1881.

The Committee stated that for many years the Russian revolutionary party had peacefully strived to raise the Russian workmen and peasants in the scale of civilization, and to promote the welfare of the Russian people generally, and did not in any way concern itself with political questions. The Russian Government had rewarded its efforts by cruel persecution: thousands of its members were in prison or in the mines of Siberia; thousands of families had been ruined or had perished miserably. At the same time the power of the officials was increased, and in no country in the world were the interests of the nation so cynically sacrificed to the luxury of the ruling caste. Being thus persecuted by the police, and deprived of any hope of being able to pursue its beneficial work among the people under the existing system, the revolutionary party had gradually entered upon the path of resistance to the agents of that system. The Government had replied by punishing resistance with death. No alternative was now left to the revolutionists between physical and moral annihilation; and they accordingly had determined either to destroy the despotism of centuries which is paralysing Russian life, or to perish in the attempt. The struggle against the foundations of despotism had then been organized, and the catastrophe which had befallen Alexander II was a single episode of that struggle. The proclamation ended by expressing a hope that all thinking men in Europe will understand the importance of the contest, and not condemn the way in which it was carried on, as it had been brought about by the inhumanity of the Russian Government, and a Russian had now no means of emancipating himself from despotism except by blood.

(b) *Narodnik* programme, October 1881.

We are above all things socialists and men of the people. We are convinced that mankind can only secure liberty, equality, and fraternity—the material prosperity of all, and the complete development of the individual—on socialistic principles; and that the development of a nation can only be permanent when it acts with independence and freedom. The food of the people and the will of the people are our most sacred and indivisible principles. The masses are living in a state of economical and political slavery. Their labour serves only to feed and maintain the parasitical classes of society. They are deprived of all the rights of citizens; nothing that exists in Russia has been created by their will, and they are not even allowed to say what they want. Over them stands a herd of plunderers, placed there and supported by the Government. All power is in its hands; and it is solely by brute force—by its soldiers, police and officials—that the empire is kept together. Yet, notwithstanding the oppression which still stifles them, the people still cling to their old ideas of the right of the peasants to the land, of communal self-government, and of freedom of speech and conscience. We, therefore, as socialists and friends of the people, consider it our first duty to liberate them from the oppression that destroys them, and to bring about a political revolution which shall place the powers of the state in their hands. By so doing we shall secure the free and independent development of the nation according to its own wishes and tendencies, and the recognition of those socialistic principles which we advocate in common with it. We believe that the people's will could only be intelligibly manifested in a constituent assembly, if such assembly were free and elected by universal suffrage, and if it acted under instructions from the electors. Our aim, therefore, is to deprive the existing Government of power in order to transfer it to a constituent assembly, elected for the purpose of revising and altering all our present political and social institutions. Our programme is:

1. A Government elected by the nation, and acting in pursuance of the national will.
2. Self-government on the widest basis, secured by all posts in the administration being made elective.
3. All the land to be given to the people.
4. All factories to become the property of the workmen.
5. Complete freedom of conscience, speech, the press, public meeting and election.
6. Replacement of the standing army by a territorial army.

132. Programme of the 'Emancipation of Labour' Group, 1883

Although the assassination of Alexander II was successful, its results were not the ones desired by the *narodniki*. Instead of frightening the régime into concessions, it provoked a new wave of repression as a consequence of which the leadership of both *narodnik* groups was executed, imprisoned, or exiled, thus reducing the effectiveness of the movement.

A number of *narodniki* (mainly of the *Chernii Peredel*) had already been doubting the effectiveness of *narodnik* methods and was experiencing the influence of Marx and his ideas. When they were forced into exile they, under the leadership of Plekhanov, formed in Switzerland the first Russian Marxist group, the 'Emancipation of Labour'. The following are substantial excerpts of the first programme of this group, drafted by Plekhanov in late 1883.

Source: G. Plekhanov, *Selected Philosophical Works* (London, Lawrence and Wishart, 1961), vol. i, pp. 400-5.

The *Emancipation of Labour* group sets itself the aim of spreading socialist ideas in Russia and working out the elements for organizing a Russian workers' socialist party.

The essence of its outlook can be expressed in the following few propositions:

1. The economic emancipation of the working class will be achieved only by the transfer to collective ownership by the working people of all means and products of production and the organization of all the functions of social and economic life in accordance with the requirements of society.

2. The modern development of technology in civilized societies not only provides the *material possibility* for such an organization but makes it *necessary and inevitable* for solving the contradictions which hinder the quiet and all-round development of these societies.

3. The radical economic revolution will entail most fundamental changes in the entire constitution of social and international relationships.

Abolishing the class struggle by destroying the classes themselves; making the economic struggle of individuals impossible and unnecessary by abolishing commodity production and the competition resulting from it; briefly, putting an end to the struggle for existence between individuals, classes and whole societies it renders unnecessary all those social organs which have developed as the weapons of that struggle during the many centuries it has been proceeding.

Without falling into utopian fantasies about the social and international organization of the future, we can already now foretell the abolition of the most important of the organs of chronic struggle inside society, namely *the state as a political organization opposed to society* and safeguarding mainly the interests of the ruling section. In exactly the same way we can already now foresee the international character of the impending economic revolution . . .

That is why the socialist parties in all countries acknowledge the international character of the present-day working class movement and proclaim the principle of international solidarity of producers.

The *Emancipation of Labour* group also acknowledges the great principles of the former International Working Men's Association (cf. No. 98) and the identity of interests among the working people of the whole civilized world.

4. Introducing consciousness where blind economic necessity now dominates, replacing the modern mastery of the product over the producer by that of the producer over the product, the socialist revolution simplifies all social relationships and gives them a purpose, at the same time providing each citizen with the real possibility of participating directly in the discussion and decision of all social matters.

This direct participation of citizens in the management of all social matters pre-supposes the abolition of the modern system of political representation and its replacement by direct popular legislation.

In their present-day struggle, the socialists must bear in mind this necessary political reform and aim at its realization by all means in their power. This is all the more necessary as the political self-education and the rule of the working class are a necessary preliminary condition of its economic emancipation. Only a completely democratic state can carry out the economic revolution which conforms to the interests of the producers and demands their intelligent participation in the organization and regulation of production . . .

It goes without saying that the practical tasks, and consequently the programme of the socialists, are bound to be more original and complicated in countries where capitalist production has not yet become dominant and where the working masses are oppressed under a double yoke—that of rising capitalism and that of obsolescent patriarchal economy.

In those countries, the socialists must at the same time organize the workers for the struggle against the bourgeoisie and wage war against the survivals of the old pre-bourgeois social relationships, which are harmful both to the development of the working class and to the welfare of the whole people.

That is precisely the position of the Russian socialists . . .

One of the most harmful consequences of this backward state of production was and still is the underdevelopment of the middle class, which, in our country, is incapable of taking the initiative in the struggle against absolutism.

That is why our socialist intelligentsia has been obliged to head the present-day emancipation movement, whose direct task must be to set up free political institutions in our country, the socialists on their side being under the obligation to provide the working class with the possibility to take an active and fruitful part in the future political life of Russia.

The first means to achieve this aim must be agitation for a democratic constitution . . .

But this aim will not be achieved, the political initiative of the workers will be unthinkable, if the fall of absolutism finds them completely unprepared and unorganized.

That is why the socialist intelligentsia has the obligation to organize the workers and prepare them as far as possible for the struggle against the present-day system of government as well as against the future bourgeois parties.

The intelligentsia must immediately set to work to organize the workers in our industrial centres, as the foremost representatives of the whole working population of Russia, in secret groups with links between them and a definite social and political programme corresponding to the present-day needs of the entire class of producers in Russia and the basic tasks of socialism . . .

The main points of the economic section of the workers' programme must be the demands:

1. of a radical revision of our agrarian relations, i.e., the condition for the redemption of the land and its distribution to peasant communities. Of the right to renounce allotments and leave the community for those peasants who find this convenient for themselves.

2. of the abolition of the present system of dues and the institution of a progressive taxation system.

3. of the legislative regulation of relations between workers . . . and employers . . .

4. of State assistance for production associations organized in all possible branches of agriculture, the mining and manufacturing industries . . .

The Emancipation of Labour group is convinced that not only the success but even the mere possibility of such a purposeful movement of the Russian working class depends in a large degree upon the work referred to above being done by the intelligentsia among the working class.

But the group assumes that the intelligentsia themselves must as a preliminary step adopt the standpoint of modern scientific socialism, adhering to the *Narodnaia Volia* traditions only inasmuch as they are not opposed to its principles.

In view of this, the Emancipation of Labour group sets itself the aim of spreading modern socialism in Russia and preparing the working class for a conscious social and political movement; to this aim it devotes all its energies, calling upon our revolutionary youth for help and collaboration.

Pursuing this aim by all means in its power, the Emancipation of Labour group at the same time recognizes the necessity for terrorist struggle against the absolute government and differs from the *Narodnaia Volia* party only on the question of the so-called seizure of power by the revolutionary party and of the tasks of the immediate activity of the socialists among the working class.

The Emancipation of Labour group does not in the least ignore the peasantry which constitutes an enormous portion of Russia's working population. But it assumes that the work of the intelligentsia, especially under present-day conditions of the social and political struggle, must be aimed first of all at the most developed part of this population, which consists of the industrial workers. Having secured the powerful support of this section, the socialist intelligentsia will have far greater hope of success in extending their activity to the peasantry as well, especially if they have by that time won freedom of agitation and propaganda. Incidentally, it goes without saying that the distribution of the forces of our socialists will have to be changed if an independent revolutionary movement becomes manifest among the peasantry, and that even at present people who are in direct touch with the peasantry could, by their work among them, render an important service to the socialist movement in Russia. The Emancipation of Labour group, far from rejecting such people, will exert all its efforts to agree with them on the basic propositions of the programme.

133. *Lenin's Draft Rules of the Russian Social-Democratic Labour Party, 1903*

The decades following the foundation of the Emancipation of Labour group in 1883 (cf. No. 132) saw the proliferation of Marxist groups all over Russia. Although there was some co-operation between them, there was no central body which could have directed and co-ordinated the social-democratic movement. An attempt to form a central organization was made in 1898, but failed because of the vigilance of the Government; the next attempt was the Party Congress held at Brussels and London in July–August 1903.

Although formally a united organization was agreed to, this Congress also laid the foundations of the Bolshevik-Menshevik split. Our document, the draft rules of the Party written by Lenin and approved by the Organizing Committee, illustrates the most important point on which differences arose: the composition and nature of the party. Lenin's draft Article 1 was rejected, and the Menshevik Martov's amendment, quoted in the footnote, adopted instead.

Source: V. I. Lenin, *Collected Works* (London, Lawrence and Wishart, 1961), vol. vi, pp. 476–8.

1. A party member is one who accepts the Party's programme and supports the Party both financially and by personal participation in one of its organizations.[1]

[1] Martov's amended Article 1, which was adopted at the Congress, reads: 'A member of the Russian Social-Democratic Labour Party is one who accepts its programme, supports the Party financially, and renders it regular personal assistance under the direction of one of its organizations.'

2. The Party Congress is the supreme organ of the Party . . .

3. The following are entitled to representation at a congress: a) the Central Committee; b) the editorial board of the Central organ; c) all local committees recognized by the Party; d) all unions of committees recognized by the Party; and e) the League Abroad. Each . . . has two deciding votes . . .

4. The Party Congress appoints the Central Committee, the editorial board of the Central Organ, and the Party Council.

5. The Central Committee co-ordinates and directs all the practical activities of the Party and administers the Central Party Treasury . . .

6. The editorial board of the Central Organ gives ideological guidance to the Party by editing the Party's Central Organ, the scientific organ, and pamphlets.

7. The Party Council is appointed by the Congress from among members of the editorial board of the Central Organ and the Central Committee and consists of five persons. The Council settles disputes and differences arising between the editorial board of the Central Organ and the Central Committee on questions of general organization and tactics . . .

8. New Committees and unions of committees are endorsed by the Central Committee.

9. Any party member and any person who has any contact with the Party is entitled to demand that any statements made by him should be transmitted in the original to the Central Committee, the Central Organ, or the Party Congress.

10. It is the duty of every Party organization to afford both the Central Committee and the editorial board of the Central Organ every opportunity of becoming acquainted with all its activities and its entire composition.

11. All Party organizations and collegiate bodies decide their affairs by a simple majority vote and have the right of co-optation . . .

12. It is the purpose of the League of Russian Revolutionary Social-Democracy Abroad to carry on propaganda and agitation abroad and also to assist the movement in Russia.

The League enjoys all the rights of committees, with the sole exception in that it renders assistance to the movement in Russia only through persons or groups specially appointed for the purpose by the Central Committee.

134. The Programme of the Union of Liberation, January 1904

The liberal movement, although it started, in informal groups, earlier than either the *narodnik* or the social-democratic one, was rather later in forming organized bodies. Meetings of 'zemstvo-liberals' took place earlier, but it was only in the twentieth century that the liberals engaged in large-scale activity. One of the more important liberal groups, the Union of Liberation, consisted of supporters of the liberal newspaper *Liberation (Osvobozhdenie)*, published abroad. At the first, secret, meeting of the Union in January 1904 the following programme was adopted.

Source: G. Fischer, *Russian Liberalism: from Gentry to Intelligentsia* (Cambridge, Mass., Harvard University Press, 1958), p. 147.

The first and main aim of the Union of Liberation is the political liberation of Russia. Considering political liberty in even its most minimal form completely incompatible with the absolute character of the Russian monarchy, the Union will seek before all else the abolition of autocracy and the establishment in Russia of a constitutional regime. In determining the concrete forms in which a constitutional regime can be realized in Russia, the Union of Liberation will make all efforts to have the political problem resolved in the spirit of extensive democracy. Above all, it recognizes as fundamentally essential that the principles of universal, equal, secret and direct elections be made the basis of the political reform.

Putting the political demands in the forefront, the Union of Liberation recognizes as essential the definition of its attitude in principle to the social-economic problems created by life itself. In the realm of social-economic policy, the Union of Liberation will follow the same basic principles of democracy, making the direct goal of its activity the defence of the interests of the labouring masses.

In the sphere of national questions, the Union recognizes the right of self-determination of different nationalities entering into the composition of the Russian state. In relation to Finland the Union supports the demand for the restoration of the [autonomous] status which existed in that country until its illegal abrogation.

135. 'Bloody Sunday', 9 January 1905

Social and political ferment in Russia became ever more acute after the outbreak of the Russo-Japanese War which strained the resources of the Russian State and, because of the defeats suffered, shook the people's remaining confidence in the Tsar and his Government. This confidence was shaken even further when, on 9 January 1905, a large, initially peaceful, demonstration, which desired to hand the following petition to the Tsar, was fired upon by troops. Social and political discontent increased from this time on, and more and more Russians engaged in overt action with the aim of forcing the Tsar to make concessions.

Source: A. J. Sack, *The Birth of the Russian Democracy* (New York, Russian Information Bureau, 1918), pp. 99–103.

Sire:

We workingmen and inhabitants of St. Petersburg . . . come to Thee, Sire, to seek for truth and defence. We have become beggars; we have been oppressed; we are burdened by toil beyond our powers; . . we are not recognized as human beings; we are treated as slaves . . . We are choked by despotism and irresponsibility . . . We have no more power, Sire; the limit of patience has been reached. There has arrived for us that tremendous moment when death is better than the continuation of intolerable tortures. We have left off working and we have declared to the masters that we shall not begin to work until they comply with our demands. We beg but little . . . The first request which we made was that our masters should discuss our needs with us; but this they refused, on the ground that no right to make this request is recognized by law. They also declared to be illegal our requests to diminish the working hours to eight hours daily, to agree with us about the prices for our work, to consider our misunderstandings with the interior administration of the mills, to increase the wages for the labour of women and of general labourers, so that the minimum daily wage should be one rouble per day, to abolish overtime work, to give us medical attention without insulting us, to arrange the workshops so that it might be possible to work there and not find in them death from awful draughts and from rain and snow. All these requests appeared to be, in the opinion of our masters and of the factory and mill administrations, illegal.

Every one of our requests was a crime, and the desire to improve our condition was regarded by them as impertinence, and as offensive to them.

Sire, here are many thousands of us, and all are human beings only in appearance. In reality in us, as in all Russian people, there is not recognized any human right, not even the right of speaking, thinking, meeting, discussing our needs . . . We have been enslaved . . . under the auspices of Thy officials. Every one of us who dares to raise a voice in defence of working-class and popular interests is thrown into gaol or is sent into banishment . . . Even to pity a beaten man . . . means to commit a heavy crime. All the people . . . are handed over to the discretion of the officials of the Government, who are thieves of the property of the State . . . The Government officials have brought the country to complete destruction . . . The people are deprived of the possibility of expressing their desires and they now demand that they be allowed to take part in the introduction of taxes and in the expenditure of them.

The workingmen are deprived of the possibility of organizing themselves in unions for the defence of their interests.

Sire, is it in accordance with divine law, by grace of which Thou reignest? . . . We are seeking here the last salvation. Do not refuse assistance to Thy people . . . Give their destiny into their own hands. Cast away from them the intolerable oppression of officials. Destroy the wall between Thyself and Thy people, and let them rule the country together with Thyself . . .

Russia is too great. Its necessities are too various and numerous for officials to rule it. National representation is indispensable . . . order immediately the convocation of representatives of the Russian land from all ranks, including representatives from the working men . . . This is the most capital of our requests . . . Yet one measure alone cannot heal our wounds . . . The following are indispensable:

I. Measures to counteract the ignorance and legal oppression of the Russian People.

1. The immediate release and return of all who have suffered for political and religious convictions, for strikes, and national peasant disorders.

2. The immediate declaration of freedom and of the inviolability of the person—freedom of speech and press, freedom of meetings, and freedom of conscience in religion.

3. Universal and compulsory elementary education of the people . . .

4. Responsibility of the ministers before the people and guarantee that the Government will be law-abiding.

5. Equality before the law of all . . .

6. Separation of the Church from the State.

II. Measures against the Poverty of the People.

1. Abolition of indirect taxes and the substitution of a progressive income tax.

2. Abolition of the redemption instalments, cheap credit, and gradual transference of the land to the people . . .

3. The orders for the military and naval ministries should be filled in Russia, and not abroad.

4. The cessation of the war by the will of the people.

III. Measures against the Oppression of Labour.

1. Abolition of the factory inspectorships.

2. Institution at factories and mills of permanent committees of elected workers which, together with the administration, would consider the complaints of individual workers. Discharge of working men should not take place otherwise than by resolution of this committee.

3. Freedom of organization of co-operative societies . . . and of trade unions . . .

4. Eight-hour working day . . .

5. Freedom of the struggle of labour against capital, immediately.

6. Normal wages, immediately.

7. Participation of working-class representatives in the working out of projects of law concerning workmen's State insurance . . .

Order and take an oath to comply with these requests, and Thou wilt make Russia happy and famous and Thou wilt impress Thy name in our hearts . . . If Thou wilt not order and wilt not answer our prayer—we shall die here on this place before Thy Palace. We have nowhere to go farther and nothing for which to go. We have only two ways—either towards liberty and happiness or into the grave . . .

136. Proclamation of the 'Bulygin Duma', 19 August 1905

Popular discontent having become ever more widespread, the Tsar and his advisers finally accepted the necessity of making concessions. In August 1905, therefore, on the submission of one of his ministers, Bulygin, Nicholas II issued a manifesto in which he promised the establishment of an elected consultative body, called State Duma. Great as this concession was, a Duma with merely consultative functions was not acceptable to the people, and thus this projected 'Bulygin Duma' never met.

Excerpts from the Tsar's manifesto follow.

Source: *London Weekly Times*, 25 August 1905, in J. H. Robinson and C. A. Beard, *Readings in Modern European History* (Boston, Ginn, 1909), vol. ii, pp. 375-7.

The Empire of Russia is formed and strengthened by the indestructible union of the Tsar with the people and the people with the Tsar. This concord and union of the Tsar and the people is the great moral force which has created Russia in the course of centuries by protecting her from all misfortunes and all attacks, and has constituted up to the present time a pledge of unity, independence, integrity, material well-being, and intellectual development in the present and in the future . . .

The time has now come . . . to summon elected representatives from the whole of Russia to take a constant and active part in the elaboration of laws, adding for this purpose to the higher State institutions a special consultative body instructed with the preliminary elaboration and discussion of measures and with the examination of the State Budget. It is for this reason that, while preserving the fundamental law regarding autocratic power, We have deemed it well to form a State Duma and to approve regulations for elections to this Duma, extending these laws to the whole territory of the Empire . . .

We reserve to Ourselves exclusively the care of perfecting the organization of the State Duma, and when the course of events has demonstrated the necessity of changes corresponding to the needs of the times and the welfare of the Empire, we shall not fail to give the matter our attention at the proper moment . . .

137. *The 'October Manifesto', 17 October 1905*

The proclamation of the establishment of a consultative assembly (cf. No. 136) did not quell disorder in Russia; on the contrary, under the impact of defeat in the Russo-Japanese War it only gained intensity. On the advice of Count Witte the Tsar, on 17 October, issued a manifesto in which he granted certain civil and political rights, and agreed to the granting of legislative functions to the State Duma. It was this document on which the 1906 Constitution (No. 140(a)) was based, and which, therefore, served as the foundation of Russian political life until the Revolution of 1917. It also served to split the oppositional movement, as a large group of the liberals, hereafter called the 'Octobrists', accepted the concessions granted as sufficient, though the majority of the liberals, now called Constitutional Democrats, continued to demand the establishment of a truly parliamentary régime.

Source: F. A. Golder, *Documents of Russian History, 1914–1917* (New York, The Century Press, 1927), pp. 627–8.

The rioting and agitation in the capitals and in many localities of Our Empire fills Our heart with great and deep grief. The welfare of the Russian Emperor is bound up with the welfare of the people, and its sorrows are His sorrows. The turbulence which has broken out may confound the people and threaten the integrity and unity of Our Empire.

The great vow of service by the Tsar obligates Us to endeavour, with all Our strength, wisdom, and power, to put an end as quickly as possible to the disturbance so dangerous to the Empire. In commanding the responsible authorities to take measures to stop disorders, lawlessness, and violence, and to protect peaceful citizens in the quiet performance of their duties, We have found it necessary to unite the activities of the Supreme Government, so as to ensure the successful carrying out of the general measures laid down by Us for the peaceful life of the State.

We lay upon the Government the execution of Our unchangeable will:

1. To grant to the population the inviolable right of free citizenship, based on the principles of freedom of person, conscience, speech, assembly, and union.

2. Without postponing the intended elections for the State Duma and in so far as possible, in view of the short time that

remains before the assembling of that body, to include in the participation of the work of the Duma those classes of the population that have been until now entirely deprived of the right to vote, and to extend in the future, by the newly created legislative way, the principles of the general right of election.

3. To establish as an unbreakable rule that no law shall go into force without its confirmation by the State Duma and that the persons elected by the people shall have the opportunity for actual participation in supervising the legality of the acts of authorities appointed by Us . . .

138. Manifesto to Better the Conditions . . . of the Peasant Population, 3 November 1905

Even before the Revolution of 1905 the Government considered some measures to alleviate the conditions of the peasants, but because of differences of opinion between its members, no decision was taken. When rural discontent and violence became more and more widespread in the course of 1905, the Tsar issued the following manifesto which provided a measure of relief, though not to the desired extent. After 1906, under the direction of Stolypin, further laws were enacted to assist the peasants, but, unfortunately, none could be included in this collection.

Source: F. A. Golder, *Documents of Russian History, 1914-1917* (New York, The Century Press, 1927), pp. 628-9.

. . . The troubles that have broken out in villages . . fill Our heart with deep sorrow . . . Violence and crime do not, however, help the peasant and may bring much sorrow and misery to the country. The only way to better permanently the welfare of the peasant is by peaceful and legal means; and to improve his condition has always been one of Our first cares . . . We have decided:

1. To reduce by half, from January 1, 1906, and to discontinue altogether after January 1, 1907, payments due from peasants for land which before emancipation belonged to large land-owners, State and Crown.

2. To make it easier for the Peasant Land Bank, by increasing its resources and by offering better terms for loans, to help the peasant with little land to buy more . . .

139. *The St. Petersburg Soviet, 13 October–3 December 1905*

The workers of the cities, particularly of St. Petersburg, had long been discontented (cf. No. 135). In late September 1905 their dissatisfaction gained practical expression in a spontaneous general strike which spread over much of the country and which was led, after its formation on 13 October, by the Council (or Soviet) of Workers' Deputies. The Soviet, whose members were elected by the workers of the factories etc., co-ordinated the activity of the workers for fifty days until its arrest on 3 December, and it established the machinery which was revived and used to advantage in 1917.

Three documents of the Soviet follow: the proclamation (a) which called off the general strike after the issue of the October Manifesto (No. 137), the resolution (b) which called a second general strike in support of the rebellion of the sailors at Kronstadt, and, finally, the so-called 'Financial Manifesto' (c) of 2 December in which the Soviet asked the population to continue its passive resistance to the Government.

Source: (a) and (b) M. J. Olgin, *The Soul of the Russian Revolution* (New York, Holt, 1917), pp. 145, 147.
      (c) A. J. Sack, *The Birth of the Russian Democracy* (New York, Russian Information Bureau, 1918), p. 123.

(a) Calling off the First General Strike, 20 October 1905.

In view of the necessity of the working-class to organize on the basis of its achieved victories and to arm for a final struggle for a Constituent Assembly on the basis of universal, equal, direct and secret suffrage which is to establish a democratic republic, the Council of Workmen's Delegates orders that the political strike be stopped at noon, October 21st. The Council is confident, however, that, should it be required by further developments, the working men will resume the strike as willingly and as devotedly as heretofore.

(b) Calling the Second General Strike, 1 November 1905.

The government continues to stride over corpses. It puts on trial before a court-martial the brave Kronstadt soldiers of the army and navy who rose to the defence of their rights and of national freedom. It put the noose of martial law on the neck of oppressed Poland.

The Council of Workmen's Delegates calls on the revolutionary proletariat of Petersburg to manifest their brotherly solidarity with the revolutionary soldiers of Kronstadt and with the revolutionary proletarians of Poland through a general political strike, which has proved to be a formidable power, and through general meetings of protest. Tomorrow, on November 2nd, at noon, the working men of Petersburg will stop work, their slogans being:

1. Down with court-martial!
2. Down with capital punishment!
3. Down with martial law in Poland and all over Russia!

(c) The 'Financial Manifesto', 2 December 1905.

[This Manifesto pointed out the main crimes of the Tsar's Government against the people and declared that the fall of the autocracy was the only way out of the abyss. To overthrow the autocratic order it was deemed necessary to take away its financial power. The Tsar's Government, becoming bankrupt, would inevitably fall. Therefore the Manifesto called upon the people:]

To refuse payment of redemption instalments and all other fiscal payments.

To demand that all payments of wages or salaries be in gold and that amounts less than five roubles be paid in hard coin, full weight.

To withdraw the deposits from the Savings Banks and from the State Bank, demanding all payments in gold.

140. *The Beginnings of 'Constitutional' Government,* *April–July 1906*

The First Duma, called together on the basis of the August and October Manifestoes (Nos 136, 137), expected to be called upon to assist in drafting a constitution. Shortly before its first meeting, however, the Government promulgated a revised version of the Fundamental Laws of the Empire (a) which was to serve instead of a constitution and which retained large powers in the hands of the Tsar and his Government.

Instead of concentrating on the measures submitted by the Government, the Duma devoted most of its attention to the discussion of a liberal reform programme, and by this soon exhausted the patience of the Tsar who dissolved it by the Proclamation that follows (b). The Second Duma was no more successful in gaining the co-operation of the Government, it also was dissolved after a brief session. The electoral law was then amended unconstitutionally by decree, and the Third Duma, elected on a much restricted franchise, was willing to give support to the Government.

Source: (a) *Jahrbuch des öffentlichen Rechts* (1908), vol. ii, pp. 423 ff.
(b) *London Weekly Times*, 27 July 1906, both in J. H. Robinson and C. A. Beard, *Readings in Modern European History* (Boston, Ginn, 1909), vol. ii, pp. 377–81.

(a) Fundamental Laws of the Russian Empire, 23 April 1906.

. . . 4. The supreme autocratic power is vested in the Tsar of All the Russias. It is God's command that his authority should be obeyed not only through fear but for conscience' sake . . .

7. The Tsar exercises the legislative power in conjunction with the Council of the Empire and the Imperial Duma.

8. The initiative in all branches of legislation belongs to the Tsar. Solely on his initiative may the Fundamental Laws of the Empire be subjected to a revision in the Council of the Empire and the Imperial Duma.[1]

9. The Tsar approves of the laws, and without his approval no law can come into existence.

10. All governmental powers in their widest extent throughout the whole Russian Empire are vested in the Tsar . . .

17. The Tsar appoints and dismisses the president of the Council, the ministers themselves, and the heads of the chief departments of administration, as well as all other officials where the law does not provide for another method of appointment and dismissal . . .

[Articles 66–81 set down fairly liberal civil rights for all subjects; some of the more important articles follow in full.]

2. No one can be prosecuted for an offence except according to the process established by law.

73. No one shall be arrested except in the cases determined by law . . .

78. Russian subjects are entitled to meet peaceably and without arms for such purposes as are not contrary to law.

79. Within the limits fixed by law every one may express his thought by word or writing and circulate them by means of the press or otherwise . . .

---

[1] Members of the State Council and of the Duma were, however, granted legislative initiative in relation to ordinary laws.

84. The Russian Empire shall be governed by laws passed according to a fixed and regular proceeding . . .

86. No new law shall go into force without the sanction of both the Council of the Empire and the Duma and the ratification of the Tsar.

[87. During the recess of the Imperial Duma, if extraordinary circumstances require the adoption of a measure which should be made the subject of legislative deliberation, the Council of Ministers may present such a measure directly to the Emperor. Such a measure shall not, however, introduce any changes in the Fundamental Laws of the Empire, or in the organization of the Council of the Empire or of the Imperial Duma, or regulations concerning the elections to the Council of the Empire or to the Imperial Duma . . .] . . .

100. The Council of the Empire shall be composed of persons appointed by . . . the Tsar, and elected persons . . .

101. The Duma shall be composed of members chosen by the inhabitants of the Russian Empire for five years, according to regulations established by law . . .

(b) Dissolution of the First Duma, 21 July 1906.

We summoned the representatives of the nation by Our will to the work of productive legislation. Confiding firmly in divine clemency and believing in the great and brilliant future of Our people, We confidently anticipated benefits for the country from their labours. We proposed great reforms in all departments of the national life. We have always devoted Our greatest care to the removal of the ignorance of the people by the light of instruction, and to the removal of their burdens by improving the conditions of agricultural work.

A cruel disappointment has befallen Our expectations. The representatives of the nation, instead of applying themselves to the work of productive legislation, have strayed into spheres beyond their competence, and have been making inquiries into the acts of local authorities established by Ourselves, and have been making comments upon the imperfections of the Fundamental Laws, which can only be modified by Our imperial will. In short, the representatives of the nation have undertaken really illegal acts, such as the appeal by the Duma to the nation.

The peasants, disturbed by such anomalies, and seeing no hope of the amelioration of their lot, have resorted in a number of districts to open pillage and the destruction of other people's property, and to disobedience of the law and of the legal authorities. But Our subjects ought to remember that an improvement in the lot of the people is only possible under conditions of perfect order and tranquillity. We shall not permit arbitrary or illegal acts, and We shall impose Our imperial will on the disobedient by all the power of the State.

We appeal to all well-disposed Russians to combine for the maintenance of legal authority and the restoration of peace in Our dear fatherland . . .

In dissolving the Duma We confirm Our immutable intention of maintaining this institution, and in conformity with this intention We fix March 5, 1907, as the date of the convocation of a new Duma . . . With unshakable faith in divine clemency and in the good sense of the Russian people, We shall expect from the new Duma the realization of Our efforts and their promotion of legislation in accordance with the requirements of a regenerated Russia . . .

XIII · THE THIRD REPUBLIC IN FRANCE, 1870-1940

FRENCH defeat in the Franco-Prussian war of 1870-1 resulted in a proclamation of the republic by the people of Paris and the formation of a republican Government of National Defence (No. 142). Although the republican forces, largely taking their stand on the Belleville programme of radical democracy (No. 141) were strong, they were defeated in the elections held in February 1871 because they were associated with a drive to continue the war. The new Assembly, the main task of which was to approve the peace settlement with Germany (No. 97), had a largely royalist and conservative majority. It was soon opposed by a revolution in Paris, the Paris Commune (No. 143), which it defeated only after prolonged bloody fighting.

There were proposals, at this stage, to re-establish the monarchy, but they failed because of the intransigence of the Pretender, the Comte de Chambord (No. 144). The royalists temporized and, when enacting fundamental laws for France (Nos 145(a) and (b)) drafted them so that a simple constitutional amendment would enable them to install a King instead of a President. But the republican feeling of the country grew too strong for them and, by 1884, established the Republic as permanent (No. 145(c)).

The anti-republican forces nevertheless remained fairly strong. Documents on the Church-State controversy which poisoned the political atmosphere of this period can be found in Section X (Nos 117, 119, 120), but there were other serious crises of which two, the Boulanger crisis (No. 146) and the Dreyfus Affair (No. 147) are illustrated.

The final victory of republican forces was followed by the strengthening of the socialist movement which in late 1904 formed a united socialist party (No. 148). The trade unions, however, still retained a large autonomy of action and most continued to adhere to the principles of syndicalism, as is shown by the Charter of Amiens, 1906 (No. 149).

Many different documents of interest could have been selected from the period of the First World War and the inter-war period, but it was considered best to concentrate on two issues only: first, the attempted *coup d'état* of the right in 1934, giving some background to the Stavisky affair (No. 150) and to the *coup* itself (No. 151), and, secondly, the formation of the Popular Front, including its programme (No. 152) and its activity in settling the internal crisis with which it was faced when taking office (No. 153).

Documents relevant to the foreign relations of the Third Republic will be found in Sections IX, XIV, and XIX.

141. *The Belleville Programme of 1869*

During the elections of 1869, Leon Gambetta stood for the con-stituency of Belleville, a suburb of Paris. To emphasize his demo-cratic leanings, he asked a committee of electors to draw up a programme of radical democracy which he undertook to make his own if elected. Although these events took place during the Second Empire, the document is inserted in this section as the Belleville Programme gained its real importance only in the early years of the Third Republic, when it became the rallying point of the Left.

Source: E. Ollivier, *L'Empire liberal*, vol. xi, *La veillée des armes* (Paris, Garnier, 1907), pp. 497–8 (trans. Ed.).

In the name of universal suffrage, which is the basis of all political and social organization, we give to our deputy the mandate of affirming the principles of radical democracy and of demanding forcefully [the following]:

The most radical application of universal suffrage, for the elections of mayors and municipal councillors . . . as well as for the election of deputies;

A redistribution of constituencies based on the number of those entitled to vote and not on that of registered voters;

That individual liberty be hereafter placed under the protec-tion of laws, and not be subject to . . . administrative arbitrari-ness;

. . . The direct responsibility of all officials;

That political offenders be tried before juries;

Complete freedom of the press . . .;

Unrestricted freedom of assembly . . . for the discussion of all religious, philosophical, political and social matters . . .;

Abolition of [financial] contributions by the State to the Church, and separation of Church and State;

Secular, free and compulsory primary education, with admission to the also free higher levels by competitive examination;

The suppression of municipal taxes on goods, the abolition of large salaries and multiple appointments, and modification of the system of taxation;

Nomination of all public officials by election;

Suppression of standing armies . . .;

The abolition of privileges and monopolies . . .;

Economic reforms, which affect the social problem, whose solution, though less important than political transformation, should be studied and sought in the name of the principles of social justice and equality . . .

142. *The Birth of the Third Republic, 4–5 September 1870*

After the defeat at Sedan and the capture of Napoleon III by the Germans the Chamber considered what action to take, but while they discussed whether establishment of a Council of Regency or the deposition of Napoleon and government by a commission of the Legislature would be best for France, the population of Paris invaded the Chamber and demanded the establishment of a republic. Under popular pressure this was done, and a republican Government appointed (a); the following day a proclamation (b) summarized the Government's policy.

Source: (a) F.-A. Hélie, *Les constitutions de la France* (Paris, Duchemin, 1880) p. 1333 (trans. Ed.).
(b) *Annual Register*, 1870, p. 172.

(a) The Proclamation of the Republic, 4 September 1870.

Citizens of Paris!

The republic is proclaimed. A Government is appointed by acclamation. It consists of the following deputies of Paris: Emmanuel Arago, Crémieux, Jules Favre, Jules Ferry, Gambetta, Garnier-Pagès, Glais-Bizoin, Pelletan, Picard, Jules Simon.

General Trochu is entrusted with full military powers for national defence. He is called to be the Head of the Government. . . .

The Government asks the citizens to remain calm; the population will not forget that it is facing the enemy.

The Government is, before all, a Government of national defence.

(b) The First Proclamation of the Government, 5 September 1870.

Frenchmen!

The people have disavowed a Chamber which hesitated to save the country when in danger. It has demanded a Republic. The friends of its representatives are not in power but in peril.

The Republic vanquished the invasion of 1792. The Republic is proclaimed!

The Revolution is accomplished in the name of right and public safety.

Citizens! Watch over the city confided to you. Tomorrow you will be, with the army, avengers of the country.

143. *The Paris Commune, 18 March–28 May 1871*

Although the republic was proclaimed in September 1870 (No. 142), the National Assembly elected in February 1871, with the main purpose of approving the peace treaty with Germany, had a conservative and royalist majority. The radical leaders of Paris, having resisted the Germans in a siege lasting four months, felt humiliated by the peace terms (No. 97) and wished to republicanize the new régime, headed by Thiers, which had its seat at Versailles. Unrest arose over some of the financial measures of the new Government and, when Government troops attempted to seize the cannons of the National Guard of Paris, open rebellion broke out on 18 March.

The Government forces initially evacuated the city, where an elected assembly, exercising both legislative and executive functions, the Paris Commune, took over power from the Central Committee of the National Guard which organized the initial resistance. The Government forces besieged the city which fell after two months of fighting, both sides exercising a great deal of cruelty and ruthlessness. The war against the Commune and the persecution of the participants afterwards created lasting bitterness between the workers of Paris and the rest of France.

Our documents include a manifesto outlining the assumptions underlying the formation of a Commune published by the Committee of the Twenty Arrondissements of the National Guard (a), excerpts from the minutes of the first business meeting of the Commune (b), and the programme of the Commune drawn up in April (c).

Source: (a) and (b): P. Vésinier, *History of the Commune of Paris* (London, Chapman and Hall, 1872), pp. 61–5, 161–9.
(c) F. Harrison, 'The Revolution of the Commune', *Fortnightly Review*, N.S. ix (1871), pp. 566–7.

(a) Manifesto of the Committee of Twenty Arrondissements, 19 March 1871.

By its revolution of the 18th March, and the spontaneous and courageous efforts of the National Guard, Paris has regained its autonomy . . . On the eve of the sanguinary and disastrous defeat suffered by France as the punishment it has to undergo for the seventy years of the Empire, and the monarchical, clerical, parliamentary, legal and conciliatory reaction, our country again rises, revives, begins a new life, and retakes the tradition of the Communes of old and of the French Revolution. This tradition, which gave victory to France, and earned the respect and sympathy of past generations, will bring independence, wealth, peaceful glory and brotherly love among nations in the future.

Never was there so solemn an hour. The Revolution which our fathers commenced and we are finishing . . . is going on without bloodshed, by the might of the popular will . . . To secure the triumph of the Communal idea . . . it is necessary to determine its general principles, and to draw up . . . the programme to be realized . . .

The Commune is the foundation of all political states, exactly as the family is the embryo of human society. It must have autonomy; that is to say, self-administration and self-government, agreeing with its particular genius, traditions, and wants; preserving, in its political, moral, national, and special groups its entire liberty, its own character, and its complete sovereignty, like a citizen of a free town.

To secure the greatest economic development, the national and territorial independence, and security, association is indispensable; that is to say, a federation of all communes, constituting a united nation.

The autonomy of the Commune guarantees liberty to its

citizens; and the federation of all the communes increases, by the reciprocity, power, wealth, markets, and resources of each member, the profit of all.

It was the Communal idea . . . which triumphed on the 18th of March, 1871. It implies, as a political form, the Republic, which is alone compatible with liberty and popular sovereignty.

The most complete liberty to speak, to write, to meet, and to associate.

Respect to the individual, and inviolability of opinion.

The sovereignty of universal suffrage, being for ever its own master, and constantly able to convoke and manifest itself.

The electoral principle for every functionary and magistrate.

The responsibility of mandataries, and consequently their permanent revocability.

The imperative mandate, that is to say, the precise statement and limitation of the power and mission of those elected . . .

Autonomy of the National Guard, formed of all electors, nominating all its chiefs and its general staff officers . . .

Suppression of the Prefecture of Police. Surveillance of the city by the National Guard under the direct command of the Commune.

Suppression of the standing army . . .

Financial organization which will permit Paris to dispose internally and freely of its budget . . .

Suppression of all subsidies to creeds, theatres, and the press.

The spread of entirely secular education . . .

The immediate opening of an inquiry to fix the responsibility on public men guilty of the disasters suffered by France; to state precisely the financial [etc.] situation of the city, the capital and the force at its disposal, and to furnish the means and elements for a general and amicable liquidation requisite for the paying up of arrears and the recovery of credit . . .

Constant and assiduous researches to find out the best means of furnishing the producer with capital, tools, markets and credit, so as to settle for ever the question of wages and horrible pauperism, and to prevent the return of their fatal consequences, sanguinary revenge and civil war.

Such is the mandate which we propose, and which we demand of you, citizens, to give to those whom you elect . . .

(b) From the Minutes of the First Business Meeting of the Commune, 29 March 1871.

On ... March 29th, the sitting of the Commune was opened with cries of '*Vive la République!*' Citizen Beslay, as the oldest member, again took the chair. He begged the Assembly to elect its President, and citizen Lefrançais was nominated ...

Citizen Eudes rose to beg of his colleagues that the new Municipal Council should be called the Commune of Paris. Citizen Ranc seconded this proposition by saying that it was indispensable to break off from the past. The name Commune of Paris would alone indicate that this great city desired to have its full and entire municipal franchise; in a word, self-government.

The name of Commune was accepted with acclamation.

The President read a proposition that the Council of the Commune should declare that the members of the Central Committee [of the National Guard] had acted like good citizens and had deserved well of the Commune. Citizen Delescluze seconded the proposition, and said, 'The members of the Committee have well deserved the thanks not only of Paris and France, but also of the universal Republic' ...

The thanks were unanimously voted ...

The Assembly, in order to facilitate the despatch of business and the examination of motions, decided on forming themselves into ten Commissions. Each Commission was to possess the same powers as the old ministries, except that of Religion, the budget of which was to be suppressed, and placed under the jurisdiction of the Commission of General Safety. In addition to these, certain particular Commissions were instituted in order to meet the pressing necessities of the moment. The ten Commissions were:

1. The Executive—This Commission is charged with the execution of the decrees of the Commune as well as of those of the other Commissions ...
2. The Military Commission, which replaces the Committee of the National Guard ...
3. The Commission of Supply, which shall superintend the victualling ...
4. The Finance Commission—This Commission is charged with establishing the budget of Paris on a new basis ...

5. The Commission of Justice . . .

6. The Commission of General Safety, with the powers of the Prefecture of Police . . .

7. The Commission of Labour, Industry and Exchange, having in its province a part of the public works and commerce. It is also entrusted with the dissemination of socialist doctrines. It has to seek means for the equalization of labour and wages . . .

8. The Commission of Public Service—This Commission is charged with the supervision of the great services, the post office, telegraphs, and public ways . . .

9. The Commission of Foreign Affairs—This Commission is empowered to entertain amicable relations with all the communes of France, so as to lead to a general federation. It is enjoined to contribute to the enfranchisement of the country by its propaganda.

It is likewise empowered, as occasion presents itself, to send representatives to the different States of Europe, and especially to Prussia, as soon as the attitude of this power towards the Commune shall become known.

10. The Commission of Instruction, having for its province the public education . . .

The proposition of citizens Assi and Varlin concerning rents was also voted with urgency . . .

The Commune organized the municipal administration of twenty arrondissements of Paris by . . . decree.

On the proposition of citizen Beslay, the question of interest on mortgages was put as the order of the day . . . urgency was rejected.

On the proposition of the Military and Finance Commission, the conscription was abolished and the National Guard declared to be the only regular armed force . . .

On the proposition of twenty-three of its members, the Assembly declared the Commune of Paris to be the only regular power. By another decree an act of accusation was instituted against the members of the Versailles Government, and their property in Paris confiscated . . .

(c) The Programme of the Commune, April 1871.

It is the duty of the Commune to confirm and ascertain the

aspirations and wishes of the people of Paris. The precise
character of the movement of the 18th of March is misunder-
stood and unknown, and is calumniated by the politicians at
Versailles. At that time Paris still laboured and suffered for the
whole of France, for whom she had prepared by her battles an
intellectual, moral, administrative and economic regeneration,
glory and prosperity. What does she demand? The recognition
and consolidation of the Republic, and the absolute independence of the Commune extended at all places in France, thus
assuring to each the integrity of its rights, and to every Frenchman the full exercise of his faculties and aptitudes as a man, a
citizen, and a producer. The independence of the Commune
has no other limits but its rights. The independence is equal
for all Communes who are adherents of the contract, the association of which ought to secure the unity of France. The inherent rights of the Commune are to vote the Communal
budget of receipts and expenses, the improving and alteration
of taxes, the direction of local services; the organization of the
property belonging to the Commune; the choice by election or
competition—with the responsibility and permanent right of
control and revocation—of the Communal magistrates and
officials of all classes; the absolute guarantee of individual
liberty and liberty of conscience; the permanent intervention
of the citizens in Communal affairs by the free manifestation of
their ideas and the free defence of their interests; guarantees
given for those manifestations by the Commune, who alone are
charged with securing the free and just exercise of the right of
meeting and publicity; and the organization of urban defence
and the National Guard, which must elect its chiefs and alone
watch over the maintenance of order in the city. Paris wishes
nothing more under the head of local guarantees on the well-
understood condition of regaining, in a grand Central Administration and Delegation from the Federal Communes, the realization and practice of those principles; but in favour of her
independence, and profiting by her liberty of action, she reserves to herself liberty to bring about as may seem good to her
administrative and economic reforms which the people demand,
and to create such institutions as may serve to develop and
further education. Produce, exchange, and credit have to
universalize power and property according to the necessities of

the moment, the wishes of those interested, and the data furnished by experience.

Our enemies deceive themselves or deceive the country when they accuse Paris of desiring to impose its will and supremacy upon the rest of the nation, and to aspire to a dictatorship which would be a veritable attempt to overthrow the independence and sovereignty of other Communes. They deceive themselves when they accuse Paris of seeking the destruction of French unity established by the Revolution. The unity which has been imposed upon us up to the present by the Empire, the Monarchy, and the Parliamentary Government is nothing but centralization, despotic, unintelligent, arbitrary, and onerous. The political unity, as desired by Paris, is a voluntary association of all local initiative, the free and spontaneous co-operation of all individual energies with the common object of the well-being, liberty, and security of all. The Communal Revolution, initiated by the people on the 18th of March, inaugurated a new era in politics, experimental, positive and scientific . . .

144. *Proclamation of the Comte de Chambord, 5 July 1871*

The monarchist majority of the National Assembly, elected in February 1871, wished to re-establish the monarchy, but was divided in its allegiance. One section, the legitimists, supported the claims of the Comte de Chambord, grandson of Charles X, the other those of the Comte de Paris, grandson of Louis Philippe. It was arranged between them that the Comte de Chambord be established as King and, having no direct heir, be succeeded by the much younger Comte de Paris, who was next in the legitimate line of descent. Difficulties arose, however, with the Comte de Chambord because, in the proclamation that follows and a number of other, later, ones, he set certain conditions for his return which, as even his legitimist supporters realized, would have been unacceptable to the French people.

Source: F. H. Brabant, *The Beginning of the Third Republic in France* (London, Macmillan, 1940), pp. 339–40.

People of France,

I am among you; you have opened the doors of France to me, and I could not refuse the happiness of seeing my country again, but I do not wish by staying any longer to furnish new pretexts for excitement at a time when there is so much restlessness . . .

As I leave France, it is in my heart to tell you that I am not separated from you; France knows I belong to her. I cannot forget that the right of the King is part of the nation's inheritance, nor can I refuse those duties towards the nation, which it imposes upon me.

These duties I shall carry out ... We will found together, and when you will a Government in conformity with the real needs of the nation, widely based on administrative decentralization and local liberties.

As a guarantee of the public liberties, to which all Christian peoples have a right, we shall grant universal suffrage, honestly practised, and the control of two Chambers. We shall resume the national movement of the end of the last century restoring to it its true character.

A minority in revolt against the wishes of France made it the occasion of a period of demoralization by falsehood, and of disorganization by violence; their criminal conspiracy imposed a revolution on a nation that only asked for reforms and, since, has driven it to the edge of an abyss ...

It is the working classes, the labourers in the country and the towns, whose welfare has been the constant object of my most anxious thought and my most welcome studies, and who have suffered the most from this social disorder. But France, cruelly disillusioned by unprecedented disasters, will understand that it is impossible to return to the truth by exchanging one error for another, that we cannot evade eternal necessities by temporary expedients.

France will recall me and I shall come to her with all that I have—my devotion on her service, my principle, and my flag.

On the question of the Flag mention has been made of conditions to which I cannot submit. People of France, I am ready to do everything to help my country to rise from her downfall and resume her position in the world; the only sacrifice I cannot make to her is that of my honour.

I belong to my time with all my heart; I pay sincere homage to all its greatness and, whatever has been the flag under which our soldiers have marched, I have admired their heroism and thanked God for all which their courage added to the treasure of our national glory.

There must be no misunderstanding or reserve between you and me. No, it is not true what ignorance and credulity have spoken of—class privileges, absolutism, and intolerance, and I know not what else—tithes and feudal rights—phantoms which the most daring calumny is trying to evoke before you. But I will not, for that, let the standard of Henri IV, François I, and Jeanne d'Arc be snatched from my hands.

With that flag the national unity was effected; with that flag your ancestors, led by mine, conquered Alsace and Lorraine, whose faithfulness to us is still a consolation in our disaster; it has conquered the barbarians in their land of Africa, which witnessed the first war-like actions of a Prince of my family. It will conquer the modern barbarians, by whom the world is menaced. I shall entrust it without fear to the courage of our army. They know it has never followed any path but that of honour. I received it as a sacred legacy from the old King, my grandfather, when he died in exile; it has always for me been bound up with the thought of my distant country. It floated over my cradle; I wish that it may overshadow my tomb. In the glorious folds of this unspotted standard I shall bring you order and freedom. People of France, Henri V cannot abandon the White Flag of Henri IV.

145. *The Constitutional Laws of the Third Republic, 1875–84*

The royalist majority in the French National Assembly long temporized over enacting constitutional laws in the hope that the difficulties with the claimants for the throne (cf. No. 144) might be settled and the monarchy might be re-established. By 1875 it became clear, however, that the temporary institutions of France had to be replaced by permanent ones. Thus a series of constitutional laws was enacted which established a republican form of government, but was so drafted that, by replacing the President with a King, they would well suit a constitutional monarchy. To facilitate the transition, amendment of these laws was made comparatively easy.

Our selections (a) and (b) consist of some of the more important provisions of the two basic laws, followed by an early amendment (c) after the republicans gained a parliamentary majority.

Source: *Annals of the American Academy of Political and Social Science* (Philadelphia), vol. iii, Supplement, March 1893, 'Constitutional and organic laws of France', pp. 42–50.

(a) Law on the Organization of the Public Powers, 25 February 1875.

1. The legislative power is exercised by two assemblies; the Chamber of Deputies and the Senate. The Chamber of Deputies is elected by universal suffrage ... The composition, the method of election, and the powers of the Senate shall be regulated by a special law.

2. The President of the Republic is chosen by an absolute majority of votes of the Senate and Chamber of Deputies united in National Assembly. He is elected for seven years. He is re-eligible.

3. The President of the Republic has the initiative of the laws, concurrently with the members of the two Chambers. He promulgates the laws when they have been voted by the two Chambers; he looks after and secures their execution. He has the right of pardon; amnesty can be granted by law only. He disposes of the armed force. He appoints to all civil and military positions. He presides over national festivals ... Every act of the President of the Republic must be countersigned by a Minister.

4. As vacancies occur ... the President of the Republic appoints, in the Council of Ministers, the Councillors of State ...

5. The President of the Republic may, with the advice of the Senate, dissolve the Chamber of Deputies before the legal expiration of its term.

6. The Ministers are [collectively] responsible to the Chambers for the general policy of the government, and individually for their personal acts. The President of the Republic is responsible in case of high treason only ...

8. The Chambers shall have the right by separate resolutions, taken in each by an absolute majority of votes, either upon their own initiative or upon the request of the President of the Republic, to declare a revision of the Constitutional Laws necessary. After each of the two Chambers shall have come to this decision, they shall meet together in National Assembly to proceed with the revision ...

(b) Law on the Relations of the Public Powers, 16 July 1875.

1. The Senate and the Chamber of Deputies shall assemble each year the second Tuesday of January, unless convened earlier by the President of the Republic. The two Chambers continue in session at least five months each year ...

3. One month at least before the legal expiration of the powers of the President of the Republic, the Chambers must be called together in National Assembly and proceed to the election of a new President. In default of a summons, this meeting shall take place as of right the fifteenth day before the expiration of those powers ...

5. The sittings of the Senate and of the Chamber of Deputies are public.

6. The President of the Republic communicates with the Chambers by messages, which are read from the tribune by a Minister. The Ministers have entrance to both Chambers and must be heard when they request it ...

9. The President of the Republic cannot declare war except by the previous assent of the two Chambers ...

12. The President of the Republic may be impeached by the Chamber of Deputies only, and tried by the Senate only. The Ministers may be impeached by the Chamber of Deputies for offences committed in the performance of their duties. In this case they are tried by the Senate. The Senate may be constituted a Court of Justice, by a decree of the President of the Republic, issued in the Council of Ministers, to try all persons accused of attempts upon the safety of the State ...

(c) Law Partially revising the Constitutional Laws, 14 August 1884.

... 2. To ... Article 8 of [the Law on Organization of the Public Powers] is added the following:
'The republican form of the government cannot be made the subject of a proposed revision. Members of families that have reigned in France are ineligible to the presidency of the Republic' ...

146. *Boulanger's Speech at Tours, 17 May 1889*

Boulanger, a republican general and a very popular figure, was a protégé of the Radicals, and Minister for War in one of the cabinets dominated by them in 1886–87. When the Government fell, he lost his post, and, in a subordinate posting, began to engage in political activities. Supported mainly by a right wing group, the League of Patriots, but also by the Left, including many workers of Paris, he was elected to the Chamber of Deputies several times, although being a serving officer he was ineligible and his elections were declared invalid. He began a campaign for a revision of the constitution and swiftly gained popularity. At one time, in January 1889, he seemed about to stage a *coup d'état* in Paris, but he let the opportunity slip by. After about two months of hesitation, in which he tried to rally further support, he fled abroad from the measures threatened by the Government and committed suicide in 1891.

The excerpts from his last speech in France, which follow, are a typical example of the ideas on which his popularity was based.

Source: A. Zévaès, *Au temps du boulangisme* (Paris, © Editions Gallimard 1930), pp. 153–4 (trans. Ed.).

... I call on all good Frenchmen to rally around me in order to strengthen the Republic by purifying it. In this appeal I don't ask anybody where he comes from ... It does not matter to me whether he rallies to the Republican idea by enthusiasm or by reason. What is important is that he rally without reservations, with a sincere desire to accomplish the common task ...

I have faith in the republican idea. I believe that when our institutions will correspond with our needs, with the aspirations of that so fundamentally democratic society which constitutes France, all doubts which might still exist will vanish. I am sure that those who come to us today with the determination to help in our great enterprise without really daring to believe in it will become the most sincere, the most devoted republicans ...

Republicans of long standing, who have fought and suffered for the Republic, are numerous in the national party ... and nothing hinders those who have not yet joined us from coming to swell our ranks and thus to prove the vanity of the baseless fears of our enemies.

When I declared the Republic to be open, I did not say that it was open to the monarchists or closed to the republicans. I said that I would open it to all men of good will, and only those are excluded who systematically refuse to deny their sentiments of personal predilection in order to work exclusively for the unity, the greatness, and the prosperity of the fatherland . . .

I am marching . . . towards the Republic, but a non-parliamentary republic, a republic which gives the country a strong Government, a republic which will protect the humble and the small, a republic which takes passionate care of the interests of the people, a republic which, lastly, respects individual liberty, first of all the liberty of conscience which is the first and most important of all the liberties. Long live France! Long live the Republic! Long live Liberty!

147. *The Dreyfus Affair*

Even the barest outlines of the Dreyfus case are too complex to be described here, and this note will confine itself to a brief description of the documents included.

The *bordereau* (a) which was the first lead to a spy in the French General Staff was found in the office of the German military attaché. It was the major piece of evidence against Captain Dreyfus, a Jewish Alsatian officer of the General Staff, who was convicted of treason and sentenced to transportation for life.

His family claimed that a miscarriage of justice had taken place and pressed for a revision. The sentence was indeed revised, and Dreyfus' conviction confirmed, but the proceedings were again questionable, and, as later evidence showed, based partly on forged evidence. When through the efforts of some altruistic officers evidence was accumulated against the real culprit, Major Esterhazy, and political pressure led to his trial, he was triumphantly acquitted, mainly because of documents forged by Major Henry of the Intelligence Branch. The *petit-bleu* (telegram letter) (b) which follows was one of the major pieces of evidence against Esterhazy.

The Dreyfus case, however, only became the Dreyfus affair, which split France and shook the foundations of the Third Republic, after Émile Zola, the author, published his open letter *J'accuse* addressed to the President of the Republic. The concluding paragraphs of this long letter follow (c).

Source: F. C. Conybeare, *The Dreyfus case* (London, Geo. Allen, 1898), pp. 30–1, 102, 228–9.

(a) The *Bordereau*, 1894.

Sir,

though I have no news to indicate that you wish to see me, nevertheless I am sending you some interesting items of information.

1. A note on the hydraulic brake of the 120, and on the way in which this piece behaved.

2. A note on the covering troops (some modifications will be entailed by the new plan).

3. A note on a modification in artillery formations.

4. A note relative to Madagascar.

5. The project of a firing manual for field artillery, 14th March 1894.

The last document is extremely difficult to procure, and I can only have it at my disposal during a very few days. The Minister of War has sent a limited number of copies to the several corps, and these corps are responsible for the return of it after the manœuvres. If, then you would like to take out of it whatever interests you, and hold it afterwards at my disposal, I will take it, unless, indeed, you would like me to have it copied *in extenso*, and then send the copy to your address.

I am just setting off to the manœuvres.

(b) The *petit-bleu*, 1896.

Address: M. le Commandant Esterhazy, 27 Rue de la Bien-faisance, Paris.

Text: I await before everything a more detailed explanation than what you gave me the other day in regard to the question at issue. In consequence I beg you to give it me in writing so that I may judge if I can continue my relations with the firm R . . . or not.

(c) The Concluding Paragraphs of Zola's *J'accuse*, 13 January 1898.

. . . I accuse Lieutenant-Colonel Du Paty de Clam of having been the diabolical contriver of the judicial error, unconscious I would fain believe; and of having afterwards defended his nefarious work for three years by machinations as ridiculous as they are guilty.

I accuse General Mercier of having made himself the accomplice, through his mere weakness of character, in one of the greatest iniquities of the century.

I accuse General Billot of having had in his hands the certain proofs of Dreyfus' innocence and of having stifled them; of having incurred the guilt of a betrayal of humanity, of a betrayal of justice, in order to serve political ends and to save a [General Staff] that was compromised.

I accuse Generals de Boisdeffre and Gonse of having made themselves accomplices in the same crime—the one, no doubt, led on by clerical passion, the other perhaps by that *esprit de corps* which makes of the War Office Bureaux an ark holy and not to be touched.

I accuse General de Pellieux and Commandant Ravary of having turned their inquiry into a work of villainy, by which I mean that the inquiry was conducted with the most monstrous partiality; and that of this partiality the report of Ravary is an imperishable monument, brazen in its audacity.

I accuse the three handwriting experts—MM. Belhomme, Varinard, and Couard—of having drawn up lying and fraudulent reports; unless, indeed, a medical examination shows them to be the victims of a diseased eyesight and judgement.

I accuse the War Office of having carried on in the press . . . an abominable campaign intended to lead astray opinion and hide its misdoings.

Lastly, I accuse the first court-martial of having violated right by condemning an accused man on a document which was kept secret, and I accuse the second court-martial of having shielded this illegality to order, committing in its turn the judicial crime of acquitting a man they knew to be guilty.

148. *Union of French Socialists Parties, 30 December 1904*

The French socialist movement long lacked the effectiveness the number of its adherents ought to have secured because of the existence of several socialist parties of differing views, ranging from syndicalism to doctrinaire Marxism. After a number of unsuccessful attempts the main socialist groups appointed a unification commission which, after four meetings in December 1904, agreed on the following declaration which, in January 1905, was accepted by all groups as the foundation document of a new, united, party.

Source: P. Louis, *Le parti socialiste en France* (Paris, Quillet, 1913), pp. 82–5 (Encyclopédie Socialiste, vol. x) (trans. Ed.).

The delegates of the [following] French organizations: Workers Socialist Revolutionary Party, Socialist Party of

DEC—z

France, French Socialist Party, and [six] autonomous [socialist regional] Federations, appointed by their respective Parties and Federations to establish unity ... declare that their organizations are ready to collaborate immediately in the task of the unification of socialist forces on the basis of the following, determined and accepted by common agreement:

1. The Socialist Party is a class party, whose aim is the socialization of the means of production and exchange, that is, the transformation of capitalist society into a collective or communist society, by the means of the economic and political organization of the proletariat. In its aim, in its ideal, in the means it uses, the Socialist Party is not a party of reform—although it will endeavour to achieve the immediate reforms demanded by the working class—but a party of class war and revolution.

2. Those elected to Parliament shall form a single group opposed to all bourgeois political factions. The socialist group in Parliament must refuse to the Government all means which assure the domination of the bourgeoisie and its maintenance in power, it must refuse, therefore, [the granting of] military votes, votes for colonial conquest, secret funds, and the whole of the budget.

The deputies can not commit the Party without its agreement even in exceptional circumstances.

In Parliament, the socialist group must devote itself to the defence and extension of the political freedom and rights of the workers, and to the pursuit and realization of reforms which improve the conditions of life ... of the working class ...

4. Freedom of discussion in the press is complete in all questions of doctrine and method, but with respect to action, all socialist newspapers must conform strictly to the decision of the Congress, interpreted by the central organization of the party ...

6. The party will take steps to ensure that its deputies shall respect their *mandat impératif*.[1]

149. The 'Charter of Amiens', October 1906

The largest French trade union federation, the *Confédération Général du Travail* (*C.G.T.*) was formed in 1895, mainly by syndicalist

---

[1] The obligation to act or vote in accordance with the instructions of the majority of their electors.

unions. But the unions represented varied in their attitude to the revolutionary general strike and to co-operation or affiliation with outside political bodies. The formation of the united socialist party in 1905 (cf. No. 148) brought matters to a head, and the *C.G.T.* Congress held at Amiens in October 1906 passed the following resolution which, by pronouncing the complete independence of trade unions from political parties, clearly showed the victory of the revolutionary, rather than the reformist, element in it.

Source: J.-B. Séverac, *Le mouvement syndical* (Paris, Quillet, 1913), pp. 282–4 (Encyclopédie Socialiste, vol. xi) (trans. Ed.).

The federal congress of Amiens confirms Article 2 of the *C.G.T.* constitution which reads: 'The *C.G.T.* unites, without regard to their political beliefs, all workers who are conscious of the struggle to be carried out for the disappearance of the wage-system and the class of employers.'

The Congress considers that this declaration is a recognition of the class war which, in the economic field, puts the workers in revolt into opposition to all forms of exploitation and oppression, material and moral, of the working class by the capitalist class.

The Congress clarified this theoretical statement by the following points:

In its day-to-day activity the trade union movement seeks the co-ordination of workers' efforts, the increase of the workers' well-being by the achievement of immediate improvements, such as the reduction of the hours of work, raising of wages, etc.

But this task is only one side of the work of the trade union movement: it prepares the total emancipation which can only be achieved by the expropriation of the capitalist class; it commends publicly the general strike as the means [to this end] and it considers that the trade union, which is today the organization of resistance, will in the future become the unit of production and distribution, the basis of social re-organization.

The Congress declares that these day-to-day and long-term tasks result from the condition of the wage-earners which weighs down the working class, and which makes it the duty of all workers, whatever political or philosophical convictions they may hold, to belong to the basic organization, the trade union.

Therefore, as far as the individual is concerned, the Congress declares the complete liberty of the trade union member to take part, outside the union, in such form of action as may suit his philosophical or political view, and it merely asks him . . . not to introduce to the union the opinions he holds outside it.

As far as the organizations are concerned, the Congress declares that, in order to attain the maximum efficacy of the union movement, the economic action must be taken directly against the employers; therefore the constituent organizations should not concern themselves, as unions, with parties and groups which, outside or parallel with the unions, may freely strive for social transformation.

150. *The Stavisky Affair, January 1934*

Right-wing organizations had been increasing in strength ever since the Dreyfus affair (No. 147) and, by the early nineteen thirties, became vocal and violent in their expressions of discontent with the Government. Their discontent was brought to an even greater pitch when, in January 1934, the scandal of the Stavisky affair compromised members of the Government.

Our selections include contemporary reports from *The Times* which give an outline of developments (a) and a proclamation of the leader of the *Camelots du Roi*, the militant wing of the *Action française* (b) which gives the right wing point of view.

Source: (a) *The Times* (London), 5, 8, 10, and 11 January 1934.
(b) A. Werth, *France in Ferment* (London, Jarrolds, 1934), pp. 90–1.

(a) Reports from *The Times*.

(1) 5 January 1934.

Although the total value of the fraudulent bonds issued on behalf of the Bayonne Municipal Pawnbroking Establishment is not yet known, reports now set the figure at about 500,000,000 francs (£4,000,000 gold). The magnitude of the swindle and the possibilities of political repercussion are causing the Government some concern.

This morning M. Chautemps, the Prime Minister, summoned the Law Officers of the Republic and of the Seine Department and the Chiefs of the Police and gave orders that no effort was to be spared to apprehend Alexandre Stavisky, who is wanted in connexion with the affair, and added that whatever the position of those implicated they must be brought to justice . . .

Meanwhile two letters written in June and September, 1932, by M. Dalimier, the Minister of Labour and now Minister of the Colonies, have been published. The first, addressed to M. Hermant, president of the General Insurance Committee declares that the writer, in accordance with a request from the Minister of Commerce, wishes to point out the desirability of facilitating the placing of municipal bonds. The second, addressed to M. Tissier, the director of the Credit Municipal of Bayonne, . . . suggests that he should approach the insurance companies for the disposal of the municipal bonds, adding that, in view of the security they offered, the bonds would in all probability be taken up without difficulty . . .

(2) 8 January 1934.
. . . An official report issued yesterday says that Stavisky was born in 1886, near Kieff. His father, a dentist, came to France in 1900 and was naturalized. In 1912 Stavisky was sentenced to 15 days imprisonment and a fine of 25 francs for fraud. He joined the French Army as a volunteer in August 1914. 'Then' —laconically says the report—'he founded a bank and was sentenced on July 15, 1915, to six months' imprisonment and a fine of 100 francs.'

In July 1926 Stavisky was again arrested on a charge of fraud. In December 1927 he was released on bail of 50,000 francs on grounds of ill health. A police doctor certified that he could be treated at the prison infirmary, but the prison doctor disagreed. On the plea that he was suffering from paraplegia, Stavisky's case was adjourned on successive occasions until last October. It stands on the list for hearing on January 26. Stavisky was known at various times by the names of Serge Alexandre, Sacha Alex, Doing de Monti, and Victor Boitel . . .

(3) 10 January 1934.
Alexandre Stavisky, the financier who, according to the statements of the police shot himself in a villa at Chamonix yesterday afternoon when about to be arrested, died early this morning . . . It is . . . presumed officially [on the basis of a post mortem examination] that Stavisky committed suicide.

There is, however, a theory, reflected in a certain section of public comment and of the Press, that he was shot by the police when they entered the villa . . .

This evening several hundred demonstrators, mainly composed of *camelots du roi*, came into collision with the public force who guarded all approaches to the neighbourhood [of the Chamber] . . . Mounted guards charged repeatedly and more than two hundred arrests were made before calm was restored . . .

(4) 11 January 1934.

Tomorrow's debate in the Chamber on the six interpellations handed in on the subject of the Stavisky affair is likely to be stormy. The interpellations seek to fix the responsibility for the political and administrative errors which the case has revealed, to protect public savings . . . and to impugn Courts and officials who have manifestly failed to do their duty . . .

The air of the lobbies has reeked for days with the miasma of distrust, suspicion of political profiteering in Stavisky's ill-gotten gains, of shares in the plunder, of collusion and interference in the course of justice . . .

(b) Proclamation of the *Camelots du Roi*, 7 January 1934.
To the People of Paris.

At a time when the Government and the Parliament of the Republic declare themselves incapable of balancing our budget, and continue to defend the topsy-turvy foundations of their régime; while they refuse to reduce the burden of taxation and are actually inflicting more taxes on the French people, a scandal breaks out. This scandal shows that, far from protecting the savings of the people, the Republican Authorities have given free course to the colossal rackets of an alien crook. A Minister, M. Dalimier, by his letters of June 25th and September 23rd, 1932, deliberately[1] provided an instrument which enabled the thief Stavisky to rob the insurance companies and the Social Insurance Fund of over half a milliard francs. He has been urged to resign; but he has refused to do so.[2] He should be in prison together with his pals Stavisky and Dubarry; instead of which, he continues to be a member of the Government

[1] The official Commission of Enquiry did not establish deliberate intention to deceive on the part of Dalimier.
[2] Dalimier later resigned his ministerial post.

whose duty it is to inquire into this affair. Dalimier is not alone; we can see behind him a crowd of other ministers and influential members of Parliament, all of whom have, in one way or another, favoured the adventurer's rackets, especially by instructing the police to leave him alone, and by suspending during many years the legal proceeding that should have been taken against him. There is no law and no justice in a country where magistrates and the police are the accomplices of criminals. The honest people of France who want to protect their own interests, and who care for the cleanliness of public life, are forced to take the law into their own hands.

At the beginning of this week, Parliament will reassemble and we urge the people of Paris to come in large numbers before the Chamber of Deputies, to cry 'Down with the Thieves' and to clamour for honesty and justice.

Maurice Pujo.

P.S. Instructions will be sent to our friends in due course.

151. *The attempted Coup d'État of the Leagues, 6 February 1934*

In an atmosphere made explosive by the Stavisky affair (No. 150) and its aftermath, a new Government was to meet the Chamber of Deputies on 6 February. For this day extremist groups, mainly right wing, concerted an armed demonstration and attack on the Chamber of Deputies with the aim of replacing the Government and the Chamber with one of their own choice. Their attempt was defeated after some bitter streetfights, and a strong coalition Government was formed to break the Leagues' power.

The following proclamations by organizations participating in the attack explain their views.

Source: A. Werth, *France in Ferment* (London, Jarrolds, 1934), pp. 143–4.

(a) Proclamation of the *Solidarité Française*, 6 February 1934.

France for the French! Take your brooms and sweep out the rubbish! We have had enough of this!

In all towns, in all villages, you, members of the *Solidarité Française*, must demonstrate at seven o'clock to-night against this grotesque regime, against the parliamentary profiteers! May your demonstration be calm, orderly, dignified and without violence. Members of the *Solidarité* of the Paris area meet in the Grands Boulevards, between the Opéra and the rue Drouot. The Government must be made to realize that the people of France have wakened and that they are determined to put an end to the reign of international revolutionaries and corrupt politicians.

(b) Appeal of the *Jeunesses Patriotes*.

People of Paris!

You will join us in the Place de Grève, outside the Town Hall, the cradle of your civic rights, and proclaim with us that the country is in danger. Led by your own representatives [several town councillors of Paris] you will tell Parliament your own 'way of thinking'. France has her eyes fixed on Paris. Paris will respond to France's appeal. Meet at seven o'clock in the Place de l'Hôtel de Ville ...

(c) The Appeal of the *Action Française*, 6 February 1934.

To the people of Paris!

Called to power in the hope that they would restore justice and order, Messrs. Frot and Daladier began their work by chasing out the policeman. They have given free rein to Socialist anarchy, and want to save the Masonic crooks.

In trying to force this abject régime on us, in trying to smother the voice of public opinion, MM. Daladier and Frot are hurling violent threats at decent people. These gentlemen are terrified and have a bad conscience, and still they hope to have things their own way.

They are making a mistake.

The people of France will respond to these acts of defiance. With the régime falling to pieces, they will assert their own rights. After the closing of the factories and offices they will meet before the Chamber to-night and crying 'Down with the Thieves!' they will tell the Government and its parliamentary supporters that they have had enough of this putrid régime.

152. *The Programme of the Popular Front, 10 January 1936*

On several earlier occasions socialists and radicals co-operated in French elections and were successful in gaining a majority. After forming a coalition Government, however, they usually found that the aims of the component groups of the *Cartel des Gauches*[1] diverged too much for a consistent Government policy to be carried out, and thus their Government fell. To avoid repetition, the groups of the Left met in January 1936 and agreed on a programme to be put into effect if they gained power after the approaching elections.

Source: G. Fraser and T. Natanson, *Léon Blum* (London, Gollancz, 1937), pp. 307–12.

POLITICAL DEMANDS

I. Defence of Liberty.

1. General amnesty.
2. Against the Fascist Leagues:
    (a) Effective disarmament, and dissolution of semi-military formations . . .
    (b) The putting into force of legal enactments in cases of incitement to murder or of attempts endangering the safety of the State.
3. The cleansing of public life, especially through the enforcement of parliamentary disqualifications (i.e. inability of a Deputy to hold certain offices).
4. The Press:
    (a) Repeal of the infamous laws and decrees restricting freedom of opinion.
    (b) Reform of the Press by . . . legislative measures . . .
    (c) The organization of State broadcasting messages, with the aim of ensuring the accuracy of information and the equality of political and social organizations at the microphone.
5. Trade union liberties:
    (a) Application and observance of trade union rights for all.
    (b) Observance of factory legislation concerning women.
6. Education and freedom of conscience:
    (a) To safeguard the development of public education, not only by the necessary grants, but also by reforms such as the extension of compulsory attendance at school up to the age of fourteen, and, in secondary education, the proper selection of pupils as an essential accompaniment of grants.
    (b) To guarantee to all concerned, pupils and teachers, full

---

[1] Left Block.

freedom of conscience, particularly by ensuring the
neutrality of education, its nonreligious character, and
the civic rights of the teaching staff.

7. Colonial territories: The setting up of a Parliamentary
Commission of Enquiry into the political, economic and cultural
situation in France's overseas territories . . .

II. Defence of Peace

1. Appeal to the people, and particularly to the working masses, for collaboration in the maintenance and organization of peace.

2. International collaboration within the framework of the League of Nations for collective security, by defining the aggressor and the automatic and joint application of sanctions in cases of aggression.

3. A ceaseless endeavour to pass from armed peace to disarmed peace, first by a convention of limitation, and then by the general, simultaneous, and effectively controlled reduction of armaments.

4. Nationalization of the war industries and suppression of private trade in arms.

5. Repudiation of secret diplomacy, international action, and public negotiations to bring back to Geneva the States which have left it, without weakening the constituent principles of the League of Nations: collective security and indivisible peace.

6. Simplification of the procedure provided in the League of Nations Covenant for the pacific adjustment of treaties which are dangerous to the peace of the world . . .

ECONOMIC DEMANDS

I. Restoration of purchasing power destroyed or reduced by the crisis.

Against unemployment and the crisis in industry

The establishment of a national unemployment fund.

Reduction of the working week without reduction of weekly wages.

Drawing young workers into employment by establishing a system of adequate pensions for aged workers.

The rapid carrying out of a scheme of large-scale works of public utility . . .

Against the agricultural and commercial crisis

Revision of prices of agricultural produce, combined with a fight against speculation and high prices, so as to reduce the gap between wholesale and retail prices.

In order to put an end to the levies taken by speculators from both producers and consumers, the setting up of a National Grain Board . . .

Support for agricultural co-operatives, supply of fertilizers at cost prices . . ., extension of agricultural credits, reduction of leasehold rents.

Suspension of distraints and the regulation of debt repayments.

Pending the complete and earliest possible removal of all the injustices inflicted by the economy decrees, the immediate repeal of measures affecting those groups whose conditions of life have been most severely damaged by these decrees.

II. Against the robbery of savings and for a better organization of credit.

Regulation of banking business.

Regulation of balance sheets issued by banks and limited liability companies.

Further regulation of the powers of directors of companies.

Prohibition of State servants who have retired, or are on the reserve list, from being members of boards of directors of companies.

In order to remove credit and savings from the control of the economic oligarchy, to transform the *Banque de France*, now a privately owned Bank, into the *Banque de la France* (i.e. to nationalize it).

Abolition of the Council of Regents of the Bank of France.

Extension of the powers of the Governor of the Bank of France, under the permanent control of a council composed of representatives of the legislative assembly, representatives of the executive authority, and representatives of the main organized forces of labour and of industrial, commercial and agricultural activity.

Conversion of the capital of the bank into bonds, with measures to safeguard the interests of smallholders.

III. AGAINST FINANCIAL CORRUPTION

Control of the trade in armaments, in conjunction with the nationalization of war industries.

Abolition of waste in the civil and military departments.

The setting up of a War Pensions Fund.

Democratic reform of the tax system so as to relax the fiscal burden with a view to economic revival, and the finding of financial resources through measures directed against large fortunes (rapid steepening of the rates of tax on incomes over 75,000 francs—reorganization of death-duties—taxation of monopoly profits in such a way as to prevent any repercussion on the prices paid by consumers).

Prevention of fraud in connexion with transferable securities.

Control of exports of capital, and punishment for evasion by the most rigorous measures, up to the confiscation of property concealed abroad or of its equivalent value in France.

153. *The Matignon Agreement, 7 June 1936*

The Popular Front (cf. No. 152) gained a majority in the elections and formed a Government under the premiership of Léon Blum. Its first task was to deal with the economic and social crisis prevalent in the country, which had led to violent strike action and even to the occupation of factories by the workers. To settle the strikes, long-drawn-out negotiations were held between employer and employee organizations under the auspices of the Minister of Labour, but they only led to an agreement after Blum himself took over the conduct of negotiations. The text of the agreement follows. It is called the 'Matignon' agreement because it was concluded in the Matignon Palace, the official residence of the Premier.

Source: V. R. Lorwin, *The French Labour Movement* (Cambridge, Mass., Harvard University Press, 1954) pp. 313–15.

The delegates of the General Confederation of French Production (CGPF) and the General Confederation of Labour (CGT) have met under the chairmanship of the Premier (Léon Blum) and have concluded the following agreement, after arbitration by the Premier:

1. The employer delegation agrees to the immediate conclusion of collective agreements.

2. These agreements must include, in particular, articles 3 and 5 below.

3. All citizens being required to abide by law, the employers recognize the freedom of opinion of workers and their right to freely join and belong to trade unions . . .

In their decisions on hiring, organization or assignment of work, disciplinary measures or dismissals, employers agree not to take into consideration the fact of membership or non-membership in a union.

If one of the contracting parties claims that the dismissal of a worker has been caused by a violation of the right to organize and belong to a union stated above, the two parties will seek to determine the facts and arrive at an equitable solution of the case in question. This does not prejudice the rights of parties to obtain reparation at law for the damage caused.

The exercise of trade union rights must not give rise to acts contrary to law.

4. The wages actually paid to all workers as of 25 May 1936 will be raised, as of the resumption of work, by a decreasing percentage ranging from 15 per cent for the lowest rates down to 7 per cent for the highest rates. In no case must the total increase in any establishment exceed 12 per cent . . .

The negotiations, which are to be launched at once, for the determination by collective agreement of minimum wages by regions and by occupations must take up, in particular, the necessary revision of abnormally low wages.

The employer delegation agrees to carry out the adjustments necessary to retain a normal relationship between salaries of nonproduction employees and hourly wages.

5. Except for special cases already regulated by law, in each establishment with more than ten workers, after an agreement between labour and management organizations (or, in the absence of those, between the interested parties), there will be two shop stewards or more . . ., in accordance with the size of the establishment. These stewards will have the right to present to management individual grievances which have not been satisfactorily adjusted . . .

6. The employer delegation promises that there will be no sanctions for strike activities.

7. The CGT delegation will ask the workers on strike to return

to work as soon as the managements of establishments have
accepted this general agreement and as soon as negotiations for
its application have begun between the managements and the
personnel of the establishments.

XIV · THE FIRST WORLD WAR

IMPORTANT documents relating to the first world war and the peace settlement could fill—indeed, have filled—many volumes. Very few documents have here been selected, and they illustrate mainly the outbreak of the war and the peace settlement.

The first four documents relate to the outbreak of the war. The letter (No. 154) in which the German Government assures the Austro-Hungarian Government of its unqualified support opens the section. It is followed by the Austro-Hungarian ultimatum to Serbia (No. 155) and the Serbian reply (No. 156) in which the Serbian Government gives qualified acceptance to the Austro-Hungarian demands. The last document on the outbreak is the German declaration of war on Russia (No. 157).

Many documents on war aims and peace proposals could have been chosen, but, in the end, it was decided to include only the most important one, President Wilson's Fourteen Points and its later elaborations and qualifications (No. 158). A contrast is provided by the Peace Treaty of Brest Litovsk (No. 159) between the Central Powers and Russia.

A few selected articles of the Treaty of Versailles (No. 160) conclude the section.

154. *The German 'Blank Cheque' to Austria, 6 July 1914*

After the assassination of Archduke Franz Ferdinand at Sarajevo on 28 June 1914, and allegations of Serbian complicity made by the Austro-Hungarian Government, intense diplomatic activity began between Austria–Hungary and Germany, closely bound together not only by the Triple Alliance (No. 102) but also by the Austro-German treaty of 1879 (No. 100). The German Emperor and Government were so convinced of the justness of the Austrian claims that, in the following telegram, they promised unqualified support to Austria–Hungary. As a result they were not consulted in advance on the terms of the Austro-Hungarian ultimatum to Serbia (No. 155).

Source: *Outbreak of the War: German Documents Collected by K. Kautsky* and ed. by M. Montgelas and W. Schücking; tr. by the Carnegie Endowment for International Peace (New York, Oxford University Press, 1924), pp. 78–9.

Telegram from the Imperial Chancellor at Berlin to the German Ambassador at Vienna, 6 July 1914.

The Austro-Hungarian Ambassador yesterday delivered to the Emperor a confidential personal letter from the Emperor Franz Joseph, which depicts the present situation from the Austro-Hungarian point of view, and describes the measures which Vienna has in view . . .

I replied . . . on behalf of His Majesty that His Majesty sends his thanks to the Emperor Franz Joseph for his letter and would soon answer it personally. In the meantime His Majesty desires to say that he is not blind to the danger which threatens Austria–Hungary and thus the Triple Alliance as a result of the Russian and Serbian Panslavic agitation. [German diplomatic assistance is promised in Romania and Bulgaria to prevent the formation of a Balkan alliance against Austria–Hungary.]

Finally, as far as concerns Serbia, His Majesty, of course, can not interfere in the dispute now going on between Austria–Hungary and that country, as it is a matter not within his competence. The Emperor Franz Joseph may, however, rest assured that His Majesty will faithfully stand by Austria–Hungary, as is required by the obligations of his alliance and of his ancient friendship.

155. *The Austro-Hungarian Note to Serbia, 23 July 1914*

The initial diplomatic flurry which occurred after the assassination of Franz Ferdinand had died away when, nearly a month later, on 23 July 1914, the Austro-Hungarian Government presented a note to the Serbian Government. The note made far-reaching demands (note particularly points 2, 4, 5, and 6) and demanded a reply within forty-eight hours. The Austro-Hungarian Government did not consult any other Government, even the German, before presenting the note.

Source: Great Britain. Foreign Office. *Collected Diplomatic Documents*

relating to the Outbreak of the European War (London,
H.M.S.O., 1915) (Cd. 7860), pp. 414–16.

On March 31st, 1909, the Royal Serbian Minister to the
Court of Vienna made the following statement, by order of his
Government:—'Serbia declares that she is not affected in her
rights by the situation established in Bosnia,[1] and that she will
therefore adapt herself to the decisions which the Powers are
going to arrive at . . . By following the councils of the Powers,
Serbia binds herself to cease the attitude of protest and resistance which she has assumed since last October, relative to the
annexation, and she binds herself further to change the direction of her present policies towards Austria–Hungary, and, in
future, to live with the latter in friendly and neighbourly
relations.'

The history of the last years, and especially the painful events
of June 28th,[2] have demonstrated the existence of a subversive
movement in Serbia whose aim it is to separate certain territories from the Austro-Hungarian Monarchy. This movement,
which developed under the eyes of the Serbian Government,
has found expression subsequently beyond the territory of the
kingdom, in acts of terrorism, a series of assassinations and
murders.

Far from fulfilling the formal obligations contained in the
declaration of March 31st, 1909, the Royal Serbian Government has done nothing to suppress this movement. She suffered
the criminal doings of the various societies and associations
directed against the Monarchy, the unbridled language of the
press, the glorification of the originators of assassinations, the
participation of officers and officials in subversive intrigues . . .

This sufferance of which the Royal Serbian Government
made itself guilty has lasted up to the moment in which the
events of June 28th demonstrated to the entire world the
ghastly consequences of such sufferance.

It becomes plain from the evidence and confessions of the
criminal authors of the outrage of June 28th, that the murder
at Sarajevo was conceived in Belgrade, that the murderers

---

[1] A reference to the annexation of Bosnia–Herzegovina by Austria–
Hungary in 1908.
[2] The assassination of the Archduke.

received the arms and bombs with which they were equipped from Serbian officers and officials who belonged to the *Narodna Obrana*, and that, lastly, the transportation of the criminals and their arms to Bosnia was arranged and carried out by leading Serbian frontier officials . . .

The Imperial and Royal Government is forced to demand official [public] assurance from the Serbian Government that it condemns the propaganda directed against Austria–Hungary, i.e. the entirety of the machinations whose aim it is to separate parts from the monarchy which belong to it, and that she binds herself to suppress with all means this criminal and terrorising propaganda . . .

The Royal Serbian Government binds itself, in addition, as follows:

1. to suppress any publication which fosters hatred of, and contempt for, the Austro-Hungarian Monarchy, and whose general tendency is directed against the latter's territorial integrity;

2. to proceed at once with the dissolution of the society *Narodna Obrana*, to confiscate their entire means of propaganda, and to proceed in the same manner against the other societies and associations in Serbia which occupy themselves with the propaganda against Austria–Hungary . . .

3. without delay to eliminate from the public instruction in Serbia . . . that which serves, or may serve, to foster propaganda against Austria–Hungary;

4. to remove from military service and the administration in general all officers and officials who are guilty of propaganda against Austria–Hungary, and whose names . . . the Imperial and Royal Government reserves the right to communicate to the Royal Government;

5. to consent that in Serbia officials of the Imperial and Royal Government co-operate in the suppression of a movement directed against the territorial integrity of the Monarchy;

6. to commence a judicial investigation against the participants of the conspiracy of June 28th, who are on Serbian territory. Officials delegated by the Imperial and Royal Government will participate in the examinations.

7. to proceed at once with all severity to arrest Major Voja

Tankosic and a certain Milan Ciganowic, Serbian State officials, who have been compromised through the result of the investigation;

8. to prevent . . . the participation of the Serbian authorities in the smuggling of arms and explosives across the frontier . . .

10. The Imperial and Royal Government expects a reply from the Royal Government at the latest until Saturday, 25th inst., at 6 p.m. A memoir concerning the results of the investigations at Sarajevo . . . is enclosed with this note.

156. *Serbian Note in Reply to Austria, 25 July 1914*

The Serbian Government's reply to the Austro-Hungarian note (No. 155) was given within the time limit stipulated and accepted most of the Austrian demands, although some of them only with qualifications. The tone of the note was so conciliatory that many Governments hoped that peace could be preserved. The Austro-Hungarian Government, however, having decided to accept only an unqualified acquiescence in their demands, broke off diplomatic relations and commenced hostilities.

Source: *Diplomatic Documents relating to the Outbreak of the European War*; ed. by J. B. Scott (New York, Oxford University Press, 1916) (Carnegie Endowment for International Peace), Pt. i, pp. 77–81.

The Royal Serbian Government has received the communication of the Imperial and Royal Government . . . and is convinced that its reply will remove any misunderstanding which may threaten to impair the good neighbourly relations between the Austro-Hungarian Monarchy and the Kingdom of Serbia . . .

The Royal Government has been painfully surprised at the allegations that citizens of the Kingdom of Serbia have participated in the preparations for the crime committed at Sarajevo; the Royal Government had expected to be invited to collaborate in an investigation of all that concerns this crime, and it stood ready, in order to prove the entire correctness of its attitude, to take measures against any persons concerning whom representations might be made to it.

Complying with the desire of the Imperial and Royal Government, it is prepared to commit for trial any Serbian subject, regardless of his station or rank, of whose complicity in the crime of Sarajevo proofs shall be produced, and more especially it undertakes to publish ... the declaration [demanded by Austria–Hungary] ...

The Royal Government further undertakes:

1. To insert, at the first ordinary convocation of the *Skuptchina*,[1] a provision into the press law for the most severe punishment of incitement to hatred and contempt of the Austro-Hungarian Monarchy, and for taking action against any publication the general tendency of which is directed against the territorial integrity of Austria–Hungary. The Government engages, at the impending revision of the Constitution, to add to Article 22 of the Constitution an amendment permitting that such publications be confiscated, a proceeding at present impossible according to the clear provisions of Article 22 ...

2. The Government possesses no proof, nor does the note of the Imperial and Royal Government furnish it with any, that the *Narodna Obrana* and other similar societies have committed up to the present any criminal act of this nature through the proceedings of any of their members. Nevertheless, the Royal Government will accept the demands of the Imperial and Royal Government and will dissolve the *Narodna Obrana* society and every other association which may be directing its efforts against Austria–Hungary.

3. The Royal Serbian Government undertakes to remove without delay from the system of public instruction in Serbia all that serves or could serve to foment propaganda against Austria–Hungary, whenever the Imperial and Royal Government shall furnish it with facts and proofs of such propaganda.

4. The Royal Government also agrees to remove from the military and the civil service all such persons as the judicial inquiry may have proved to be guilty of acts directed against the territorial integrity of the Austro-Hungarian Monarchy, and it expects the Imperial and Royal Government to communicate to it at a later date the names and the acts of these officers and officials for the purpose of the proceedings which are to be taken against them.

5. The Royal Government must confess that it does not clearly understand the meaning or the scope of the demand made by

---

[1] The Serbian Parliament.

the Imperial and Royal Government that Serbia shall undertake to accept the collaboration of officials of the Imperial and
Royal Government upon Serbian territory, but it declares that
it will admit such collaboration as agrees with the principle of
international law, with criminal procedure, and with good
neighbourly relations.

6. It goes without saying that the Royal Government considers
it a duty to begin an enquiry against all such persons as are, or
eventually may be, implicated in the plot of the 28 June, and
who may happen to be within the territory of the Kingdom. As
regards the participation in this inquiry of Austro-Hungarian
agents or authorities . . . the Royal Government cannot accept
such an arrangement, as it would constitute a violation of the
Constitution and of the law of criminal procedure; nevertheless, in concrete cases communications as to the results of the investigation in question might be given to the Austro-Hungarian agents.

7. The Royal Government proceeded, on the very evening of
the delivery of the note, to arrest Major Voja Tankosich. As
regards Milan Ciganovitch, who is a subject of the Austro-
Hungarian Monarchy . . ., it has not yet been possible to arrest
him. The Austro-Hungarian Government is requested . . . to
supply as soon as possible . . . the presumptive evidence of guilt
as well as the possible proofs of guilt . . . for the purposes of the
Serbian inquiry.

8. The Serbian Government will reinforce and extend the
measures which have been taken for suppressing the illicit
traffic in arms and explosives across the frontier . . .

If the Imperial and Royal Government is not satisfied with
this reply, the Serbian Government, considering that it is not to
the common interest to take precipitate action in the solution
of this question, is ready, as always, to accept a pacific understanding, either by referring this question to the decision of the
International Tribunal at the Hague, or to the Great Powers . . .

157. *German Declaration of War on Russia, 1 August 1914*

After the Austro-Hungarian rejection of the Serbian reply and the
commencement of hostilities between Austria–Hungary and Serbia,
Russia, which had an interest in supporting the latter, decided, after

some hesitation, to mobilize. This caused the German Government to call for a cancellation of the Russian mobilization orders and, when its demands were not satisfied, to declare war on Russia in the note that follows.

Source: Great Britain. Foreign Office. *Collected Diplomatic Documents relating to the Outbreak of the European War* (London, H.M.S.O., 1915) (Cd. 7860), pp. 294–5.

The Imperial German Government have used every effort since the beginning of the crisis to bring about a peaceful settlement. In compliance with a wish expressed to him by His Majesty the Emperor of Russia, the German Emperor had undertaken, in concert with Great Britain, the part of mediator between the Cabinets of Vienna and St. Petersburg; but Russia, without waiting for any result, proceeded to a general mobilization of her forces both on land and sea. In consequence of this threatening step, which was not justified by any military proceedings on the part of Germany, the German Empire was faced by a grave and imminent danger. If the German Government had failed to guard against this peril, they would have compromised the safety and the very existence of Germany. The German Government were, therefore, obliged to make representations to the Government of His Majesty the Emperor of All the Russias and to insist upon a cessation of the aforesaid military acts. Russia having refused to comply with (not having considered it necessary to answer)[1] this demand, and having shown by this refusal (this attitude)[1] that her action was directed against Germany, I have the honour, on the instructions of my Government, to inform your Excellency as follows:

His Majesty the Emperor, my august Sovereign, in the name of the German Empire, accepts the challenge, and considers himself at war with Russia.

158. *President Wilson's War Aims, 1918*

Most Governments formulated and published their war aims, but none gained the importance of President Wilson's Fourteen Point programme (a), announced on 8 January 1918. Qualified and

[1] The words in brackets occur in the original. It must be supposed that two variations had been prepared in advance, and that, by mistake, they were both inserted in the note.

extended by the Four Principles (b), Four Ends (c), and Five Particulars (d) announced at various times later in the year, this programme was accepted, with some qualifications, by the major Allies of the United States of America. It was understood when concluding the armistice with Germany that this programme would serve as the basis for the peace settlement with Germany. No such obligation was entered into with respect to the other Central Powers, but the Fourteen Points and their supplements were officially understood to be the basis of the peace settlement.

Source: *Congressional Record*, vol. lvi, (1918) (65 Congr. 2d Sess.), pp. 680–1, 1937, 8671, 10887.

(a) The Fourteen Points, 8 January 1918.

... We entered this war because violations of right had occurred which touched us to the quick and made the life of our own people impossible unless they were corrected and the world secured once for all against their recurrence. What we demand in this war, therefore, is nothing peculiar to ourselves. It is that the world be made fit and safe to live in; and particularly that it be made safe for every peace-loving nation which, like our own, wishes to live its own life, determine its own institutions, be assured of justice and fair dealing by the other peoples of the world as against force and selfish aggression. All the peoples of the world are in effect partners in this interest, and for our own part we see very clearly that unless justice be done to others it will not be done to us. The programme of the world's peace, therefore, is our programme; and that programme, the only possible programme, as we see it, is this:

1. Open covenants of peace openly arrived at, after which there shall be no private international understandings of any kind, but diplomacy shall proceed always frankly and in the public view.
2. Absolute freedom of navigation upon the seas, outside territorial waters, alike in peace and in war, except as the seas may be closed in whole or in part by international action for the enforcement of international covenants.
3. The removal, so far as possible, of all economic barriers and the establishment of an equality of trade conditions among all the nations consenting to the peace and associating themselves for its maintenance.

4. Adequate guarantees given and taken that national armaments will be reduced to the lowest point consistent with domestic safety.

5. A free, open-minded, and absolutely impartial adjustment of all colonial claims, based upon a strict observance of the principle that in determining all such questions of sovereignty the interests of the population concerned must have equal weight with the equitable claims of the government whose title is to be determined.

6. The evacuation of all Russian territory and such a settlement of all questions affecting Russia as will secure the best and freest co-operation of the other nations of the world in obtaining for her an unhampered and unembarrassed opportunity for the independent determination of her own political development and national policy and assure her of a sincere welcome into the society of free nations under institutions of her own choosing; and, more than a welcome, assistance also of every kind that she may need and may herself desire. The treatment accorded Russia by her sister nations in the months to come will be the acid test of their goodwill, of their comprehension of her needs as distinguished from their own interests, and of their intelligent and unselfish sympathy.

7. Belgium, the whole world will agree, must be evacuated and restored, without any attempt to limit the sovereignty which she enjoys in common with all other free nations. No other single act will serve as this will serve to restore confidence among the nations in the laws which they have themselves set and determined for the government of their relations with one another. Without this healing act the whole structure and validity of international law is forever impaired.

8. All French territory should be freed and the invaded portions restored, and the wrong done to France by Prussia in 1871 in the matter of Alsace-Lorraine, which has unsettled the peace of the world for nearly fifty years, should be righted, in order that peace may once more be made secure in the interest of all.

9. A readjustment of the frontiers of Italy should be effected along clearly recognizable lines of nationality.

10. The peoples of Austria–Hungary, whose place among the nations we wish to see safeguarded and assured, should be

accorded the freest opportunity of autonomous development.

11. Romania, Serbia, and Montenegro should be evacuated;
occupied territories restored; Serbia accorded free and secure
access to the sea; and the relations of the several Balkan states
to one another determined by friendly counsel along historically
established lines of allegiance and nationality; and international guarantees of the political and economic independence
and territorial integrity of the several Balkan states should be
entered into.

12. The Turkish portions of the present Ottoman Empire
should be assured a secure sovereignty, but the other nationalities which are now under Turkish rule should be assured an
undoubted security of life and an absolutely unmolested opportunity of autonomous development, and the Dardanelles should
be permanently opened as a free passage to the ships and commerce of all nations under international guarantees.

13. An independent Polish state should be erected which
should include the territories inhabited by indisputably Polish
populations, which should be assured a free and secure access
to the sea, and whose political and economic independence and
territorial integrity should be guaranteed by international
covenant.

14. A general association of nations must be formed under
specific covenants for the purpose of affording mutual guarantees of political independence and territorial integrity to great
and small states alike.

(b) The 'Four Principles', 11 February 1918.

... The principles to be applied are these:

First, that each part of the final settlement must be based
upon the essential justice of that particular case and upon such
adjustments as are most likely to bring a peace that will be
permanent;

Second, that peoples and provinces are not to be bartered
about from sovereignty to sovereignty as if they were mere
chattels and pawns in a game, even the great game, now forever
discredited, of the balance of powers, but that

Third, every territorial settlement involved in this war must be made in the interest and for the benefit of the population concerned, and not as part of any mere adjustment or compromise of claims amongst rival states; and

Fourth, that all well-defined national aspirations shall be accorded the utmost satisfaction that can be accorded them without introducing new or perpetuating old elements of discord and antagonism that would be likely in time to break the peace of Europe and consequently of the world.

(c) The 'Four Ends', 4 July 1918.

There can be but one issue. The settlement must be final. There can be no compromise. No halfway decision would be tolerable. No halfway decision is conceivable. These are the ends for which the associated peoples of the world are fighting and which must be conceded them before there can be peace:

1. The destruction of every arbitrary power anywhere that can separately, secretly, and of its single choice disturb the peace of the world; or, if it cannot be presently destroyed, at the least its reduction to virtual impotence.

2. The settlement of every question, whether of territory, of sovereignty, or economic arrangement, or of political relationship, upon the basis of the free acceptance of that settlement by the people immediately concerned, and not upon the basis of the material interest or advantage of any other nation or people which may desire a different settlement for the sake of its own exterior influence or mastery.

3. The consent of all nations to be governed in their conduct towards each other by the same principles of honour and of respect for the common law of civilized society that govern the individual citizens of all modern states in their relations with one another, to the end that all promises and covenants may be sacredly observed, no private plots or conspiracies hatched, no selfish injuries wrought with impunity, and a mutual trust established upon the handsome foundations of a mutual respect for right.

4. The establishment of an organization of peace which shall make it certain that the combined power of free nations will check every invasion of right and serve to make peace and jus-

tice the more secure by affording a definite tribunal of opinion to which all must submit and by which every international readjustment that cannot be amicably agreed upon by the peoples directly concerned shall be sanctioned.

(d) The 'Five Particulars', 27 September 1918.

. . . But these general terms do not disclose the whole matter. Some details are needed to make them sound less like a thesis and more like a practical programme. These, then, are some of the particulars, and I state them with the greater confidence because I can state them authoritatively as representing the Government's interpretation of its own duty with regard to peace.

First. The impartial justice to be meted out must involve no discrimination between those to whom we wish to be just and those to whom we do not wish to be just. It must be a justice that plays no favourites and knows no standard but the equal rights of the several peoples concerned.

Second. No special or separate interest of any single nation or any group of nations can be made the basis of any part of the settlement which is not consistent with the common interest of all.

Third. There can be no leagues or alliances or special covenants and understandings within the general and common family of the league of nations.

Fourth. And more specifically, there can be no special, selfish, economic combinations within the league and no employment of any form of economic boycott or exclusion except as the power of economic penalty by exclusion from the markets of the world may be vested in the league of nations itself as a means of discipline and control.

Fifth. All international agreements and treaties of every kind must be made known in their entirety to the rest of the world.

159. *The Peace Treaty of Brest-Litovsk, 3 March 1918*

By the time of the February Revolution in Russia the Central Powers were in a clearly victorious position in Russia, however great difficulties they may have faced on the other fronts. Nevertheless the Provisional Government of Russia considered itself bound to continue the war until its victorious conclusion, even though it was ill supported by a disorganized and war-weary army and people. None of its efforts made any difference to the Russian position, except insofar as it contributed to a swing of support to the Bolshevik Party, which promised the speedy conclusion of peace.

Shortly after the October Revolution the new Bolshevik Government asked the Central Powers for an armistice and then negotiated the peace treaty that follows. The very harsh terms insisted on by the Central Powers, particularly the Germans, were opposed by many Soviet leaders, but in the end, largely on pressure from Lenin, they were accepted, Russia not being in a position to continue the war in any case.

Source: *International Conciliation*, 1918, pp. 422–5.

1. The Central Powers and Russia declare the state of war between them to be terminated and are resolved henceforth to live in peace and friendship with one another.

2. The contracting nations will refrain from all agitation or provocation against other signatory Governments . . .

3. The regions lying west of the line agreed upon by the contracting parties and formerly belonging to Russia, shall no longer be under Russian sovereignty. It is agreed that the line appears from the appended map, No. 1., which, as agreed upon, forms an essential part of the peace treaty[1] . . . The regions in question will have no obligation whatever toward Russia, arising from their former relations thereto. Russia undertakes to refrain from all interference in the internal affairs of these territories and to let Germany and Austria determine the future fate of these territories in agreement with their populations.

4. Germany and Austria agree, when a general peace is concluded and Russian demobilization is fully completed, to evacuate the regions east of the line designated in Article 3 . . . Russia will do everything in her power to complete as soon as possible the evacuation of the Anatolian provinces and their orderly return to Turkey. The districts of Erivan, Kars, and Batum will likewise without delay be evacuated by Russian troops. Russia will not interfere in the reorganization of the constitutional or international conditions of these districts, but

[1] Finland, the Baltic States, Poland, and the Ukraine were to be detached from Russia.

leaves it to the populations of the districts to carry out the reorganization . . .

5. Russia will without delay carry out the complete demobilization of her army, including the forces newly formed by the present Government. Russia will further transfer her warships to Russian harbours and leave them there until a general peace or immediately disarm . . .

6. Russia undertakes immediately to conclude peace with the Ukraine People's Republic . . . Ukrainian territory will be immediately evacuated by the Russian troops and the Russian Red Guard . . . Esthonia and Livonia will likewise be evacuated without delay . . . Finland and the Åland Islands will also forthwith be evacuated . . .

9. The contracting parties mutually renounce indemnification of their war costs . . . as well as indemnification for war damages . . .

160. *The Treaty of Versailles, 28 June 1919*

After months of negotiations among themselves the Allied and Associated Powers agreed, with some difficulty, on the Peace Treaty with Germany, which the German Government had to accept without alteration. The most important paragraphs of the treaty follow.

Part I of the Treaty is the Covenant of the League of Nations, incorporated in the peace treaty to ensure its acceptance by all Allied Governments. As the peace treaty is a document which concludes a war, and, in a sense, a whole period of history, while the Covenant, on the other hand, was supposed to be the foundation of a new era, it was considered to be expedient to include the text of the Covenant not here, but at the beginning of Section XIX, International Affairs, 1919–39.

Source: *The Treaty of Peace between the Allied and Associated Powers and Germany* . . . signed at Versailles, June 28th, 1919 (London, H.M.S.O., 1919) (Cmd. 153).

PART I

The Covenant of the League of Nations . . .

[A substantial part of the Covenant will be found as the initial document (No. 206) of Section XIX, International Affairs, 1919–39.]

PART II

Boundaries of Germany . . .

PART III

Political clauses for Europe . . .

Section III. Left Bank of the Rhine.

42. Germany is forbidden to maintain or construct any fortifications either on the left bank of the Rhine or on the right
bank to the west of a line drawn 50 kilometres to the east of
the Rhine.

43. In the area defined above the maintenance and the
assembly of armed forces, either permanently or temporarily,
and military manoeuvres of any kind, as well as the upkeep
of all permanent works for mobilization, are in the same way
forbidden.

44. In case Germany violates in any manner whatever the
provisions of Articles 42 and 43, she shall be regarded as committing a hostile act against the Powers signatory of the present
Treaty and as calculated to disturb the peace of the world.

Section IV. Saar Basin.

45. As compensation for the destruction of the coal mines in
the north of France and as part payment towards the total
reparation due from Germany for the damage resulting from
the war, Germany cedes to France in full and absolute possession,
with exclusive rights of exploitation, unencumbered and free
from all debts and charges of any kind, the coal-mines situated
in the Saar Basin . . .

49. Germany renounces in favour of the League of Nations, in
the capacity of trustee, the government of the territory [of the
Saar Basin] . . .

At the end of fifteen years from the coming into force of the
present Treaty the inhabitants of the said territory shall be
called upon to indicate the sovereignty under which they desire
to be placed.

Section V. Alsace-Lorraine.

The High Contracting Parties recognizing the moral obligation to redress the wrong done by Germany in 1871 both to

the rights of France and to the wishes of the population of
Alsace and Lorraine, which were separated from their country
in spite of the solemn protest of their representatives at the
Assembly of Bordeaux, agree upon the following Articles:
51. The territories which were ceded to Germany in accordance
with the Preliminaries of Peace signed at Versailles on February 26, 1871 (No. 97), and the Treaty of Frankfurt of May 10,
1871, are restored to French sovereignty . . .

Section VI. Austria.

80. Germany acknowledges and will respect strictly the independence of Austria, within the frontiers which may be
fixed in a Treaty between that State and the Principal Allied
and Associated Powers; she agrees that this independence shall
be inalienable, except with the consent of the Council of the
League of Nations.

Section VIII. Poland.

87. Germany, in conformity with the action already taken by
the Allied and Associated Powers, recognizes the complete
independence of Poland, and renounces in her favour all rights
and title over the territory [defined in detail] . . .

The boundaries of Poland not laid down in the present Treaty
will be subsequently determined by the Principal Allied and
Associated Powers.
88. In the portion of Upper Silesia included within the boundaries described below, the inhabitants will be called upon to
indicate by a vote whether they wish to be attached to Germany
or to Poland . . .

Section IX. East Prussia.

[The districts of Allenstein (Art. 94) and Marienwerder (Art.
96) will also be allocated according to a plebiscite of inhabitants.] . . .

Section XIV. Russia . . .

116. . . . Germany accepts . . . the abrogation of the Brest-
Litovsk Treaties (No. 159) . . .

PART IV

German rights and interests outside Germany.

118. In territory outside her European frontiers as fixed by the present Treaty, Germany renounces all rights, titles and privileges whatever in or over territory which belonged to her or to her allies, and all rights, titles and privileges whatever their origin which she held as against the Allied and Associated Powers . . .

Section I. German Colonies.

119. Germany renounces in favour of the Principal Allied and Associated Powers all her rights and titles over her oversea possessions . . .

PART V

Military, naval and air clauses.

In order to render possible the initiation of a general limitation of the armaments of all nations, Germany undertakes strictly to observe the military, naval and air clauses which follow.

Section I. Military clauses . . .

160. (1) By a date which must not be later than March 31, 1920, the German Army must not comprise more than seven divisions of infantry and three divisions of cavalry. After that date the total number of effectives in the Army . . . must not exceed one hundred thousand men, including officers and establishments of depots. The Army shall be devoted exclusively to the maintenance of order within the territory and to the control of the frontiers. The total effective strength of officers, including the personnel of staffs . . . must not exceed four thousand . . .

(3) . . . The Great German General Staff and all similar organizations shall be dissolved and may not be reconstituted in any form . . .

164. Up till the time at which Germany is admitted as a member of the League of Nations the German Army must

not possess an armament greater than the amounts fixed ...
Germany agrees that after she has become a member of the
League of Nations the armaments fixed ... shall remain in
force until they are modified by the Council of the League ...
168. The manufacture of arms, munitions, or any war material,
shall only be carried out in factories or works the locations of
which shall be communicated to and approved by the Governments of the Principal Allied and Associated Powers, and the
number of which they retain the right to restrict ...
169. Within two months from the coming into force of the
present Treaty German arms, munitions and war material,
including anti-aircraft material, existing in Germany in excess
of the quantities allowed, must be surrendered to the Governments of the Principal Allied and Associated Powers to be
destroyed or rendered useless ...
171. ... The manufacture and the importation into Germany
of armoured cars, tanks and all similar constructions suitable
for use in war are ... prohibited ...
173. Universal compulsory military service shall be abolished
in Germany. The German Army may only be constituted and
recruited by means of voluntary enlistment.
174. The period of enlistment for non-commissioned officers
and privates must be twelve consecutive years ...
175. The officers who are retained in the Army must undertake
the obligation to serve in it up to the age of forty-five years at
least. Officers newly appointed must undertake to serve on the
active list for twenty-five consecutive years at least ...

Section II. Naval clauses.

181. ... The German naval forces in commission must not
exceed 6 battleships ..., 6 light cruisers, 12 destroyers, 12
torpedo boats, or an equal number of ships constructed to
replace them ... No submarines are to be included ...
191. The construction or acquisition of any submarine, even
for commercial purposes, shall be forbidden in Germany ...

Section III. Air Clauses.

198. The armed forces of Germany must not include any
military or naval air forces ...

D E C—BB

Section IV. Inter-Allied Commissions of Control.

203. All the military, naval and air clauses contained in the present Treaty, for the execution of which a time-limit is prescribed, shall be executed by Germany under the control of Inter-Allied Commissions specially appointed for this purpose by the Principal Allied and Associated Powers.

PART VII

Penalties.

227. The Allied and Associated Powers publicly arraign William II of Hohenzollern, formerly German Emperor, for a supreme offence against international morality and the sanctity of treaties.

A special tribunal will be constituted to try the accused, thereby assuring him the guarantees essential to the right of defence. It will be composed of five judges, one appointed by each of the following Powers, namely the United States of America, Great Britain, France, Italy and Japan. In its decisions the tribunal will be guided by the highest motives of international policy, with a view to vindicating the solemn obligations of international undertakings and the validity of international morality. It will be its duty to fix the punishment which it considers should be imposed . . .

PART VIII

Reparation.

231. The Allied and Associated Governments affirm and Germany accepts the responsibility of Germany and her allies for causing all the loss and damage to which the Allied and Associated Governments and their nationals have been subjected as a consequence of the war imposed upon them by the aggression of Germany and her allies.

232. The Allied and Associated Governments recognize that the resources of Germany are not adequate, after taking into account permanent diminutions of such resources which will result from other provisions of the present Treaty, to make complete reparation for all such loss and damage. The Allied

and Associated Governments, however, require, and Germany undertakes, that she will make compensation for all damage done to the civilian population of the Allied and Associated Powers and to their property during the period of the belligerency of each . . .

233. The amount of the above damage . . . shall be determined by an Inter-Allied Commission, to be called the *Reparation Commission* . . . The Commission shall . . . draw up a schedule of payments prescribing the time and manner for securing and discharging the entire obligation within a period of thirty years from May 1, 1921 . . .

235. In order to enable the Allied and Associated Powers to proceed at once to the restoration of their industrial and economic life, pending the full determination of their claims, Germany shall pay in such instalments and in such manner (whether in gold, commodities, ships, securities or otherwise) as the Reparation Commission may fix, during 1919, 1920 and the first four months of 1921, the equivalent of 20,000,000,000 gold marks . . .

PART XIV

Guarantees.

428. As a guarantee for the execution of the present Treaty by Germany, the German territory situated to the west of the Rhine, together with the bridgeheads, will be occupied by Allied and Associated troops for a period of fifteen years . . .

XV · THE RUSSIAN REVOLUTION, FEBRUARY 1917 TO JANUARY 1918

THE World War, although initially supported with enthusiasm by most of the Russian population, soon created great stresses in Russian society and increased privation and discontent to levels previously unknown. The inefficiency of the Russian Government, which refused to co-operate with the Duma, only aggravated the situation. When a spontaneous revolution broke out at Petrograd[1] in February 1917, liberal (mainly Cadet) members of the Duma pressed the Tsar (No. 161) to appoint a parliamentary Government which would have the support of the population. Upon the refusal, and then abdication, of the Tsar the Duma formed a Provisional Government which was to introduce long-desired reforms (No. 163). At the same time, however, the workers and soldiers of Petrograd (and later of the rest of the country) formed Soviets on the 1905 model (cf. No. 139) which established effective control over the workers, and, perhaps more importantly, most of the armed forces (No. 162).

The Soviets, in accordance with traditional Marxist doctrine, initially supported the Provisional Government, Lenin being the only important leader who wanted power to be transferred to the Soviets immediately (No. 164).

Co-operation between the Soviet and the Provisional Government was not easy, as is shown by the crisis of the Miliukov note on war aims (No. 165), though when socialist ministers entered the ministry the moderate majority of the Soviets gave closer support to it than before (No. 166(a)) and maintained this support even during the armed rising of the 'July Days' (No. 167).

Opposition to the Government, and to Soviet participation

---

[1] The German-sounding name St. Petersburg was changed to Petrograd in 1915.

in it, continued to grow, however. The workers and peasants wanted 'Peace, Bread and Land' in the terms of the Bolshevik slogan, and considered that a Government with a bourgeois majority would not achieve this (No. 166(b), 167(b)). But there was opposition on the Right wing, too. General Kornilov, the Commander-in-Chief, wished to depose the Government because of its ineffectiveness in prosecuting the war and maintaining order (No. 168). He was defeated mainly because of the actions of the Bolshevik Red Guard.

The Bolsheviks' part in the defeat of Kornilov increased popular support for them; their propaganda, expressed in Lenin's April Theses (No. 164), now truly corresponded with the people's wish. The Bolshevik Central Committee, upon Lenin's prodding, resolved to organize an armed rising (No. 169), which was supported by the workers and soldiers of Petrograd, and took place successfully (No. 170) on the day when the Second Congress of Soviets was to meet.

The Congress of Soviets, dominated by Bolsheviks, and Left-wing Socialist Revolutionaries who had joined them, assumed power (No. 171(a)), passed a number of decrees, including one on peace (No. 171(b)) and one on land (No. 171(c)), and appointed a Council of People's Commissars to put Soviet policy into effect. One of the most important of the decrees of the People's Commissars was that on Workers' Control (No. 172), a first step towards the establishment of a socialist society.

Elections to a Constituent Assembly, first promised in February, took place in November, and it met on 5 January 1918. It was dominated by a Right-wing Socialist Revolutionary and Menshevik majority, which would not fall in with the wishes of the Bolshevik-dominated Central Soviet Executive Committee and rejected a draft declaration on the Right of the Workers (No. 173(a)). Such signs of independence were not acceptable to the Bolshevik-dominated Soviet bodies, and they dissolved the Constituent Assembly after its first day of sitting.

All dates in this section are stated according to the Julian Calendar used in Russia at the time. Russia changed to the Gregorian Calendar on 1 February 1918.

161. *Telegrams to the Tsar, 26–27 February 1917*

The February Revolution in Petrograd broke out spontaneously. The war-weary population was soon joined by the garrison, and the authority of the Government disintegrated. The only official body still active was the State Duma (reinforced by some elected members of the State Council) which, although dissolved by the Tsar, resolved on 27 February not to disperse. Hoping to save the situation, the President of the State Duma, Rodzianko, and a group of elected members of the State Council, acquainted the Tsar with the situation by telegrams, and pressed him to appoint a ministry which would have the support of the people. Their appeals remained unheeded.

Source: F. A. Golder, *Documents of Russian History, 1914–1917* (New York, The Century Press, 1927), pp. 278–9.

(a) Rodzianko's Telegram, 26 February 1917.

The situation is serious. The Capital is in a state of anarchy. The Government is paralyzed; the transport service is broken down; the food and fuel supplies are completely disorganized. Discontent is general and on the increase. There is wild shooting on the streets; troops are firing at each other. It is urgent that some one enjoying the confidence of the country be entrusted with the formation of a new Government. There must be no delay. Hesitation is fatal. I pray God that at this hour the responsibility may not fall upon the monarch.

(b) Rodzianko's Telegram, 27 February 1917.

The situation is growing worse. Measures should be taken immediately, as tomorrow will be too late. The last hour has struck, when the fate of the country and dynasty is being decided.

(c) Telegram of Members of the State Council, 27/28 February 1917.

We, [six] members of the State Council by election, realizing the danger that threatens our country, turn to you in fulfilment of our conscientious duty before you and Russia.

Owing to the complete collapse of transportation... factories and mills have shut down. This forced unemployment, combined with the acute food crisis... has driven the

popular masses into despair. This situation has been accentuated by the feeling of detestation and grave suspicion of the
authorities which has sunk deeply into the hearts of the people.

All these factors have brought on a popular uprising, which
the army has joined. Never having had the confidence of Russia
and now thoroughly discredited, the authorities are quite
powerless to handle the dangerous situation.

Your Majesty, the further keeping of the present Government in power means the complete breakdown of law and order
and will bring with it inevitable defeat in war, ruin of the
dynasty, and great miseries for Russia.

We think that the last and only remedy is for Your Imperial
Majesty to make a complete change in the internal policy and
in agreement with the repeated requests of the popular representatives, classes, and public organizations, call together at once
the legislative chambers; dismiss the present Council of Ministers; and ask some one who has the confidence of the people,
to submit to you, for confirmation, a list of names for a new
cabinet capable of governing the country in complete harmony
with the representatives of the people . . .

162. *Order No. 1 of the Petrograd Soviet, 1 March 1917*

One of the first steps of the workers of Petrograd was the revival
of the body which was temporarily so successful in 1905, the Soviet
of Workers' (later Workers' and Soldiers') Deputies (cf. No. 139).
Although members of the Duma formed a Provisional Committee,
and later a Provisional Government (No. 163) whose authority was
nominally accepted by everyone, the only body which held any real
authority over the workers and soldiers was the Soviet. The Soviet's
authority over the soldiers was formalized in the following order.
Source: F. A. Golder, *Documents of Russian History, 1914–1917* (New
   York, The Century Press, 1927), pp. 386–7.

To the garrison of the Petrograd District, to all the soldiers
of the guard, army, artillery, and navy, for immediate and
strict execution, and to the workers of Petrograd for their
information:

The Soviet of Workers' and Soldiers' Deputies has resolved:

1. In all companies, battalions, regiments, . . . committees from
the elected representatives of the lower ranks . . . shall be
chosen immediately.

2. In all those military units which have not yet chosen their representatives to the Soviet of Workers' Deputies, one representative from each company shall be selected . . .

3. In all its political actions, the military branch is subordinated to the Soviet of Workers' and Soldiers' Deputies, and to its own committees.

4. The orders of the military commission of the State Duma shall be executed only in such cases as do not conflict with the orders and resolutions of the Soviet . . .

5. All kinds of arms . . . must be kept at the disposal and under the control of the company and battalion committees, and in no case be turned over to officers, even at their demand.

6. In the ranks and during the performance of the duties of the service, soldiers must observe the strictest military discipline, but outside the service and the ranks, in their political, general civic and private life, soldiers cannot in any way be deprived of those rights which all citizens enjoy. In particular, standing at attention and compulsory saluting, when not on duty, is abolished . . .

163. *Formation and Programme of the Provisional Government, 3 March 1917*

The State Duma formed a Provisional Committee on 27 February to re-establish order in Petrograd and to establish contact with revolutionary leaders. With the disintegration of all authority, the Committee saw that the functions of the old Government had to be taken over by a new one and appointed, after consultation with the Soviet, a Provisional Government to carry on the administration and undertake the most urgent reforms. The following proclamation announced the formation of the Provisional Government and its programme.

Source: F. A. Golder, *Documents of Russian History, 1914–1917* (New, York, The Century Press, 1927), pp. 308–9.

Citizens:

The Provisional Executive Committee of the members of the Duma, with the aid and support of the garrison of the capital and its inhabitants, has triumphed over the dark forces of the Old Régime to such an extent as to enable it to organize a more stable executive power. With this idea in mind, the Provisional Committee has appointed as ministers of the first Cabinet representing the public, men whose past political and public life assures them the confidence of the country.

Prince George E. Lvov, Prime Minister and Minister of the Interior.

P. N. Miliukov, Minister of Foreign Affairs.

A. I. Guchkov, Minister of War and Marine.

M. I. Tereshchenko, Minister of Finance.

A. A. Manuilov, Minister of Education.

A. I. Shingarev, Minister of Agriculture.

N. V. Nekrasov, Minister of Transportation.

A. I. Konovalov, Minister of Commerce and Industry.

A. F. Kerensky, Minister of Justice.

V. L. Lvov, Holy Synod.

The Cabinet will be guided in its actions by the following principles:

1. An immediate general amnesty for all political and religious offences, including terrorist acts, military revolts, agrarian offences, etc.

2. Freedom of speech and press; freedom to form labour unions and to strike. These political liberties should be extended to the army in so far as war conditions permit.

3. The abolition of all social, religious and national restrictions.

4. Immediate preparation for the calling of a Constituent Assembly, elected by universal and secret vote, which shall determine the form of government and draw up the Constitution for the country.

5. In place of the police, to organize a national militia with elective officers, and subject to the local self-governing body.

6. Elections to be carried out on the basis of universal, direct, equal and secret suffrage.

7. The troops that have taken part in the revolutionary movement shall not be disarmed or removed from Petrograd.

8. On duty and in war service, strict military discipline should be maintained, but when off duty, soldiers should have the same public rights as are enjoyed by other citizens.

The Provisional Government wishes to add that it has no

intention of taking advantage of the existence of war conditions to delay the realization of the above-mentioned measures
of reform.

164. *Lenin's April Theses, 4 April 1917*

The Bolshevik leader, Lenin, did not return from his exile in
Switzerland until 3 April 1917. At Petrograd he found the Social
Democrats, including the Bolsheviks, supporting the Provisional
Government, a course with which he strongly disagreed. On the
following day, therefore, he held a speech on 'The tasks of the
Proletariat in the present revolution' of which the 'theses' that
follow formed part. They were published in the Bolshevik news-
paper *Pravda* on 7 April, and caused violent controversy even among
Bolsheviks.

Source: V. I. Lenin, *Selected Works in Three Volumes* (London,
    Lawrence and Wishart, n.d.), vol. ii, pp. 45–8.

1. In our attitude towards the war, which also under the new
Government of Lvov and Co. unquestionably remains on
Russia's part a predatory imperialist war owing to the capitalist nature of that Government, not the slightest concession to
'revolutionary defencism' is permissible.

The class-conscious proletariat can give its consent to a
revolutionary war, which would really justify revolutionary
defencism, only on condition: (a) that the power pass to the
proletariat and the poorest sections of the peasants . . .; (b)
that all annexations be renounced in deed and not in word;
(c) that a complete break be effected in actual fact with all
capitalist interests.

In view of the undoubted honesty of the broad sections of
the mass believers in revolutionary defencism, who accept the
war only as a necessity, and not as a means of conquest, in
view of the fact that they are being deceived by the bourgeoisie,
it is necessary with particular thoroughness, persistence and
patience to explain their error to them, to explain the inseparable connexion existing between capital and the imperialist war, and to prove that without overthrowing capital
it is impossible to end the war by a truly democratic peace . . .

2. It is a specific feature of the present situation in Russia that
it represents a *transition* from the first stage of the revolution—

which, owing to the insufficient class-consciousness and organization of the proletariat, placed power in the hands of the bourgeoisie—to its *second* stage, which must place power in the hands of the proletariat and the poorest sections of the peasants.

This transition is characterized, on the one hand, by a maximum of legally recognized rights (Russia is *now* the freest of all the belligerent countries in the world); on the other, by the absence of violence in relation to the people, and, finally, by the unreasoning confidence of the people in the Government of capitalists, the worst enemies of peace and socialism.

This peculiar situation demands of us an ability to adapt ourselves to the *special* conditions of Party work among unprecedentedly large masses of proletarians who have just awakened to political life.

3. No support for the Provisional Government; the utter falsity of all its promises should be explained, particularly those relating to the renunciation of annexations. Exposure in place of the impermissible, illusion-breeding 'demand' that *this* Government, a Government of capitalists, should cease to be an imperialist Government.

4. Recognition of the fact that in most of the Soviets of Workers' Deputies our Party is in a minority, and so far in a small minority, as against a *bloc of all* the petty-bourgeois opportunists . . .

It must be explained to the people that the Soviets of Workers' Deputies are the *only possible* form of revolutionary government, and that therefore our task is, as long as *this* government yields to the influence of the bourgeoisie, to present a patient, systematic, and persistent *explanation* of the errors of their tactics . . .

As long as we are in the minority we carry on the work of criticizing and exposing errors and at the same time we preach the necessity of transferring the entire state power to the Soviets . . . so that the people may overcome their mistakes by experience.

5. Not a parliamentary republic—to return to a parliamentary republic from the Soviets of Workers' Deputies would be a retrograde step—but a republic of Soviets of Workers', Agricultural Labourers' and Peasants' Deputies throughout the country, from top to bottom.

Abolition of the police, the army, and the bureaucracy.

The salaries of all officials, all of whom are to be elected and to be subject to recall at any time, not to exceed the average wage of a competent worker.

6. In the agrarian programme the most important part to be assigned to the Soviets of Agricultural Labourers' Deputies.

Confiscation of all landed estates.

Nationalization of *all* lands in the country, the disposal of the land to be put in the charge of the local Soviets of Agricultural Labourers' and Peasants' Deputies. The organization of separate Soviets of Deputies of Poor Peasants . . .

7. The immediate amalgamation of all banks in the country into a single national bank . . .

8. It is not our immediate task to 'introduce' socialism, but only to bring social production and distribution of products at once under the *control* of the Soviets of Workers' Deputies . . .

10. A new International. We must take the initiative in creating a revolutionary International, an International against the *social-chauvinists* . . . (Cf. No. 197).

165. *Miliukov's Note on War-Aims, and its Explanation, 18–21 April 1917*

The Soviets, and the majority of the politically minded workers accepted the Provisional Government's policy of continuing a war of defence against the Central Powers, provided that any peace concluded would not be an imperialist peace, but a just one, 'without annexations and indemnities'. A political crisis therefore arose when the Foreign Minister, Miliukov, handed a Note on Russian war aims (a) to the representatives of the Allied Powers in which this popular wish was apparently disregarded. Popular demonstrations led to the Provisional Government explaining away Miliukov's statement (b). Miliukov had to resign, and a new Government was formed which, for the first time, included socialists.

Source: A. J. Sack, *The Birth of the Russian Democracy* (New York, Russian Information Bureau, 1918), pp. 272–4.

(a) Part of Miliukov's Note on War-Aims, 18 April 1917.

. . . The declaration of the Provisional Government, imbued with the new spirit of free democracy, naturally cannot afford the least pretext for assumption that the demolition of the old structure has entailed any slackening on the part of Russia in the common struggle of all the Allies. On the contrary, the nation's determination to bring the world war to a decisive victory has been accentuated . . .

This spirit has become still more active by the fact that it is concentrated on the immediate task, which touches everybody so closely, of driving back the enemy who invaded our territory. It is understood . . . that the Provisional Government, in safeguarding the right acquired for our country, will maintain a strict regard for its agreements with the Allies of Russia.

Firmly convinced of the victorious issue of the present war, and in perfect agreement with our Allies, the Provisional Government is likewise confident that the problems which were created by this war will be solved by concluding a lasting peace, and that, inspired by identical sentiments, the Allied Democracies will find means of establishing the guarantees and penalties necessary to prevent any recourse to sanguinary war in the future.

(b) Explanation issued by the Provisional Government, 21 April 1917.

The Note was subjected to long and detailed examination by the Provisional Government, and was unanimously approved. This note, in speaking of a decisive victory, had in view a solution of the problems mentioned in the communication of [March 27] and which was thus specified:

'The Government deems it to be its right and duty to declare now that free Russia does not aim at the domination of other nations or at depriving them of their national patrimony, or at occupying by force foreign territories, but that its object is to establish a durable peace on the basis of the rights of nations to decide their own destiny. The Russian Nation does not lust after the strengthening of its power abroad at the expense of other nations. Its aim is not to subjugate or humiliate any one. In the name of the higher principles of equity, the Russian people have broken the chains which fettered the Polish Nation, but it will not suffer that its own country shall emerge from the great struggle humiliated or weakened in its vital forces.'

In referring to the 'penalties and guarantees' essential to a durable peace the Provisional Government had in view the reduction of armaments, the establishment of international tribunals, etc.

This explanation will be communicated by the Minister of Foreign Affairs to the Ambassadors of the Allied Powers.

166. *The First Congress of Soviets, 3–24 June 1917*

The First All-Russian Congress of Soviets, consisting of representatives from all over Russia, met early in June and discussed, among other matters, the conditions under which socialists might be allowed to take part in the coalition Government (a), support of which was reaffirmed by the Congress. It also had to listen to a Bolshevik protest against the so-called June Offensive, a major war effort, Russia's last, which was organized by Kerensky (b).

Source: W. H. Chamberlin, *The Russian Revolution 1917–1921* (New York, Macmillan, 1935), vol. i, pp. 451–3.

(a) Resolutions of the First Congress of Soviets, 8 June 1917.

1. . . . That under the conditions which were created by the first ministerial crisis the handing over of all power only to the bourgeois elements would have inflicted a blow upon the revolutionary cause;

2. That the passing of all power to the Soviets of Workers' and Soldiers' Deputies in the present period of the Russian Revolution would have considerably weakened its forces, would have prematurely pushed away from it elements which are still able to serve it, and would have threatened the Revolution with disaster;—

Therefore, the All-Russian Soviet Congress approves the action of the Petrograd Soviet in finding a remedy for the crisis of April 20–21 (cf. No. 165) in creating a Coalition Government on the basis of a decisive and logical democratic platform . . .

The Congress urges the Provisional Government to carry out more vigorously and logically the democratic platform which it has accepted, and especially:

(a) To struggle insistently for the speediest achievement of a general peace without annexations and contributions on the basis of self-determination of the peoples;

(b) To carry out the further democratization of the Army and to strengthen its fighting capacity;

(c) To adopt the most energetic measures for combating breakdown in the fields of finance, economic life and food supply, with the direct participation of the working masses . . .

(g) The Congress especially demands the convocation at the earliest possible moment of the All-Russian Constituent Assembly . . .

(b) Bolshevik Protest against the June Offensive, 19 June 1917.

On the first day of the All-Russian Congress of Soviets of Workers' and Soldiers' Deputies we presented a statement, in which we pointed out that a policy directed toward the kindling of imperialist war, toward new stirring up of chauvinist passions, a policy of immediate offensive, is beneficial only to the counter-revolution, that this policy has been dictated . . . by Anglo-French, American and Russian imperialists, that a policy of launching an offensive places in danger all the conquests of the Revolution.

The demonstration of June 18 in St. Petersburg showed very clearly that the vanguard of the Russian Revolution—the Petrograd proletariat and the Petrograd revolutionary garrison— demonstrated its solidarity with the above mentioned viewpoint of our Party.

Today Kerensky's order for an offensive, dated June 16, is published.

We state that the entire responsibility for this policy falls on the Provisional Government and on the Parties, the Mensheviki and the Socialist Revolutionaries, which support it. We confirm the declaration which we made on the first day of the Congress. Along with the enormous majority of the Petrograd workers and soldiers we express our deep conviction that the end of the War can be brought about not by an offensive on the front, but only by the revolutionary efforts of the workers of all countries.

167. *The 'July Days', 3–5 July 1917*

In the first days of July large-scale, apparently spontaneous, demonstrations took place in Petrograd which, on 4 July, were endorsed by the Bolshevik Central Committee. The aim of the rising was to force the dismissal of the capitalist ministers and the transfer of power to the Soviets (cf. No. 164, points 3–5). The Central Executive

Committee of the Congress of Soviets rejected the demonstrators' demands, and the rising was put down by troops. As a consequence of the Bolshevik-backed rising Lenin and other leading Bolsheviks had to go into hiding.

Part of a resolution (a) of the Central Executive Committee follows, contrasted with statements (b) giving the demonstrators' point of view.

Source: W. H. Chamberlin, *The Russian Revolution 1917–1921* (New York, Macmillan, 1935), vol. i, pp. 455–7.

(a) Resolution of the Soviet Executive Committee, 3 July 1917.

. . . Despite the repeated warning of the Soviet some military units came out on the streets with arms in their hands . . . They demanded that the Executive Committee should take all power into its own hands. Proposing that governmental authority should belong to the Soviets, they were the first to attack this governmental authority. The All-Russian Executive bodies of the Soviets of Workers' and Peasants' Deputies indignantly repudiate any attempt to bring pressure on their free will . . . Those who ventured to call out armed men for this purpose are responsible for the blood which has flowed . . . These actions are equivalent to treason to our revolutionary Army, which is defending the conquests of the Revolution . . .

The All-Russian organizations of the Soviets of Workers' and Peasants' Deputies protest against these evil signs of undiscipline, which undermine any form of government by the people, not excepting the future government of the Constituent Assembly. The All-Russian Executive Committees . . . demand once for all a stoppage of such outbreaks, which disgrace revolutionary Petrograd. The Executive Committees . . . summon all who defend the Revolution and its conquests to await the decision of the authorized representative body of the democracy in the matter of the crisis of governmental authority. All who prize the cause of freedom must submit to this decision, in which the voice of all revolutionary Russia will be pronounced.

(b) Statement of the Representatives of Fifty-Four Factories at the Session of the All-Russian Soviet Executive Committee, 4 July 1917.

Fifty-four factories are represented here. It isn't necessary to talk about what has happened . . . Our demand is the general demand of the workers: all power to the Soviets of Workers' and Soldiers' Deputies. This demand has been presented to you . . .

We demand the withdrawal of the ten capitalist ministers. We trust the Soviet, but not those whom the Soviet trusts. Our comrades, the Socialist ministers, entered into an agreement with the capitalists, but these capitalists are our mortal enemies. We demand that the land should be seized immediately, that control over industry should be established immediately, we demand struggle against the threatening hunger . . .

The present moment seems to us very dangerous. The ground is shaking. The Revolution develops. The masses do not desire the power of bourgeois ministers. The masses go beyond the limits of organization . . . The will of the democracy is quite clear: the transfer of power into the hands of the Soviets . . .

168. *General Kornilov's Appeal, 27 August 1917*

Kerensky, Premier since 7 July, called a State Conference in Moscow to organize support for the Provisional Government. After sitting for three days, 12–14 August, the Conference dispersed without having achieved anything concrete beyond bringing out into the open the enmity between the Premier and the recently appointed Commander-in-Chief, General Kornilov.

On 25 August Kornilov, at the head of mainly Cossack troops, began an attack on Petrograd in order to take over the Government. He issued the following appeal to gain popular support, but without success; his movement was defeated, largely by Bolshevik propaganda and the efforts of the Bolshevik Red Guard.

Source: A. J. Sack, *The Birth of the Russian Democracy* (New York, Russian Information Bureau, 1918), pp. 476–7.

. . . Russians, our great country is dying, the hour of death is approaching. I am compelled to come out into the open.

I, General Kornilov, declare that the Provisional Government, under the pressure of the Bolshevik majority in the Soviets, is playing into the hands of the German General Staff, and while the landing of the hostile forces is expected on the Riga coast, the Government is killing the Army and ruining the country.

The consciousness of imminent danger to the country bids me at this hour of stress to call upon all Russians to stand up for the defence of the country, which is practically dying. Every one in

whose breast beats the heart of a Russian, all who believe in
God pray to the Lord that he work a miracle—the miracle of
saving the country.

I, General Kornilov, the son of a peasant and the descendant
of a Cossack, tell you, one and all, that I personally do not want
anything except to save Russia, and I pledge myself to secure
for the people, through victory over the foreign foe, the convocation of the Constituent Assembly, in which the people
themselves will decide upon their destiny and will choose the
form of their new political life. To betray Russia into the hands
of her old enemy, the Teuton, and to make the Russian people
slaves to the Germans—I cannot bear the thought of it, and
prefer to die on the field of battle so as not to see the Russian
land disgraced. People of Russia, the fate of Russia is in your
hands.

169. *Resolutions of the Bolshevik Central Committee,* *10 and 16 October 1917*

After the defeat of Kornilov, Kerensky, whose position was greatly
weakened by the rising, tried a number of expedients to bolster the
Provisional Government. His efforts were unsuccessful, however, as
the spirit of dissatisfaction became widespread and violent all over
Russia, but particularly in the cities. It was reflected in the fact that
the Bolsheviks gained a majority, for the first time, in both the
Petrograd and Moscow Soviets.

Lenin was still in hiding in Finland at this time, and in his
absence the Bolshevik Central Committee did little to bring about
a new revolution. After a number of his letters remained without
effect, Lenin secretly went to Petrograd and there persuaded the
Central Committee that an early armed insurrection was essential.
The Central Committee's resolution (a), confirmed by a resolution
of 16 October (b), follows.

Source: V. I. Lenin, *Selected Works in Three Volumes* (London,
      Lawrence and Wishart, n.d.), vol. ii, pp. 479, 482.

(a) The Resolution of 10 October 1917.

The Central Committee recognizes that the international
position of the Russian revolution (the revolt in the German
navy which is an extreme manifestation of the growth throughout Europe of the world socialist revolution; the threat of peace
by the imperialists with the object of strangling the revolution

in Russia) as well as the military situation (the indubitable decision of the Russian bourgeoisie and Kerensky and Co. to surrender Petrograd to the Germans), and the fact that the proletarian party has gained a majority in the Soviets—all this, taken in conjunction with the peasant revolt and the swing of popular confidence towards our Party (the elections in Moscow), and, finally, the obvious preparations being made for a second Kornilov affair (the withdrawal of troops from Petrograd, the dispatch of Cossacks to Petrograd, the encircling of Minsk by Cossacks, etc.)—all this places the armed uprising on the agenda.

Considering therefore that an armed uprising is inevitable, and that the time for it is fully ripe, the Central Committee instructs all Party organizations to be guided accordingly, and to discuss and decide all practical questions (the Congress of Soviets of the Northern Region, the withdrawal of troops from Petrograd, the action of our people in Moscow and Minsk, etc.) from this point of view.

(b) Resolution of 16 October 1917.

The meeting fully welcomes and fully supports the resolution of the Central Committee (No. 169(a)) and calls upon all organizations and all workers and soldiers to make all-round, energetic preparations for an armed uprising and to support the centre set up for that purpose by the Central Committee; the meeting expresses its complete confidence that the Central Committee and the Soviet will indicate in good time the favourable moment and the most appropriate methods of attack.

170. *Proclamation of the Military Revolutionary Committee of the Petrograd Soviet on the Success of the Revolution, 25 October 1917*

The armed insurrection organized by the Bolsheviks finally took place on the night 24/25 October, the night before the Second Congress of Soviets was to meet, and was immediately successful. The following proclamation announced the victory of the revolution.

Source: V. I. Lenin, *Selected Works in Three Volumes* (London, Lawrence and Wishart, n.d.), vol. ii, p. 495.

To the Citizens of Russia!

The Provisional Government has been deposed. State power has passed into the hands of the organ of the Petrograd Soviet of Workers' and Soldiers' Deputies—the Revolutionary Military Committee, which heads the Petrograd proletariat and garrison.

The cause for which the people have fought, namely, the immediate offer of a democratic peace, the abolition of landlord ownership, workers' control over production, and the establishment of Soviet Power—this cause has been secured.

Long live the revolution of workers, soldiers, and peasants!

171. *The Second Congress of Soviets, 25–27 October 1917*

When the Congress met on 25 October, it was faced with the defeat of the Kerensky Government and the victory of the Revolution. The majority, consisting of Bolsheviks and Left-wing Socialist Revolutionaries, decided that the Soviets should assume power (a), appointed a Council of People's Commissars, under the chairmanship of Lenin, and, on the following day, passed decrees on peace (b) and land (c).

Source: (a) and (c): J. Bunyan and H. H. Fisher, *The Bolshevik Revolution 1917–1918* (Stanford, Calif., Stanford University Press, 1934), pp. 121–2, 129–31.

(b) F. A. Golder, *Documents of Russian History, 1914–1917* (New York, The Century Press, 1927), pp. 620–3.

(a) Proclamation on the Assumption of Power, 25 October 1917.

To All Workers, Soldiers, and Peasants:

The Second All-Russian Congress of Soviets of Workers' and Soldiers' Deputies has opened . . . Supported by an overwhelming majority of the workers, soldiers, and peasants, and basing itself on the victorious insurrection of the workers and the garrison of Petrograd, the Congress hereby resolves to take governmental power into its own hands.

The Provisional Government is deposed and most of its members are under arrest.

The Soviet authority will at once propose a democratic peace to all nations and an immediate armistice on all fronts. It will safeguard the transfer without compensation of all land . . . to the peasant committees; it will defend the soldiers' rights, . . .

it will establish workers' control over industry, it will ensure the convocation of the Constituent Assembly on the date set, it will supply the cities with bread and the villages with articles of first necessity, and it will secure to all nationalities inhabiting Russia the right of self-determination.

The Congress resolves that all local authority shall be transferred to the Soviets of Workers', Soldiers', and Peasants' Deputies . . .

(b) Decree on Peace, 26 October 1917.

The Workers' and Peasants' Government . . . proposes to all warring peoples and their Governments that negotiations leading to a just peace begin at once.

The just and democratic peace for which the great majority of war-exhausted, tormented toilers and labouring classes of all belligerent countries are thirsting; the peace for which the Russian workers and peasants are so insistently and loudly clamouring since the overthrow of the Tsarist regime is, in the opinion of the Government, an immediate peace without annexation (i.e. without the seizure of foreign lands and the forcible taking over of other nationalities) and without indemnity.

The Russian Government proposes that this kind of peace be concluded immediately between all the warring nations. It offers to take decisive steps at once, without the least delay, without waiting for a final confirmation of all the terms of such a peace by conferences of popular representatives of all countries and all nations . . .

To prolong this war because the rich and strong nations cannot agree how to divide the small and weak nationalities which they have seized is, in the opinion of the Government, a most criminal act against humanity, and it solemnly announces its decision to sign at once terms of peace bringing this war to an end on the indicated conditions . . .

Moreover, the Government declares that it does not regard the above mentioned terms of peace in the light of an ultimatum. It will agree to examine all other terms. It will insist only that whatever belligerent nation has anything to propose, it should do so quickly, in the clearest terms, leaving out all double meanings and all secrets in making the proposal. The Government does away with all secret diplomacy and is determined to carry on all negotiations quite openly in the view of all people. It will proceed at once to publish all secret treaties, ratified or concluded by the Government of landowners and capitalists . . . The Government annuls, immediately, and unconditionally, the secret treaties, in so far as they have for their object . . . to give benefits and privileges to the Russian landowners and capitalists, to maintain or to increase annexation by the Great Russians . . .

The Government proposes to all Governments and peoples of all belligerent countries to conclude at once an armistice of no less than three months . . . In making these peace proposals to the Governments and peoples of all warring countries the Provisional Government of Workers and Peasants of Russia appeals in particular to the intelligent workers of the three foremost nations of mankind, and the leading participators in this war, England, France and Germany. The toilers of these countries have rendered the greatest service to the cause of progress and Socialism by their great examples . . . These examples of proletarian heroism and historical development lead us to believe that the workers of the named countries will understand the task before them to free humanity from the horrors of war and its consequences. By decisive, energetic and self-sacrificing efforts in various directions, these workers will help us not only to bring the peace negotiations to a successful end, but to free the toiling and exploited masses from all forms of slavery and all exploitation.

(c) The Land Decree, 26 October 1917.

1. The Landlord's right to the land is hereby abolished without compensation.

2. . . . All lands . . . are transferred to the *volost*[1] land committees and the *uezd*[1] Soviet of Peasants' Deputies until the Constituent Assembly meets . . .

4. The following Land Mandate drawn up by the editorial board of the *Izvestiia*[2] of the All-Russian Soviet of Peasants' Deputies on the basis of two hundred and forty-two peasant

---

[1] Districts of different levels.   [2] Bulletin.

petitions . . . shall everywhere regulate the realization of the great land reforms until their final solution by the Constituent Assembly.

CONCERNING THE LAND . . .

1. The right of private ownership of land is abolished forever. Land cannot be sold, bought, leased, mortgaged, or alienated in any manner whatsoever. All lands . . . are alienated without compensation, become the property of the people, and are turned over for the use of those who till them . . .
2. All the underground resources, minerals [etc.] as well as forests and water of national importance, are transferred to the state for its exclusive use . . .
3. Intensively cultivated holdings . . . are to be not divided but turned into model farms . . .
6. All Russian citizens (irrespective of sex) who are willing to till the land, either by themselves or with the assistance of their families or in collective groups, are entitled to the use of the land, as long as they are able to cultivate it. Hired labour is not permitted . . .
8. All the alienated land goes into one national land fund. Its distribution among the toilers is in charge of the local and central self-governing bodies . . .
The lands of peasants and Cossacks of average means shall not be confiscated.

172. *Decree on Workers' Control, 14 November 1917*

In accordance with the announced policy of the Congress of Soviets (cf. No. 171(a)) one of the early measures of the Council of People's Commissars was the establishment of workers' control of industry, a first step towards the establishment of a socialist economy.

Source: J. Bunyan and H. H. Fisher, *The Bolshevik Revolution 1917–1918* (Stanford, Calif., Stanford University Press, 1934), pp. 308–10.

1. In the interests of a systematic regulation of national economy, Workers' Control is introduced in all industrial, commercial, agricultural [and similar] enterprises which are hiring people to work for them in their shops or which are giving them

work to take home. This control is to extend over the production, storing, buying and selling of raw materials and finished products as well as over the finances of the enterprise.

2. The workers will exercise this control through their elected organizations, such as factory and shop committees, Soviet of elders, etc. . . .

3. Every large city, gubernia, and industrial area is to have its own Soviet of Workers' Control . . .

4. Until the meeting of the Congress of the Soviets of Workers' Control an All-Russian Soviet of Workers' Control will be organized in Petrograd.

5. Commissions of trained inspectors . . . will be established in connexion with the higher organs of Workers' Control and will be sent out . . . to investigate the financial and technical side of enterprises.

6. The organs of Workers' Control have the right to supervise production, fix the minimum of output, and determine the cost of production . . .

8. The rulings of the organs of Workers' Control are binding on the owners of enterprises and can be annulled only by decisions of the higher organs . . .

10. In all enterprises the owners and the representatives of the workers and employees elected to the Committee on Workers' Control are responsible to the State for the order, discipline, and safety of the property. Persons guilty of hiding raw materials or products, of falsifying accounts, and of other similar abuses are criminally liable . . .

173. *The Constituent Assembly, 5 January 1918*

At the time of the October Revolution preparations for the elections to a Constituent Assembly, promised repeatedly since February, were fairly well advanced, and the new Soviet Government was not in the position to stop the elections. When the Constituent Assembly met on 5 January 1918, the majority of its members belonged to the right wing of the Socialist Revolutionary Party, the Bolsheviks and the left Socialist Revolutionaries being in the minority.

The All-Russian Central Executive Committee of the Soviets had formulated a Declaration of Rights of the Working and Exploited People (a) which was moved for adoption by the Bolshevik Delegation but was rejected by the Assembly. As it seemed clear after the first day of sitting that the temper of the representatives was against that of the Bolsheviks, the Central Executive Committee prevented further meetings of the Assembly and decreed its dissolution (b).

Source: (a) W. H. Chamberlin, *The Russian Revolution 1917–1921* (New York, Macmillan, 1935), vol. i, pp. 491–3.
   (b) J. Bunyan and H. H. Fisher, *The Bolshevik Revolution 1917–1918* (Stanford, Calif., Stanford University Press, 1934), pp. 384–6.

(a) Declaration of the Rights of the Working and Exploited People.

I

1. Russia is declared a Republic of Soviets of Workers', Soldiers' and Peasants' Deputies. All power in the centre and in the localities belongs to these Soviets.
2. The Soviet Russian Republic is established on the basis of a free union of free peoples, as a federation of Soviet national republics.

II

Setting as its fundamental task the destruction of any exploitation of man by man, the complete abolition of the division of society into classes, the merciless suppression of the exploiters, the establishment of a socialist organization of society and the victory of socialism in all countries, the Constituent Assembly further resolves:

1. In order to realize the socialization of the land, private property in land is abolished and the entire land reserve is declared the general property of the people and is handed over to the workers without any purchase, on the principle of equalized use of the land.

All forests, minerals and waters of general state significance, all livestock and machinery, all estates and agricultural enterprises are declared national property.
2. The Soviet law on workers' control and on the Supreme Economic Council is confirmed for the purpose of assuring the power of the workers over the exploiters, as a first step toward the complete passing of the factories, mines, railroads and other means of production and transportation into the possession of the Soviet Workers' and Peasants' Republic.

3. The passing of all the banks into the possession of the workers' and peasants' State is confirmed as one of the conditions of the liberation of the working masses from the yoke of capital.

4. General liability to labour service is introduced for the purpose of destroying the parasite classes of society and for the organization of economic life.

5. The arming of the workers, the organization of a socialist Red Army of workers and peasants and the complete disarmament of the propertied classes are decreed in order to assure all power for the workers and in order to remove any possibility of the restoration of the power of the exploiters.

III

1. Expressing an unbending determination to tear humanity out of the claws of finance capital and imperialism, which has flooded the earth with blood in the present, most criminal, of all wars, the Constituent Assembly fully adheres to the Soviet Government's policy of tearing up the secret treaties, organizing the broadest fraternization with the workers and peasants of the armies which are now fighting against each other and achieving, at any cost, by revolutionary measures, a democratic peace between peoples, without annexations and contributions, on the basis of free self-determination of the nations.

2. With the same objectives in view the Constituent Assembly insists on a complete breach with the barbarous policy of bourgeois civilization, building up the welfare of the exploiters in a few chosen nations on the enslavement of hundreds of millions of the working population in Asia, in the colonies in general, and in little countries . . .

IV

Being elected on the basis of Party lists which were made up before the October Revolution, when the people could not rise up with all its masses against the exploiters, did not know all the strength of the resistance of the latter in defending their class privileges, when the people had still not started practically to create a socialist society, the Constituent Assembly would consider it fundamentally incorrect, even from the formal standpoint, to oppose itself to the Soviet régime.

In substance the Constituent Assembly assumes that now, at a time of decisive struggle of the people against its exploiters, there can be no place for the exploiters in any executive bodies. Power must belong entirely and exclusively to the working masses and to their authorized form of representation—Soviets of Workers', Soldiers' and Peasants' Deputies.

Supporting the Soviet régime and the decrees of the Council of People's Commissars, the Constituent Assembly recognizes that its own functions are confined to a general working out of the fundamental principles of the socialist reorganization of society . . .

(b) Decree dissolving the Constituent Assembly, 6 January 1918.

From the very beginning of the Russian Revolution the Soviets . . . came to the front as a mass organization. It brought the toiling and exploited classes together and led them in the fight for full political and economic freedom. During the first period of the revolution the Soviets increased, developed, and grew strong. They learned by experience the futility of compromising with the bourgeoisie . . .

The Constituent Assembly which was elected on the lists made out before the October Revolution represents the old order when the compromisers and Cadets were in power.

At the time of voting for the Socialist Revolutionists the people were not in a position to decide between the Right Wing —partisans of the bourgeoisie—and the Left Wing—partisans of socialism. This accounts for the fact that the Constituent Assembly, the crown of the bourgeois-parliamentary republic, stands in the way of the October Revolution and the Soviet Government . . .

The labouring classes have learned by experience that the old bourgeois parliament has outlived its usefulness, that it is quite incompatible with the task of establishing socialism, and that the task of overcoming the propertied classes and of laying the basis of a socialistic society cannot be undertaken by a national institution but only by one representing a class such as the Soviet. To deny full power to the Soviets . . . in favour of a bourgeois parliamentarism or the Constituent Assembly would be a step backward and the death blow of the October workers'-peasants' revolution.

The Constituent Assembly which opened on January 5 has . . . a majority of Socialist-Revolutionists of the Right, the party of Kerensky . . . It is natural that this party should refuse to consider the . . . recommendation of the sovereign organ of the Soviet Government and should refuse to recognize the 'Declaration of the Rights of the Toiling and Exploited People', the October Revolution, and the Government of the Soviet. By these very acts the Constituent Assembly has cut every tie that bound it to the Soviet of the Russian Republic. Under the circumstances the Bolsheviks and Socialist-Revolutionists of the Left . . . had no choice but to withdraw from the Constituent Assembly.

The majority parties of the Constituent Assembly—the Socialist-Revolutionists and the Mensheviks—are carrying on an open war against the Soviet, calling . . . for its overthrow, and in this way helping the exploiters in their efforts to block the transfer of the land and factories to the toilers.

It is clear that this part of the Constituent Assembly can be of help only to the bourgeois counter-revolution in its efforts to crush the power of the Soviets.

In view of the above the Central Executive Committee hereby decrees: The Constituent Assembly is dissolved.

XVI · FASCIST ITALY

No documents in Italian history have been included in this collection between the time of unification and the rise of Mussolini. There were no events of outstanding importance in this period, and, although the time between the end of the war and the rise of Mussolini might have warranted some attention, no document of this period proved to be sufficiently suitable.

Therefore the section opens with the 1919 programme of the Fascist Party (No. 174), symptomatic of Mussolini's thinking at this period, but soon discarded. It is followed by documents relating to the assumption of power, the order which began the March on Rome (No. 175(a)) and part of Mussolini's first parliamentary speech as Prime Minister (No. 175(b)). The remainder of the section is devoted to documents illustrating the structure of the Fascist State.

The laws on the abolition of the Prime Minister's direct responsibility to Parliament (No. 176(a)) and on the power to make laws by decree (No. 176(b)) gave Mussolini a free hand for the re-organization of the State, particularly after a party body, the Grand Council of Fascism became one of the supreme organs of the State (No. 179). This re-organization aimed at the creation of a Corporative State, the most original contribution of Fascism to the body of political and social ideas, and several selections (Nos 177, 178, 181, 182) deal with its development.

The Treaty of the Lateran (No. 180(a)), which settled the long controversy between the Papacy and Italy (cf. No. 115) and the Concordat concluded at the same time (No. 180(b)) are also included.

Documents relating to the Ethiopian affair, and to Italy's role in international affairs, will be found in Section XIX.

174. *The Fascist Programme of 1919*

The programme of the Fascist Party formulated by Mussolini in 1919 is interesting as a revelation of his thinking at the time. He soon changed his views as circumstances changed and in fact hardly one of the points of this programme was ever carried out.

Source: Count Carlo Sforza, *Contemporary Italy* (London, F. Muller, 1946), p. 244.

1. A Constituent National Assembly will proceed, as the Italian Section of the Constituent International Assembly of the peoples, to a radical transformation of the political and economic bases of the life of the community.

2. Proclamation of the Italian Republic. Decentralization of the executive power; autonomous administration of the regions and communes entrusted to their respective legislative organization. Sovereignty of the people, exercised by universal suffrage of all citizens of the two sexes; the people retaining the initiative of referendum and veto.

3. Abolition of the Senate. Abolition of the political police. The Magistrature to be elected independently of the executive power.

4. Abolition of all titles of nobility and all orders of knighthood.

5. Abolition of obligatory military service.

6. Liberty of opinion and conscience, of religion, of assembly, of the press.

7. A system of education in the schools, common and professional, open to all.

8. The greatest attention to social hygiene.

9. Suppression of incorporated joint stock companies, industrial or financial. Suppression of all speculation by banks and stock exchanges.

10. Control and taxation of private wealth. Confiscation of unproductive income.

11. Prohibition of work of children under the age of sixteen. An eight-hour work day.

12. Reorganization of production on a co-operative basis and direct participation of the workers in the profits.

13. Abolition of secret diplomacy.

14. An international policy based on the solidarity of the

peoples and on their individual independence within the framework of a federation of States.

175. *Mussolini gains Power, October–November 1922*

As the normal political institutions of Italy showed more and more
signs of being unworkable in 1922, and as his movement gained
support, Mussolini prepared plans for a *coup* through which he
would gain power. In October, in the midst of a Government crisis,
everything was ready and the Fascists, under the direction of a
quadrumvirate (a Committee of four generals presided over by
Mussolini) ordered a march on Rome (a). There was little resistance
and, on 30 October, Mussolini was appointed Prime Minister of
a Fascist-dominated coalition Government, which, although it
could count only on a small minority Fascist group in Parliament,
went ahead with its business confidently (b).

Source: B. Mussolini, *My Autobiography* [by R. W. Child] Rev. ed.
(London, Hutchinson, 1939), pp. 167–8, 186–7.

(a) Proclamation by the Quadrumvirate, 26 October 1922.

Fascisti! Italians!

The time for determined battle has come! Four years ago the
National Army loosed at this season the final offensive, which
brought it to victory.[1] Today the army of the Black-shirts takes
again possession of that victory, which has been mutilated, and
going directly to Rome brings victory again to the glory of that
capital. From now on *principi* and *triari*[2] are mobilized. The
martial law of Fascism now becomes a fact. By order of the
Duce all the military, political, and administrative functions of
the party management are taken over by a secret Quadrumvirate of Action with dictatorial powers.

The Army, the reserve and safeguard of the Nation, must not
take part in this struggle. Fascism renews its highest homage
given to the Army of Vittorio Veneto. Fascism, furthermore,
does not march against the police, but against a political class
both cowardly and imbecile, which in four long years has not
been able to give a Government to the nation. Those who form
the productive class must know that Fascism wants to impose
nothing more than order and discipline upon the nation and to

---

[1] The victory of Vittorio Veneto.
[2] Names of Fascist formations.

help to raise the strength which will renew progress and prosperity. The people who work in the fields and in the factories, those who work on the railroads or in offices, have nothing to fear from the Fascist Government. Their just rights will be protected. We will even be generous with unarmed adversaries.

Fascism draws its sword to cut the multiple Gordian knots which tie and burden Italian life. We call God and the spirit of our five hundred thousand dead to witness that only one impulse sends us on, that only one passion burns within us—the impulse and the passion to contribute to the safety and greatness of our country.

Fascisti of all Italy! Stretch forth like Romans your spirits and your fibres! We must win! We will.

Long live Italy! Long live Fascism!

(b) Mussolini's speech in the Chamber of Deputies, 16 November 1922.

. . . From further communications you will know the Fascist programme in its details. I do not want, as long as I can avoid it, to rule against the Chamber; but the Chamber must feel its own position. That position opens the possibility that it may be dissolved in two days or in two years. We ask full powers, because we want to assume full responsibility. Without full powers you know very well that we could not save one lira—I say, one lira. We do not want to exclude the possibility of voluntary co-operation, for we will cordially accept it, if it comes from deputies, senators, or even from competent private citizens. Every one of us has a religious sense of our difficult task. The country cheers us and waits. We will not give it words, but facts. We formally and solemnly promise to restore the budget to health. And we will restore it. We want to make a foreign policy of peace, but at the same time one of dignity and steadiness. We will do it. We intend to give the nation a discipline. We will give it. Let none of our enemies of yesterday, of today, of tomorrow, be illusioned in regard to our permanence in power. Foolish and childish illusions, like those of yesterday.

Our Government has a formidable foundation in the conscience of the nation. It is supported by the best, the newest Italian generation. There is no doubt that in these last years a great step toward the unification of spirits has been made. The Fatherland has again found itself bound together from north to south, from the continent to the generous islands, which will never be forgotten, from the metropolis to the active colonies of the Mediterranean and the Atlantic Ocean. Do not, gentlemen, address more vain words to the nation. Fifty-two applications to speak about my communications to Parliament are too many. Let us, instead of talking, work with pure heart and ready mind to assure the prosperity and the greatness of the country.

May God assist me in bringing to a triumphant end my hard labour.

176. *The Establishment of the Dictatorship, 1925–26*

Although Mussolini's Government, aided by electoral manipulation, held quite a strong position in the country, it was still technically and at times really hampered by parliament. The following two laws, passed within a few weeks of each other, did a great deal to free Mussolini from any control and to give him dictatorial power.

Source: Rappard's *Source Book on European Government* (New York, Van Nostrand, 1937).

(a) Law on the Powers and Prerogatives of the Head of the Government, 24 December 1925.

1. The executive power is exercised by His Majesty the King through his Government. The Government consists of the Prime Minister Secretary of State and the Ministers Secretaries of State.

The Prime Minister is Head of the Government.

2. The Head of the Government . . . is appointed and recalled by the King and is responsible to the King for the general policy of the Government . . .

3. The Head of the Government . . . directs and co-ordinates the activities of the Ministers, settles disputes among them, calls meetings of the Council of Ministers and presides over them . . .

6. No bill or motion may be submitted to either of the Houses of Parliament without the consent of the Head of the Government.

The Head of the Government has the power to request that a bill, rejected by one of the Houses of Parliament, be voted upon again three months after the first vote. In such cases the vote is by ballot without previous debate . . .

The Head of the Government also has the power to request that a bill rejected by one of the Houses be submitted to the other House to be voted upon after due examination . . .

(b) Law on the Power of the Executive Branch to make Decrees having the Force of Laws, 31 January 1926.

1. By Royal Decree, after deliberation in the Council of Ministers and hearing in the Council of State, regulations having the force of laws may be issued concerning the following, even in matters heretofore regulated by law:
(1) The execution of laws.
(2) The use of powers belonging to the executive branch.
(3) The organization and functioning of the State administrations and of their personnel; the organization of public institutions and concerns . . .

Expenditures provided for by a Finance Act must continue to be authorized by an Act of Parliament . . .
3. By Royal Decree, after deliberation in the Council of Ministers, regulations having the force of laws may be issued in the following cases:
(1) When the Government is empowered and delegated to do so by a law . . .
(2) When the case is exceptional by reason of its urgency or absolute necessity; whether or not a case is exceptional shall be judged only by Parliament.

In cases referred to in paragraph (2) . . . the Royal Decree shall contain a clause providing for presentation to Parliament for ratification; the Decree ceases to have effect unless it is submitted to one of the Houses of Parliament for ratification, and this should be done not later than at the third session after the publication of the Decree . . .

177. *Law concerning the Legal Discipline of Collective Labour Relations, 3 April 1926*

By establishing compulsory professional and trade associations and prescribing the conclusion of collective contracts, both under the control of the Government, this law went a long way towards laying the foundations of the Corporative State. At the same time, by prohibiting strikes and lockouts, and by providing Labour Courts, it ensured the maintenance of industrial peace and the protection of the economic interests of the State.

Source: Rappard's *Source Book on European Government* (New York, Van Nostrand, 1937), pp. III 32–43.

I

1. Associations of employers and of labourers, intellectual or manual, may be legally recognized if they can prove that they meet the following requirements:

(1) In the case of associations of employers, that the employers voluntarily registered as members employ at least ten per cent of the workers in the trade and district which the association represents; in the case of associations of employees, that the employees voluntarily registered as members include at least ten per cent of the workers in the trade and district which the association represents.

(2) That, besides protecting the economic and moral interests of its members, the association effectively carries out plans for the insurance, instruction and moral and patriotic education of its members.

(3) That the director of the association gives proof of his ability, morality, and unswerving loyalty to the nation.

2. When the conditions prescribed in the foregoing article are met, legal recognition can be given to associations of persons independently engaged in an art, trade, or profession . . .

3. The associations referred to . . . shall consist either of employers only or of employees only.

Associations of employers and those of employees may be united by means of central co-ordinating bodies with a common hierarchy of higher officers . . .

4. The associations referred to . . . shall be recognized by Royal Decree on the proposal of the Minister concerned . . .

5. Legally recognized associations have legal personality and legally represent all the employers, labourers, employees, artists or professional men of the particular class for which they are formed within the territorial limits of the association, whether they are registered as members or not . . .

Only legally recognized associations may appoint representatives of employers or employees to all councils, corporations, or other bodies in which such representation is provided for by law.

6. Associations may be communal, district, provincial, regional, inter-regional, or national.

Federations or unions of several associations, and confederations of several federations may also be legally recognized . . .

Only one association may be legally recognized for any one class of employers, employees, artists or professional men . . .

Whenever a national confederation shall have been recognized . . ., the recognition of federations or associations which do not form part of these confederations shall be prohibited . . .

10. Collective labour contracts made by the legally recognized associations . . . are obligatory on all employers [etc.] in the classes referred to in the contracts or represented in the associations . . .

The central co-ordinating bodies . . . may establish . . . general norms and conditions for labour, valid for all employers and employees of the class to which said norms refer . . .

11. The provisions of this law . . . on the legal recognition of syndical associations do not apply to associations of employees of the State, the Provinces, the municipalities, or public philanthropic institutions . . .

All associations of officers, non-commissioned officers, and soldiers in the army, navy, and air forces, and of other armed bodies of the State, Provinces, and municipalities, and associations of magistrates . . ., and of officials [etc.] of the Ministries . . . are, therefore, forbidden . . .

II

13. All controversies arising as to the regulation of collective labour relations, whether they concern the application of collective contracts and other existing regulations, or whether they concern demands for new labour conditions, are subject to the jurisdiction of the Courts of Appeal acting as Labour Courts . . .

17. Only legally recognized associations have the right to take action in disputes arising out of collective labour contracts, and such action must be taken against legally recognized associa-

tions, when they exist; otherwise against a trustee specially appointed by the President of the Court of Appeal . . .

Only legally recognized associations can represent in Court all the employers or employees of the class in the district for which they are formed . . .

III

18. Lockouts and strikes are prohibited . . .

178. *The Charter of Labour, 21 April 1927*

The Charter of Labour is important mainly because it sets down the philosophical and constitutional principles of the Corporative State, though it also sets out in some detail the criteria to be observed in drawing up collective contracts. It further sets out the welfare and educational measures which the State intends to implement. Most of the later legislation and judicial practice in connexion with labour relations and corporations is based on its provisions.

Source: *British and Foreign State Papers*, vol. cxxvii (1927 pt. 2), pp. 756–61.

The Corporative State and its Organization

1. The Italian nation is an organism with objects, life and means of action superior in power and duration to those of the individuals or groups which compose it. It is a moral, political and economic unit which is integrally realized in the Fascist State.

2. Labour in all its organized and executive forms, intellectual, technical and manual, is a social duty. In this aspect, and in this aspect alone, it is under the protection of the State.

Production as a whole is a unit from the national point of view; its objectives are single and are summed up in the welfare of individuals and the development of the national power.

3. Syndical or professional organization is free. But only the syndicate which is legally recognized and subject to the control of the State has the right legally to represent the entire category of employers or workers for which it is constituted, to protect their interests as against the State and other professional associations, to conclude collective labour contracts binding upon all belonging to the category, to impose contributions

upon them and to exercise in respect of them delegated functions of public interest.

4. In the collective labour contract the solidarity between the various factors of production finds its concrete expression, through the conciliation of the opposing interests of employers and workers and their subordination to the higher interests of production.

5. The Labour Magistracy is the organ by which the State intervenes to settle labour disputes, whether they turn upon the observance of agreements and of other existing regulations, or upon the establishment of new conditions of labour.

6. The legally recognized professional associations assure the juridical equality of employers and workers, maintain discipline in production and labour and promote their improvement.

The corporations form the unitary organization of the forces of production and integrally represent their interests.

In virtue of this integral representation, the interests of production being national interests, the corporations are recognized by law as organs of the State.

As representatives of the unitary interests of production, the corporations may issue regulations of an obligatory character governing labour relationships, and also on the co-ordination of production whenever they have had the necessary powers to that end from the component associations.

7. The corporative State considers private initiative in the field of production to be the most effective and most useful instrument in the national interest . . .

9. The intervention of the State in economic production takes place only when private initiative is lacking or is insufficient or when the political interests of the State are involved. Such intervention may take the form of control, encouragement and direct management.

10. In collective labour disputes judicial action may not be initiated unless the corporative organ has first made an attempt at conciliation . . .

Collective Labour Contracts and Labour Guarantees

11. The professional associations are obliged to regulate, by means of collective contracts, labour relations between the categories of employers and workers whom they represent . . .

12. The action of the syndicate, the work of conciliation of the corporative organs and the decision of the Labour Magistracy guarantee the equivalence of wages to the normal requirements of life, the possibilities of production and the yield of the labour.

The decision of wages is withdrawn from the scope of any general regulation and is entrusted to agreements between the parties in collective contracts . . .

15. The worker has the right to a weekly day of rest, falling on Sunday . . .

16. After one year of uninterrupted service the worker, in undertakings which operate continuously, has the right to an annual period of holiday with pay . . .

19. Breaches of discipline and acts which disturb the normal functioning of the business, committed by workers, shall be punished, according to the gravity of the offence, by fine, suspension from work and, in serious cases, by immediate dismissal without indemnity . . .

Labour Exchanges

22. The State alone ascertains and controls the phenomenon of employment and unemployment, the comprehensive index of the conditions of production and labour.

23. The Labour Exchanges are constituted on the basis of parity under the control of the corporative organs of the State. Employers must engage workmen through these offices. They have the privilege of selection within the limits of the persons enrolled in the registers of the Exchange, giving preference to members of the Fascist party and of the Fascist syndicates according to their seniority on the lists . . .

Welfare, Assistance, Education and Instruction

26. Social measures are a further manifestation of the principle of collaboration towards which employers and employees must contribute proportionately. The State, through the corporative organs and professional associations, will endeavour as far as possible to co-ordinate and unify the system and institutions providing for welfare work.

27. The Fascist State proposes to accomplish:

(1) The improvement of accident insurance.

(2) The improvement and extension of maternity insurance.

(3) Insurance against occupational illnesses and tuberculosis as the first step towards general insurance against all illness.

(4) Improvement of insurance against involuntary unemployment.

(5) The adoption of special endowment insurance for young workers . . .

179. *Law respecting the Constitution and Functions of the Grand Council of Fascism, 9 December 1928*

The Grand Council of Fascism was formed in 1925 as the supreme policy-making body of the Fascist Party. Its functions within the Party were, however, gradually taken over by the Party's National Directorate and the Grand Council became more concerned with wider issues. In the law that follows it was transformed from an organ of the Party into an organ of the State with very wide powers.

Source: *British and Foreign State Papers*, vol. cxxix (1928 pt. 2), pp. 757–60.

1. The Fascist Grand Council is the supreme organ which co-ordinates all the activities of the régime which emerged from the revolution of October 1922. It has deliberative functions in the cases determined by law, and, furthermore, gives opinions on any other political, economic or social question of national interest which may be put to it by the Head of the Government.

2. The Head of the Government . . . is . . . the President of the Fascist Grand Council . . .

3. The Secretary of the National Fascist Party is Secretary of the Grand Council . . .

4. The following are members of the Grand Council for an unlimited time:

(1) The members of the quadrumvirate of the march on Rome (cf. No. 175(a)).

(2) Persons who, in their capacity as members of the Government, have formed part of the Grand Council for at least three years.

(3) The Secretaries of the National Fascist Party who have left office since 1922.

5. The following are members of the Grand Council by reason of their duties, and for the entire duration of these duties:

(1) The Presidents of the Senate and of the Chamber of Deputies.

(2) The Ministers . . .

(3) The Under-Secretary of State to the President of the Council.

(4) The Commandant-General of the Volunteer Militia for National Security.

(5) The members of the Directorate of the National Fascist Party.

(6) The Presidents of the Italian Academy and of the Fascist Cultural Institute.

(7) The President of the National Balilla Organization.

(8) The President of the Special Tribunal for the Defence of the State.

(9) The Presidents of the National Fascist Confederations of Syndicates legally recognized.

(10) The President of the National Co-Operative Organization . . .

11. The Grand Council takes decisions:

(1) Upon the list of deputies . . .

(2) Upon the statutes, orders and policy of the National Fascist Party.

(3) Upon the appointment and dismissal of the . . . members of the Directorate of the National Fascist Party.

12. The views of the Grand Council must be ascertained on all questions of a constitutional character.

Bills dealing with the following subjects are always considered as having a constitutional character:

(1) The succession to the Throne, the powers and the prerogatives of the King.

(2) The composition and functioning of the Grand Council, the Senate of the Kingdom and the Chamber of Deputies.

(3) The attributes and prerogatives of the Head of the Government . . .

(4) The faculty of the Executive Power to issue juridical regulations.

(5) The organization of the syndicates and corporations.

(6) The relations between the State and the Holy See.

(7) International treaties involving modifications of the territory of the State and the colonies, or renunciation of territorial acquisitions.

180. *The Lateran Agreements, 11 February 1929*

There were no official relations between Italy and the Holy See since the occupation of Rome by Italian forces in 1870, and the Italian Law of Guarantees (No. 115) was not accepted by the Pope. Participation of Catholics in the political life of the Italian State was prohibited by a succession of Popes and was only permitted, and then tacitly, during the First World War. One of Mussolini's concerns was to settle this problem, and with the Holy See indicating a willingness to accept the existing situation if Italy were willing to make some concessions, a treaty (a) regularizing the relations of the Papacy and Italy was concluded in 1929. It was accompanied by a Concordat (b), some articles of which follow.

Source: *British and Foreign State Papers*, vol. cxxx (1929 pt. 1), pp. 791–814.

(a) The Treaty of the Lateran, 11 February 1929.

1. Italy recognizes and reaffirms the principle embodied in article 1 of the statute of the Kingdom dated the 4th March 1848 (cf. No. 86) according to which the Roman Catholic Apostolic religion is the sole religion of the State.

2. Italy recognizes the sovereignty of the Holy See in the international domain . . .

3. Italy recognizes the full ownership and the exclusive and absolute dominion . . . of the Holy See over the Vatican . . .

4. The sovereignty and exclusive jurisdiction over the Vatican City, which Italy recognizes as appertaining to the Holy See, precludes any intervention therein on the part of the Italian Government and any authority other than that of the Holy See . . .

8. Considering the person of the Supreme Pontiff as sacred and inviolable, Italy declares any attempt against the same, and any incitement to commit such an attempt, to be punishable with the same penalties as are prescribed in the case of an attempt . . . against the person of the King . . .

11. The central bodies of the Catholic Church shall be exempt from any interference on the part of the Italian State . . .

25. By a special convention, signed at the same time as the present treaty . . . provision is made for the liquidation of the sums due to the Holy See by Italy . . .

26. . . . The law dated 13 May 1871 (No. 115) and any other provisions contrary to the present treaty are abrogated . . .

(b) Concordat between the Holy See and Italy, 11 February
1929.

1. In accordance with article 1 of the treaty (No. 180(a)),
Italy shall assure to the Catholic Church the free exercise of
spiritual power and the free and public exercise of worship, as
well as of its jurisdiction in ecclesiastical matters . . .
2. The Holy See shall communicate and correspond freely with
the bishops, the clergy and the whole Catholic world without
any interference on the part of the Italian Government . . .
5. No ecclesiastic may be engaged or remain in an employment
or office of the Italian State or of public bodies subordinate
thereto without the consent of the diocesan ordinary . . .
19. The selection of archbishops and bishops shall appertain to
the Holy See.
    Before proceeding to the appointment . . . the Holy See shall
communicate to the Italian Government the name of the person
selected in order to ensure that the latter have no objections of
a political nature to such appointment . . .
20. Before taking over their dioceses bishops shall take an oath
of allegiance to the Head of the State . . .
21. The bestowal of ecclesiastical benefices shall devolve upon
the ecclesiastical authorities . . .
34. Desiring to restore to the institution of marriage, which is
the basis of the family, a dignity in conformity with the Catholic
traditions of its people, the Italian State recognizes the civil
effects of the sacrament of marriage as governed by canon
law . . .
    Actions for the nullity of marriage and the annulment of
marriages solemnized but not consummated shall be reserved
to the competence of ecclesiastical courts and departments . . .
As regards suits for personal separation, the Holy See agrees
that these shall be justiciable by the civil judicial authority . . .

181. *Law Reforming the National Council of Corporations,*
20 March 1930

A further step towards the building of the Corporative State (cf.
Nos 177, 178) was the formation of the National Council of Corporations, representative of the associations of employers and employees

formed in accordance with the law of 1926 (No. 177). Note the wide powers given to this Council.

Source: *British and Foreign State Papers*, vol. cxxxiii (1930 pt. 2), pp. 650–62.

. . . 4. The National Council of Corporations shall be composed of seven sections, as follows:

(1) A section for the liberal professions and the arts . . .

(2) A section for industry and artisans . . .

(3) A section for agriculture.

(4) A section for commerce.

(5) A section for land transport and internal navigation.

(6) A section for sea and air transport . . .

(7) A section for banks . . .

5. When the subject for decision is of interest to the entire syndical and corporative order of the State, and in the cases specifically prescribed by the present law, the sections of the Council shall be convoked in General Assembly . . .

6. For the treatment of individual subjects of a general character and of a prevalently technical order . . . permanent special commissions composed of members of the General Assembly may be constituted . . .

10. The National Council of Corporations shall be called upon to give its views on the following special subjects:

(1) The application and integration of the principles contained in the Labour Charter (No. 178) . . .

(2) Legislative bills and the promulgation of rules in conformity with the law of the 31st January 1926 (No. 176(b)) when these have as their object the regulation of production and labour.

(3) The protection on the part of the syndical associations of the interests of their category . . .

(4) The promotion of the increase in production . . .

(5) The activities of the corporative organs and institutions having as their object the increase, co-ordination and perfecting of production, culture and national art . . .

(6) The relations between the different syndical associations, their complementary bodies and the corporative organs and institutions . . .

(7) The co-ordination of the relief activities assigned to the syndical associations . . .

(8) Questions relating to the syndical organization of the various professional categories.

(9) The recognition of syndical association . . .

(13) The regional and national co-ordination of labour exchanges . . .

(14) Constitution of the individual corporations . . .

(15) Scientific and popular propaganda for the better understanding of the principles upon which the corporative system is based.

(16) The fixing of syndical dues.

In general, the National Council of Corporations may be called upon to give its opinion on any question whatever relating to national production . . .

15. The Central Corporative Committee shall be constituted within the National Council of Corporations.

The task of the Central Corporative Committee shall be to co-ordinate the activity of the Council; to substitute itself, in the intervals between the sessions thereof, for the General Assembly in matters requiring urgent discussion . . . and to give its opinion on questions reflecting the political orientations of the syndical activity with regard to the national problems of production and to the moral aims of the corporative organization . . .

182. *Law on Corporations, 5 February 1934*

Although Corporations, bodies uniting all organizations of employers and employees in a field, had been mentioned in earlier legislation (Nos 177, 178), and a National Council of Corporations had been formed (cf. No. 181), the formation of Corporations only took place after the Law of Corporations, part of which follows, was enacted in 1934. Although some further changes in corporative structure were made later, all important features of the Corporative State were settled by the passing of this law and the regulations based on it.

Source: Rappard's *Source Book on European Government* (New York, Van Nostrand, 1937), pp. III 59–62.

1. The Corporations mentioned in the sixth clause of the Labour Charter (No. 178) . . . shall be established by decree of the Head of the Government on proposal of the Minister of

Corporations with the approval of the Central Corporative Committee (cf. No. 181, Art. 15) . . .

4. In the Corporations in which occupations from various branches of economic activity are represented special sections may be formed whose recommendations must be approved by the Corporation.

5. The Head of the Government, in matters pertaining to various branches of economic activity, may order that two or more Corporations meet together . . .

7. The associations combined in a Corporation become autonomous as syndical bodies but continue to belong to their respective Confederations . . .

8. . . . A Corporation shall make rules for the collective regulation of economic matters and for the unified direction of production . . .

10. A Corporation, within its own field, shall have the power to fix rates . . . for economic employment and services, as well as prices for goods offered to the public . . .

12. A Corporation shall pass judgment on all questions that commonly interest the particular branch of economic production for which it is established, whenever it is so requested by the public administration concerned . . .

XVII · GERMANY 1918–39

THE section on inter-war Germany opens with two documents illustrating the policy of the new Socialist Government of Germany (No. 183) which are followed by selected articles of the Weimar Constitution (No. 184).

Several documents have been selected to show the effect reparations were having on Germany and the Germans. Two relate to the occupation of the Ruhr area by French and Belgian troops in 1923 (No. 186), while another provides a summary of the Dawes Plan on Reparations of 1924 (No. 187). The following selection (No. 188) illustrates German right-wing attitudes to reparations and the Young Plan of 1929 rather than the Young Plan itself.

Only two documents are included from the period between the onset of the depression and Hitler's assumption of power. These are the declaration of the Social-Democratic Party when its ministers resigned from the Müller coalition Government in 1930 (No. 189) and the declaration made by Social-Democratic deputies later in the year (No. 190) which explains why they continued to tolerate the Brüning Government. Any really informative material from the time between 1930 and January 1933 would be of the nature of memoir or description, and would not, therefore, fall within the scope of this collection.

Apart from the 1920 programme of the National Socialist German Workers' Party (NSDAP) (No. 185) three groups of documents were included from the period of national socialist domination. The emergency ordinance of 28 February 1933 (No. 191) and the enabling law of 24 March 1933 (No. 192) provided the legal foundations on which Hitler built up his dictatorship. The documents of the *Gleichschaltung* or 'co-ordination' (No. 193) show the steps by which Hitler transformed the Weimar Republic into a state which conformed to his ideas. The Nürnberg laws of 1935 and related measures (No. 194) illustrate the way in which Hitler's racial ideas were translated into practice.

The basic document for Germany's international relations in this period is the Treaty of Versailles (No. 160). Many other relevant documents will be found in Section XIX.

183. The German Revolution, November 1918

The description of the mutinies, riots, formation of workers' and soldiers' councils on the Soviet model, etc., which led to the appointment and then resignation of Prince Max of Baden as Chancellor, to the appointment of Ebert, the leader of the majority Social-Democrats, as Chancellor, and the abdication of Emperor William II, is beyond the scope of this note. The formulation of a socialist Government was welcomed by many who thought it would lead to a socialist republic; but Ebert had a true sense of democracy and wanted to ascertain and obey the will of the majority; it was therefore without his knowledge and against his will that Scheidemann proclaimed the republic (a). Two versions of Scheidemann's speech are current. The shorter version, which follows, was published in a newspaper of the day. There is some evidence that the longer version was written by Scheidemann from memory some time later.

A decree setting out the programme of the new Government follows (b).

Source: (a) E. R. Huber, *Dokumente zur deutschen Verfassungsgeschichte* (Stuttgart, Kohlhammer, 1966), vol. iii, pp. 1–2 (trans. Ed.).

      (b) *International Conciliation*, 1919, pp. 545–6.

(a) Scheidemann Proclaims the Republic, 9 November 1918.

We have won all along the line; what is old no longer exists. Ebert has been appointed Chancellor. Deputy Lt. Göhre is seconded to the Minister of War [to countersign his orders]. The task now is to consolidate our victory; nobody can hinder us in it.

The Hohenzollern have abdicated. Take care, that this proud day be not besmirched by anything. It will always be a day of honour in the history of Germany. Long live the German Republic!

(b) Programme of the New Government, 12 November 1918.

To the German People!

The Government which the Revolution has produced, whose political convictions are purely socialist, is undertaking the task of realizing the socialist programme. They now make the following announcements, which will have the force of law:

1. The state of siege is abolished.

2. The right of association and meeting is subject to no limitations, not even for officials and State workers.

3. The censorship ceases to exist . . .

4. Expression of opinion, whether by word of mouth or in writing, is free.

5. Freedom of religious practice is guaranteed. No one shall be compelled to perform any religious act.

6. An amnesty is granted for all political punishments. Trials now proceeding for such crimes are quashed.

7. The Law of (compulsory) National Auxiliary Service is abolished with the exception of the provisions referring to the settlement of disputes . . .

9. The laws protecting Labour, which were abandoned at the beginning of the war, are herewith restored. Further orders of a social-political nature will be published shortly. On January 1, 1919, at latest, the eight-hour day will come into force. The Government will do all that is possible to secure sufficient opportunities of work. An Order *re* the support of unemployed is ready. It divides the burden between the Empire (Federal), state, and municipality. In the sphere of sickness insurance, the insurance obligation will be increased beyond the present limit of 2,500 marks. The housing difficulty will be dealt with by the building of houses. Efforts will be made to secure regular feeding of the people. The Government will maintain ordered production, will protect property against private interference, as well as the freedom and security of individuals. All elections to public bodies are immediately to be carried out according to the equal, secret, direct, and universal franchise on the basis of proportional representation for all male and female persons of not less than twenty years of age; this franchise also holds for the Constituent Assembly, concerning which more detailed orders will follow.

D E C—EE

184. *The Weimar Constitution, 11 August 1919*

A constituent assembly was elected in January 1919, its two main tasks being the enacting of a constitution and the conclusion of peace. It met on 6 February at the provincial town of Weimar—hence the name 'Weimar Republic'—since Berlin and the other large cities were still in the throes of a Spartacist (extreme left wing) rising. The Assembly elected Ebert as President of the Republic, it agreed, under strong protest, to the Treaty of Versailles (No. 160), and enacted a constitution, some provisions of which follow. Care has been taken to include all articles referred to in later documents.

Source: *British and Foreign State Papers*, vol. cxii (1919), pp. 1063-94.

This constitution has been framed by the united German people, inspired by the determination to restore and establish their Federation upon a basis of liberty and justice, to be of service to the cause of peace both at home and abroad, and to promote social progress.

1. The German Federation is a republic . . .

5. The executive power is exercised in Federal affairs through the institutions of the Federation in virtue of the Federal Constitution, and in State affairs by the officials of the State, in virtue of the Constitution of the States.

6. The Federal Government has the sole legislative power as regards: (1) Foreign relations; (2) Colonial affairs; (3) Nationality, right of domicile, immigration, emigration and extradition; (4) Military organization; (5) The monetary system; (6) The customs departments, as well as uniformity in the sphere of customs, trade, and freedom of commercial intercourse; (7) The postal and telegraph services, including the telephone service.

7. The Federal Government has legislative powers as regards: (1) Civic rights; (2) Penal power; (3) Judicial procedure . . .; (6) The press, trade unions, and the rights of assembly; . . . (9) Labour laws . . .; (15) Traffic in foodstuffs and luxuries as well as in articles of daily necessity; . . . (20) Theatres and cinemas; . . .

13. Federal law overrides state law . . .

20. The Reichstag is an assembly composed of the deputies of the German people.

21. The deputies are representatives of the whole people. They

are subject to their conscience only, and not bound by any mandates.

22. The deputies are elected by the universal, equal, direct and secret suffrage of all men and women above the age of twenty, upon the principles of proportional representation . . .

25. The President of the Federation may dissolve the Reichstag, but only once for any one reason. The general election will take place not later than sixty days after the dissolution . . .

41. The President of the Federation is elected by the whole German people. Every German who has completed his thirty-fifth year is eligible . . .

47. The President of the Federation has supreme command over all the armed forces of the Federation.

48. In the case of a State not fulfilling the duties imposed on it by the Federal Constitution or the Federal laws, the President of the Federation may enforce their fulfilment with the help of armed forces.

Where public security and order are seriously disturbed or endangered within the Federation, the President of the Federation may take the measures necessary for their restoration, intervening in case of need with the help of armed forces. For this purpose he is permitted, for the time being, to abrogate, either wholly or partially, the fundamental laws laid down in articles 114, 115, 117, 118, 123, 124, and 153.

The President of the Federation must, without delay, inform the Reichstag of any measures taken in accordance with paragraphs one and two of this Article. Such measures shall be withdrawn upon the demand of the Reichstag.

Where there is danger in delay, the State Government may take provisional measures of the kind described in paragraph 2 for its own territory. Such measures shall be withdrawn upon the demand of the President of the Federation or the Reichstag . . .

52. The Federal Government consists of the Chancellor of the Federation and the Federal Ministers.

53. The President . . . appoints and dismisses the Chancellor . . . and, on the latter's recommendation, the . . . Ministers.

54. The Chancellor . . . and the . . . Ministers require, for the administration of their office, the confidence of the Reichstag. Any one of them must resign, should the confidence of the House be withdrawn by an express resolution.

56. The Chancellor . . . determines the main lines of policy, for which he is responsible to the Reichstag . . .

60. A Reichsrat is formed for the representation of the German States in Federal legislation and administration . . .

68. Bills are introduced by the Federal Government or by members of the Reichstag.

69. The introduction of bills by the Federal Government requires the consent of the Reichsrat.

72. The promulgation of a Federal law shall be deferred by two months if one third of the Reichstag demands it. Laws which both the Reichstag and the Reichsrat declare to be urgent may, however, be promulgated by the President of the Federation, in spite of such demand.

73. A law passed by the Reichstag shall, before its promulgation, be submitted to the decision of the people, if the President of the Federation so determines, within one month.

A law, the promulgation of which is deferred on the proposal of at least one-third of the Reichstag, shall be submitted to the decision of the people if desired by one-twentieth of those entitled to the franchise.

A decision of the people shall also take place if one-tenth of those entitled to the franchise petitions for the submission of a proposed law . . .

75. A resolution of the Reichstag shall not be annulled unless a majority of those entitled to the franchise participates in the voting.

76. The Constitution may be altered by legislation. But decisions of the Reichstag as to such alteration come into effect only if two-thirds of the legal total of members be present, and if at least two-thirds of those present have given their consent . . .

114. Personal liberty is inviolable. No encroachment on, or deprivation of, personal liberty by public authority is permissible, unless supported by law.

Persons who have been deprived of their liberty shall be informed—at the latest on the following day—by what authority and on what grounds the deprivation of liberty has been ordered; opportunity shall be given them without delay to make objection against such deprivation.

115. The residence of every German is a sanctuary for him, and inviolable; exceptions are admissible only in virtue of laws . . .

117. Every German has the right, within the limits of the general laws, to express his opinion freely by word, writing, printed matter or picture, or in any other manner . . .

123. All Germans have the right, without notification or special permission, to assemble peacefully and without arms.

Open-air meetings may be made notifiable by a Federal law, and in case of immediate danger to public security may be forbidden.

124. All Germans have the right to form unions and societies, provided their objects do not run counter to the penal laws . . .

142. Art, science, and the teaching of both, are free.

The State guarantees their protection and participates in furthering them . . .

151. The organization of economic life must correspond to the principles of justice, with the aim of ensuring for all conditions worthy of a human being. Within these limits the economic freedom of the individual must be guaranteed . . .

153. Property is guaranteed by the Constitution . . .

157. Labour is under the special protection of the Federation . . .

185. *Programme of the NSDAP, 25 February 1920*

Insignificant in 1920, the National Socialist German Workers' Party soon gained notoriety, and, later, in 1933, full power. Its programme is therefore included as a matter of interest.

Source: Rappard's *Source Book on European Government* (New York, Van Nostrand, 1937), pp. IV 9-13.

The programme of the National Socialist German Workers' Party is a time programme. The leaders decline, after achievement of the purposes laid down in the programme, to set up new goals only for the purpose of making possible the continuance of the party through the artificially stimulated dissatisfaction of the masses.

1. We demand the union of all Germans in one Great Germany by the right of self-determination of peoples.

2. We demand the equality of the German nation with all other nations and abrogation of the Treaties of Versailles (No. 160) and St. Germain.[1]

---

[1] The peace treaty with Austria.

3. We demand land and territory (colonies) for the feeding of our people and for the settlement of our surplus population.

4. Only those who are members of the nation can be citizens. Only those who are of German blood, without regard to religion, can be members of the German nation. No Jew can, therefore, be a member of the nation.

5. He who is not a citizen shall be able to live in Germany only as a guest and must live under laws governing foreigners.

6. The right to decide on the leadership and on the laws of the state may belong only to citizens. Therefore we demand that every public office, of whatever sort . . . shall be filled only by citizens. We fight against the corrupting parliamentary system of filling offices with people chosen because of their party viewpoint without regard to character and ability.

7. We demand that the state be obliged, in the first instance, to provide the possibility of work and life for the citizen . . .

8. All further immigration of non-Germans is to be prevented. We demand that all non-Germans who have immigrated to Germany since the second of August 1913 shall be compelled to leave the Reich immediately.

9. All citizens must possess the same rights and duties.

10. The first duty of every citizen is to work productively with mind or body. The activities of individuals must not transgress the interests of the community but must be for the common good.

THEREFORE WE DEMAND

11. The elimination of income which is acquired without labour or effort.

BREAKING OF THE INTEREST SLAVERY

12. Out of regard to the frightful sacrifice in goods and blood which every war demands from the nation, personal enrichment through war must be designated as a crime against the nation. We demand, therefore, summary confiscation of all war profits.

13. We demand the nationalization of all trusts.

14. We demand profit-sharing in large concerns.

15. We demand a large-scale extension of the old-age pension system.

16. We demand the creation of a sound middle class and its

maintenance, immediate communalization of large department stores and their rental at low cost to small merchants, the strictest control of all small merchants in their dealings with the national government, the states, or the communes.

17. We demand land reform adapted to our national needs, the enactment of a law for the uncompensated expropriation of land for public purposes, the elimination of land interest and the prevention of land speculation.

18. We demand the most ruthless campaign against everyone who injures the public interest by his actions. Those who commit crimes against the people, usurers, profiteers and so forth, must be punished by death, without respect to religion or race.

19. We demand that the Roman Law, which serves the materialistic world order, shall be replaced by a legal system for all Germany.

20. In order to make possible the attainment of higher education for every capable and industrious German and thereby the entrance into a leading position, the state has the responsibility of providing for a fundamental extension of our entire education system. The teaching plans of all educational institutions must be adapted to the demands of practical life. An understanding of national consciousness must be taught to the children at the earliest possible age. We demand the education at state expense of especially gifted children of poor parents without regard to profession or position.

21. The state must care for the improvement of the people's health through the protection of mother and child, through the forbidding of child labour, through development of physical capability by means of legislative provision of a gymnastic and sports duty and through the greatest support of all associations engaged in physical education of youth.

22. We demand the abolition of the mercenary army and the formation of a people's army.

23. We demand legislative action against conscious political lies and their propagation through the press. In order to make possible the creation of a German press, we demand that:

(a) All editors and contributors of newspapers which appear in German, must be citizens.

(b) Non-German newspapers must have the special permission of the state . . .

(c) Every financial participation in German newspapers or the influencing by non-Germans is to be forbidden and we demand as punishment for violation the closing of such newspaper plant, as well as the immediate expulsion from the Reich of the participating non-German.

Newspapers which work against the public welfare are to be forbidden. We demand legislative action against an artistic and literary tendency which exerts a destructive influence over our national life and the closing of institutions which conflict with these demands.

24. We demand the freedom of all religions in the state in so far as they do not endanger its welfare or offend against the morals and sense of decency of the German race.

The party as such represents the standpoint of a positive Christianity without binding itself to a particular belief. It fights the Jewish materialistic spirit within and without and is convinced that a permanent convalescence of our nation can only succeed from within on the foundation of:

PUBLIC INTEREST BEFORE PRIVATE INTEREST

25. For the carrying out of all these we demand: the creation of a strong central power in the Reich; absolute authority of the political central parliament over the entire Reich and all its organizations.

The formation of professional and trade chambers for the carrying out of the general laws of the Reich in the individual federal states.

The leaders of the party promise to work ruthlessly for the carrying out of the points above set forth even to the extent of risking their lives for the programme.

186. *The Occupation of the Ruhr, 1923*

French and Belgian troops occupied the most important industrial area of Germany, the Ruhr, in January 1923 in order to ensure that payment and delivery of reparations (cf. No. 160, Articles 232-5) take place on schedule. The German Government protested in vain, suspended reparations payments, and called for passive resistance. The first proclamation that follows (a) is the appeal by the Government calling for passive resistance, the second (b) issued in September when the direct and indirect effects of the occupation and of inflation had completely disrupted German economic life calls off the resistance. Negotiations with the creditor powers and the appointment of an expert committee to recommend a new scheme of reparations (cf. No. 187) soon followed.

Source: E. R. Huber, *Dokumente zur deutschen Verfassungsgeschichte* (Stuttgart, Kohlhammer, 1966), vol. iii, pp. 277, 280–1 (trans. Ed.).

(a) Directive on Passive Resistance, 19 January 1923.

The action of the French and Belgian Governments in the Ruhr area constitutes a gross violation of international law and of the Treaty of Versailles (No. 160). As a consequence all orders and ordinances directed to German officials in the course of this action are legally invalid. The Governments of the Reich, of Prussia, Bavaria, Hessen and Oldenburg therefore direct [all officials] not to obey the ordinances of the occupation Powers but only the ordinances of their own Governments . . .

(b) Proclamation calling off Passive Resistance, 26 September 1923.

On 11 January French and Belgian troops occupied . . . the German Ruhr territory. Since then, the Ruhr Territory and the Rhineland had to suffer severe oppression. Over 180,000 German men, women, old people and children have been driven from house and home. Millions of Germans no longer know what personal freedom is. Countless acts of violence have accompanied the occupation, more than one hundred fellow Germans lost their lives, hundreds are still languishing in prison.

A spirit of justice and of patriotism rose against the unlawfulness of the invasion. The population refused to work under foreign bayonets. For this loyalty and constancy . . . the whole German people gives them thanks.

The Reich Government undertook to do what it could for the suffering compatriots. An ever increasing amount of the means of the Reich has been claimed by this task. In the past week support for the Ruhr and the Rhineland amounted to 3,500 billion[1] marks. In the current week a doubling of this sum is

[1] One billion equals 1,000,000 million. The U.S. dollar stood at 126 million marks on the day of the proclamation, having risen from 4·6 million marks in just over a month.

expected. Economic life in Germany, occupied or unoccupied, is disrupted. Perseverance in our present course threatens the terribly serious danger that it will be impossible to establish a stable currency, to maintain economic activity, and thus even to secure a bare existence for our people.

In the interest of Germany's future as well as in the interest of the Rhineland and the Ruhr this danger must be averted. To save the life of the people and of the State we face today the bitter necessity of breaking off the struggle . . .

187. *The 'Dawes Plan', 1924*

When Germany, under Stresemann's chancellorship, discontinued resistance in the Ruhr area (No. 186(b)) and declared its willing-ness to resume the payment of reparations, an expert committee under the chairmanship of the American Dawes was appointed to make recommendations. The report of the committee was accepted by the Governments concerned and formed the basis of a number of treaties which regulated reparations from that time. Note that the obligation to pay reparations was still not limited in time.

The following is part of a summary of the report, prepared by the expert committee itself.

Source: *International Conciliation*, 1924, pp. 149–57.

I. The Attitude of the Committee.

a. The standpoint adopted has been that of business and not politics.

b. Political factors have been considered only in so far as they affect the practicability of the plan.

c. The recovery of debt, not the imposition of penalties, has been sought.

d. The payment of that debt by Germany is her necessary contribution to repairing the damage of the war.

e. It is in the interest of all parties to carry out this plan in that good faith which is the fundamental of all business. Our plan is based upon this principle.

f. The reconstruction of Germany is not an end in itself; it is only part of the larger problem of the reconstruction of Europe.

g. Guarantees proposed are economic, not political.

II. German Economic Unity.

For success in stabilizing currency and balancing budgets, Germany needs the resources of German territory as defined by the Treaty of Versailles, and free economic activity therein.

III. Military Aspects—Contingent Sanctions
and Guarantees.

a. Political guarantees and penalties are outside our jurisdiction.

b. The military aspect of this problem is beyond our terms of reference.

c. Within the unified territory, the plan requires that, when it is in effective operation:

1. if any military organization exists, it must not impede the free exercise of economic activities;

2. there shall be no foreign economic control or interference other than that proposed by the plan.

d. But adequate and productive guarantees are provided.

IV. The Committee's Task.

a. Stabilization of currency and the balancing of budgets are interdependent, though they are provisionally separable for examination.

b. Currency stability can only be maintained if the budget is normally balanced; the budget can only be balanced if a stable and reliable currency exists.

c. Both are needed to enable Germany to meet her internal requirements and Treaty payments.

V. Economic Future of Germany.

a. Productivity is expected from increasing population, technical skill, material resources and eminence in industrial science.

b. Plant capacity has been increased and improved since the war . . .

IX. Normal Resources from which Payments are Made.

Germany will pay Treaty charges from three sources:
A. Taxes; B. Railways; C. Industrial debentures . . .

X. Summary of Provision for Treaty Payments.

a. 1. Budget Moratorium Period.
1st year—From foreign loans and part interest on railway
bonds.
   Total of   One thousand million gold marks.
2nd year—From part interest on railway bonds and on industrial debentures, budget contribution, through sale of
500 million g.m. railway shares.
   Total of   1,220 million g.m.
   2. Transition Period.
3rd year—From interest on railway bonds and on industrial
debentures, from transport tax and from budget.
   Total of   1,200 million g.m.
4th year—[from the same sources]
   Total of   1,750 million g.m.
5th year—[from the same sources]
   Total of   2,500 million g.m.
Thereafter 2,500 millions plus a supplement computed on the
index of prosperity.
Interest on the securities, but not the proceeds of their sale,
is included in these figures.
b. The first year will begin to run from the date when the plan
shall have been accepted and put into effective execution.

XI. Inclusive Amounts and Deliveries in Kind.

a. The above sums cover all amounts for which Germany may
be liable to the Allied and Associated Powers.
b. Deliveries in kind are to be continued, but are paid for out
of balances in the Bank . . .

XVII. The Nature of the Plan.

a. The plan is an indivisible unit.

b. The aim of the plan is:

1. To set up machinery to provide the largest annual payments from Germany;

2. to enable maximum transfers to be made to Germany's creditors;

3. to take the question of 'what Germany can pay' out of the field of speculation and put it in the field of practical demonstration;

4. to facilitate a final and comprehensive agreement upon all the problems of reparations and connected questions, as soon as circumstances make this possible.

188. *Initiative and Referendum on the Young Plan, 1929*

Until 1929 Germany fulfilled her obligations under the Dawes Plan (No. 187) but it was felt that the increased payments envisaged for 1930 and after would be beyond her capacity. A new expert committee, under the American Young, was therefore appointed early in 1929, and finally settled the total amount to be paid by Germany, reduced the annual instalments, and recommended the liberation of Germany from international control. The substance of these recommendations was embodied in the Hague agreements of August 1929.

Although the Young Plan seemed to be advantageous as compared with the Dawes Plan, there was strong opposition to it in Germany. The Nationalist and National Socialist Parties organized an initiative under the provisions of Article 73 of the Constitution (No. 184), gaining support from 10·02% of those entitled to vote. The text of the law to be introduced follows.

The proposal was, however, defeated in the referendum, although a large majority of those voting was in favour of it, because there was only a 14·59% participation in the voting instead of the more than half required by Article 75 of the Constitution.

Source: E. R. Huber, *Dokumente zur deutschen Verfassungsgeschichte* (Stuttgart, Kohlhammer, 1966), vol. iii, pp. 402–3 (trans. Ed.).

1. The Government is to advise . . . the foreign Powers that the forced acknowledgement of war guilt in the Versailles Treaty (No. 160) is contrary to historical truth, is based on false premises, and is not binding in international law.

2. The Government must endeavour to have Articles 231

as well as 429 and 430[1] of the Versailles Treaty formally invalidated.

It must also endeavour to have the occupied [Rhineland] territories evacuated immediately and unconditionally, without any further control over German territory, independently of the acceptance or rejection of the decisions of the Hague Conference [on reparations].

3. New burdens and obligations toward foreign Powers must not be accepted if they are based on the recognition of war guilt.

The burdens and obligations which are to be accepted by Germany on the basis of the proposals of the Paris Experts[2] and the agreements resulting from them are included in this provision . . .

189. *Appeal of the SPD Executive, 28 March 1930*

All Governments of the Weimar Republic were coalition Governments, consisting of at least four parties. Because of their divergent interests, no Government could last for very long. The strongest Governments were those of the Great Coalition, in which the strongest party, the SPD, shared with the Centre, the Democrats, the Bavarian People's Party and the German People's Party (*Deutsche Volkspartei*). Such a Government came into power in June 1928 and lasted for nearly two years. It broke up because the widely disparate interests of the SPD and the *Deutsche Volkspartei* could not agree on the policy to be followed in the exceptional circumstances of the depression. The SPD left the Government for the reasons set out below, and thus, with the appointment of Brüning as Chancellor, the weight of the Government moved towards the right.

Source: E. R. Huber, *Dokumente zur deutschen Verfassungsgeschichte* (Stuttgart, Kohlhammer, 1966), vol. iii, pp. 412-14 (trans. Ed.).

To the Working Population!

The Reich Government of Hermann Müller resigned on 27 March 1930. The struggle over unemployment insurance . . . has led to an open crisis.

Securing support for the huge army of . . . unemployed is and remains an aim of Social Democracy, a reduction of benefits is the aim of the *Deutsche Volkspartei*. This contrast led to the crisis.

[1] Articles 429 and 430 refer to the military occupation of the Rhineland.
[2] The Young Committee.

Last year already there was a strong attack on unemployment insurance. Social Democracy and the trade unions . . .
defeated it. They were successful in maintaining unemployment
benefits. But the social reaction was not satisfied.

The social reaction wants to destroy unemployment insurance, so that necessity will force the worker to accept reductions
in wages without opposition.

Social Democracy wanted to put unemployment insurance
on a sound basis by increasing contributions and maintaining
State subsidies. This . . . was opposed by the *Deutsche Volkspartei*.

Therefore it refused the proposal of the Reich Government
of 5 March, which envisaged a 4% increase in contributions
and State subsidies of 200 millions. This proposal, made
by ministers from the *Volkspartei*, was agreed to by Social
Democracy.

[The other partners in the coalition Government tried to
mediate, but the compromise proposals would all probably have
led to a reduction of unemployment benefits. Social Democracy
was willing to make concessions in other fields, like agreeing to
the raising of indirect, reduction of direct, taxes, in order to
gain agreement to a maintenance of the unemployment benefits, but this was not acceptable.]

The attack of the *Deutsche Volkspartei* is not only against unemployment insurance. It is directed against the whole of the
social welfare activity of the Reich, States and municipalities,
and thus against the basis of existence of the working class.

The Social-Democratic Party used its influence in the coalition Government to ward off the social reactionary plan of the
employers' associations . . .

Social Democracy will continue the fight which it had fought
within the Government even outside it.

We don't know what developments we may have to face.
Serious conflicts threaten.

The working masses must preserve a closer unity than ever,
ready for defence and for attack . . .

190. *Declaration of Social-Democratic Deputies of the Reichstag,*
18 October 1930

Brüning's Government also found it difficult to gain Reichstag
support for its policy for dealing with the economic crisis, though it

was initially kept in office by the Social Democrats, who would
not support any moves against him. The following declaration sets
out their reason for doing so.

Source: E. R. Huber, *Dokumente zur deutschen Verfassungsgeschichte*
(Stuttgart, Kohlhammer, 1966), vol. iii, p. 430 (trans. Ed.).

Social Democracy has fought against the Brüning Cabinet in
the elections. It still opposed this Government strongly. Nevertheless it has not moved a non-confidence motion against it, and
it has rejected the no-confidence motions moved by National
Socialists, Communists, and others. This does not mean that
Social Democracy has confidence in the present Government . . .
    The Social-Democratic group can bring about the fall of the
Government any day if it combines with National Socialists,
Communists or Nationalists, but it can never form a Government with such allies. Therefore, and because it has a sense of
responsibility for the working class—it refuses support to no-
confidence motions of other parties—of parties like the National
Socialists or the Nationalists, which are openly inimical to the
workers, or like the Communists, who, by their tactics, weaken
the working class and strengthen Fascism.
    Social Democracy and the free trade unions are the bastion
against the domination of Fascism in Germany. The whole
working class must support the parliamentary struggle of the
Social-Democratic deputies . . . with all its power.

191. *Ordinance for the Protection of the People and State,
28 February 1933*

Hitler accepted the Chancellorship on 30 January 1933 only on
condition that new Reichstag elections, refused by the President to
Chancellor Schleicher, would be held on 5 March. In the period
of the campaign, on 27 February, the building of the Reichstag was
burned down. The National Socialists claimed the fire was the
result of a Communist conspiracy, and persuaded President Hinden-
burg to issue the following ordinance, directed 'against Communist
acts of violence' but in fact used by Hitler against all his political
opponents.

Source: *British and Foreign State Papers*, vol. cxxxvi (1933), pp. 7-9.

In virtue of article 48, paragraph 2, of the Constitution of the Reich (No. 184), the following is ordered as a protection against Communist acts of violence imperilling the State:

1. Articles 114, 115, 117, 123, 124 and 153 of the Constitution of the German Reich (No. 184) are invalidated until further notice. Restrictions on personal freedom, on the right of free expression of opinion, including freedom of the press, and on rights of association and assembling, encroachments on the secrecy of letters, post, telephone and telegraph, and orders for domiciliary searches and for the confiscation of or restrictions on property, are therefore permissible even outside the legal bounds otherwise set for this purpose.

2. If in any State the necessary steps for the restoration of public safety and order are not taken, the Government of the Reich may thus far temporarily take over the powers of the supreme State authorities . . . [The rest of the ordinance contains the punishments prescribed for infringement of this ordinance, and of general laws; punishment by death is prescribed for crimes of violence.]

192. *Law to relieve the Distress of the People and the Reich, 24 March 1933*

When the new Reichstag met, with Communist deputies prevented from attending, Hitler introduced the following 'enabling law' which, in effect, suspended the Constitution and gave Hitler unlimited power to issue laws. Only the Social Democrats opposed the measure, and thus Hitler gained the majority prescribed in Article 76 of the Constitution (No. 184) even though the NSDAP only had 43·9% of the seats of the Reichstag.

Source: *British and Foreign State Papers*, vol. cxxxvi (1933), pp. 9–10.

1. Laws of the Reich can be passed not only in the manner prescribed by the constitution of the Reich but also by the Government of the Reich . . .

2. Laws passed by the Government of the Reich can be at variance with the constitution of the Reich so long as they do not deal with the actual institution of the Reichstag or of the Reichsrat. The rights of the President of the Reich remain untouched.

D E C—FF

3. Laws passed by the Government of the Reich will be drawn up by the Chancellor of the Reich and published . . .

193. *The 'Gleichschaltung', 1933–34*

The word *Gleichschaltung*, of which there is no exact English equivalent but which is usually translated as 'co-ordination', was used in Germany to describe the process by which Hitler transformed Germany from a federal parliamentary State into a unitary dictatorship while never formally repudiating the Weimar Constitution. The laws which follow illustrate the steps taken to establish the Chancellor as the only effective power, and to establish Party domination in Germany.

Source: (a) to (d) *British and Foreign State Papers*, vol. cxxxvi (1933), pp. 10–15, 22–3.

     (e) Rappard's *Source Book on European Government* (New York, Van Nostrand, 1937), p. IV 16.

(a) Provisional Law for Establishing Uniformity between the States and Reich, 31 March 1933.

1. (1) The Governments of the States are authorized to pass State laws otherwise than by the procedure contemplated in the State constitution . . .

4. (1) The representative bodies of the States . . . are hereby dissolved . . .

(2) They shall be formed afresh in accordance with the number of votes cast within each State for the electoral lists in the Reichstag election of the 5th March 1933. No seats will be allotted to electoral lists of the Communist Party . . .

12. (1) The self-governing municipal bodies . . . are hereby dissolved.

(2) They will be formed afresh in accordance with the number of valid votes cast in the area in question at the Reichstag elections of the 5th March 1933. No account will be taken of votes cast for Communist Party lists . . .

(b) Second German Law for Establishing Uniformity between the States and the Reich, 7 April 1933 (as modified to 14 October 1933).

1. (1) The President of the Reich, on the proposal of the Chancellor of the Reich, shall appoint Reich Governors (*Reichstatt-*

halter) in the German States, with the exception of Prussia. The Reich Governor has the duty of assuring the observance of the main lines of policy laid down by the Chancellor of the Reich. He possesses the following authority in the realm of State power:

  (i) Appointment and dismissal of the head of the State Government . . .
  (ii) Dissolution of the Diet and ordering of fresh elections . . .
  (iii) Drafting and promulgation of State laws . . .
  (iv) Appointment and dismissal . . . of directly employed State officials and judges . . .
  (v) The right of pardon . . .

2. (1) The Reich Governor may not at the same time be a member of a State Government . . .

3. (1) The Reich Governor may at any time be removed from office by the President of the Reich on the proposal of the Chancellor . . .

4. Votes of no confidence passed by the State Diet against the head and members of the State Governments are not permitted . . .

(c) Law forbidding the Formation of Parties, 14 July 1933.

1. The only political party existing in Germany is the National Socialist German Workers' Party.

2. Whoever takes steps to maintain the organized existence of another political party or to form a new political party will . . . be punished with penal servitude up to 3 years or with imprisonment from 6 months to 3 years.

(d) Law to secure the Unity of the Party and the State, 1 December 1933.

1. (1) As a result of the victory of the National Socialist revolution, the National Socialist German Workers' Party is the custodian of the German national sentiment and is indissolubly connected with the State . . .

2. In order to guarantee the closest co-operation between the officials of the Party and of the S.A. and the public authorities, the Deputy of the Leader and the Chief of Staff of the S.A. shall be members of the Government of the Reich.

3. (1) There devolve on members of the National Socialist

German Workers' Party and of the S.A. . . . . as the leading and controlling force in the National Socialist State, additional duties towards Leader, people and State . . .

6. The public authorities must, within the limits of their competence, render official and legal assistance to the officials of the Party and of the S.A. who are entrusted with the exercise of Party and S.A. jurisdiction . . .

(e) Law for the New Structure of the Reich, 30 January 1934.

1. The state legislatures are abolished.

2. (1) The rights of the states are transferred to the Reich.

(2) The state cabinets are subordinate to the national cabinet.

3. The Reich governors come under the supervision of the national minister of the interior.

4. The national cabinet is empowered to prepare a new constitution.

5. The national minister of the interior decrees the necessary legal ordinances and administrative provisions for the execution of this law . . .

194. *The Nürnberg Laws, 1935*

Anti-Semitism was endemic in Germany even before the First World War, but Hitler and his followers went much further: they developed a racial ideology (cf. No. 185, particularly Article 4) based on an alleged superiority of the Aryan race of which the Germans are the purest strain. To maintain this purity and to avoid its contamination by allegedly inferior races, a series of laws was passed on 15 September 1935. Parts of two of these laws and of ordinances based on them follow.

Source: *British and Foreign State Papers*, vol. cxxix (1935), pp. 481–3, 485–9.

(a) German Citizenship Law, 15 September 1935.

1. (1) A national is a person who belongs to the protective association of the German Reich and as a result is under special obligations to it.

(2) Nationality is acquired in accordance with the provisions of the Reich and State nationality laws.

2. (1) Only a national of German or similar blood, who proves

by his behaviour that he is willing and able loyally to serve the German people and Reich, is a citizen of the Reich . . .

(b) Law for the Protection of German Blood and German Honour, 15 September 1935.

Inspired by the realization that the purity of German blood is the pre-requisite for the continued existence of the German people, and animated by the inflexible determination to assure the German nation for all time, the Reichstag has unanimously passed the following law, which is promulgated herewith:

1. (1) Marriages between Jews and nationals of German or similar blood are forbidden. Marriages concluded in spite of this are invalid, even if they have been contracted with a view to circumventing this law . . .
2. Extra-marital intercourse between Jews and nationals of German or similar blood is forbidden.
3. Jews may not employ in their households female nationals of German or similar blood under 45 years of age.
4. (1) Jews are forbidden to hoist the Reich and national flags and to show the Reich colours.
They are, on the other hand, allowed to show the Jewish colours . . .

(c) First Ordinance under the Reich Citizenship Law, 14 November 1935.

1. (1) . . . Nationals of German or similar blood who possessed the right to vote at Reichstag elections at the time of the entry into force of the Reich citizenship law . . . shall be provisionally regarded as Reich citizens . . .
2. (2) A person of mixed Jewish blood is one descended from one or two grandparents of full Jewish race, provided that he is not regarded as a Jew within the meaning of Art. 5, paragraph 2. A grandparent shall be regarded forthwith as a full Jew if he has been a member of the Jewish religious community . . .
4. (1) A Jew may not be a citizen of the Reich. He has no vote in political matters; he may not fill public office.
(2) Jewish officials will be retired on the 31st December 1935 . . .

5. (1) A Jew is a person descended from at least three grand-parents of fully Jewish blood . . .

(2) A person is also regarded as a Jew if he or she is a national of mixed Jewish blood descended from two grandparents who are full Jews if:

(a) At the time of the enactment of the law he or she belonged to the Jewish religious community or joined it after that date.

(b) At the time of the enactment of the law he or she was married to a Jewess or Jew or contracted such a marriage after that date . . .

(d) First Ordinance for the Execution of the Law for the Protection of German Blood and German Honour, 14 November 1935.

. . . 2. Marriages between Jews and nationals of mixed Jewish blood who have only one fully Jewish grandparent shall also belong to the category of marriages forbidden . . .

3. (1) Nationals of mixed Jewish blood with two grandparents who are full Jews require the permission of the Reich Minister for the Interior and the deputy of the Leader . . . in order to contract a marriage with nationals of German or similar blood or with nationals of mixed Jewish blood who have only one full Jewish grandparent . . .

4. A marriage shall not be contracted between nationals of mixed Jewish blood who have only one full Jewish grand-parent . . .

XVIII · RUSSIA AND THE SOVIET UNION,[1] 1918–39

AFTER the dissolution of the Constituent Assembly (No. 173), the Third Congress of Soviets formally laid the foundations of a Soviet State (No. 195), the principles of which were elaborated in the 1918 constitution of the Russian Socialist Federated Soviet Republic (RSFSR)[1] (No. 196). The ensuing years, described officially as the period of civil war and foreign intervention, were difficult ones for the new régime which had to fight anti-revolutionary forces and foreign troops at the same time as it was reorganizing the economic and social system of the State. Foreign Communist parties, now organized in the Third, or Communist, International (No. 197) could be of little assistance as many of them were looking for assistance from the RSFSR themselves. The result of these difficulties was economic and social disruption, and a running down of productive forces which could not be reversed by strictly socialist means because of great popular discontent, of which the insurrection of the Kronstadt sailors (No. 198) was the most noticeable sign.

To pacify the country and build up its productive capacity the Communist Party agreed to a New Economic Policy (NEP) which introduced a modified market economy in the field of agriculture (No. 200), light industry and small-scale commerce. To maintain the unity and coherence of the Communist Party in such adverse conditions, its Tenth Congress agreed to a resolution on party unity (No. 199) which in later years was often used to defeat groups within the Party which opposed the policy of the leadership. It is regretted that no really informative document on the intra-party struggles of this period could be included.

[1] The name 'Soviet Union' or, more correctly, 'Union of Soviet Socialist Republics', came into official use in late 1922 when Transcaucasian provinces joined the RSFSR.

Greater emphasis than under NEP was placed on the development of heavy industry by the resolutions of the Fourteenth Party Congress in 1925 (No. 201) which led in 1928, after the defeat by Stalin of the Left Opposition, to the introduction of the five-year plans, and, later in the same year, after the defeat of the Right Opposition, to the collectivization of agriculture and the elimination of the kulaks as a class (No. 202).

The Great Purges of the nineteen thirties are illustrated by some brief documents taken from Khrushchev's secret speech of 1956 (No. 204) while the structure of the Communist Party and of the USSR in this period is elucidated by excerpts from the party rules of 1934 (No. 203) and the 1936 constitution of the Soviet Union (No. 205).

195. *Resolution of the Third Congress of Soviets, 28 January 1918*

The Third Congress of Soviets convened a few days after the dissolution of the Constituent Assembly (No. 173). In meetings between 21 and 31 January it drew up the basic outlines of the new state and society.

The following resolution sets the seal on the assumption of power by the Soviets.

Source: J. Bunyan and H. H. Fisher, *The Bolshevik Revolution 1917–1918* (Stanford, Calif., Stanford University Press, 1934), pp. 396–7.

1. The Russian Socialist Soviet Republic is a federation of Soviet republics founded on the principle of a free union of the peoples of Russia.
2. The highest organ of government in the federation is the All-Russian Congress of Soviets of Workers', Soldiers', Peasants', and Cossacks' Deputies, meeting at least once every three months.
3. The All-Russian Congress of Soviets . . . selects the All-Russian Central Executive Committee. In the interim between the Congresses the All-Russian Central Executive Committee is the highest organ of government.
4. The Government of the federation, the Soviet of People's Commissars, is elected or dismissed in whole or in part by the All-Russian Congress of Soviets or the All-Russian Central Executive Committee.

5. The manner in which separate Soviet Republics and particular territories having peculiar customs and national organizations may participate in the federal government, as well as the delimitation of the respective spheres of federal and regional administration within the Russian Republic, shall be determined immediately upon the formation of regional Soviet republics by the All-Russian Central Executive Committee and the Central Executive Committee of these republics.

6. All local matters are settled exclusively by the local Soviets. Higher Soviets have the right to regulate affairs between the lower Soviets and to settle differences that may arise between them. The Central Soviet Government sees to it that the fundamental principles of the federation are not violated and represents the Russian Soviet Federation as a whole. The central Government looks after matters that concern the states as a whole, but it must not encroach on the rights of the separate regions that make up the federation.

7. The Central Executive Committee of the Soviets is charged with the drafting of a constitution for the Russian Federated Soviet Republic [to be] submitted at the next Congress of Soviets.

196. The Constitution of the RSFSR, 10 July 1918

The Fifth Congress of Soviets which met in July 1918 adopted a full-scale constitution based on the principles enunciated at the Second (No. 171) and Third (No. 195) Congresses. Section I of this Constitution, 'Declaration of Rights of the Labouring and Exploited People', repeats the Declaration of the same title submitted to, but rejected by, the Constituent Assembly (No. 173(a)). Brief selections from other parts of the Constitution have been chosen to show some of the principles underlying the Soviet State and its structure.

Source: Howard L. McBain and Lindsay Rogers, *The New Constitutions of Europe* (Garden City, New York, Doubleday Page & Co., 1922), pp. 385–400.

. . . SECTION II

GENERAL PROVISIONS OF THE CONSTITUTION OF THE [RSFSR] . . .

9. The fundamental problem of the constitution of the [RSFSR] involves, in view of the present transition period,

the establishment of a dictatorship of the urban and rural proletariat and the poorest peasantry in the form of a powerful All-Russian Soviet authority, for the purpose of abolishing the exploitation of men by men and of introducing Socialism, in which there will be neither a division into classes nor a state of autocracy.

10. The Russian Republic is a free Socialist society of all the working people of Russia. The entire power, within the boundaries of the [RSFSR], belongs to all the working people of Russia, united in urban and rural Soviets . . .

18. The [RSFSR] considers work the duty of every citizen of the Republic, and proclaims as its motto: 'He shall not eat who does not work' . . .

SECTION III

CONSTRUCTION OF THE SOVIET POWER

24. The All-Russian Congress of Soviets is the supreme power of the [RSFSR] . . .

25. The All-Russian Congress of Soviets is composed of representatives of urban Soviets . . . and of representatives of the provincial congresses of Soviets . . .

28. The All-Russian Congress elects an All-Russian Central Executive Committee of not more than 200 members . . .

30. In the periods between the convocation of the Congresses, the All-Russian Central Executive Committee is the supreme power of the Republic . . .

32. The All-Russian Central Executive Committee directs in a general way the activity of the Workers' and Peasants' Government and of all organs of the Soviet authority in the country, and it co-ordinates and regulates the operation of the Soviet constitution and of the resolutions of the All-Russian Congresses and of the central organs of the Soviet power . . .

35. The All-Russian Central Executive Committee forms a Council of People's Commissars for the purpose of general management of the affairs of the [RSFSR] . . .

53. Congresses of Soviets are composed as follows:

(1) Regional: of representatives of the urban and county Soviets . . . or of representatives of the provincial Congresses . . .

(2) Provincial: of representatives of urban and rural Soviets . . .

(3) County: of representatives of rural Soviets . . .

(4) Rural: of representatives of all village Soviets in the Volost (district) . . .

55. Every Congress of Soviets (regional, provincial, county and rural) elects its Executive organ—an Executive Committee . . .

57. Soviets of Deputies are formed:

(1) In cities, one deputy for each one thousand inhabitants; the total to be not less than 50 and not more than 1,000 members.

(2) All other settlements (towns, villages, hamlets, etc.) of less than 10,000 inhabitants one deputy for each 100 inhabitants; the total to be not less than 3 and not more than 50 deputies for each settlement . . .

58. The Soviet of Deputies elects an Executive Committee to deal with current affairs . . .

64. The right to vote and to be elected to the Soviets is enjoyed by the following citizens, irrespective of religion, nationality, domicile, etc . . . of both sexes, who shall have completed their eighteenth year . . .:

(1) All who have acquired the means of living through labour that is productive and useful to society, and also persons engaged in housekeeping, which enables the former to do productive work . . .

(2) Soldiers of the army and navy of the Soviets.

(3) Citizens of the two preceding categories who have to any degree lost their capacity to work . . .

65. The following persons enjoy neither the right to vote nor the right to be voted for, even though they belong to one of the categories enumerated above, namely:

(1) Persons who employ hired labour in order to obtain from it an increase in profits.

(2) Persons who have an income without doing any work, such as interest from capital, receipts from property, etc.

(3) Private merchants, trade and commercial brokers.

(4) Monks and clergy of all denominations.

(5) Employees and agents of the former police, the gendarme corps, and the Okhrana,[1] also members of the former reigning dynasty . . .

---

[1] The Imperial secret police.

197. *Statutes of the Communist International (Comintern),*
4 August 1920

The Second International (cf. No. 109) disintegrated at the outbreak of the First World War and by the end of the war it was clear that moderate socialists, or Social-democrats, would not again be able to form a common body with the extremists, the Communists. It was on Russian Communist initiative that an international meeting was convened at Moscow between 2-6 March 1919 to found an international Communist body. The statutes which follow were adopted by the second meeting of the Comintern in August 1920.

Source: *The Communist International 1919–1943* by Jane Degras (Oxford University Press under the auspices of the Royal Institute of International Affairs), vol. i, 1956, pp. 162–6.

In 1864 the International Workingmen's Association, the First International, was founded in London. Its provisional rules ran as follows:

[See the first six paragraphs of No. 98.]

The Second International, founded in Paris in 1889, undertook to carry on the work of the First International. But in 1914, at the beginning of the world slaughter, it suffered complete breakdown. Undermined by opportunism and shattered by the treachery of its leaders, who went over to the side of the bourgeoisie, the Second International collapsed.

The Communist International, founded in March 1919 in the capital of the Russian Federal Soviet Republic, Moscow, solemnly declares before the entire world that it undertakes to continue and to carry through to the end the great work begun by the First International Workingmen's Association.

The Communist International was formed after the conclusion of the imperialist war of 1914–18, in which the imperialist bourgeoisie of the different countries sacrificed 20 million men . . . Without the overthrow of capitalism the repetition of such robber wars is not only possible, but inevitable.

It is the aim of the Communist International to fight by all available means, including armed struggle, for the overthrow of the international bourgeoisie and for the creation of an international Soviet republic as a transitional stage to the complete abolition of the State. The Communist International considers the dictatorship of the proletariat the only possible way to liberate mankind from the horrors of capitalism. And the Communist International considers the Soviet power the historically given form of this dictatorship of the proletariat.

The imperialist war bound the destinies of the proletariat of each country very closely to the destinies of the proletariat of all other countries. The imperialist war once again confirmed what was written in the statutes of the First International: the emancipation of the workers is not a local, nor a national, but an international problem.

The Communist International breaks once and for all with the traditions of the Second International, for whom in fact only white-skinned peoples existed. The task of the Communist International is to liberate the working people of the entire world . . .

The Communist International supports to the full the conquests of the great proletarian revolution in Russia . . . and calls on the proletariat of the entire world to take the same path. The Communist International undertakes to support every Soviet republic, wherever it may be formed.

The Communist International recognizes that in order to hasten victory, the Workingmen's Association which is fighting to annihilate capitalism and create communism must have a strongly centralized organization. The Communist International must, in fact and in deed, be a single communist party of the entire world. The parties working in the various countries are but its separate sections. The organizational machinery of the Communist International must guarantee the workers of each country the opportunity of getting the utmost help from the organized proletariat of other countries at any given moment.

For this purpose the Communist International ratifies the following statutes:

1. The new international association of workers is established to organize joint action by the proletariat of the different countries which pursue the one goal: the overthrow of capitalism, the establishment of the dictatorship of the proletariat and of an international Soviet republic which will completely

abolish all classes and realize socialism, the first stage of communist society.

2. The new international association of workers is called 'The Communist International'.

3. All parties belonging to the Communist International bear the name 'Communist Party of such and such a country (section of the Communist International)'.

4. The supreme authority in the Communist International is the world congress of all the parties and organizations which belong to it . . .

5. The world congress elects the Executive Committee of the Communist International, which is the directing body of the Communist International in the period between its world congresses . . .

8. The chief work of the Executive Committee falls on the party of that country where, by decision of the world congress, the Executive Committee has its seat. The party of the country in question shall have five representatives with full voting powers on the Executive Committee. In addition the ten to thirteen most important communist parties, the list to be ratified by the regular world congress, shall each have one representative with full voting power . . .

9. The Executive Committee conducts the entire work of the Communist International from one congress to the next, publishes, in at least four languages, the central organ of the Communist International . . . issues any necessary appeals . . . and issues instructions which are binding on all parties and organizations belonging to the Communist International. The Executive Committee of the Communist International has the right to demand that parties belonging to the International shall expel groups or persons who offend against international discipline, and it also has the right to expel from the Communist International those parties which violate decisions of the world congress . . .

12. The general situation all over Europe and America compels communists throughout the world to create illegal communist organizations side by side with the legal organization. The Executive Committee is obliged to see that this is put into effect everywhere . . .

14. Trade unions adhering to the communist platform and

organized internationally under the leadership of the Communist International, shall form a trade union section of the Communist International . . .

198. *Demands of the Kronstadt Sailors, 1 March 1921*

The period of civil war and foreign intervention and the concurrent reorganization of the country on socialist lines created a critical economic and social situation. Productivity fell, famine threatened, and the Government and the Party were in a precarious position. Discontent was strong, particularly in the countryside. It gained violent expression in the insurrection of the sailors at the naval base of Kronstadt, near Petrograd. The sailors' demands were not accepted, and the insurrection was crushed ruthlessly, but, partly as a result, far-reaching concessions soon followed.

Source: W. H. Chamberlin, *The Russian Revolution 1917–1921* (New York, Macmillan, 1935), vol. ii, pp. 495–6.

Having heard the report of the representatives of the Crews, despatched by the General Meeting of the Crews from the ships to Petrograd in order to learn the state of affairs in Petrograd we decided:

1. In view of the fact that the present Soviets do not represent the will of the workers and peasants, immediately to re-elect the Soviets by secret voting, with free preliminary agitation among all workers and peasants before the elections.
2. Freedom of speech and press for workers, peasants, Anarchists and Left Socialist Parties.
3. Freedom of meetings, trade unions and peasant associations.
4. To convene . . . a nonparty conference of workers, soldiers and sailors of Petrograd City, Kronstadt and Petrograd Province.
5. To liberate all political prisoners of Socialist Parties, and also all workers, peasants, soldiers and sailors who have been imprisoned in connexion with working class and peasant movements.
6. To elect a commission to review the cases of those who are imprisoned in gaols and concentration camps.
7. To abolish all Political Departments, because no single party may enjoy privileges in the propaganda of its ideas and receive funds from the state for this purpose. Instead of these

Departments locally elected cultural-educational commissions must be established and supported by the state.

8. All 'cordon detachments'[1] are to be abolished immediately.

9. To equalize rations for all workers, harmful departments being excepted.

10. To abolish all Communist fighting detachments in all military units, and also various Communist guards at factories. If such detachments and guards are needed they may be chosen from the companies in military units and in factories according to the judgement of the workers.

11. To grant the peasant full right to do what he sees fit with his land and also to possess cattle, which he must maintain and manage with his own strength, but without employing hired labour . . .

15. To permit free artisan production with individual labour.

The resolutions were adopted by the Meeting [of the Crews of the Ships of the Line] unanimously, with two abstentions.

199. *Resolution on Party Unity, 16 March 1921*

Discontent with the economic and social policy of the Soviet Government (cf. No. 198) was so widespread by 1921 that the Communist leadership realized Soviet rule could only be maintained if the Communist Party closed its ranks and presented a united front. The following resolution was adopted by the Tenth Party Congress with the aim of preventing organized opposition to the leadership from arising within the Party, and thus of ensuring strong, united leadership in the critical situation. This was all the more necessary as the New Economic Policy (NEP), introduced a few days later (No. 200), could be regarded as a retreat from Marxist principles and therefore could provoke well-justified criticism from Party members. The resolution was used extensively in the following years to deal with groups in opposition to the leadership within the Party.

Source: W. H. Chamberlin, *The Russian Revolution 1917–1921* (New York, Macmillan, 1935), vol. ii, pp. 497–9.

1. The Congress directs the attention of all members of the Party to the fact that the unity and solidarity of its ranks . . . is especially necessary at the present moment, when a number

---

[1] Requisitioning detachments which searched passengers on the trains for food.

of circumstances increase the waverings among the petty-
bourgeois population of the country.

2. On the other hand, even before the general Party discussion
about the trade unions, some signs of fractionalism were manifested in the Party. Groups grew up with special platforms
and with a desire to maintain a separate existence to a certain
degree and to create their own group discipline.

All class-conscious workers must clearly recognize the harm
and impermissibility of any kind of fractionalism, which inevitably leads in fact to the weakening of energetic work and
to the strengthening of the repeated attempts of enemies who
have crept into the governing Party to deepen the differences
and to exploit them for counter-revolutionary purposes . . .

3. Propaganda in this question must consist, on one hand, in a
detailed explanation of the harm and danger of fractionalism
. . .; on the other hand, in an exposition of the peculiarity of
the latest tactical devices of the enemies of the Soviet régime . . .

4. Every Party organization must very strictly see to it that the
absolutely necessary criticism of the failings of the Party, that
any analysis of the general policy of the Party or appraisal of
its practical experience . . . should be submitted not for the
consideration of groups which have formed on the basis of
some 'platform' etc., but for the consideration of all the
members of the Party . . .

6. The Congress gives instructions that all groups which have
been organized on the basis of some platform should be immediately dissolved and commissions all organizations to watch
out very closely, so that no fractional demonstrations may be
permitted. Nonfulfilment of this decision of the Congress must
bring as its consequence unconditional and immediate expulsion from the Party.

200. *The New Economic Policy: Decree on the Tax in Kind, 23 March 1921*

The decree that follows, the first measure in the New Economic
Policy (NEP), showed a retreat from strictly Marxist principles.
By replacing requisitioning with the tax in kind, the Government
took the first step towards the establishment of a modified market
economy. This step was soon followed by the handing back of light
and small-scale industry to private ownership and management.

The State retained heavy industry, banking and foreign trade in
its own hands.

Source: W. H. Chamberlin, *The Russian Revolution 1917–1921* (New
York, Macmillan, 1935), vol. ii, pp. 499–501.

1. In order to assure an efficient and untroubled economic
life on the basis of a freer use by the farmer of the products of
his labour and of his economic resources, in order to strengthen
the peasant economy and raise its productivity and also in
order to calculate precisely the obligation to the State which
falls on the peasants, requisitioning, as a means of state collection of food supplies, raw material and fodder, is to be
replaced by a tax in kind.

2. This tax must be less than what the peasant has given up to
this time through requisitions . . .

3. The tax is to be taken in the form of a percentage or partial
deduction from the products raised in the peasant holding,
taking into account the harvest, the number of eaters in the
holding and the number of cattle.

4. The tax must be progressive; the percentage must be lower
for the holdings of middleclass and poorer peasants and town
workers . . .

The industrious peasants who increase the amount of land
planted and the number of cattle in their holdings and those
who increase the general productivity of their holdings receive
privileges in paying the tax in kind . . .

7. The responsibility for paying the tax rests with each individual household . . .

8. All the reserves of food, raw material and fodder which
remain with the peasants after the tax has been paid are at
their full disposition and may be used by them for improving
and strengthening their holdings, for increasing personal
consumption and for exchange for products of factory and hand
industry and of agriculture.

Exchange is permitted within the limits of local economic
turnover, both through co-operative organizations and through
markets.

9. Those farmers who wish to deliver to the state the surplus
in their possession after the tax has been paid must receive,
in exchange for the voluntary delivery of this surplus, objects
of general consumption and agricultural machinery . . .

201. *Stalin's Report on Industrialization, 3 December 1927*

The modified market economy introduced by NEP had been under attack for some time by the 'Left Opposition', which wanted the capitalist elements of the system eliminated and much greater emphasis put on the heavy industries, when, at the Fourteenth Party Congress (the so-called 'industrialization Congress') of 1925 Stalin introduced some resolutions dealing with industrialization. It was on the basis of these resolutions that the Five Year Plans were introduced in 1928, after Stalin succeeded in exiling Trotsky and breaking the Left Opposition.

The resolutions of the Fourteenth Congress are here summed up by Stalin's report, on behalf of the Central Committee of the Party, to the Fifteenth Party Congress in 1927.

Source: J. V. Stalin, *Works* (London, Lawrence and Wishart, 1955), vol. x, pp. 298–9.

The Fourteenth Congress of our Party instructed the Central Committee to direct the development of our national economy from the standpoint of the following principal tasks:

firstly, that our policy should promote the progressive growth of production in the national economy as a whole;

secondly, that the Party's policy should promote the acceleration of the rate of development of industry and ensure for industry the leading role in the whole of the national economy;

thirdly, that in the course of development of the national economy, the socialist sector of the national economy, the socialist forms of economy, should be ensured ever-increasing relative importance at the expense of the private-commodity and capitalist sectors;

fourthly, that our economic development as a whole, the organization of the new branches of industry, the development of certain branches for raw materials, etc., should be conducted along such lines that the general development should ensure the economic independence of our country, that our country should not become an appendage of the capitalist system of world economy;

fifthly, that the dictatorship of the proletariat, the bloc of the working class and the peasant masses, and the leadership by the working class in this bloc, should be strengthened, and

sixthly, that the material and cultural conditions of the working class and of the rural poor should be steadily improved . . .

202. *Stalin's Speech on Agrarian Policy, 27 December 1929*

A natural concomitant of industrialization (cf. No. 201) was the reorganization of agriculture to eliminate the capitalist elements existing under NEP and to free resources and labour for industry. A policy of collectivization and of eliminating the kulaks as a class began after the breaking of the power of the Right Opposition, in 1928. This agrarian policy was summed up by Stalin in a speech at the end of 1929, excerpts of which follow.

Source: J. V. Stalin, *Works* (London, Lawrence and Wishart, 1955), vol. xii, pp. 172–5.

. . . The characteristic feature in the work of our Party during the past year is that we, as a party, as the Soviet Power:

a) have developed an offensive along the whole front against capitalist elements in the countryside;

b) that this offensive, as you know, has yielded and continues to yield very appreciable, *positive* results.

What does this mean? It means that we have passed from the policy of *restricting* the exploiting tendencies of the kulaks to the policy of *eliminating* the kulaks as a class. It means that we have carried out, and are continuing to carry out, one of the decisive turns in our whole policy.

Until recently the Party adhered to the policy of *restricting* the exploiting tendencies of the kulaks . . . Was this policy correct? Yes, it was absolutely correct at the time. Could we have undertaken such an offensive against the kulaks some five years or three years ago? Could we then have counted on success in such an offensive? No, we could not. That would have been the most dangerous adventurism. It would have been a very dangerous playing at an offensive. For we should certainly have failed, and our failure would have strengthened the position of the kulaks. Why? Because we did not yet have in the countryside strong points in the form of a wide network of state farms and collective farms which could be the basis for a determined offensive against the kulaks. Because at that time we were not yet able to *replace* the capitalist production of the kulaks by the socialist production of the collective farms and state farms . . .

An offensive against the kulaks is a serious matter. It should not be confused with declamations against the kulaks. Nor should it be confused with a policy of pin-pricks against the kulaks, which the Zinoviev-Trotsky opposition did its utmost to impose upon the Party. To launch an offensive against the kulaks means that we must smash the kulaks, eliminate them as a class. Unless we set ourselves these aims, an offensive would be mere declamation, pin-pricks, phrase-mongering, anything but a real Bolshevik offensive. To launch an offensive against the kulaks means that we must prepare for it and then strike at the kulaks, strike so hard as to prevent them from rising to their feet again . . .

Today, we have an adequate material base for us to strike at the kulaks, to break their resistance, to eliminate them as a class, and to *replace* their output by the output of the collective farms and state farms . . .

203. *Rules of the Communist Party of the Soviet Union, 10 February 1934*

Excerpts from the rules of the CPSU, adopted by the Seventeenth Party Congress, are here included to give some information about the party structure during the nineteen thirties.

Source: Rappard's *Source Book on European Government* (New York, Van Nostrand, 1937), pp. V 34–52.

The All-Union Communist Party (Bolsheviks), being a section of the Communist International (cf. No. 197), is the organized vanguard of the proletariat of the Union of Soviet Socialist Republics (USSR), the highest form of its class organization.

The Party effects the leadership of the proletariat, the toiling peasantry and all toiling masses in the struggle for the dictatorship of the proletariat, for the victory of socialism.

The Party leads all organs of the proletarian dictatorship and ensures the successful construction of socialist society.

The Party is a unified militant organization held together by conscious, iron proletarian discipline. The Party is strong because of its coherence, unity of will and unity of action which are incompatible with any deviation from its programme, with any violation of Party discipline or with factional groupings within the Party. The Party demands from all its members active and self-sacrificing work to carry out the programme and rules of the Party, to fulfil all decisions of the Party and its organs, to ensure unity within the Party and the consolidation of the fraternal international relations among the toilers of the nationalities of the USSR as well as among the proletarians of the whole world ...

1. A Party member is anyone who accepts the programme of the Party, who works in one of its organizations, submits to its decisions, and pays membership dues ...

18. The guiding principle of the organizational structure of the Party is democratic centralism, which signifies:

(a) The application of the elective principle to all leading organs of the Party, from the highest to the lowest;

(b) The periodic accountability of the Party organs to their respective Party organizations;

(c) Strict Party discipline and subordination of the minority to the majority;

(d) The absolutely binding character of the decisions of the higher organs upon the lower organs and upon all Party members ...

23. The scheme of the Party organization is as follows:

(a) USSR—All-Union Congress—Central Committee of the Party;

(b) Regions, ... republics—Regional Conferences, Congresses of the national Communist Parties—Regional Committees, Central Committees of the national Communist Parties.

(c) Cities, districts—city, district conferences—city, district committees.

(d) Factories, villages, collective farms, machine-tractor stations, Red Army units, offices—general meetings, primary Party organization conferences—primary Party committees (mill Party committee, factory Party committee, Red Army unit Party bureau etc.).

27. The supreme body of the Party is the Congress ...

29. The Congress ... elects a Central Committee, a Commission of Party Control, a Central Auditing Commission, and nominates the members of the Commission of Soviet Control ...

32. The Central Committee organizes a Political Bureau for political work, an Organizational Bureau for the general

guidance of the organizational work, and a Secretariat for current work of an organizational or executive nature.

33. ... The Central Committee directs the work of the central Soviet and public organizations through the Party groups in them ...

36. The Commission of Party Control:

(a) Controls the fulfilment of decisions of the Party and of the Central Committee of the Party;

(b) Brings proceedings against those who have violated Party discipline;

(c) Brings proceedings against those who have violated Party ethics ...

50. The primary Party organization connects the mass of the workers and peasants with the leading organs of the Party. Its tasks are:

(1) Agitational and organizational work among the masses for the Party slogans and decisions;

(2) The attraction of sympathizers and new members and their political training;

(3) Assistance to the City Committee or District Committee ... in its day-to-day work of organization and agitation;

(4) The mobilization of the masses at the factories, at the Soviet farms, at the collective farms, etc., for the fulfilment of the production plan, for the consolidation of labour discipline and the development of shock-brigade work;

(5) The struggle against laxity and mismanagement at the factories [etc.] and day-to-day solicitude for the improvement of the living conditions of the workers and collective farmers;

(6) Active participation, as a Party organ, in the economic and political life of the country ...

57. The free and business-like discussion of questions of Party policy in individual organizations or in the Party as a whole is the inalienable right of every Party member derived from internal Party democracy. Only on the basis of internal Party democracy is it possible to develop Bolshevik self-criticism and to strengthen Party discipline, which must be conscious and not mechanical. But extensive discussion, especially discussion on an All-Union scale, of questions of Party policy must be so organized that it cannot lead to attempts by an insignificant minority to impose its will upon the vast majority of the Party, or to

attempts to form factional groupings which break the unity of the Party, to attempts at a split which may shake the strength and endurance of dictatorship of the proletariat, to the delight of the enemies of the working class. Therefore a wide discussion on an All-Union scale can be regarded as necessary only if: (a) this necessity is recognized by at least several local Party organizations whose jurisdiction extends to a region or a republic; (b) if there is not a sufficiently solid majority in the Central Committee itself on very important questions of Party policy; (c) if in spite of the existence of a solid majority in the Central Committee which advocates a definite standpoint, the Central Committee still deems it necessary to test the correctness of its policy by means of a discussion in the Party. Only compliance with these conditions can safeguard the Party against an abuse of internal Party democracy by anti-Party elements; only under those conditions can internal Party democracy be counted on to be of profit to the cause and not to be used to the detriment of the Party and the working class.

58. The maintenance of Party unity, the relentless struggle against the slightest attempt at a factional fight or a split and the strictest Party and Soviet discipline are the foremost duties of all Party members and of all Party organizations. In order to realize strict discipline within the Party and in all Soviet work, and attain the greatest possible unity with the elimination of all factionalism, the Central Committee of the Party has the right, in the case of a violation of discipline, or of a revival or development of factionalism, to inflict any Party penalty including expulsion from the Party, and in the case of members of the Central Committee—demotion to candidateship and as an extreme measure, expulsion from the Party. The convocation of the plenum of the Central Committee, to which all alternate members of the Central Committee and all members of the Commission of Party Control are invited, must be a condition precedent for the application of such an extreme measure to any member of the Central Committee, alternate members of the Central Committee, or member of the Commission of Party Control. If such a general meeting of the most responsible leaders of the Party by a two-thirds' vote recognizes the necessity of demoting a member of the Central Committee or of the Commission of Party Control to a candidate,

or of expelling him from the Party, such measure must be immediately carried out . . .

204. *The Purges, 1931–39*

From the beginning of the nineteen thirties, when it became clear that the ambitious objectives of the first Five Year Plan could not be achieved, a series of purges began which went on until 1939. Beginning with non-party experts and technicians, the purges gradually extended into the Party. By the end of our period the majority of Soviet leadership and of the Soviet High Command, anybody who could be considered a potential threat to Stalin's position, was eliminated either by execution, or by imprisonment in a forced labour camp.

The following three documents, which became available only through Khrushchev's Special Report to the Twentieth Party Congress, may serve to illustrate the purges.

Source: *The Anti-Stalin Campaign and International Communism: a Selection of Documents* ed. by the Russian Institute, Columbia University (New York, Columbia University Press, 1956), pp. 25, 26, 41.

(a) Order of the Central Executive Committee, 1 December 1934.

1. Investigative agencies are directed to speed up the cases of those accused of the preparation or execution of acts of terror.

2. Judicial organs are directed not to hold up the execution of death sentences pertaining to crimes of this category in order to consider the possibility of pardon, because the Presidium of the Central Executive Committee [of the] USSR does not consider as possible the receiving of petitions of this sort.

3. The organs of the Commissariat of Internal Affairs [NKVD] are directed to execute death sentences against criminals of the above-mentioned category immediately after the passage of sentences.

(b) Stalin's and Zhdanov's Telegram to the Political Bureau, 25 September 1936.

We deem it absolutely necessary and urgent that Comrade Yezhov be nominated to the post of People's Commissar for Internal Affairs. Yagoda has definitely proved himself to be incapable of unmasking the Trotskyite-Zinovievite bloc. The OGPU[1] is 4 years behind in this matter. This is noted by all Party workers and by the majority of the representatives of the NKVD.

(c) Stalin's Telegram to Party Secretaries and the NKVD, 20 January 1939.

The Central Committee of the All-Union Communist Party (Bolsheviks) explains that the application of methods of physical pressure in NKVD practice is permissible from 1937 on in accordance with permission of the Central Committee . . . It is known that all bourgeois intelligence services use methods of physical influence against the representatives of the socialist proletariat and that they use them in their most scandalous form. The question arises as to why the socialist intelligence service should be more humanitarian against the mad agents of the bourgeoisie, against the deadly enemies of the working class and the kolkhoz[2] workers. The Central Committee of the All-Union Communist Party (Bolsheviks) considers that physical pressure should still be used obligatorily, as an exception applicable to known and obstinate enemies of the people, as a method both justifiable and appropriate.

205. The Constitution of the USSR, 5 December 1936

A new constitution of the USSR was drafted in early 1936 and the draft was submitted to public discussion by the population. It was finally passed, with some amendments suggested by public meetings, by the Congress of Soviets in December 1936.

The brief excerpts from the text are intended to illustrate the changes in the structure of the Soviet Union. The Constitution of 1918 (No. 196) may serve as a basis for comparison.

Source: Rappard's *Source Book on European Government* (New York, Van Nostrand, 1937), pp. V 107–29.

1. The Union of Soviet Socialist Republics (USSR) is a socialist state of workers and peasants.
2. The political foundation of the USSR is formed by the Soviets of toilers' deputies which have grown and become

---

[1] The 'Unified State Political Administration', the secret police.
[2] Collective farm.

strong as a result of the overthrow of the power of the landlords and capitalists and the conquests of the dictatorship of the proletariat.

3. All power in the USSR belongs to the toilers of the town and village in the form of Soviets of toilers' deputies.

4. The economic foundation of the USSR consists in the socialist system of economy and socialist ownership of the implements and means of production, firmly established as a result of the liquidation of the capitalist system of economy, the abolition of private ownership of the implements and means of production and the abolition of exploitation of man by man.

5. Socialist ownership in the USSR has either the form of state ownership (public property) or the form of co-operative and collective-farm ownership (property of individual collective farms, property of co-operative association) . . .

9. Alongside the socialist system of economy, which is the dominant form of economy in the USSR, the law allows small private economy of individual peasants and handicraftsmen based on individual labour and excluding the exploitation of the labour of others . . .

12. Work in the USSR is the obligation and matter of honour of each citizen capable of working, according to the principle: 'He who does not work shall not eat'. In the USSR the principle of socialism is being realized: 'From each according to his ability, to each according to his work' . . .

13. The USSR is a federal state, formed on the basis of the voluntary association of the Soviet Socialist Republics with equal rights . . .

30. The supreme organ of state power of the USSR is the Supreme Council [Soviet] of the USSR . . .

32. The legislative power of the USSR is exercised exclusively by the Supreme Council of the USSR.

33. The Supreme Council of the USSR consists of two Chambers: the Council of the Union and the Council of Nationalities.

34. The Council of the Union is elected by election districts by the citizens of the USSR on the basis of one deputy per 300,000 of population.

35. The Council of Nationalities is elected by the citizens of the USSR, by Union republics and autonomous republics, by autonomous regions and national districts, on the basis of 25

deputies from each Union republic, 11 deputies from each autonomous republic, 5 deputies from each autonomous region and one deputy from each national district . . .

48. The Supreme Council of the USSR elects, at a joint session of both chambers, the Presidium of the Supreme Council of the USSR . . .

56. The Supreme Council of the USSR at a joint session of both chambers forms the Government of the USSR—the Council of People's Commissars of the USSR . . .

64. The supreme executive and administrative organ of state power in the USSR is the Council of People's Commissars of the USSR . . .

94. The organs of state power in territories, provinces, autonomous provinces, regions, districts, cities and villages . . . are Soviets of toilers' deputies . . .

95. The Soviets of toilers' deputies of territories [etc.] are elected by the toilers of the respective territory [etc.] . . .

126. In accordance with the interests of the toilers and for the purpose of developing the organizational self-expression and political activity of the masses of the people, citizens of the USSR are ensured the right of combining in public organizations: trade unions, co-operative associations, youth organizations, sport and defence organizations, cultural, technical and scientific societies, and for the most active and conscientious citizens from the ranks of the working class and other strata of the toilers, of uniting in the All-Union Communist Party (of Bolsheviks), which is the vanguard of the toilers in their struggle for strengthening and developing the socialist system and which represents the leading nucleus of all organizations of the toilers, both public and state . . .

134. Deputies to all Soviets of toilers' deputies, the Supreme Council of the USSR [etc.] are elected by the electors on the basis of universal, equal and direct suffrage by secret ballot.

135. Elections of the deputies are universal: all citizens of the USSR who have reached the age of 18, irrespective of race or nationality, religion, educational qualifications, residential qualifications, social origin, property status and past activity, have the right to participate in elections of deputies and to be elected, with the exception of the mentally deficient and persons deprived of electoral rights by the courts . . .

141. Candidates are put forward for election according to electoral districts.

The right to put forward candidates is granted to social organizations and societies of the toilers: Communist Party organizations, trade unions, co-operatives, youth organizations and cultural societies . . .

XIX · INTERNATIONAL AFFAIRS,
1919–39

THE Covenant of the League of Nations (No. 206) which opens this section was to be the foundation stone of a new era of international relations characterized by the maintenance of peace and international co-operation. But the Covenant, which formed part of the Treaty of Versailles (No. 160) and the other peace treaties, did not assure the former Central Powers of equal treatment; they were not immediately admitted to the League of Nations, and remained under Allied control throughout most of the nineteen twenties (cf. Nos 186, 187, 188). It was only in 1922 that Germany was again treated as an equal by another Great Power, and even then it was by the Soviet Union (No. 207), another outcast.

The powers of the League of Nations to deal with threats to peace were not as strong as might have been desired; attempts were made at an early date to strengthen them, the most important such attempt being the Geneva Protocol (No. 208). This proposal went too far for the British Government, and thus was not adopted. It was thought, however, that the conclusion of regional treaties like the Locarno settlement (No. 209) and, later, the General Pact for the Renunciation of War (No. 210), would ensure the maintenance of peace.

Yet the Manchurian crisis (No. 211) showed the League's powers and its will to enforce its principles to be deficient, and this fact was further underlined by the collapse of the long-drawn-out disarmament negotiations when Germany, now under Hitler, withdrew from the Disarmament Conference and the League of Nations (No. 212). Even when Germany unilaterally denounced the military clauses of the Treaty of Versailles (No. 213) the League could take no effective action; the proposals put to the League Council by a special conference between France, Great Britain, and Italy (No. 214) were ineffectual.

The League did take action when Italy invaded Ethiopia (No. 215) but its action hardly hindered Italy and resulted in a joint front being formed by Italy and Germany which later denounced the Locarno agreements and re-occupied the Rhineland (No. 216) without earning more than verbal protests. The German-led block of Italy, Japan, and several small States was finally formalized by the Anti-Comintern Pact (No. 217) initially concluded between Germany and Japan. The friendship between Germany and Italy was also assisted by the Spanish Civil War (No. 218) in which these two powers almost openly assisted Franco's forces against the Republican Government.

The remaining documents illustrate the further steps leading up to the outbreak of the Second World War: the *Anschluss* of Austria in March 1938 (No. 219), the Munich Agreement (No. 220) which began the dismemberment of Czechoslovakia, and, finally, the German-Polish dispute and the outbreak of the war (No. 221).

206. *The Covenant of the League of Nations, 28 June 1919*

Although it forms Part I of the Treaty of Versailles (No. 160), the Covenant of the League of Nations is included at the beginning of this section because it served as the fundamental document in the international relations of the inter-war period.

The United States of America is mentioned several times in the Covenant, which is here included in its original form. The United States Senate rejected the Treaty of Versailles, and thus prevented the U.S.A. becoming a member of the League at the outset. The U.S.A. never became a member, although on several occasions (e.g. the Manchurian crisis, cf. No. 211) it co-operated closely with the League Council.

Source: *Treaty of Peace between the Allied and Associated Powers and Germany* . . . (London, H.M.S.O., 1919) (Cmd. 153).

THE HIGH CONTRACTING PARTIES

In order to promote international co-operation and to achieve international peace and security

by the acceptance of obligations not to resort to war,

by the prescription of open, just and honourable relations between nations, by the firm establishment of the understandings of international law as the actual rule of conduct among Governments, and

by the maintenance of justice and a scrupulous respect for all treaty obligations in the dealings of organized peoples with one another,

agree to this Covenant of the League of Nations.

1. The original members of the League of Nations shall be those of the signatories which are named in the Annex to this Covenant and also such of those other States named in the Annex as shall accede without reservation to this Covenant . . .

Any fully self-governing State, Dominion or Colony not named in the Annex may become a Member of the League if its admission is agreed to by two-thirds of the Assembly, provided that it shall give effective guarantees of its sincere intention to observe its international obligations, and shall accept such regulations as may be prescribed by the League in regard to its military, naval, and air forces and armaments.

Any Member of the League may, after two years' notice of its intention so to do, withdraw from the League . . .

2. The action of the League under this Covenant shall be effected through the instrumentality of an Assembly and of a Council, with a permanent Secretariat.

3. The Assembly shall consist of representatives of the Members of the League.

The Assembly shall meet at stated intervals and from time to time as occasion may require at the Seat of the League or at such other place as may be decided upon.

The Assembly may deal at its meetings with any matter within the sphere of action of the League or affecting the peace of the world.

At meetings of the Assembly each Member of the League shall have one vote, and may have not more than three representatives.

4. The Council shall consist of representatives of the Principal Allied and Associated Powers[1] together with representatives of four other Members of the League. These four Members of

[1] U.S.A., British Empire, France, Italy, and Japan. The U.S.A. did not ratify the Treaty of Versailles and thus did not become a member of the League.

the League shall be selected by the Assembly from time to time in its discretion . . .

With the approval of the majority of the Assembly, the Council may name additional Members of the League whose representatives shall always be members of the Council; the Council with like approval may increase the number of members of the League to be selected by the Assembly for representation on the Council.

The Council shall meet from time to time as occasion may require, and at least once a year, at the Seat of the League or at such other place as may be decided upon.

The Council may deal at its meetings with any matter within the sphere of action of the League or affecting the peace of the world.

Any Member of the League not represented on the Council shall be invited to send a representative to sit as a member at any meeting of the Council during the consideration of matters specially affecting the interests of that Member of the League.

At meetings of the Council, each Member of the League represented on the Council shall have one vote, and may have not more than one representative.

5. Except where otherwise expressly provided in this Covenant or by the terms of the present Treaty, decisions at any meeting of the Assembly or of the Council shall require the agreement of all the Members of the League represented at the meeting.

All matters of procedure at meetings of the Assembly or of the Council . . . may be decided by a majority of the Members . . .

6. The permanent Secretariat shall be established at the Seat of the League. The Secretariat shall comprise a Secretary-General and such secretaries and staff as may be required . . .

7. The Seat of the League is established at Geneva . . .

8. The Members of the League recognize that the maintenance of peace requires the reduction of national armaments to the lowest point consistent with national safety and the enforcement by common action of international obligations.

The Council, taking account of the geographical situation and circumstances of each State, shall formulate plans for such reduction for the consideration and action of the several Governments.

D E C—HH

Such plans shall be subject to reconsideration and revision at least every ten years.

After these plans shall have been adopted by the several Governments, the limits of armaments therein fixed shall not be exceeded without the concurrence of the Council.

The Members of the League agree that the manufacture by private enterprise of munitions and implements of war is open to grave objections. The Council shall advise how the evil effects attendant upon such manufacture can be prevented, due regard being had to the necessities of those Members of the League which are not able to manufacture the munitions and implements of war necessary for their safety.

The Members of the League undertake to interchange full and frank information as to the scale of their armaments, their military, naval and air programmes, and the condition of such of their industries as are adaptable to war-like purposes.

9. A permanent Commission shall be constituted to advise the Council on the execution of the provisions of Articles 1 and 8 and on military, naval and air questions generally.

10. The Members of the League undertake to respect and preserve as against external aggression the territorial integrity and existing political independence of all Members of the League. In case of any such aggression or in case of any threat or danger of such aggression the Council shall advise upon the means by which this obligation shall be fulfilled.

11. Any war or threat of war, whether immediately affecting any of the Members of the League or not, is hereby declared a matter of concern to the whole League, and the League shall take any action that may be deemed wise and effectual to safeguard the peace of nations. In case any such emergency should arise the Secretary-General shall on the request of any Member of the League forthwith summon a meeting of the Council.

It is also declared to be the friendly right of each Member of the League to bring to the attention of the Assembly or of the Council any circumstance whatever affecting international relations which threatens to disturb international peace or the good understanding between nations upon which peace depends.

12. The Members of the League agree that if there should arise between them any dispute likely to lead to a rupture, they will

submit the matter either to arbitration or to inquiry by the Council, and they agree in no case to resort to war until three months after the award by the arbitrators or the report by the Council.

In any case under this Article the award of the arbitrators shall be made within a reasonable time, and the report of the Council shall be made within six months after the submission of the dispute.

13. The Members of the League agree that whenever any dispute shall arise between them which they recognize to be suitable for submission to arbitration and which cannot be satisfactorily settled by diplomacy, they will submit the whole subject-matter to arbitration.

Disputes as to the interpretation of a treaty, as to any question of international law, as to the existence of any fact which if established would constitute a breach of any international obligation, or as to the extent and nature of the reparation to be made for any such breach, are declared to be among those which are generally suitable for submission to arbitration.

For the consideration of any such dispute the court of arbitration to which the case is referred shall be the court agreed on by the parties to the dispute or stipulated in any convention existing between them.

The Members of the League agree that they will carry out in full good faith any award that may be rendered, and that they will not resort to war against a Member of the League which complies therewith. In the event of any failure to carry out such an award, the Council shall propose what steps should be taken to give effect thereto.

14. The Council shall formulate and submit to the Members of the League for adoption plans for the establishment of a Permanent Court of International Justice. The Court shall be competent to hear and determine any dispute of an international character which the parties thereto submit to it. The Court may also give an advisory opinion upon any dispute or question referred to it by the Council or by the Assembly.

15. If there should arise between Members of the League any dispute likely to lead to a rupture, which is not submitted to arbitration in accordance with Article 13, the Members of the League agree that they will submit the matter to the Council.

Any party to the dispute may effect such submission by giving notice of the existence of the dispute to the Secretary-General, who will make all necessary arrangements for a full investigation and consideration thereof.

For this purpose the parties to the dispute will communicate to the Secretary-General, as promptly as possible, statements of their case, with all the relevant facts and papers, and the Council may forthwith direct the publication thereof.

The Council shall endeavour to effect a settlement of the dispute, and if such efforts are successful, a statement shall be made public giving such facts and explanations regarding the dispute and the terms of settlement thereof as the Council may deem appropriate.

If the dispute is not thus settled, the Council either unanimously or by a majority vote shall make and publish a report containing a statement of the facts of the dispute and the recommendations which are deemed just and proper in regard thereto.

Any Member of the League represented on the Council may make public a statement of the facts of the dispute and of its conclusions regarding the same.

If a report by the Council is unanimously agreed to by the members thereof other than the representatives of one or more of the parties to the dispute, the Members of the League agree that they will not go to war with any party to the dispute which complies with the recommendations of the report.

If the Council fails to reach a report which is unanimously agreed to by the members thereof, other than the representatives of one or more of the parties to the dispute, the Members of the League reserve to themselves the right to take such action as they shall consider necessary for the maintenance of right and justice.

If the dispute between the parties is claimed by one of them, and is found by the Council, to arise out of a matter which by international law is solely within the domestic jurisdiction of that party, the Council shall so report, and shall make no recommendation as to its settlement.

The Council may in any case under this Article refer the dispute to the Assembly. The dispute shall be so referred at the request of either party to the dispute, provided that such requests be made within fourteen days after the submission of the dispute to the Council.

In any case referred to the Assembly, all the provisions of this Article and of Article 12 relating to the action and powers of the Council shall apply to the action and powers of the Assembly, provided that a report made by the Assembly, if concurred in by the representatives of those Members of the League represented on the Council and of a majority of the other Members of the League, exclusive in each case of the representatives of the parties to the dispute, shall have the same force as a report by the Council concurred in by all the members thereof other than the representatives of one or more of the parties to the dispute.

16. Should any Member of the League resort to war in disregard of its covenants under Articles 12, 13 or 15, it shall *ipso facto* be deemed to have committed an act of war against all other Members of the League, which hereby undertake immediately to subject it to the severance of all trade or financial relations, the prohibition of all intercourse between their nationals and the nationals of the covenant-breaking State, and the prevention of all financial, commercial and personal intercourse between the nationals of the covenant-breaking State and the nationals of any other State, whether a Member of the League or not.

It shall be the duty of the Council in such case to recommend to the several Governments concerned what effective military, naval or air force the Members of the League shall severally contribute to the armed forces to be used to protect the covenants of the League.

The Members of the League agree, further, that they will mutually support one another in the financial and economic measures which are taken under this Article, in order to minimize the loss and inconvenience resulting from the above measures, and that they will mutually support one another in resisting any special measures aimed at one of their number by the covenant-breaking State, and that they will take the necessary steps to afford passage through their territory to the forces of any of the Members of the League which are co-operating to protect the covenants of the League.

Any Member of the League which has violated any covenant

of the League may be declared to be no longer a Member of the League by a vote of the Council concurred in by the representatives of all the other Members of the League represented thereon.

17. In the event of a dispute between a Member of the League and a State which is not a Member of the League, or between States not Members of the League, the State or States not Members of the League shall be invited to accept the obligations of Membership in the League for the purposes of such dispute . . .

18. Every treaty or international engagement entered into hereafter by any Member of the League shall be forthwith registered with the Secretariat and shall as soon as possible be published by it. No such treaty or international engagement shall be binding until so registered.

19. The Assembly may from time to time advise the reconsideration by Members of the League of treaties which have become inapplicable and the consideration of international conditions whose continuance might endanger the peace of the world.

20. The Members of the League severally agree that this Covenant is accepted as abrogating all obligations or understandings *inter se* which are inconsistent with the terms thereof, and solemnly undertake that they will not hereafter enter into any engagements inconsistent with the terms thereof . . .

21. Nothing in this Covenant shall be deemed to affect the validity of international engagements, such as treaties of arbitration or regional understandings like the Monroe doctrine, for securing the maintenance of peace.

22. To those colonies and territories which as a consequence of the late war have ceased to be under the sovereignty of the States which formerly governed them and which are inhabited by peoples not yet able to stand by themselves under the strenuous conditions of the modern world, there should be applied the principle that the well-being and development of such peoples form a sacred trust of civilization and that securities for the performance of this trust should be embodied in this Covenant.

The best method of giving practical effect to this principle is that the tutelage of such peoples should be entrusted to advanced nations who by reason of their resources, their experience or their geographical position can best undertake this responsibility, and who are willing to accept it, and that this tutelage should be exercised by them as Mandatories on behalf of the League.

The character of the mandate must differ according to the stage of the development of the people, the geographical situation of the territory, its economic condition and other similar circumstances.

Certain communities formerly belonging to the Turkish Empire have reached a stage of development where their existence as independent nations can be provisionally recognized subject to the rendering of administrative advice and assistance by a Mandatory until such time as they are able to stand alone. The wishes of these communities must be a principal consideration in the selection of the Mandatory.[1]

Other peoples, especially those of Central Africa, are at such a stage that the Mandatory must be responsible for the administration of the territory under conditions which will guarantee freedom of conscience and religion, subject only to the maintenance of public order and morals, the prohibition of abuses such as the slave trade, the arms traffic and the liquor traffic, and the prevention of the establishment of fortifications or military and naval bases and of military training of the natives for other than police purposes and the defence of territory, and will also secure equal opportunities for the trade and commerce of other Members of the League.[2]

There are territories, such as South-West Africa and certain of the South Pacific Islands, which, owing to the sparseness of their population or their small size, or their remoteness from the centres of civilization, or their geographical contiguity to the territory of the Mandatory, and other circumstances, can best be administered under the laws of the Mandatory as integral portions of its territory, subject to the safeguards above mentioned in the interests of the indigenous population.[3]

In every case of mandate, the Mandatory shall render to the Council an annual report in reference to the territory committed to its charge.

[1] The so-called A-class mandates.
[2] The so-called B-class mandates.
[3] The so-called C-class mandates.

The degree of authority, control, or administration to be exercised by the Mandatory shall, if not previously agreed upon by the Members of the League, be explicitly defined in each case by the Council.

A permanent Commission shall be constituted to receive and examine the annual reports of the Mandatories and to advise the Council on all matters relating to the observance of the mandates.

23. Subject to and in accordance with the provisions of international conventions existing or hereafter to be agreed upon, the Members of the League:

(a) will endeavour to secure and maintain fair and humane conditions of labour for men, women, and children, both in their own countries and in all countries to which their commercial and industrial relations extend, and for that purpose will establish and maintain the necessary international organizations;

(b) undertake to secure just treatment of the native inhabitants of territories under their control;

(c) will entrust the League with the general supervision over the execution of agreements with regard to the traffic in women and children and the traffic in opium and other dangerous drugs;

(d) will entrust the League with the general supervision of the trade in arms and ammunition with the countries in which the control of this traffic is necessary in the common interest;

(e) will make provision to secure and maintain freedom of communications and of transit and equitable treatment for the commerce of all Members of the League . . .

(f) will endeavour to take steps in matters of international concern for the prevention and control of disease.

24. There shall be placed under the direction of the League all international bureaux already established by general treaties if the parties to such treaties consent. All such international bureaux and all commissions for the regulation of matters of international interest hereafter constituted shall be placed under the direction of the League . . .

ANNEX

Original members of the League of Nations signatories of the Treaty of Peace

United States of America	Cuba	Nicaragua
Belgium	Ecuador	Panama
Bolivia	France	Peru
Brazil	Greece	Poland
British Empire	Guatemala	Portugal
Canada	Haiti	Romania
Australia	Hedjaz	Serb-Croat-Slovene
South Africa	Honduras	State[1]
New Zealand	Italy	Siam
India	Japan	Czecho-Slovakia
China	Liberia	Uruguay

States invited to accede to the Covenant

Argentine Republic, Chili, Colombia, Denmark, Netherlands, Norway, Paraguay, Persia, Salvador, Spain, Sweden, Switzerland, Venezuela.

207. *The Treaty of Rapallo, 16 April 1922*

In April 1922 the European Governments held a conference at Genoa, with German and Russian participation, to settle the main economic questions facing Europe. The conference did not in fact settle anything, largely because Soviet Russia would not recognize pre-revolutionary foreign debts as was demanded by France. During the conference, however, negotiations were conducted by the two isolated States, Germany and Russia, which resulted in the following treaty, the first diplomatic break-through for either of the parties since the end of the war.

Source: *British and Foreign State Papers*, vol. cxviii (1923 pt. 2), pp. 586–90.

1. The two Governments agree that the settlement ... of questions arising from the time when a state of war existed between Germany and Russia shall be effected on the following basis:

(a) [The Parties] renounce mutually all compensation in respect of the costs of the war and of war losses ... also ... all

---

[1] Later called Yugoslavia.

compensation in respect of civilian losses caused . . . by the so-called exceptional war legislation or by compulsory measures taken by State Departments on the other side.

(b) The public and private legal relations between the two States . . . will be settled on a basis of reciprocity.

(c) Germany and Russia mutually renounce all compensation in respect of costs incurred on both sides for prisoners of war . . .

2. Germany renounces all claims arising from the application up to the present of the laws and measures of the Russian Socialist Federal Soviet Republic to German nationals or their private rights and to the rights of the German Reich and States in regard to Russia . . . provided that the Government of the Russian Socialist Federal Soviet Republic does not give satisfaction to like claims put forward by other States.

3. Diplomatic and consular relations will immediately be resumed . . .

5. Both Governments will endeavour reciprocally to meet the economic needs of the other side in an accommodating spirit . . .

208. The 'Geneva Protocol', 2 October 1924

The Covenant of the League of Nations (No. 206) sets out in Articles 12–16 the method to be followed in settling international disputes, but it leaves room for some doubt and latitude in carrying them out. There had been some interest, particularly among the smaller States, in defining procedures and obligations rather more clearly, and for this purpose a draft treaty of mutual assistance was proposed in 1923. It did not gain acceptance, and was superseded by another attempt in 1924, the so-called 'Geneva Protocol' which was to serve as a supplement to the Covenant.

Although accepted by the League Assembly on 2 October 1924, the Protocol did not gain effect because the British Government refused to ratify it. It was considered too strong, mainly because it prescribed the automatic application of sanctions in Articles 10–11.

Source: *Resolutions and Recommendations adopted by the League of Nations Assembly . . . 1924* (Geneva, League of Nations, 1924), pp. 20–7.

1. The signatory States undertake to make every effort in their power to secure the introduction into the Covenant of amendments on the lines of the provisions contained in the following articles . . .

2. The signatory States agree in no case to resort to war . . .
except in case of resistance to acts of aggression or when acting
in agreement with the Council or the Assembly of the League
of Nations in accordance with the provisions of the Covenant
and of the present Protocol.

[The following articles elaborate the provisions of Article 15 of
the Covenant (No. 206).]

7. In the event of a dispute arising between two or more signatory States, these States agree that they will not, either before
the dispute is submitted to proceedings for pacific settlement or
during such proceedings, make any increase of their armaments
or effectives . . . nor will they take any measure of military,
naval, air, industrial or economic mobilization, nor, in general,
any action of a nature likely to extend the dispute or render it
more acute . . .

If . . . enquiries and investigations . . . establish an infraction
of the provisions of the first paragraph of the present Article, it
shall be the duty of the Council to summon the State or States
guilty of the infraction to put an end thereto . . .

10. Every State which resorts to war in violation of the undertakings contained in the Covenant or in the present Protocol is
an aggressor. Violation of the rules laid down for a demilitarized
zone shall be held equivalent to resort to war.

In the event of hostilities having broken out, any State shall
be presumed to be an aggressor, unless a decision of the Council,
which must be taken unanimously, shall otherwise declare:

1. If it has refused to submit the dispute to the procedure of
pacific settlement provided by Articles 13 and 15 of the Covenant as amplified by the present Protocol, or to comply with a
judicial sentence or arbitral award or with a unanimous recommendation of the Council, or has disregarded a unanimous
report of the Council, a judicial sentence or an arbitral award
recognizing that the dispute between it and the other belligerent State arises out of a matter which by international law is
solely within the domestic jurisdiction of the latter State;
nevertheless, in the last case the State shall only be presumed
to be an aggressor if it has not previously submitted the question
to the Council or the Assembly, in accordance with Article 11
of the Covenant.

2. If it has violated provisional measures enjoined by the

Council for the period while the proceedings are in progress as contemplated by Article 7 of the present Protocol.

Apart from the cases dealt with in paragraphs 1 and 2 of the present Article, if the Council does not at once succeed in determining the aggressor, it shall be bound to enjoin upon the belligerents an armistice, and shall fix the terms, acting, if need be, by a two-thirds majority and shall supervise its execution.

Any belligerent which has refused to accept the armistice or has violated its terms shall be deemed an aggressor.

The Council shall call upon the signatory States to apply forthwith against the aggressor the sanctions provided by Article 11 of the present Protocol, and any signatory State thus called upon shall thereupon be entitled to exercise the rights of a belligerent.

11. As soon as the Council has called upon the signatory States to apply sanctions, as provided in the last paragraph of Article 10 of the present Protocol, the obligations of the said States, in regard to the sanctions of all kinds mentioned in paragraphs 1 and 2 of Article 16 of the Covenant, will immediately become operative in order that such sanctions may forthwith be employed against the aggressor.

Those obligations shall be interpreted as obliging each of the signatory States to co-operate loyally and effectively in support of the Covenant of the League of Nations, and in resistance to any act of aggression, in the degree which its geographical position and its particular situation as regards armaments allow.

In accordance with paragraph 3 of Article 16 of the Covenant the signatory States give a joint and several undertaking to come to the assistance of the State attacked or threatened, and to give each other mutual support by means of facilities and reciprocal exchanges as regards the provision of raw materials and supplies of every kind, openings of credits, transport and transit, and for this purpose to take all measures in their power to preserve the safety of communications by land and by sea of the attacked or threatened State.

If both parties to the dispute are aggressors within the meaning of Article 10, the economic and financial sanctions shall be applied to both of them . . .

14. The Council shall alone be competent to declare that the

application of sanctions shall cease and normal conditions be re-established . . .

209. The Locarno Treaties, 16 October 1925

The reparations question having been settled by the acceptance of the Dawes Plan (No. 187) it was considered necessary to come to a political settlement with Germany before her admission to the League of Nations would be considered. A multilateral conference at Locarno developed a German proposal, made some two years before, and a series of treaties was agreed upon. They were initialled at the conclusion of the Conference and formally signed at London on 1 December 1925.

The main agreement was the Treaty of Mutual Guarantee (a) between Germany, Belgium, France, Great Britain, and Italy, in which Germany's Western boundaries and the status of the demilitarized zone were recognized by Germany and guaranteed by the latter two Powers. This treaty was supplemented by Arbitration Conventions between Germany and Belgium (b) and Germany and France. Although a multilateral recognition and guarantee of Germany's Eastern frontiers could not be agreed upon, arbitration treaties between Germany and Czechoslovakia and Germany and Poland were concluded, guaranteed by separate treaties, not strictly part of the Locarno settlement, between France and Poland and France and Czechoslovakia (c).

Our selections include part of the Treaty of Mutual Guarantee (a), part of the Arbitration Convention between Germany and Belgium (b) (identical in text with Germany's arbitration agreements with France, Poland and Czechoslovakia), and the treaty between France and Czechoslovakia (c) (identical in text with the Franco-Polish treaty).

Source: *League of Nations Treaty Series*, liv (1926/27), 291–7, 305–13, 361–3.

(a) Treaty of Mutual Guarantee between Germany, Belgium, France, Great Britain and Italy, initialled on 16 October 1925.

1. The High Contracting Parties collectively and severally guarantee, in the manner provided in the following articles, the maintenance of the territorial *status quo* resulting from the frontiers between Germany and Belgium and between Germany and France and the inviolability of the said frontiers as fixed by or in pursuance of the Treaty of Peace signed at Versailles on the 28th June, 1919 (No. 160) and also the observance of the

stipulations of Articles 42 and 43 of the said treaty concerning the demilitarized zone.

2. Germany and Belgium, and also Germany and France, mutually undertake that they will in no case attack or invade each other or resort to war against each other.

This stipulation shall not, however, apply in the case of—

1. The exercise of the right of legitimate defence, that is to say, resistance to a violation of the undertaking contained in the previous paragraph or to a flagrant breach of Articles 42 or 43 of the said Treaty of Versailles, if such breach constitutes an unprovoked act of aggression and by reason of the assembly of armed forces in the demilitarized zone immediate action is necessary.

2. Action in pursuance of Article 16 of the Covenant of the League of Nations (No. 206).

3. Action as the result of a decision taken by the Assembly or by the Council of the League of Nations or in pursuance of Article 15, paragraph 7, of the Covenant of the League of Nations, provided that in this last event the action is directed against a State which was the first to attack.

3. In view of the undertakings entered into in Article 2 . . ., Germany and Belgium and Germany and France undertake to settle by peaceful means and in the manner laid down herein all questions of every kind which may arise between them and which it may not be possible to settle by the normal methods of diplomacy . . .

4. 1. If one of the High Contracting Parties alleges that a violation of Article 2 of the present Treaty or a breach of Articles 42 or 43 of the Treaty of Versailles has been or is being committed, it shall bring the question at once before the Council of the League of Nations.

2. As soon as the Council of the League of Nations is satisfied that such violation or breach has been committed, it will notify its finding without delay to the Powers signatory of the present Treaty, who severally agree that in such case they will each of them come immediately to the assistance of the Power against whom the act complained of is directed.

3. In case of a flagrant violation . . . by one of the High Contracting Parties, each of the other Contracting Parties hereby undertakes immediately to come to the help of the party

against whom such a violation or breach has been directed . . .
5. The provisions of Article 3 of the present Treaty are placed
under the guarantee of the High Contracting Parties . . .

(b) Arbitration Convention between Germany and Belgium,
   initialled on 16 October 1925.

1. All disputes of every kind between Germany and Belgium
with regard to which the Parties are in conflict as to their
respective rights, and which it may not be possible to settle
amicably by the normal methods of diplomacy, shall be submitted for decision either to an arbitral tribunal or to the
Permanent Court of International Justice . . .
2. Before any resort is made to arbitral procedure or to
procedure before the Permanent Court of International
Justice, the dispute may, by agreement between the parties, be
submitted, with a view to amicable settlement, to a permanent
international commission styled the Permanent Conciliation
Commission, constituted in accordance with the present convention . . .
4. The Permanent Conciliation Commission mentioned in
Article 2 shall be composed of five members, who shall be
appointed as follows, that is to say: the German Government
and the Belgian Government shall each nominate a commissioner chosen from among their respective nationals, and shall
appoint, by common agreement, the three other commissioners
from among the nationals of third Powers; these three commissioners must be of different nationalities, and the German
and Belgian Governments shall appoint the president of the
commission from among them . . .
[Articles 5-16 regulate procedure to be followed in the Permanent Conciliation Commission.]
17. All questions on which the German and Belgian Governments shall differ without being able to reach an amicable
solution by means of the normal methods of diplomacy the
settlement of which cannot be attained by means of a judicial
decision as provided in Article 1 of the present Convention, and
for the settlement of which no procedure has been laid down by
other conventions in force between the parties, shall be submitted to the Permanent Conciliation Commission, whose duty

it shall be to propose to the parties an acceptable solution and in any case to present a report . . .

18. If the two Parties have not reached an agreement within a month from the termination of the labours of the Permanent Conciliation Commission the question shall, at the request of either Party, be brought before the Council of the League of Nations, which shall deal with it in accordance with Article 15 of the Covenant of the League (No. 206) . . .

(c) Treaty between France and Czechoslovakia, 16 October 1925.

1. In the event of Czechoslovakia or France suffering from a failure to observe the undertakings arrived at this day between them and Germany with a view to the maintenance of general peace, France, and reciprocally Czechoslovakia, acting in application of Article 16 of the Covenant of the League of Nations (No. 206), undertake to lend each other immediately aid and assistance, if such a failure is accompanied by an unprovoked recourse to arms.

In the event of the Council of the League of Nations, when dealing with a question brought before it in accordance with the said undertakings, being unable to succeed in making its report accepted by all its members other than the representatives of the parties to the dispute, and in the event of Czechoslovakia or France being attacked without provocation, France, or reciprocally Czechoslovakia, acting in application of Article 15, paragraph 7, of the Covenant of the League of Nations, will immediately lend aid and assistance . . .

210. *General Pact for the Renunciation of War, 27 August 1928*

A declaration of principles rather than a treaty containing specific obligations, the following multilateral treaty was a result of negotiations between the French Premier, Briand, and the U.S. Secretary of State, Kellogg. Hence it is often referred to as the Kellogg-Briand Pact, or, from the place where it was signed, the Pact of Paris. It was initially signed by representatives of the recognized Great Powers (Germany, U.S.A., France, Great Britain, Italy, Japan) and of the three other Locarno Powers (Belgium, Czechoslovakia, and Poland). Many other States adhered at a later time.

Source: *League of Nations Treaty Series*, xciv (1929), 59–64.

1. The High Contracting Parties solemnly declare in the names of their respective peoples that they condemn recourse to war for the solution of international controversies, and renounce it as an instrument of national policy in their relations with one another.

2. The High Contracting Parties agree that the settlement or solution of all disputes or conflicts of whatever nature or of whatever origin they may be, which arise among them, shall never be sought except by pacific means.

3. ... This Treaty shall ... remain open as long as may be necessary for adherence by all the other Powers of the world ...

211. *Recommendations of the League of Nations Assembly on the Manchurian Dispute, 24 February 1933*

The dispute between China and Japan over Manchuria broke out in 1931 and was referred to the League of Nations. The League dispatched a fact-finding committee (called the Lytton Committee after its chairman) which, after a long investigation, submitted a lengthy report. The Assembly, on 24 February 1933, adopted the findings of the Lytton Report and added a set of recommendations for settlement of the dispute which follows. The recommendations were not acceptable to Japan which thereupon left the League.

Source: *League of Nations Official Journal, Special Supplement No. 112,* 1933, pp. 73-6.

Statement of the Recommendations ...

Section I

The recommendations of the Assembly take into account the very special circumstances of this case and are based on the following principles, conditions and considerations:

(a) The settlement of the dispute should observe the provisions of the Covenant of the League (No. 206), the Pact of Paris (No. 210) and the Nine-Power Treaty of Washington[1] ...

(b) The settlement of the dispute should observe the provisions of Parts I and II of the Assembly resolution of March 11, 1932.

[1] Article 1 of this Treaty provides: 'The Contracting Powers, other than China, agree to respect the sovereignty, the independence, and the territorial and administrative integrity of China.'

In that resolution ... the Assembly considered that the provisions of the Covenant were entirely applicable to the present dispute, more particularly as regards:

(1) The principle of a scrupulous respect for treaties;

(2) The undertaking entered into by Members of the League of Nations to respect and preserve as against external aggression the territorial integrity and existing political independence of all the Members of the League;

(3) Their obligation to submit any dispute which may arise between them to procedures for peaceful settlement ...

(c) In order that a lasting understanding may be established between China and Japan on the basis of respect for the international undertakings mentioned above, the settlement of the dispute must conform to the principles and conditions laid down by the Commission of Enquiry in the following terms:

'1. Compatibility with the interests of both China and Japan...

2. Consideration for the interests of the Union of Soviet Socialist Republics ...

3. Conformity with existing multilateral treaties ...

4. Recognition of Japan's interests in Manchuria ...

5. The establishment of new treaty relations between China and Japan ...

6. Effective provision for the settlement of future disputes ...

7. Manchurian autonomy. The Government in Manchuria should be modified in such a way as to secure, consistently with the sovereignty and administrative integrity of China, a large measure of autonomy ... The new civil régime must be so constituted and conducted as to satisfy the requirements of good government.

8. Internal order and security against external aggression. The internal order of the country should be secured by an effective local gendarmerie force, and security against external aggression should be provided by the withdrawal of all armed forces other than the gendarmerie, and by the conclusion of a treaty of non-aggression between the countries interested.

9. Encouragement of an economic *rapprochement* between China and Japan ...

10. International co-operation in Chinese reconstruction ...'

Section II

The provisions of this section constitute the recommendations of the Assembly under Article 15, paragraph 4, of the Covenant.

Having defined the principles, conditions and considerations applicable to the settlement of the dispute,
The Assembly recommends as follows:

1. Whereas the sovereignty over Manchuria belongs to China,
A. Considering that the presence of Japanese troops outside the zone of the South Manchuria Railway and their operations outside this zone are incompatible with the legal principles which should govern the settlement of the dispute . . .,

The Assembly recommends the evacuation of these troops [as] the first object of the negotiations recommended hereinafter . . .

B. Having regard to the local conditions special to Manchuria, the particular rights and interests possessed by Japan therein, and the rights and interests of third States,

The Assembly recommends the establishment in Manchuria . . . of an organization under the sovereignty of, and compatible with the administrative integrity of, China. This organization should provide a wide measure of autonomy, should be in harmony with local conditions, and should take account of the multilateral treaties in force, the particular rights and interests of Japan, the rights and interests of third States, and, in general, the principles and conditions reproduced in Section I (c) above . . .

2. Whereas, in addition to the questions dealt with in the two recommendations 1A and 1B, the report of the Commission of Enquiry mentions in the principles and conditions for a settlement of the dispute set out in Section I (c) above certain other questions affecting the good understanding between China and Japan . . .,

The Assembly recommends the parties to settle these questions on the basis of the said principles and conditions.

3. Whereas the negotiations necessary for giving effect to the foregoing recommendations should be carried on by means of a suitable organ,

The Assembly recommends . . . the negotiations between the parties should take place with the assistance of a Committee set up by the Assembly. . . .

Section III

In view of the special circumstances of the case, the recommendations made do not provide for a mere return to the *status quo* existing before September 1931. They likewise exclude the maintenance and recognition of the existing régime in Manchuria, such maintenance and recognition being incompatible with the fundamental principles of existing international obligations and with the good understanding between the two countries on which peace in the Far East depends.

It follows that, in adopting the present report, the Members of the League intend to abstain, particularly as regards the existing régime in Manchuria, from any act which might prejudice or delay the carrying out of the recommendations of the said report. They will continue not to recognize this régime either *de jure* or *de facto*. They intend to abstain from taking any isolated action with regard to the situation in Manchuria and to continue to concert their action among themselves as well as with the interested States not Members of the League . . .

212. German Withdrawal from the Disarmament Conference and the League of Nations, 14 October 1933

Although the German Government continued to participate in disarmament negotiations after Hitler became Chancellor, the German line gradually hardened. When rather far-reaching German demands were rejected, Hitler, in the proclamation that follows, announced Germany's withdrawal both from the Disarmament Conference and the League of Nations.

Source: *Documents on International Affairs 1933* (Oxford University Press under the auspices of the Royal Institute of International Affairs), pp. 287-9.

Filled with the sincere desire to accomplish the work of the peaceful internal reconstruction of our nation and of its political and economic life, former German Governments, trusting in the grant of a dignified equality of rights, declared their willingness to enter the League of Nations and to take part in the Disarmament Conference.

In this connexion Germany suffered a bitter disappointment. In spite of our readiness to carry through German disarmament . . . other Governments could not decide to redeem the pledges signed by them in the Peace Treaty.

By the deliberate refusal of real moral and material equality of rights to Germany, the German nation and its Governments have been profoundly humiliated.

After the German Government had declared, as a result of the equality of rights expressly laid down on December 11, 1932, that it was again prepared to take part in the Disarmament Conference, the German Foreign Minister and our delegates were informed . . . that this equality of rights could no longer be granted to present-day Germany.

As the German Government regards this action as an unjust and humiliating discrimination against the German nation, it is not in a position to continue, as an outlawed and second-class nation, to take part in negotiations which could only lead to further arbitrary results.

While the German Government again proclaims its unshaken desire for peace, it declares to its great regret that, in view of these imputations, it must leave the Disarmament Conference. It will also announce its departure from the League of Nations.

It submits this decision . . . to the judgement of the German nation[1] . . .

213. German Denunciation of the Military Clauses of the Treaty of Versailles, 16 March 1935

The Provisions of Part V (the military, naval, and air clauses) of the Treaty of Versailles (No. 160) were always a sore point with the Germans. Germany left the League of Nations (cf. No. 212) over the issue of equality of armaments, and when further negotiations on the limitation of armaments were unsuccessful, Hitler announced the decision to rearm (a) and published a law reintroducing compulsory military service (b).

Source: *Documents on International Affairs 1935* (Oxford University Press under the auspices of the Royal Institute of International Affairs), vol. i, pp. 58–64.

[1] The referendum approved this decision by a large majority.

(a) Proclamation by Hitler, 16 March 1935.

When in November 1918 the German people, trusting in the promises given in President Wilson's Fourteen Points (No. 158(a)), grounded arms after four and a half years' honourable resistance in a war whose outbreak they had never desired, they believed they had rendered a service not only to tormented humanity, but also to a great idea . . .

Our people trustingly seized upon the idea of a new order in the relations between peoples, an order which was to be ennobled on one hand by doing away with the secrecy of diplomatic cabinet policies and on the other hand by abandoning the terrible methods of war . . .

The idea of the League of Nations has perhaps in no nation awakened more fervent acclaim than in Germany . . .

The German people, and especially their Governments of that time, were convinced that, by fulfilment of the conditions of disarmament laid down in the Versailles Treaty and in accordance with the promises of that Treaty, the beginning of international general disarmament would be marked and guaranteed.

For only in a two-sided fulfilment of the task by the Treaty could there lie a moral and sensible justification for a demand which, one-sidedly imposed and executed, had necessarily to lead to an eternal discrimination, and thereby to a declaration of inferiority of a great nation.

Under such conditions, however, a peace treaty of this sort could never create the conditions for a true inward reconciliation of peoples, nor for the pacification of the world achieved in this manner, but could only set up a hatred that would gnaw eternally.

Germany has, according to the investigation of the Inter-Allied Control Commission, fulfilled the disarmament conditions imposed upon her . . . the German people had the right to expect the redemption also by the other side of obligations undertaken . . . But while Germany as one party to the Treaty had fulfilled its obligations, the redemption of the obligation on the part of the second partner to the Treaty failed to become a fact. That means: the High Contracting Parties of the former victor States have one-sidedly divorced themselves from the obligations of the Versailles Treaty. Not alone did they refrain from disarming . . . No. Not even was there a halt in the armaments race, on the contrary, the increase of armaments . . . became evident . . .

The world . . . has again resumed its cries of war, just as though there never had been a World War nor the Versailles Treaty. In the midst of these highly armed warlike States . . . Germany was, militarily speaking, in a vacuum, defencelessly at the mercy of every threatening danger.

The German people recall the misfortune and suffering of fifteen years' economic misery and political and moral humiliation. It was, therefore, understandable that Germany began loudly to demand the fulfilment of the promises made by other States to disarm . . .

[A long review of negotiations, of German proposals and undertakings, and their rejection, follows.]

The German Government must, however, to its regret, note that for months the rest of the world has been rearming continuously and increasingly. It sees in the creation of a Soviet Russian Army of 101 divisions, that is, in an admitted peace strength of 960,000 men, an element that at the time of the conclusion of the Versailles Treaty could not have been divined. It sees in the forcing of similar measures in other States further proofs of the refusal to accept the disarmament ideas as originally proclaimed . . .

In these circumstances the German Government considers it impossible still longer to refrain from taking the necessary measures for the security of the Reich or even to hide the knowledge thereof from other nations . . .

What the German Government, as the guardian of the honour and interests of the German nation, desires is to make sure that Germany possesses sufficient instruments of power not only to maintain the integrity of the German Reich, but also to command international respect and value as co-guarantor of general peace.

For in this hour the German Government renews before the German people, before the entire world, its assurance of its determination never to proceed beyond the safeguarding of German honour and the freedom of the Reich, and especially does it not intend in rearming Germany to create any instrument for warlike attack but, on the contrary, exclusively for defence and thereby for the maintenance of peace.

In so doing, the German Reich's Government expresses the confident hope that the German people, having again reverted to their own honour, may be privileged in independent equality to make their contribution for the pacification of the world in free and open co-operation with other nations and their Governments . . .

(b) German Law on Military Service, 16 March 1935.

1. Service in defensive forces is predicated on universal military service.

2. The German peace army, including police units which have been incorporated in the army, shall comprise twelve corps commands and thirty-six divisions . . .

214. *The Stresa Conference, 11–14 April 1935*

After the German renunciation (No. 213) of the military clauses of the Treaty of Versailles (No. 160), British, French, and Italian Ministers met at Stresa to discuss the implications of this step and concert their policy. Their most important resolutions follow: the joint resolution (a) of the three Powers, the resolution proposed on their behalf by France to the League of Nations Council (and duly adopted on 17 April 1935) (b), an Anglo-Italian declaration (c) and a Final Declaration (d).

Source: (a), (c), and (d): *Documents on International Affairs 1935* (Oxford University Press under the auspices of the Royal Institute of International Affairs), vol. i, pp. 80–2.
(b) *League of Nations Official Journal*, 1935, pp. 550–1.

(a) Joint Resolution of the Stresa Conference, 14 April 1935.

The Representatives of the Governments of Italy, France and the United Kingdom have examined at Stresa the general European situation in the light of the results of the exchanges of views which have taken place in recent weeks, of the decision taken on March 16 (No. 213) by the German Government, and of the information obtained by British Ministers during the visits recently paid by them to several European capitals. Having considered the bearing of this situation on the policy defined in the arrangements reached respectively in Rome and in London, they found themselves in complete agreement on the various matters discussed.

1. They agreed upon a common line of conduct to be pursued in the course of the discussion of the request presented to the Council of the League of Nations by the French Government.

2. The information which they have received has confirmed their view that the negotiations should be pursued for the development which is desired in security in Eastern Europe . . .

5. In approaching the problem of armaments . . . it was regretfully recognized that the method of unilateral repudiation adopted by the German Government . . . had undermined public confidence in the security of a peaceful order. Moreover, the magnitude of the declared programme of German rearmament . . . had invalidated the quantitative assumptions upon which efforts for disarmament had hitherto been based and shaken the hopes by which those efforts were inspired.

The Representatives of the three Powers, nevertheless, reaffirm their earnest desire to sustain peace by establishing a sense of security, and declare for themselves that they remain anxious to join in every practicable effort for promoting international agreement on the limitation of armaments . . .

(b) French Recommendations to the Council of the League of Nations, 16 April 1935.

The Council,
Considering,

(1) That the scrupulous respect of all treaty obligations is a fundamental principle of international life and an essential condition of the maintenance of peace;

(2) That it is an essential principle of the law of nations that no Power can liberate itself from the engagements of a treaty nor modify the stipulations thereof unless with the consent of the other contracting parties;

(3) That the promulgation of the Military Law of March 16th, 1935, by the German Government conflicts with the above principles;

(4) That, by this unilateral action, the German Government confers upon itself no right;

(5) That this unilateral action, by introducing a new disturbing

element into the international situation, must necessarily appear to be a threat to European security;

Considering, on the other hand,

(6) That the British Government and the French Government, with the approval of the Italian Government, had communicated to the German Government as early as February 3rd, 1935, a plan for a general settlement, to be freely negotiated, for the organization of security in Europe and for a general limitation of armaments in a system of equality of rights, while ensuring the active cooperation of Germany in the League of Nations;

(7) And that the unilateral action of Germany above referred to was not only inconsistent with this plan, but was taken at a time when negotiations were actually being pursued:

I. Declares that Germany has failed in the duty which lies upon all the members of the international community to respect the undertakings which they have contracted, and condemns any unilateral repudiation of international obligations;

II. Invites the Governments which took the initiative in the plan of February 3rd, 1935, or which gave their approval to it, to continue the negotiations so initiated, and in particular to promote the conclusion, within the framework of the League of Nations, of the agreements which may appear necessary to attain the object defined in this plan, due account being taken of the obligations of the Covenant, with a view to assuring the maintenance of peace;

III. Considering that the unilateral repudiation of international obligations may endanger the very existence of the League of Nations as an organization for maintaining peace and promoting security;

Decides:

That such repudiation, without prejudice to the application of the measures already provided in international agreements, should, in the event of its having relation to undertakings concerning the security of people and the maintenance of peace in Europe, call into play all appropriate measures on the part of Members of the League and within the framework of the Covenant;

Requests a Committee composed of   to propose for this purpose measures to render the Covenant more effective in the organization of collective security and to define in particular the economic and financial measures which might be applied, should in the future a State, whether a Member of the League of Nations or not, endanger peace by the unilateral repudiation of its international obligations.

(c) Anglo-Italian Declaration, 14 April 1935.

The following joint Declaration was made by the Representatives of Italy and the United Kingdom in reference to the Treaty of Locarno:

The Representatives of Italy and of the United Kingdom, the Powers which participate in the Treaty of Locarno (No. 209(a)) only in the capacity of guarantors, formally reaffirm all their obligations under that Treaty, and declare their intention, should the need arise, faithfully to fulfil them . . .

(d) Final Declaration, 14 April 1935.

The three Powers, the object of whose policy is the collective maintenance of peace within the framework of the League of Nations, find themselves in complete agreement in opposing, by all practicable means, any unilateral repudiation of treaties which may endanger the peace of Europe, and will act in close and cordial collaboration for this purpose.

215. *The Ethiopian Crisis*

When a dispute occurred between Ethiopia and Italy in late 1934 the arbitral machinery of the Italo-Ethiopian Treaty of 1928 was invoked and the dispute was notified to the League of Nations. There was a long delay, with no settlement forthcoming. Then, on 2 October, Italy invaded Ethiopia and Ethiopia invoked Article 16 of the League Covenant (No. 206) on 5 October; the Council appointed a Committee whose report (a) it adopted on 7 October. The matter proceeded to the Assembly, which appointed a Co-Ordination Committee (b) which made proposals for the imposition of sanctions (c) against Italy.

Later in the year France and Great Britain proposed a settlement, the so-called Hoare-Laval treaty (d) which, however, favoured Italy to such an extent that it had to be withdrawn.

The economic sanctions proved ineffective and they were lifted by the Assembly, after the final Italian victory, on 4 July 1936.

Source: (a) *League of Nations Official Journal*, 1935, pp. 1223-5.

(b) and (c) *League of Nations Official Journal Special Supplement, No. 145*, 1935, pp. 2, 14–16, 19–21, 24–6.
(d) *League of Nations Official Journal*, 1936, p. 40.

(a) Report of the Council Committee, 7 October 1935.

I.

1. At its meeting on October 5th, the Council . . . set up a Committee . . . 'to study the situation and report to the Council so as to enable it to take decisions with full knowledge of the matters involved'.

2. In order to study this situation, brought about by events subsequent to October 2nd, it was the Committee's duty to specify these events and to determine their character in relation to the obligations of the Covenant.

The Committee accordingly considered whether there had been a resort to war in disregard of Articles 12, 13 or 15 of the Covenant. This involves two questions:

(1) Does a state of war exist between Italy and Ethiopia?

(2) If so, has the war been resorted to in disregard of Articles 12, 13 or 15 of the Covenant?

3. With a view to replying to these questions, the following particulars were collected and classified:

[The Committee here quotes official Italian sources on the progress of the war.]

These events occurred before the draft report in pursuance of Article 15, paragraph 4, of the Covenant had been submitted to the Council.

II.

(a) Under Articles 12, 13 and 15 of the Covenant, it is the duty of all Members of the League of Nations to submit any dispute in which they may be engaged with another Member of the League, and which is likely to lead to a rupture, either to arbitrators or judicial settlement, or to enquiry by the Council. Under Article 12, the Members of the League agree 'in no case to resort to war until three months after the award by the arbitrators of the judicial decision, or the report by the Council'. 'The report of the Council shall be made within six months after the submission of the dispute.' In the present case, the Council decided on September 26th, 1935, that the procedure of Article 15 had become applicable on September 4th.

(b) The Ethiopian Government requested the Council to examine its dispute with Italy under Article 15 in the first place on March 17th, 1935, with a view to the settlement of the Italo-Ethiopian dispute arising out of the Walwal incident, and subsequently after the submission by the Italian Government on September 4th of the memorandum apprising the Council of Italy's grievances against Ethiopia, which went far beyond the Walwal incident.

(c) In presenting his Government's memorandum on September 4th, the representative of Italy told the Council that Italy reserved 'full liberty to adopt any measures that may become necessary to ensure the safety of its colonies and to safeguard its own interests'.

In the observations which the Italian representative made on September 22nd on the subject of the suggestions of the Committee of Five, he said that 'a case like that of Ethiopia cannot be settled by the means provided by the Covenant'.

(d) Without prejudice to the other limitations to their right to have recourse to war, the Members of the League are not entitled, without having first complied with the provisions of Articles 12, 13 and 15, to seek a remedy by war for grievances they consider they have against other Members of the League. The adoption by a State of measures of security on its own territory and within the limits of its international agreements does not authorize another State to consider itself free from its obligations under the Covenant.

(e) The Pact of Paris of August 27th, 1928 (No. 210), to which Italy and Ethiopia are parties, also condemns 'recourse to war . . .'

(f) The Ethiopian Government, at the meeting of the Council on October 5th, invoked Article 16 of the Covenant. Under the terms of that article 'should any Member of the League resort to war in disregard of its covenants under Articles 12, 13 or 15, it shall *ipso facto* be deemed to have committed an act of war against all other members of the League . . .'

(g) When a Member of the League invokes Article 16 of the Covenant, each of the other Members is bound to consider the circumstances of the particular case. It is not necessary that war should have been formally declared for Article 16 to be applicable.

III.

After an examination of the facts stated above, the Committee has come to the conclusion that the Italian Government has resorted to war in disregard of its covenants under Article 12 of the Covenant of the League of Nations.

(b) Recommendation by the Assembly, 10 October 1935.

The Assembly,

Having taken cognizance of the opinions expressed by the members of the Council at the Council's meeting of October 7, 1935;

Taking into consideration the obligations which rest upon the Members of the League of Nations in virtue of Article 16 of the Covenant and the desirability of co-ordination of the measures which they may severally contemplate;

Recommends that Members of the League of Nations, other than the parties, should set up a Committee, composed of one delegate, assisted by experts, for each Member, to consider and facilitate the co-ordination of such measures and, if necessary, to draw attention of the Council or the Assembly to the situations requiring to be examined by them.

(c) Declarations and Proposals of the Co-Ordination Committee, October 1935.

(1) Resolution of 16 October 1935.

The Committee of Co-Ordination,

Considering that it is important to ensure rapid and effective application of the measures which have been and may subsequently be proposed by the Committee;

Considering that it rests with each country to apply these measures in accordance with its public law and, in particular, the powers of its Government in regard to execution of treaties:

Calls attention to the fact that the Members of the League,

being bound by the obligations which flow from Article 16 of the Covenant, are under a duty to take the necessary steps to enable them to carry out these obligations with all requisite rapidity.

(2) Proposal I—Export of Arms, Ammunition and Implements of War, 11 October 1935.

With a view to facilitating for the Governments of the Members of the League of Nations the execution of their obligations under Article 16 of the Covenant, the following measures should be taken forthwith:

(1) The Governments of the Members of the League of Nations which are enforcing at the moment measures to prohibit or restrict the exportation . . . of arms, ammunition and implements of war to Ethiopia will annul these measures immediately.
(2) The Governments . . . will prohibit immediately the exportation, re-exportation or transit to Italy or Italian possessions of arms, munitions and implements of war enumerated in the attached list[1] . . .
Each Government is requested to inform the Committee, through the Secretary General of the League, within the shortest possible time of the measures which it has taken in conformity with the above provisions.

(3) Proposal II—Financial Measures, 14 October 1935.

[First sentence as under Proposal I.]
The Governments of the Members of the League of Nations will forthwith take all measures necessary to render impossible the following operations:

(1) All loans to or for the Italian Government . . .
(2) All banking and other credits to or for the Italian Government . . .
(3) All loans to or for any public authority, person or corporation in Italian territory . . .
(4) All banking or other credits to or for any public authority, person or corporation in Italian territory . . .

[1] List not included.

(4) Proposal III—Prohibition of Importation of Italian Goods, 19 October 1935.

[First sentence as under Proposal I.]

(1) The Governments of the Members of the League of Nations will prohibit the importation into their territories of all goods (other than gold or silver bullion or coin) consigned from or grown, produced or manufactured in Italy or Italian possessions, from whatever place arriving . . .

(5) Proposal IV—Embargo on Certain Exports to Italy, 19 October 1935.

[First sentence as under Proposal I.]

(1) The Governments of the Members of the League of Nations will extend the application of paragraph (2) of Proposal I of the Co-Ordination Committee to the following articles as regards their exportation and re-exportation to Italy and Italian possessions, which will accordingly be prohibited:

(a) Horses, mules, donkeys, camels and all other transport animals;

(b) Rubber;

(c) Bauxite, aluminium and alumina (aluminium oxide), iron-ore and scrap iron;

Chromium, manganese, nickel, titanium, tungsten, vanadium, their ores and ferro-alloys (and also ferro-molybdenum, ferro-silicon, ferro-silico-manganese and ferro-silico-manganese-aluminium);

Tin and tin-ore.

List (c) above includes all crude forms of the minerals and metals mentioned and their ores, scrap and alloys . . .

(d) The Hoare-Laval Proposals, 10 December 1935.

I. *Exchange of Territories.*

The Governments of the United Kingdom and France agree to recommend to His Majesty the Emperor of Ethiopia the acceptance of the following exchanges of territory between Ethiopia and Italy.

(a) . . . Cession to Italy of eastern Tigre . . .

(b) Rectification of frontiers between the Danakil country and Eritrea . . .

(c) Rectification of frontiers between the Ogaden and Italian Somaliland . . .

(d) Ethiopia will receive an outlet to the sea with full sovereign rights. It seems that this outlet should be formed preferably by the cession, to which Italy would agree, of the port of Assab and of a strip of territory giving access to this port along the frontier of French Somaliland . . .

II. *Zone of Economic Expansion and Settlement.*

The United Kingdom and French Governments will use their influence at Addis Ababa and at Geneva to the end that the formation in Southern Ethiopia of a zone of economic expansion and settlement reserved to Italy should be accepted by His Majesty the Emperor and approved by the League of Nations.

The limits of this zone would be: on the East, the rectified frontier between Ethiopia and Italian Somaliland; on the North, the 8th parallel; on the West, the 35th meridian; on the South, the frontier between Ethiopia and Kenya.

Within this zone, which would form an integral part of Ethiopia, Italy would enjoy exclusive economic rights which might be administered by a privileged company or by any other like organization . . .

The control of the Ethiopian administration in the zone would be exercised, under the sovereignty of the Emperor, by the services of the scheme of assistance drawn up by the League of Nations. Italy would take a preponderating, but not an exclusive, share in these services, which would be under the direct control of one of the principal advisers attached to the Central Government. The principal adviser in question, who might be of Italian nationality, would be the assistant, for the affairs in question, of the Chief Adviser delegated by the League of Nations to assist the Emperor. The Chief Adviser would not be a subject of one of the Powers bordering on Ethiopia.

The services of the scheme of assistance, in the capital as well as in the reserved zone, would regard it as one of their essential duties to ensure the safety of Italian subjects and the free development of their enterprises . . .

D E C—KK

216. *German Memorandum respecting the Termination of the Treaty of Locarno and the Re-Occupation of the Rhineland, 7 March 1936*

The increase in German power moved the Governments of France and the Soviet Union to conclude a treaty of mutual assistance in 1935, which came up for ratification in the French Parliament in March 1936. Before ratification was actually agreed to, the German Government, in the following memorandum, declared the Franco-Soviet Treaty to be an infringement of the Locarno Pact; it, therefore, declared the Pact as terminated, and occupied the demilitarized zone of the Rhineland. Protests, but no other interference, ensued.

Source: *British and Foreign State Papers*, vol. cxl (1936), pp. 518–21.

. . . The latest debates and decisions of the French Parliament have shown that France, in spite of the German representations, is determined to put the pact with the Soviet Union definitively into force. A diplomatic conversation has even revealed that France already regards herself as bound by her signature of this pact on the 2nd May 1935. In the face of such a development of European politics, the German Government, if they do not wish to neglect or to abandon the interests of the German people which they have the duty of safeguarding, cannot remain inactive.

The German Government have continually emphasized during the negotiations of the last years their readiness to observe and fulfil all the obligations arising from the Rhine Pact (Locarno Agreements, No. 209) as long as the other contracting parties were ready on their side to maintain the pact. This obvious and essential condition can no longer be regarded as fulfilled by France. France has replied to the repeated friendly offers and peaceful assurances made by Germany by infringing the Rhine Pact through a military alliance with the Soviet Union exclusively directed against Germany. In this manner, however, the Locarno Rhine Pact has lost its inner meaning and ceased in practice to exist. Consequently Germany regards herself for her part as no longer bound by this dissolved treaty . . . In accordance with the fundamental right of a nation to secure its frontiers and ensure its possibilities of defence, the German Government have today restored the full and unrestricted sovereignty of Germany in the demilitarized zone of the Rhineland.

... The German Government declare themselves ready to conclude new agreements for the creation of a system of peaceful security for Europe on the basis of the following proposals:

(1) The German Government declare themselves ready to enter into negotiations with France and Belgium with regard to the creation of a zone demilitarized on both sides ...
(2) The German Government propose ... the conclusion of a non-aggression pact between Germany, France and Belgium ...
(3) The German Government desire to invite Great Britain and Italy to sign this treaty as guarantor Powers ...
(5) The German Government are prepared ... to conclude an air pact calculated to prevent in an automatic and effective manner the danger of sudden air attacks.
(6) The German Government repeat their offer to conclude with the States bordering Germany in the east non-aggression pacts ...
(7) Now that Germany's equality of rights and the restoration of her full sovereignty over the entire territory of the German Reich have finally been attained, the German Government consider the chief reason for their withdrawal from the League of Nations to be removed. They are therefore willing to re-enter the League of Nations. In this connexion they express the expectation that in the course of a reasonable period the question of colonial equality of rights and that of the separation of the League Covenant from its Versailles setting may be clarified through friendly negotiations.

217. *The Anti-Comintern Pact, 25 November 1936*

Italy, until 1935 (cf. No. 214) strongly anti-German, was alienated from the Western Powers over Ethiopia (cf. No. 215) and therefore moved closer to Germany. Co-operation between the two States in supporting General Franco in the Spanish Civil War brought the two dictators closer still, until a 'Berlin–Rome Axis' was established. This was supplemented by an agreement directed against the Communist International (cf. No. 197) initially concluded between Germany and Japan, to which Italy and a number of Eastern European States adhered.

Source: *British and Foreign State Papers*, vol. cxl (1936), pp. 529–30.

The Government of the German Reich and the Imperial Japanese Government;

In recognition of the fact that the aim of the Communist International, called 'the Comintern', is the disintegration of, and the commission of violence against, existing States with all means at its command;

In the conviction that the toleration of interference by the Communist International in the domestic affairs of nations not only endangers their internal peace and social welfare, but also threatens world peace;

Desiring to co-operate for defence against Communist disintegration, have agreed as follows:

1. The high contracting States agree mutually to keep one another informed concerning counter-measures and to carry out the latter in close collaboration.

2. The high contracting States will jointly invite third States whose internal peace is menaced by the disintegrating work of the Communist International to adopt defensive measures in the spirit of the present agreement or to participate in the present agreement . . .

218. *The Spanish Civil War, 1936–39*

General Franco's manifesto, with which the Civil War began, and the war aims formulated some time later by the Republican Government ((a) (1) and (2)) give some information about the internal aspects of the Civil War, but greater emphasis is laid in our selection on the international aspects. Although Germany, Italy and the Soviet Union nearly openly assisted one or other of the parties, they nevertheless took part in the work of the Non-Intervention Committee whose task was the prevention of foreign interference in the Civil War. The Non-Intervention Agreement, to which all European States adhered, prohibited the supply of war materials to either party, and the entry into Spain of volunteers for their armed forces. A scheme of observation (b) was set up by the Committee to police the observance of these prohibitions.

The Republican Government also appealed to the League of Nations for assistance; the League was shown by its resolutions to be sympathetic, but ineffectual (c).

Source: (a) (1) *Historia de la Cruzada Espanola* (Madrid, 1939–43), vol. ii, p. 71 (trans. Ed.).

   (2) *League of Nations Official Journal*, January–June 1938, p. 533.

   (b) International Committee for the Application of the Agreement regarding Non-Intervention in Spain.

Resolution . . . relating to a Scheme of Observation (London, H.M.S.O., 1937) (Cmd. 5399).
(c) *League of Nations Official Journal*, 1937, pp. 18–19, 35, 333–4.

(a) War aims of the Contending Parties.

(1) Franco's First Manifesto, 18 July 1936.

Spaniards!

The Nation calls to her defence all of you who feel a holy love for Spain, you who, in the ranks of the Army and the Navy, have made a profession of faith in the service of our Country, you who have sworn to defend her with your lives against her enemies.

The situation in Spain is becoming more critical every day; anarchy reigns over most of the countryside and in the towns; authorities appointed by the Government preside over, if they do not foment, the revolts . . .

Revolutionary strikes of all kinds paralyse the life of the Nation; they destroy her sources of wealth and produce a famine which reduces the workers to despair.

In obedience to orders from foreign leaders, who count on the complicity or negligence of governors and officials, most violent attacks on monuments and artistic treasures are carried out by revolutionary bands.

Gravest offences are committed in the cities and the countryside while the forces of public order remain in their quarters, corroded by the desperation caused by [the necessity] of blindly obeying leaders who intend to dishonour them. The Army, the Navy, and other armed organizations are the target of the vilest and most slanderous attacks precisely on the part of those who ought to protect their good name.

States of emergency and alert are only imposed to gag the people, to keep Spain ignorant of what goes on outside everybody's own city or town, and to imprison pretended political enemies.

The Constitution is gravely violated by all and is suffering total eclipse . . .

The Magistracy, whose independence is guaranteed by the Constitution, is weakened and undermined by persecution . . .

Electoral pacts made at the expense of the integrity of the Country, combined with attacks on government offices and strongrooms to falsify election returns, constitute the masquerade of legality which now rules us. There is no restraint on the thirst for power, on the illegal dismissal of moderate elements, on the glorification of the revolutions in Asturias and Catalonia—all violations of the Constitution. . . .

To the blind revolutionary spirit of the masses (deceived and exploited by soviet agents who conceal the bloody reality of that [Soviet] régime which has sacrificed twenty-five million people to its survival) is allied the malice and negligence of the authorities at every level who, sheltered behind the bungling of the [Central] Power, lack the authority and prestige to impose order and the rule of liberty and justice.

Can we tolerate for another day the disgraceful spectacle we are giving to the world?

Can we abandon Spain to her enemies by cowardly and traitorous behaviour, surrender her without struggle, without resistance?

No! Traitors may do so, but not we who have sworn to defend her.

We offer you justice and equality before the law; peace and love between Spaniards; liberty and fraternity, freed from licence and tyranny; work for all; social justice achieved without rancour or violence; and an equitable distribution of wealth without destroying or endangering the Spanish economy.

But, before this, war without quarter to the political exploiters, to the deceivers of the honest worker, to the foreigners and their would-be imitators, who intend, directly or indirectly, to destroy Spain . . .

Since the purity of our intentions prevents us stifling such achievements [of the recent past] as represent progress in social and political betterment, and since the spirit of hatred and revenge has no place in our heart, we shall know how to salvage from the inevitable wreck of certain legislative projects all that is compatible with the internal peace of Spain and the greatness we desire for her, making real in our Country, for the first time, and in this order, the threefold watchword of FRATERNITY, LIBERTY AND EQUALITY.

Spaniards: long live Spain!!!

Long live the honourable Spanish People!!!

The Commandant General of the Canary Islands

(2) War Aims of the Republican Government, 30 April 1938.

The Government of National Union, which has the confidence of all the parties and trade union organizations in loyal Spain, and claims that it represents all Spanish citizens who support constitutional legality, solemnly declares, to its compatriots and to the world at large, that its war aims are the following:

1. To secure the absolute independence and complete integrity of Spain—a Spain entirely free of all foreign interference, be its character and origin what they may, with her peninsular and island territory and other possessions intact and safe . . .

2. To liberate our territory from the foreign military forces that have invaded it, and from those elements who have repaired to Spain since July 1936 and who, under pretext of technical collaboration, are interfering in and seeking to dominate for their own profit, the legal and economic life of Spain.

3. A popular republic represented by a vigorous State based upon the principles of pure democracy and acting through a Government endowed with the full authority conferred by a popular vote taken by universal suffrage . . .

4. The legal and social structure of the Republic will be the outcome of the national will, freely expressed through a plebiscite which will be held as soon as the struggle has come to an end . . .

5. Respect for regional liberties, without any diminution of the unity of Spain . . .

6. The Spanish State will guarantee the full rights of the citizen in civic and social life, freedom of conscience, and the free practice of religious beliefs and observances.

7. The State will guarantee legally owned and legitimately acquired property, within the limits prescribed by the higher interest of the nation and the protection of productive elements. Without interfering with individual initiative, it will prevent the accumulation of wealth from leading to the exploitation of the citizen and the subjugation of the community, and thus counteracting the State's controlling influence in economic and social life . . .

8. There will be a far-reaching agrarian reform . . . The New Spain will be based on broad, solid, democratic foundations, and the peasant will own the land he tills.

9. The State will guarantee the workers' rights by means of up-to-date social legislation . . .

10. The cultural, physical and moral improvement of the race will be a primary and basic concern of the State.

11. The Spanish Army will be at the service of the nation, and will be free from any hegemony of tendency or party . . .

12. The Spanish State reaffirms the constitutional doctrine of the renunciation of war as an instrument of national policy. Faithful to pacts and treaties, Spain will support the policy symbolized by the League of Nations . . .

13. A complete amnesty will be granted to all Spaniards who are willing to co-operate in the immense task of rebuilding and exalting Spain . . .

(b) Resolution of the International Non-Intervention Committee relating to a Scheme of Observation, 8 March 1937.

The Governments represented on the International Committee . . . having approved the resolution . . . by the Committee to the effect that the Agreement should be extended . . . to cover the recruitment in, the transit through or the departure from, their respective countries of persons of non-Spanish nationality proposing to proceed to Spain . . . for the purpose of taking part in the present conflict; and

(2) Having deemed it expedient to establish a system of observation round the frontiers of Spain . . . for the purpose of ascertaining whether the Agreement is being observed; and

(3) His Majesty's Government in the United Kingdom having accepted an invitation by the Portuguese Government to observe the carrying out of the Agreement in Portugal . . .

(5) The Committee . . . agrees . . . that the system of observation . . . shall be carried out in the manner indicated in the Annex.

Annex.

1. The system of observation will be administered by a Board . . . consisting of a Chairman . . . and of five members nominated by the Representatives of the Governments of the United Kingdom, France, Germany, Italy and the U.S.S.R.

2. The Board will have power to decide all questions relating

to the administration of the scheme, but it will be the duty of the Board to submit all matters raising questions of principle to the International Committee for decision . . .

3. In view of the fact that a special arrangement has been reached between the United Kingdom and Portuguese Governments . . . regarding the Portuguese frontiers, there shall be stationed on the French side of the Franco-Spanish frontier and on the British side of the Gibraltar-Spanish frontier an international staff charged with the observation of the enforcement of the Non-Intervention Agreement.

4. For the purposes of the scheme, the Franco-Spanish frontier will be divided into zones, each of which will be in the charge of an 'Administrator' who will be responsible for the system of observation to be established in that zone to the 'Chief Administrator' who will be responsible for the whole frontier. Part of the international staff will be stationed at railway and road crossings over the frontier, and part will be equipped on a mobile basis.

5. The facilities to be accorded to, and the duties of the Administrators have been defined as follows:

(1) . . . The Chief Administrator and the Administrators and their subordinates shall be granted . . . full facilities . . .

(2) These facilities will include—

(a) the right of free entry at any time into railway establishments and similar premises;

(b) the right . . . of making such inspections as they may think proper in the premises referred to in (a) above, for the purpose of establishing whether any arms or war material are being exported into Spain, or whether foreign nationals are entering that country for the purpose of taking service in the present conflict . . .

(c) the right (i) to call upon the responsible authorities for documents relating to the nature of particular consignments of goods, and (ii) to examine the passports of persons proceeding to Spain . . .

(3) It will be the duty of the Chief Administrator in France and of the Administrator at Gibraltar—

(a) when called upon by the Board, to investigate, and to report on, any particular case in respect of which a complaint has been submitted . . .

(b) whenever . . . he has satisfied himself that a consignment of arms or war material . . . has been exported into Spain or that foreign nationals have entered Spain for the purpose of taking service in the present conflict . . . to submit forthwith identical reports in regard thereto—(i) to the Board; (ii) to an official nominated for the purpose by the Government of the country in which he is stationed . . .

6. All ships having the right to fly the flags of the countries which are parties to the Non-Intervention Agreement (other than naval vessels) proceeding to Spain . . . will

(a) . . . embark at one of the ports specified in paragraph 12 below two or more 'Observing Officers' appointed by the International Committee whose duty it will be to observe the unloading of the ship in Spanish ports . . .

10. . . . (c) The duties of the Observing Officers, when on board vessels in Spanish ports, will be to take . . . all steps which they may consider necessary to satisfy themselves

(i) whether any arms or war material . . . are being unloaded; and

(ii) whether . . . any foreign nationals intending to take service in the present conflict are being disembarked;

(iii) on leaving any Spanish port that no passenger or member of the crew, who may have left the ship while in port, has failed to return in contravention of the Non-Intervention Agreement . . .

23. In order to ensure that the procedure . . . for sea observation is duly observed, a system of naval observation will be established around the Spanish coasts.

24. The duty of naval observation will be undertaken by the Governments of the United Kingdom, France, Germany and Italy.

25. For the purpose of naval observation the Spanish coasts will be divided into zones, and the responsibility for observation within each zone will rest exclusively upon the Naval Power exercising observation in that zone . . .

27. The duties of naval observation . . . will only be exercised within a distance of ten sea miles from any point on the Spanish coast . . .

30. Each of the Governments exercising naval observation will—

(a) report immediately to the International Committee the arrival in any Spanish port in one of the zones for which it is responsible of any ship the name of which has not been notified as having submitted to observation, and will notify to the International Committee the name of any ship which refuses to submit to observation when the need for such observation has been pointed out to it . . .

(b) submit periodical reports to the International Committee, giving full particulars regarding the arrival of all ships entering Spanish ports within the zones for which it is responsible . . .

(c) At the League of Nations.

(1) Appeal by the Spanish Government, 27 November 1936.

In notes addressed to the Powers parties to the Non-Intervention Agreement, in a letter to the Secretary-General of the League of Nations and in my speech to the Assembly of the League, the Spanish Government has denounced the armed intervention of Germany and Italy in favour of the rebels in the Spanish civil war—such intervention constituting the most flagrant violation of international law. This intervention has culminated in the recognition of the chief of the rebels set up as a Government by the 'wire-pullers' of the same Powers. Such a proceeding is virtually an act of aggression against the Spanish Republic. The declared intention of the rebels of forcibly preventing free commerce with the ports controlled by the Government claims attention as a factor likely to create international difficulties—difficulties which, as is well known, Franco declared his intention of provoking from the outset of the rebellion. These difficulties are increased by the fact that the rebels have been recognized by Germany and Italy, which, and particularly one of them, as is proved by information in the possession of the Government of the Republic, are preparing to co-operate with them in the naval sphere as they have done in the air and on land. These facts, through their very simultaneity, constitute for the Spanish Government a circumstance affecting international relations which threatens to disturb international peace or the good understanding between nations upon which peace depends. On behalf of the Spanish Government, I therefore request Your Excellency in the supreme interests of peace and in virtue of Article 11 of the Covenant (No. 206), to take the necessary steps to enable the Council to proceed, at the earliest possible moment, to an examination of the situation outlined above.

Julio Alvarez del Vayo, Minister for Foreign Affairs
of the Spanish Republic

(2) Resolution of the League of Nations Council, 12 December 1936.

The Council . . .

I.

Noting that it has been requested to examine a situation which, in the terms of Article 11 of the Covenant (No. 206), is such as to affect international relations and to threaten to disturb international peace or the good understanding between nations upon which peace depends;

Considering that that good understanding ought to be maintained irrespective of the internal régimes of States;

Bearing in mind that it is the duty of every State to respect the territorial integrity and political independence of other States, a duty which, for Members of the League of Nations, has been recognized by the Covenant:

Affirms that every State is under an obligation to refrain from intervening in the internal affairs of another State;

II.

Considering that the setting-up of a Committee of Non-Intervention and the undertakings entered into in that connexion arise out of the principles stated above;

Having been informed that new attempts are made in the Committee to make its action more effective, in particular by instituting measures of supervision, the necessity for which is becoming increasingly urgent:

Recommends the Members of the League represented on the London Committee to spare no pains to render the non-intervention undertakings as stringent as possible, and to take appropriate measures to ensure forthwith that the fulfilment of the said undertakings is effectively supervised; . . .

IV.

Notes that there are problems of a humanitarian character in connexion with the present situation, in regard to which coordinated action of an international and humanitarian character is desirable as soon as possible;

Recognizes, further, that, for the reconstruction which Spain may have to undertake, international assistance may also be desirable;

And authorizes the Secretary-General to make available the assistance of the technical services of the League of Nations should a suitable opportunity occur.

(3) Resolution of the League of Nations Council, 29 May 1937.

The Council . . .

I.

Confirming the principles and recommendations set forth in its resolution of December 12th, 1936 (No. 218 (c) (2)), and, in particular, the duty of every State to respect the territorial integrity and political independence of other States, a duty which, for Members of the League of Nations, has been recognized in the Covenant (No. 206):

(1) Observes with regret that the development of the situation in Spain does not seem to suggest that the steps taken by Governments on the recommendations of the Council have as yet had the full effect desired;

(2) Notes that an international scheme of supervision of the non-intervention undertakings assumed by the European Governments is now in force;

(3) Notes with very great satisfaction the action taken by the London Non-Intervention Committee with a view to the withdrawal of all non-Spanish combatants taking part in the struggle in Spain;

(4) Expresses the firm hope that such action will be taken in consequence of this initiative as may ensure with the utmost speed the withdrawal from the struggle of all the non-Spanish combatants participating therein; this measure is at present, in

the Council's opinion, the most effective remedy for a situation the great gravity of which, from the standpoint of the general peace, it feels bound to emphasize and the most certain means of ensuring the full application of the policy of non-intervention;

(5) Urges Members of the League, represented on that Committee, to spare no effort in this direction;

(6) Expresses the hope that the early success of these efforts will lead without delay to the cessation of the struggle and give the Spanish people the possibility of deciding its own destiny;

II.

(1) Profoundly moved by the horrors resulting from the use of certain methods of warfare, condemns the employment, in the Spanish struggle, of methods contrary to international law and the bombing of open towns;

(2) Desires to emphasize its high appreciation of the efforts of unofficial institutions and certain Governments to save civilians, especially women and children, from these terrible dangers.

219. *The Anschluss of Austria, March 1938*

The first major extension of German territory came through the incorporation or *Anschluss* of Austria in March 1938. Following on internal disturbances in Austria, largely caused by the illegal Austrian National Socialist Party, there was German intervention in Austrian affairs. A meeting between Hitler and the Austrian Chancellor Schuschnigg resulted in an agreement as a result of which National Socialists gained a part in the Government. To bolster his own position, Schuschnigg decided to ask the people in a plebiscite whether they wanted to continue the independent existence of Austria, or be incorporated in Germany. This is the referendum our first selection (a) refers to. Because of continuing and increasing tension, the plebiscite was postponed; the Germans considered this as a breach of faith and occupied Austria. Schuschnigg protested in a broadcast message (b). The plebiscite was then conducted under German auspices and resulted in an overwhelming majority voting for joining Germany.

Source: *Documents on International Affairs 1938* (Oxford University Press under the auspices of the Royal Institute of International Affairs), vol. ii, pp. 64–6.

(a) Proclamation by the Austrian Chancellor concerning the Plebiscite, 9 March 1938.

For a free, German Austria!

People of Austria! For the first time in the history of our fatherland the leadership of the State calls for an open profession of faith in our homeland. Next Sunday, March 13, is the day of the plebiscite. All of you, whatever may be your occupation or class, men and women of free Austria, you are called upon to make a profession of faith before the whole world. You are to say whether you are willing to go with us on the path which we are treading, which has as its aim social harmony and equality of rights, the final overcoming of party schisms, German peace at home and abroad, and a policy of work.

For a free and German, independent and social, Christian and united Austria! For peace and work! And for equality of rights for all those who acknowledge their faith in their nation and fatherland! That is the object of my programme. To achieve this aim is our task, and the historic need of the hour.

Not a word of the formula which is placed before you as a question can be allowed to fail. Whoever answers 'Yes' serves the interests of all, and above all of peace. I therefore call on you, fellow-countrymen, to show that you are in earnest in meaning to inaugurate a new era of unity in the interests of your homeland. We must show the world our will to live. And so, people of Austria, stand up as one man and vote 'Yes'! . . .

(b) Broadcast by Dr. Schuschnigg, 11 March 1938.

Men and women of Austria!

Today we have been confronted with a difficult and decisive situation. I am authorized to report to the Austrian people on the events of the day.

The Government of the German Reich presented the Federal President with an ultimatum with a time-limit, according to which he had to appoint as Federal Chancellor a prescribed candidate, and constitute a Government in accordance with the proposals of the Government of the German Reich. Otherwise it was intended that German troops should march into Austria at the hour named.

I declare before the world that the reports which have been

spread in Austria that there have been labour troubles, that streams of blood have flowed, and that the Government was not in control of the situation and could not maintain order by its own means, are fabrications from A to Z.

The Federal President authorizes me to inform the Austrian people that we yield to force. Because we are not minded, at any cost and even in this grave hour, to shed German blood, we have ordered our armed forces, in case the invasion is carried out, to withdraw without resistance and to await the events of the next hours . . .

So I take my leave in this hour of the Austrian people with a German word and a heartfelt wish—God protect Austria!

220. *The Munich Agreement, 29 September 1938*

After the *Anschluss* of Austria, Czechoslovakia, or, to be more precise, the condition of the some three million Germans in the border areas of Czechoslovakia, became the focus of German attention. War between the two States threatened repeatedly, and mediation was attempted by the Western Powers. The final outcome was a four-power conference at Munich at which the German demands were accepted by the Powers in the following agreement. Czechoslovakia was finally dismembered in March 1939, Bohemia and Moravia being occupied by Germany, Slovakia becoming independent, and the Carpatho–Ukraine returned to Hungary.

Source: *British and Foreign State Papers*, vol. cxlii (1938), pp. 438–41.

Agreement for the Cession by Czechoslovakia to Germany of Sudeten German Territory.

Germany, the United Kingdom, France and Italy, taking into consideration the agreement, which has been already reached in principle for the cession to Germany of the Sudeten German territory, have agreed on the following terms and conditions governing the said cession and the measures consequent thereon, and by this agreement they each hold themselves responsible for the steps necessary to secure its fulfilment:

1. The evacuation will begin on the 1st October.
2. The United Kingdom, France and Italy agree that the evacuation of the territory shall be completed by the 10th October . . .

3. The conditions governing the evacuation will be laid down in detail by an international commission composed of representatives of Germany, the United Kingdom, France, Italy and Czechoslovakia.

4. The occupation by stages of the predominantly German territory by German troops will begin on the 1st October. The four territories marked on the attached map[1] will be occupied by German troops [between 1st and 7th October]. The remaining territory of preponderantly German character will be ascertained by the aforesaid international commission forthwith and be occupied by German troops by the 10th of October.

5. The international commission referred to . . . will determine the territories in which a plebiscite is to be held. These territories will be occupied by international bodies until the plebiscite has been completed . . .

6. The final determination of the frontiers will be carried out by the international commission . . .

Annex to the agreement.

His Majesty's Government in the United Kingdom and the French Government have entered into the above agreement on the basis that they stand by the offer . . . relating to an international guarantee of the new boundaries of the Czechoslovak State against unprovoked aggression.

When the question of the Polish and Hungarian minorities in Czechoslovakia has been settled, Germany and Italy for their part will give a guarantee to Czechoslovakia.

221. *The Outbreak of the Second World War, September 1939*

Tension between Germany and Poland, mainly resulting from the situation in Danzig and the so-called Polish corridor, grew after the dismemberment of Czechoslovakia. Great Britain and France were determined to safeguard Polish independence and announced their guarantee. They also conducted negotiations with a view to concluding a treaty of mutual assistance with the Soviet Union, but they were unsuccessful: the Soviet Union concluded a treaty with Germany instead.

The British Government tried to mediate between Germany and

---

[1] Map not reproduced.

Poland, but reminded Germany that they would intervene on Poland's behalf if necessary (a). Great Britain also concluded a treaty of mutual assistance with Poland (b). When Germany invaded Poland on 1 September, the British Government sent an ultimatum to Germany (c). This was rejected (d) and thus the Second World War began.

Source: *Documents concerning German-Polish Relations and the Outbreak of Hostilities between Great Britain and Germany on September 3, 1939* (London, H.M.S.O., 1939) (Cmd. 6106), pp. 37–9, 96–8, 175–8.

(a) Letter of the British Prime Minister to the German Chancellor, 22 August 1939.

Your Excellency will have already heard of certain measures taken by His Majesty's Government, and announced in the press . . .

These steps have, in the opinion of His Majesty's Government, been rendered necessary by the military movements which have been reported from Germany, and by the fact that apparently the announcement of a German–Soviet Agreement is taken in some quarters in Berlin to indicate that intervention by Great Britain on behalf of Poland is no longer a contingency that need be reckoned with. No greater mistake could be made. Whatever may prove to be the nature of the German–Soviet Agreement, it cannot alter Great Britain's obligation to Poland which His Majesty's Government have stated in public repeatedly and plainly, and which they are determined to fulfil.

It has been alleged that, if His Majesty's Government had made their position more clear in 1914, the great catastrophe would have been avoided. Whether or not there is any force in that allegation, His Majesty's Government are resolved that on this occasion there shall be no such tragic misunderstanding.

If the case should arise, they are resolved, and prepared, to employ without delay all the forces at their command, and it is impossible to foresee the end of hostilities once engaged. It would be a dangerous illusion to think that, if war once starts, it will come to an early end even if a success on any one of the several fronts on which it will be engaged should have been secured.

Having thus made our position perfectly clear, I wish to repeat to you my conviction that war between our two peoples would be the greatest calamity that could occur. I am certain that it is desired neither by our people, nor by yours, and I cannot see that there is anything in the questions arising between Germany and Poland which could not and should not be resolved without the use of force, if only a situation of confidence could be restored to enable discussions to be carried on in an atmosphere different from that which prevails today.

We have been, and at all times will be, ready to assist in creating conditions in which such negotiations could take place . . .

But I am bound to say that there would be slender hope of bringing such negotiations to successful issue unless it were understood beforehand that any settlement reached would, when concluded, be guaranteed by other Powers. His Majesty's Government would be ready, if desired, to make such contribution as they could to the effective operation of such guarantees . . .

(b) Agreement of Mutual Assistance between Great Britain and Poland, 25 August 1939.

1. Should one of the Contracting Parties become engaged in hostilities with a European Power in consequence of aggression by the latter against that Contracting Party, the other Contracting Party will at once give the Contracting Party engaged in hostilities all the support and assistance in its power.

2. (1) The provisions of Article 1 will also apply in the event of any action by a European Power which clearly threatened, directly or indirectly, the independence of one of the Contracting Parties, and was of such a nature that the Party in question considered it vital to resist it with armed forces.

(2) Should one of the Contracting Parties become engaged in hostilities with a European Power in consequence of action by that Power which threatened the independence or neutrality of another European State in such a way as to constitute a clear menace to the security of that Contracting Party, the provisions of Article 1 will apply, without prejudice, however, to the rights of the other European State concerned.

3. Should a European Power attempt to undermine the independence of one of the Contracting Parties by processes of economic penetration or in any other way, the Contracting

Parties will support each other in resistance to such attempts. Should the European Power concerned thereupon embark on hostilities against one of the Contracting Parties, the provisions of Article 1 will apply . . .

(c) Telegram from the British Foreign Secretary to the British Ambassador at Berlin, 3 September 1939, 5 a.m.

Please seek interview with Minister for Foreign Affairs at 9 a.m. today, Sunday, or, if he cannot see you then, arrange to convey at that time to representative of German Government the following communication:

'In the communication which I had the honour to make to you on 1st September I informed you, on the instructions of His Majesty's Principal Secretary of State for Foreign Affairs, that, unless the German Government were prepared to give His Majesty's Government in the United Kingdom satisfactory assurances that the German Government had suspended all aggressive action against Poland and were prepared promptly to withdraw their forces from Polish Territory, His Majesty's Government in the United Kingdom would, without hesitation, fulfil their obligations to Poland.

Although this communication was made more than twenty-four hours ago, no reply has been received but German attacks upon Poland have been continued and intensified. I have accordingly the honour to inform you that, unless not later than 11 a.m., British Summer Time, today 3rd September, satisfactory assurances to the above effect have been given by the German Government and have reached His Majesty's Government in London, a state of war will exist between the two countries as from that hour.'

If the assurance referred to in the above communication is received, you should inform me by any means at your disposal before 11 a.m. today 3rd September. If no such assurance is received here by 11 a.m., we shall inform the German representative that a state of war exists as from that hour.

(d) German reply to British Ultimatum, 3 September 1939, 11.20 a.m.

The German Government have received the British Government's ultimatum of the 3rd September, 1939 (No. 220(c)). They have the honour to reply as follows:

1. The German Government and the German people refuse to receive, accept, let alone to fulfil, demands in the nature of ultimata made by the British Government.

2. On our eastern frontier there has for many months already reigned a condition of war. Since the time when the Versailles Treaty (No. 160) first tore Germany to pieces, all and every peaceful settlement was refused to all German Governments. The National Socialist Government also has since the year 1933 tried again and again to remove by peaceful negotiations the worst rapes and breaches of justice of this treaty. The British Government have been among those who, by their intransigent attitude, took the chief part in frustrating every practical revision. Without the intervention of the British Government—of this the German Government and German people are fully conscious—a reasonable solution doing justice to both sides would certainly have been found between Germany and Poland. For Germany did not have the intention nor had she raised the demands of annihilating Poland. The Reich demanded only the revision of those articles of the Versailles Treaty which already at the time of the formulation of that dictate had been described by understanding statesmen of all nations as being in the long run unbearable, and therefore impossible for a great nation and also for the entire political and economic interests of Eastern Europe. British statesmen, too, declared the solution in the East which was then forced upon Germany as containing the germ of future wars. To remove this danger was the desire of all German Governments and especially the intention of the new National Socialist People's Government. The blame for having prevented this peaceful revision lies with the British Cabinet policy.

3. The British Government have—an occurrence unique in history—given the Polish State full powers for all actions against Germany which that State might conceivably intend to undertake. The British Government assured the Polish Government of their military support in all circumstances, should Germany defend herself against any provocation or attack. Thereupon the Polish terror against the Germans living in the territories

which had been torn from Germany immediately assumed unbearable proportions. The Free City of Danzig was, in violation of all legal provisions, first threatened with destruction economically and by measures of customs policy, and was finally subjected to a military blockade and its communications strangled. All these violations of the Danzig Statute, which were well known to the British Government, were approved and covered by the blank cheque given to Poland. The German Government, though moved by the sufferings of the German population which was being tortured and treated in an inhuman manner, nevertheless remained a patient onlooker for five months, without undertaking even on one single occasion any similar aggressive action against Poland. They only warned Poland that these happenings would in the long run be unbearable, and that they were determined, in the event of no other kind of assistance being given to this population, to help them themselves. All these happenings were known in every detail to the British Government. It would have been easy for them to use their great influence in Warsaw in order to exhort those in power there to exercise justice and humaneness and to keep to the existing obligations. The British Government did not do this . . . The British Government, therefore, bear the responsibility for all the unhappiness and misery which have now overtaken and are about to overtake many peoples.

4. After all efforts at finding and concluding a peaceful solution had been rendered impossible by the intransigence of the Polish Government covered as they were by England, after the conditions resembling civil war, which had existed already for months at the eastern frontier of the Reich, had gradually developed into open attacks on German territory, without the British Government raising any objections, the German Government determined to put an end to this continual threat, unbearable for a great Power, to the external and finally also to the internal peace of the German people, and to end it by those means which, since the Democratic Governments had in effect sabotaged all other possibilities of revision, alone remained at their disposal for the defence of the peace, security and honour of the Germans. The last attacks of the Poles threatening Reich territory they answered with similar measures. The German Government do not intend, on account of any sort

of British intentions or obligations in the East, to tolerate conditions which are identical with those conditions which we observe in Palestine which is under British protection. The German people, however, above all do not intend to allow themselves to be ill-treated by Poles.

5. The German Government, therefore, reject the attempt to force Germany, by means of a demand having the character of an ultimatum, to recall its forces which are lined up for the defence of the Reich, and thereby to accept the old unrest and the old injustice. The threat that, failing this, they will fight Germany in the war, corresponds to the intention proclaimed for years past by numerous British politicians. The German Government and the German people have assured the English people countless times how much they desire an understanding, indeed close friendship, with them. If the British Government hitherto always refused these offers and now answer them with an open threat of war, it is not the fault of the German people and of their Government, but exclusively the fault of the British Cabinet or of those men who for years have been preaching the destruction and extermination of the German people. The German people and their Government do not, like Great Britain, intend to dominate the world, but they are determined to defend their own liberty, their independence, and above all their life. The intention . . . of carrying the destruction of the German people even further than was done through the Versailles Treaty is taken note of by us, and we shall therefore answer any aggressive action on the part of England with the same weapons and in the same form.